Europe's Foreign and Security Policy
The Institutionalization of Cooperation

The emergence of a common security and foreign policy has been one of the most contentious issues accompanying the integration of the European Union. In this book, Michael Smith examines the specific ways foreign policy cooperation has been institutionalized in the EU, the way institutional development affects cooperative outcomes in foreign policy, and how those outcomes lead to new institutional reforms. Smith explains the evolution and performance of the institutional procedures of the EU using a unique analytical framework, supported by extensive empirical evidence drawn from interviews, case studies, official documents and secondary sources. His perceptive and well-informed analysis covers the entire history of EU foreign policy cooperation, from its origins in the late 1960s up to the start of the 2003 constitutional convention. Demonstrating the importance and extent of EU foreign/security policy, the book will be of interest to scholars, researchers and policymakers.

MICHAEL E. SMITH is Assistant Professor of Political Science, Georgia State University, Atlanta.

D0928244

Themes in European Governance

Series Editors
Andrea Føllesdal
Johan P. Olsen

Editorial Board

Stefano Bartolini	Beate Kohler-Koch	Percy Lehning
Andrew Moravscik	Ulrich Preuss	Thomas Risse
Fritz W. Scharpf	Philip Schlesinger	Helen Wallace
Albert Weale	J. H. H. Weiler	

The evolving European systems of governance, in particular the European Union, challenge and transform the state, the most important locus of governance and political identity and loyalty over the past two hundred years. The series *Themes in European Governance* aims to publish the best theoretical and analytical scholarship on the impact of European governance on the core institutions, policies and identities of nation-states. It focuses upon the implications for issues such as citizenship, welfare, political decision-making, and economic, monetary, and fiscal policies. An initiative of Cambridge University Press and the Programme on Advanced Research on the Europeanization of the Nation-State (ARENA), Norway, the series includes contributions in the social sciences, humanities and law. The series aims to provide theoretically informed studies analyzing key issues at the European level and within European states. Volumes in the series will be of interest to scholars and students of Europe both within Europe and world-wide. They will be of particular relevance to those interested in the development of sovereignty and governance of European states and in the issues raised by multilevel governance and multinational integration throughout the world.

Other books in the series:

Paulette Kurzer *Markets and Moral Regulation: Cultural Change in the European Union*

Christoph Knill *The Europeanisation of National Administrations: Patterns of Institutional Change and Persistence*

Tanja Börzel *States and Regions in the European Union: Institutional Adaptation in Germany and Spain*

Liesbet Hooghe *The European Commission and the Integration of Europe: Images of Governance*

Gallya Lahau *Immigration and Politics in the New Europe: Reinventing Borders*

Gary Marks and Marco R. Steenbergen *European Integration and Political Conflict*

Frank Schimmelfennig *The EU, NATO and the Integration of Europe: Rules and Rhetoric*

Europe's Foreign and Security Policy

The Institutionalization of Cooperation

Michael E. Smith

CAMBRIDGE
UNIVERSITY PRESS

PUBLISHED BY THE PRESS SYNDICATE OF THE UNIVERSITY OF CAMBRIDGE
The Pitt Building, Trumpington Street, Cambridge, United Kingdom

CAMBRIDGE UNIVERSITY PRESS
The Edinburgh Building, Cambridge, CB2 2RU, UK
40 West 20th Street, New York, NY 10011–4211, USA
477 Williamstown Road, Port Melbourne, VIC 3207, Australia
Ruiz de Alarcón 13, 28014 Madrid, Spain
Dock House, The Waterfront, Cape Town 8001, South Africa

http://www.cambridge.org

First published 2004
Reprinted 2004

Printed in the United Kingdom at the University Press, Cambridge

Typeface Plantin 10/12 pt.   *System* LATEX 2ε [TB]

A catalogue record for this book is available from the British Library

Library of Congress Cataloging-in-Publication data
Smith, Michael E. (Michael Eugene), 1965–
Europe's foreign and security policy: the institutionalization of cooperation /
Michael E. Smith.
      p.   cm. – (Themes in European governance)
Includes bibliographical references and index.
ISBN 0 521 83135 0 – ISBN 0 521 53861 0 (pb.)
1. Europe – Foreign relations – 1989–   2. European Union countries – Foreign
relations.   3. European Union countries – Politics and government.
4. Security, International.   5. European Union – Foreign relations.
I. Title.   II. Series.
D860.S65   2003
327′.094 – dc21   2003048990

ISBN 0 521 83135 0 hardback
ISBN 0 521 53861 0 paperback

For Pen
with love

Contents

Part III   Residual institutional issues

Tables

Acknowledgments

It is somehow appropriate that a book on international cooperation should begin by acknowledging the generous support of individuals and institutions on two continents. I would first like to thank Wayne Sandholtz for his extensive advice and unfailing encouragement throughout the entire process, from conception to research to writing. I could not have asked for a better mentor for this project. Roy Ginsberg's detailed studies of EU foreign policy actions helped to inspire this volume; he also graciously provided extensive comments on earlier drafts of the manuscript. The other members of my dissertation committee, Russell Dalton and Patrick Morgan, added their votes of confidence to my efforts at key stages and for that I am grateful.

I would also like to thank several scholars whose large body of work on the EU provided much of the empirical evidence for the analysis presented here. They were also kind enough to take interest in my work and lend their insights to the project. In addition to Roy Ginsberg, these scholars include David Allen, Simon Bulmer, Fraser Cameron, Jim Caporaso, Thomas Grunert, Christopher Hill, John Peterson, and Michael Smith. I am also grateful to the members of two "Institutionalization of Europe" workshops led by Wayne Sandholtz, Alec Stone Sweet, and Neil Fligstein, who helped stimulate some of the ideas presented here. Special mention goes to Simon Nuttall, who shared his detailed knowledge of the history of EU foreign and security policy with me and saved me from a number of errors. Any that remain, of course, are entirely my own.

This research was supported financially by several institutions: the Council for European Studies, the US Institute for International Education (Fulbright fellowship), the University of California Institute on Global Conflict and Cooperation/MacArthur Foundation, the UC-Irvine Regent's fellowship program, the European Union Center of the University System of Georgia, and the Bicentennial Swedish-American Fund of the Swedish Government Information Service. The Centre for European Studies in Brussels provided a very stimulating environment for my initial explorations into the EU; the manuscript also benefited from presentations at meetings of the European Union Studies Association, the Council for European Studies, and the International Studies Association, as well as graduate student conferences at Columbia University, Georgetown University, and Harvard University. Small portions of the argument have appeared in the *Journal of Common Market Studies* and the *Journal of European Public Policy*, and I appreciate the input given by the editors of those journals (Iain Begg, John Peterson, and Jeremy Richardson).

My editor at Cambridge University Press, John Haslam, expertly guided me through the book production process, and I am especially grateful to the two external reviewers he chose for their sound advice on improving the final manuscript. I would also like to thank the numerous officials involved in EU foreign policy who agreed to be interviewed for this project. It would have been impossible to develop my arguments about the relationship between institutionalization and cooperation without the valuable inside knowledge provided by these individuals. The same is true for officials from the US mission to the European Union who monitor the foreign policy of the EU and shared their opinions of it with me.

Finally, I would like to thank my family for their generous emotional (and financial) support of my scholarly ambitions. I would not have had the courage to take this path without them. My last word of thanks is reserved for the person to whom this book is dedicated, my wife Penny, for her love, patience, and encouragement.

Abbreviations

ACP	African, Caribbean, and Pacific States
ASEAN	Association of Southeast Asian Nations
ASEM	Asia–Europe Meeting
CACM	Central American Common Market
CAP	Common Agricultural Policy
CEEC	Central Eastern European Countries
CFSP	Common Foreign and Security Policy
CIS	Commonwealth of Independent States
COREPER	Committee of Permanent Representatives
COREU	*Correspondance Européenne* system
CSCE	Conference on Security and Cooperation in Europe
CTBT	Comprehensive Test Ban Treaty
EC	European Community
ECB	European Central Bank
ECJ	European Court of Justice
ECSC	European Coal and Steel Community
ECU	European Currency Unit
EDC	European Defense Community
EEC	European Economic Community
EFTA	European Free Trade Association
EIB	European Investment Bank
EP	European Parliament
EU	European Union
EPC	European Political Cooperation
ESDP	European Security and Defense Policy
EURATOM	European Atomic Energy Community
GAC	General Affairs Council
GATT	General Agreement on Tariffs and Trade
IGC	Intergovernmental Conference
JHA	Justice and Home Affairs
KEDO	Korean Peninsula Energy Development Organization
MAPE	Multinational Advisory Police Element in Albania

MBFR	Mutual and Balanced Force Reduction
MPLA	Movimento Popular de libertação de Angola
NATO	North Atlantic Treaty Organization
NPT	Nuclear Non-Proliferation Treaty
OAS	Organization of American States
OECD	Organization for Economic Cooperation and Development
OSCE	Organization for Security and Cooperation in Europe
PHARE	Poland-Hungary Assistance for Recovering Economies Program
PLO	Palestine Liberation Organization
QMV	Qualified majority voting
RRF	Rapid Reaction Force
RRM	Rapid Reaction Mechanism
SEA	Single European Act
TACIS	Technical Assistance to the Commonwealth of Independent States
TEU	Treaty on European Union
UN	United Nations
WEU	Western European Union
WTO	World Trade Organization

Introduction: foreign and security policy in the European Union

Nothing is possible without men; nothing lasts without institutions.

Jean Monnet

On November 19, 1970, Europe's novel experiment in regional economic integration quietly delved into uncharted territory. In Munich, at the former Prussian embassy to the Kingdom of Bavaria, European Union (EU) foreign ministers met for the first time under the rubric of a new institutional framework, "European Political Cooperation" (EPC). This meeting represented the latest in a long series of efforts to coordinate the foreign policies of EU member states in areas other than economic affairs. The EU's previous attempts to coordinate such policies, such as the European Defense Community and the European Political Community of the 1950s, and the Fouchet Plans of the 1960s, had failed miserably because of fundamental disagreements about the means and ends of European foreign policy cooperation. Thanks to this legacy, EPC was greeted with considerable uncertainty and skepticism when the EU foreign ministers met in Munich. The meeting aroused little public attention, and EPC participants themselves expected the profound differences in their foreign policy traditions, domestic political cultures, administrative capacities, and global relationships to inhibit their attempts to find a collective voice in world politics.

In addition, not only was EPC's scope of action so indeterminate that it threatened to invite more conflict than cooperation, but its mechanisms to induce such cooperation were feeble and peculiar. It was not based on a treaty, nor did it have any permanent organizational machinery. Its rules were extremely vague and its instruments for collective action few. Perhaps the only thing the EU foreign ministers could agree upon – but for different reasons – was that EPC should be kept strictly separate from supranational European Community (EC) procedures and that security or defense matters were not appropriate subjects for discussion in the EPC framework.

Given its obscure goals, its modest institutional support, the difficult problems Europe hoped to confront with it (such as the Middle East), the entrenched foreign policy traditions of its member states, and the hostile attitude of the US toward it, EPC should never have left the planning stage. If it did persist, it should have been little more than a "talking shop" for diplomats, very similar to other political dialogues based within regional organizations (such as the Association of Southeast Asian Nations or the Organization of American States) or held during periodic summits (such as the Group of 7 [G-7] industrialized nations) which also possessed no capacity for coordinated external actions. Yet this novel diplomatic experiment – "the world's most advanced model of collective diplomacy" (von der Gablentz 1979: 688) in the words of one enthusiastic participant – surprised its participants and critics alike over the next two decades. The very first meeting of EPC foreign ministers in Munich laid the groundwork for sustained discussions of the Middle East and East–West relations, which resulted in the Euro-Arab Dialogue and the Conference on Security and Cooperation in Europe a few years later. These two difficult subjects occupied EPC for years while other issues were gradually added to the agenda, extending foreign policy cooperation into uncharted territory. During this time the institutional framework of EPC developed and expanded far beyond what was anticipated or even desired by EU member states. Finally, although EPC was established outside EC structures, it quickly grew more sensitive to Community policies and procedures so that, by the time of the Maastricht Treaty on European Union in 1991, EPC was replaced by a "Common Foreign and Security Policy" (CFSP) and both the EC and the CFSP were tied together legally under the new single institutional framework known as the "European Union." By this time powerful taboos against discussing security issues had been overcome and cooperation in this area found its way into the Maastricht Treaty, though in a somewhat equivocal way. Today, discussions regarding defense cooperation and a common European military force are commonplace in the EU, and specific plans to further those ends have been agreed.

Thus, despite the legacy of failure and the climate of uncertainty surrounding the first tentative meetings in EPC, EU member states creatively improved and expanded their cooperation in foreign policy, a process which continues to this day. How they managed this feat is the subject of this book. In particular, I examine the relationship between institutional development and foreign policy cooperation among EU member states. Toward this end I advance a theory of institutionalization and describe the specific mechanisms that encouraged EU states to cooperate in this area. I also provide empirical evidence of such cooperation, linking it to institutional changes in EPC/CFSP.

The puzzles of European foreign policy

The EU's attempt to cooperate in foreign policy has attracted an increasing amount of attention in the growing literature on Europe's external relations. There is little consensus, however, on the relationship between EU foreign policy and international politics. Some scholars, particularly American ones, see EPC/CFSP as a pretentious waste of time or even a failure, particularly when it is unable to solve complex international problems (Art 1996; Gordon 1997–98; Hoffman 2000). Others see it as a nuisance, one that only interferes with, or even undermines, the efforts of powerful states (again, chiefly the US) to maintain global stability. Both attitudes, particularly when based on single episodes such as the Middle East or the Balkans, miss important aspects of EU foreign policy that easily justify a closer look at its development and functioning. And although a number of excellent case studies on individual EPC/CFSP actions exist, there are more elemental, and in my view, theoretically interesting questions about Europe's cooperation in foreign and security policy. In particular, this volume focuses on five closely related sets of questions.[1]

1   *The existence, endurance, and expansion of EU foreign policy*

Perhaps the most important questions are also the most general: why should a regional economic organization struggle for so long to develop its own foreign policy? Why does the EU persist in attempting to speak with a single voice in world politics, even when this might frustrate its most important ally, the United States? And why did EPC not only succeed where the European Defense Community and European Political Community had failed, but persist and expand as well, even in the face of numerous internal and external challenges? As "the simplest, leanest, most cost-effective form of international cooperation yet devised" (Hurd 1981: 388), EU member states could have kept EPC as a passive forum to share information, as it was designed; instead they repeatedly attempted to both strengthen and make greater use of the mechanism. Taboos over what had been considered issues inappropriate for EPC (such as security) were gradually broken, and changes in the mechanism itself were built

---

[1] For similar expositions of the most important questions concerning EPC, see Hill 1988a; Weiler and Wessels 1988.

onto previous innovations, so that member states did not feel threatened
by a radical expansion of their cooperation in this sensitive area. This
theme – progressive adaptation in the midst of continuity – is a defining
feature of EPC/CFSP. However, this is not to say that there were no
setbacks; in fact, in explaining continuity we must also confront the fact
that European foreign policy cooperation has disappointed its advocates
in some areas. Still, it has advanced in a fairly logical cycle involving
crisis or opportunity, small-scale innovation, and institutional consolidation (or codification), until the sequence repeated itself and gradually
took European foreign relations in new directions.

2   *EU foreign policy and the external world*

Another set of puzzles concerns the impact made by EU foreign policy
on non-members, and the influence of external forces on the EU system
itself. This topic is often framed as the emergence of the EU as an international political actor (Taylor 1979; Ginsberg 1989; Crawford and
Schulze 1990; Rummel 1990; Hill 1993; Holland 1997a; Piening 1997;
Peterson and Sjursen 1998; Whitman 1998; Bretherton and Vogler 1999;
Ginsberg 1999, 2001). The EU's impact on the world is in part a function of policy effectiveness, and could be used as an indirect measure
of cooperation. However, while critics of Europe's global ambitions frequently point to EPC's failure to "solve" (or even to positively impact
on) complex international problems such as the Arab-Israeli conflict or
the breakup of Yugoslavia, they also unfairly and too readily overlook the
more fundamental purposes of EU foreign policy cooperation. EPC was
not created to help Europe solve international problems; it was created
to prevent international problems from disrupting the Community and,
to a lesser extent, to make sure a common European voice was heard in
international affairs.

In terms of the first task EU foreign policy has proved a resounding success; foreign policy issues have rarely if ever disrupted the daily business
of the EC. And although some might argue that the close involvement of
the US in European affairs encouraged common European positions on
world politics, there also have been numerous opportunities for discord
within Europe and between Europe and the US. In fact, disagreement
with a number of American foreign policies provided a major incentive
for EU states to cooperate, as I demonstrate in this volume.[2] EU foreign policy has helped to moderate these potential areas of disagreement

[2] As Nuttall (1992a: 3) once put it, "A consistent feature [of EPC] has been the need to
find a way of expressing policies which are not those of the United States."

by framing disputes over foreign policy in terms of collective interests and rules, and often has gone beyond these activities by also promoting a collective European response to major questions of international affairs. In this sense one can say that EPC has changed from a defensive or passive approach to cooperation (preventing any external disruption of the Community) to a more positive, proactive one (asserting European interests and values beyond its borders); or in other words, from negative to positive integration. As a result, the EU is still taken far more seriously as an international *political* actor by other states (even the US), regional groupings, and international organizations than many observers appreciate. However, this is not to argue that EU foreign policy is a positive force for the outside world, or even for world peace. This study does not attempt to address this question directly, although I do touch upon it as necessary. Instead, the primary normative criterion used in this volume is whether foreign policy cooperation benefits those for whom it was originally intended: the member states of the EU.

3   EU foreign policy and European integration

The question of whether European foreign policy cooperation has an impact on the world beyond the EU is an important one. To a large extent, this has involved finding ways to convert Europe's considerable economic resources into external political power, which raises another set of research questions. As observers often point out, the EC's external economic activities are far more extensive than what takes place within the EPC/CFSP domain (Smith 1998). Sanctions, bilateral aid, and development policies are the only real tools possessed by "civilian powers" such as the EU; still, for EPC/CFSP to co-opt these policies for external political ends, thus drawing itself closer to the treaty-based Community, was a major advancement. Moreover, the EU has become increasingly concerned about improving the coherence among its external policy domains, in part to enhance its role in world politics (Coignez 1992; Neuwahl 1994; Krenzler and Schneider 1997; Smith 2001b). This has not been an easy task, and it raises the more fundamental questions of why a regional institution devoted to economic cooperation among its citizens and firms should require its own global foreign policy, and how that institution attempts to reconcile its economic and political aspirations.

To complicate matters further, there may be inherent differences between international cooperation in economic and political/security affairs. The stakes are perceived to be higher in areas of "high politics," and it is often very difficult to assess and distribute the gains, if any, from foreign policy cooperation. Economic integration represents a clear goal (the elimination of internal barriers and the harmonization of EU barriers with those of the outside world) that can be explicitly measured according to agreed timetables. A common foreign policy, however, does not share these characteristics; it can mean only a constant process of policy coordination (though informed by general principles, such as respect for human rights and democracy), often driven by changing external circumstances or crises. This may involve the creation of entirely new standards (not just the elimination of old ones), sometimes at the expense of existing national foreign policy interests. Finally, many economic issues involve a fairly high degree of consensual knowledge about the effects of economic conditions on behavior, such as the relationship between exchange rates and economic activity (Jervis 1978; Haas 1980; Lipson 1984).

This distinction between high and low politics helps explain why the EU first developed its authority in less-controversial economic areas while attempts at European defense cooperation in the 1950s failed. Unlike many economic goals, such as a single market or single currency, there is no clear "end product" to be achieved with a "common" foreign and security policy. Such a common policy, like political "integration" and political "union," implies a final stage when the mechanism, in actual practice, can mean only a continuing process of action that evolves over time. Accordingly, students of international cooperation in general, and of European integration in particular, have been preoccupied with socioeconomic policy areas, often to the exclusion of other forms of cooperation. There are also far more socioeconomic institutions in the international system than security-related institutions, which helps bias the literature on cooperation and regional integration in favor of the former. Indeed, one of the founding fathers of functional integration theory, Ernst Haas, explicitly excluded security and defense cooperation from his theory, which focused on spillover in economic policy sectors (Haas 1961). And when compared to other (EC) policy areas, EU foreign policy does seem seriously deficient; compared to international relations in general, however, it is a unique success. By focusing on supranational EC processes (or worse, foreign policymaking within states) as their benchmark for success, both integration theorists and theorists of national foreign policymaking fail to appreciate the central fact that EU foreign policy is being undertaken by states which previously had (and still have) such strong incentives and capabilities to pursue independent foreign policies, and whose pursuit of such policies once led to unprecedented misery on a global scale. Yet EPC was also quite novel in the extent to which it became increasingly linked to, and deferential to, supranational procedures within the EC. This process raises our next question regarding EU foreign policy: how it actually functions.

4   *The mechanisms and resources of European foreign policy*

The general blurring of the distinctions between high and low politics, between economic and foreign/security policy cooperation, and between the EC and EPC/CFSP, can be appreciated by a more detailed examination of the still-evolving institutions and procedures of EU foreign policy, and how they relate to those of the EC (and individual EU member states) in other areas. This constitutes a fourth major area of EU foreign policy research (Holland 1991b; Rummel 1992; Ginsberg 1995, 1997a; Cameron 1998, 1999; White 2001) and is a central focus of this study. Process always matters in fully explaining any policy decision, whether those of states or international institutions, and whether achieved by virtue of self-interested bargains or other social behaviors. More specifically, if the characteristics of cooperative issue-areas are reflected in institutional design, then we would expect that EU foreign policy cooperation would operate differently from the EC's socioeconomic policies, where the Commission has the sole authority to introduce legislation, the Council of Ministers (and in some cases, the European Parliament [EP]) has the right to modify and approve legislation, and the European Court of Justice (ECJ) can render legally binding decisions on EU member states, firms, and citizens. EU foreign policy is quite different from this process, but the argument must be substantially qualified.

One must first keep in mind that European integration has always involved the use of *economic* cooperation to reduce *political* conflicts among EU member states, and organizations such as the Commission are the driving force behind the policies used to achieve economic cooperation. Thus economic integration itself was supposed to promote, indirectly, political reconciliation, stability, and cooperation in Europe. Internal political integration of this sort might lead to foreign policy cooperation and external actions, but integration theorists assumed this connection rather than specified how it would be established or developed. In addition, EU member states have often disagreed over the extent to which Europe's external political relations should be handled by Brussels. As a result, some member states have attempted to keep EPC (and the CFSP) a strictly *intergovernmental* mechanism (at least in legal terms) to avoid "contaminating" it by existing supranational organizations and procedures in the EC. Other pro-integrationist states feared the reverse: the contamination of the EC's supranational aspects by the intergovernmental features of EPC. Both fears contributed to the explicit procedural separation of EC affairs from foreign policy when EPC was first established. Despite this separation, however, EPC *was* institutionalized and it grew much closer to the EC, eventually becoming formally linked to it as the CFSP in the new European Union framework. How EPC/CFSP involves aspects of both intergovernmentalism and supranationalism (among other processes), and the extent to which it affects the more general process of European integration, are the central concerns of this volume.

5   EU foreign policy and domestic politics

Finally, other researchers have been more concerned with the relationship between domestic politics and EU foreign policy, an increasing area of interest in other EU policy areas as well. Since EPC was established as an intergovernmental system, it seems appropriate to consider state governments, interests, and institutions at the first stage of analysis. According to many observers, national foreign policies are the primary "inputs" into the process of EU foreign policy, and they have received much attention (Hill 1983b; Pfetsch 1994; Carlsnaes and Smith 1994; Stavridis and Hill 1996; Hill 1996; and Manners and Whitman 2000). However, since EU foreign policy has also become increasingly rule-governed over the past three decades, we must also consider the possibility that policy outcomes are the result of some unique combination of EU and domestic influence that varies across time, EU states, and types of foreign policy actions. In addition, these outcomes typically are not major history-making reforms of the EU; some have suggested that bargains such as the Single European Act and the Treaty on European Union favor, and may even strengthen, the position of heads of government/state (Moravcsik 1994). This is not the case with EPC/CFSP; while its outcomes are important policy decisions of the EU, they are not wholly determined by heads of state and they may involve EC institutions in ways that treaty negotiations do not.

It is possible to take these arguments even further and consider that EU member states are fundamentally changed by virtue of their participation in foreign policy cooperation, in ways and with mechanisms that can be empirically validated. This argument is in line with the assumptions about institutions and policy adaptation noted above. Moreover, if cooperation takes the form of consensus-building and peer pressure, rather than trading favors or accepting the decisions of an independent supranational authority, then we must also consider that state interests or preferences are susceptible to other forms of political influence which have not been fully appreciated by analysts of international cooperation. Finally, if common actions reflect common interests, and common interests reflect a common identity, then loyalties or even a distinct European identity can be forged as a result of increasing economic and political cooperation. My examination of the performance record of EPC/CFSP in this volume shows it is possible to discern some persistent features of the EU's external identity from the way it behaves in world politics, and to see evidence of changes of policy within individual states by virtue of their participation in the system. Although I cannot fully explore all potential changes in the domestic politics of EU member states resulting from EU foreign policy cooperation, there is enough such activity taking place to warrant close attention in this study and in future research.

An institutional approach to European foreign policy

How do we explain EPC/CFSP and thus answer some of these important questions? Unfortunately, the wide variety of questions asked about EPC/CFSP has complicated the search for general theoretical explanations of it. As I suggested above, it is inappropriate to judge or explain EU foreign policy by comparing it to other EU policy domains, even those involving external economic relations, since it is not based on the same legal foundation or procedural mechanisms found in the EC. Although we can rely on some insights from the literature on economic integration, this approach alone cannot explain the complex dynamics of EPC/CFSP. Nor is it appropriate to rely exclusively on the literature on foreign policymaking within states, which typically follows the unitary rational actor assumption. The EU's foreign policymaking system is certainly not unified or even centralized, and it operates according to different rationales depending on the circumstances, a point I will explain in more detail in the next chapter. And as long as the EU is based on international treaty law, its member states reserve the right to participate according to their own self-interests. Finally, it is inappropriate to compare EU foreign policy to cooperation within military alliances, such as NATO. The stakes here are not nearly as high as those involving defense, and EU states have only recently begun serious discussions on joint military operations within the context of European integration.

Thus, this volume examines EPC/CFSP largely in terms of its inherent nature as an example of institutionalized multilateral cooperation among sovereign, independent states. European integration is largely an ongoing discourse about institutions: how to translate very *general* common values or aspirations into *specific* collective policies or behaviors, internal and external, through the application of norms and rules. Institutional development is central to European integration, but we need not privilege the supranational institutions of the EC (such as the Commission and the ECJ), which is the tendency of many institutional analyses of European integration. Instead, I examine the tensions, connections, and resolutions between intergovernmental and supranational methods of community-building, focusing on how behavioral precedents have been set and followed in the area of foreign policy, despite strict limits on the initiation of policy by the Commission and the adjudication of disputes by the ECJ.

Moreover, although the EU's foreign and security policy cooperation is a unique ambition among regional economic organizations, it is not strictly *sui generis*: some of its institutional elements can be found in other forums for international cooperation, and the activities of EU organizational actors in this domain are closely related to functions they perform in other EC policy areas. As a result, the organization and functioning of EPC/CFSP can offer more general theoretical lessons about the nature of international cooperation; in fact, the puzzle can be reformulated in this way: how have EU states managed to intensify their cooperation in foreign policy since 1970 without fully subordinating these efforts to the supranational Community method and while respecting the individual interests and sovereignty of EU states? Although certain historical elements, such as Franco-German reconciliation and leadership, play a role in this story, constant debates and compromises over institutional questions have been equally important. Institutions can be reproduced while history cannot, and the lessons learned by the EU in this domain can thus shed light on institutionalized cooperation in other domains.

More specifically, I argue that this cooperation is theoretically and empirically interesting for three reasons. First, EPC/CFSP represents international cooperation in what might be considered an emerging, even unusual, issue-area: it is motivated for reasons beyond economic gain or defense. EU foreign policy is largely an "aspirational" institution similar to international cooperation in areas such as human rights, development assistance, and labor standards (Botcheva and Martin 2001). For the most part, EPC/CFSP does not provide direct material benefits to EU member states in terms of either security or wealth, yet they continue to pursue it. Second, and partly due to its aspirational goals, this cooperation was achieved with an innovative and flexible set of institutional procedures, one that is still expanding and that has not been adequately explored by theorists of international relations. Aspirational institutions are usually weak (i.e., they involve no strict enforcement mechanisms), yet EU states have achieved a significant degree of cooperation in foreign policy while strengthening EPC/CFSP as an institution. Third, EPC/CFSP involves highly developed, industrialized states with vastly different capabilities and powerful historical reasons to prefer autonomy or independence, especially in foreign policy. Western Europe is largely responsible for the international state system (not to mention realist-based balance-of-power policies), and I hope to determine how and why the states of this region, through the EU, pursue such symbolic or aspirational goals by pooling their sovereignty with new institutional mechanisms.

I defend my choice of an institutional approach to EPC/CFSP in more detail in the next chapter. In general, my approach draws upon the "new institutionalism" literature (which involves both "historical institutionalism" and "sociological institutionalism") in the hopes of providing a coherent way to synthesize competing views about the nature of European foreign policy cooperation. The fundamental argument is that there is a two-way relationship between institutional development and changes in state behavior, which profoundly influences international cooperation. When institutions are weak or vaguely specified, then they should have little impact on state behavior. When institutions are more robust, with clear goals and unequivocal rules, then states should change their behavior in accordance with those goals and rules. If, over time, the same institution develops from a weak agreement to a formal organization, then we should see corresponding changes in state behavior.

This is precisely what occurred with EU foreign policy. Since 1970 it has developed from an informal, intergovernmental "gentlemen's agreement" with unwritten rules into a system of formal and informal legal obligations, plus organizations with budgets, staffs, and permanent headquarters. EPC was not organized according to functional principles, where the issue-area was well defined, goals were agreed upon in advance, costs and benefits could be easily determined, and the distribution of same could be negotiated according to a stable set of rules. The process was far more haphazard, involving trial and error, improvisation, and incremental change. Specifically, EU states improved their prospects for cooperation by shifting from a *bargaining* style of cooperation to a *problem-solving* style of cooperation. Where bargaining involves the satisfaction of *self-interests* through trade-offs and incentives, problem-solving involves an appeal to *common interests* and the use of ostracism or peer-pressure to sanction potential defectors (Scharpf 1988). These common interests are not self-evident; they must be determined through institutionalized interactions. This non-coercive style of cooperation can promote and upgrade common views in ways that are discouraged by self-interested, bargaining-centered approaches to collective action.

At the same time, states did not approach each external problem independently; previous interactions helped condition future behavior. This fact is central to the institutional logic of cooperation presented in this volume. EPC/CFSP provides a good case to explore institutionalization because we can see how the system changed as layers were added to it, affecting external policies, EU member states, and relations with EC organizations and procedures. Since EPC was created as an intergovernmental system with modest institutional support and weak links to the EC, we can see how alterations to these characteristics over the years progressively influenced cooperation in this domain. In other words, institution-building and policymaking occurred simultaneously in EPC; developing EPC as an institution was itself a form of foreign policy cooperation that encouraged additional expressions of collective action.

The case of EU foreign policy thus demonstrates that institutions can be designed and developed to encourage international cooperation in ways that go beyond transaction-costs approaches, or beyond bargaining, in two senses: beyond the great history-making decisions of inter-governmental conferences which often involve institutional reform, and beyond the *quo pro quo* policymaking negotiations which take place within many other international institutions. Institutional mechanisms are the filter through which external and internal demands are focused on the EU; they make collective behavior stable over time and help condition state interests. By explaining how these mechanisms change, we can also explain changes in cooperation.

However, I do not intend to explain the origins, purpose, and functioning of all institutional elements involved in EU foreign policy.[3] Nor will I catalogue all EU foreign policies that may have been affected by institutional change. My purpose is far more narrow: I hope to achieve a better understanding of the interplay between the EU's higher profile foreign policies and its more significant institutional elements, both of which will be defined more clearly in the chapters ahead. I must therefore strike a balance between comprehensiveness and analytical clarity to find meaningful and generalizable lessons about institutionalized cooperation and European integration.

A note on terminology and methodology

This study spans the entire history of institutionalized foreign policy co-operation in the EU from 1970 to 2002, making it necessary to clarify my use of several terms. As the above discussion suggests, EU foreign policy took two institutional forms. The first, European Political Cooperation, entered into effect with the Luxembourg Report in 1970. It was considered a form of cooperation parallel to but legally apart from the EC; it was not formally linked to existing EC treaties until the Single European Act in 1987. Nor did EPC become a treaty until that point; it operated as an informal agreement among its member states for sixteen

---

[3] For such an analysis, which is far more descriptive than explanatory, see Macleod, Henry, and Hyett 1996.

years. The second form involves the current CFSP, which legally re-placed EPC following the 1991 Treaty on European Union (Maastricht Treaty). It entered into effect on November 1, 1991, along with the rest of the Maastricht Treaty. The terms "EU foreign policy," "European foreign policy," or "foreign/security policy cooperation" are used inter-changeably to refer to activities under either of these mechanisms; the terms EPC and the CFSP are used as appropriate to the historical pe-riod under discussion. "Defense cooperation" primarily involves military matters and was not taken up until the Maastricht Treaty (nor has it re-sulted in many concrete EU policy actions); it is not a major focus of this study. I therefore distinguish defense cooperation, where military force is the exclusive or primary policy tool, from foreign/security policy cooper-ation, where diplomatic or economic tools tend to dominate. I also use the term "state" as a generic term to refer to government representatives and their supporting officials and institutions; occasionally the analysis makes it necessary to distinguish between (temporary) governments and (more permanent) bureaucratic officials. I define my use of the terms "institution," "organization," and "cooperation" in later chapters.

Under Maastricht the EC was subsumed under a new structure, the European Union (EU). I generally favor the term "EU" throughout the study to refer to the basic institutional framework in which European foreign policy is embedded; I only use the term "EC" (even during the pre-Maastricht era) to refer to the policies, procedures, and institutions of that pillar. This includes the original European Communities set up by the 1957 Treaty of Rome (the European Coal and Steel Commu-nity, the European Economic Community, and the European Atomic Energy Community), and their associated bodies. Also, since the EU has increased in membership since its birth, I use various terms to de-note this change depending on the historical period under discussion: the Six (Belgium, France, West Germany, Italy, Luxembourg, and the Netherlands), the Nine (the Six plus Denmark, Ireland, and the United Kingdom), the Ten (the Nine plus Greece), and the Twelve (the Ten plus Portugal and Spain). Note also that I use the term "Germany" to refer to unified West and East Germany; "West Germany" and "East Germany" are used only when the discussion requires a distinction between the two countries.

Methodologically, students of EPC/CFSP are faced with the problem that this policy area is still highly secret in that deliberations are not open to outsiders and minutes of EPC/CFSP meetings are not available to the public. Although an archive of EPC/CFSP documents exists in the Council Secretariat General, the EU has not taken any efforts to re-view and release them despite my requests. Given the sensitivity of these documents and the fact that they concern the foreign policies of up to fifteen member states, it is understandable that the EU is reluctant to embark upon a potentially embarrassing de-classification exercise. Thus, like most students of EPC/CFSP, my analysis uses evidence from existing published sources, including historical accounts, memoirs, case studies, and original document research. Additionally, I relied upon confidential interviews and informal conversations with approximately sixty officials involved with EPC/CFSP. These officials were interviewed (some multiple times) during three trips to Europe in 1995–96, 2001, and 2002. Some of these officials were present at the creation of EPC at the Hague summit in 1969; others began working for the CFSP following Maastricht. All EU member states were represented in this sample, as well as the following institutions:

* The European Commission (officials from the Legal Service, the Commission's general secretariat, its external relations unit, and officials from the cabinets of seven individual external relations commissioners).
* The Committee of Permanent Representatives, or COREPER (including both staff officials, such as CFSP counselors, and the permanent ambassadors to the EU); all fifteen EU member states were covered.
* The Council of Ministers Secretariat General (including the CFSP unit and the Council legal service).
* The European Parliament.
* Foreign ministries of several EU member states.
* The US mission to the European Union in Brussels.

I was also able to interview several members of the "Reflection Group," a group of high-ranking EU member state foreign ministry officials who prepared the agenda for the 1996–97 Intergovernmental Conference (IGC) of the EU, as well as several IGC negotiators themselves after the IGC began in March 1996. Finally, I made a short trip to Brussels in 2001 to assess the impact of the Amsterdam Treaty on EU foreign policy and another to Stockholm in 2002 to explore how holding the EU presidency affects a new EU member state, particularly in the foreign policy realm. All of these officials were asked a consistent set of theoretically informed questions to provide supporting evidence for the analysis that follows.

Part I

Institutions and foreign policy cooperation: the theoretical and empirical terrain

1 The institutionalization of cooperation: an analytical framework

Foreign and security policy cooperation has long been one of the most ambitious goals of those who favor a more united Europe, yet the original mechanism to achieve this goal, European Political Cooperation, was vague in its scope and severely limited in terms of institutional design.[1] By the time of the Treaty on European Union twenty years later, however, the limited "talking shop" of EPC had been formally institutionalized into a legally binding policymaking process capable of producing common positions and joint actions on a wide range of global problems. Today virtually no major foreign policy issue goes unexamined by the EU, and cooperation is under serious consideration in related areas such as security and defense. How can we explain this cooperation, and in what ways did institutionalization affect EU foreign policymaking? The key challenge here is to understand the various processes by which an informal, extra-legal, ad hoc, improvised system gradually fostered the achievement of cooperative outcomes *and* progressively enhanced its own procedures to improve the prospects for those outcomes.

As much of this activity took place outside the institutions and procedures of the European Community, an explanation of EU foreign policy may benefit from more general explanations of institutional development rather than other theories, such as functionalism, specifically developed to explain European economic integration. This means taking into account the reciprocal links between institutional development and the propensity of states to cooperate to achieve joint gains. This relationship is dynamic and circular: cooperation can encourage actors to build institutions, but institutions themselves should foster cooperative outcomes, which later influence the process of institution-building through feedback mechanisms. Causality runs in both directions, and institutionalization and cooperation can be treated as either dependent or independent variables

---

[1] Note that my focus on EU foreign policy cooperation differs from an analysis of political *integration*, which involves foreign policy cooperation plus a host of other factors, such as electoral practices and judicial cooperation.

depending on one's research interests. To capture the feedback dynamics between these behaviors, we can assess both causal paths separately, but in sequence. In other words, by analyzing the entire history of institutionalized foreign policy cooperation in the EU, I can first demonstrate that, in general, institutionalization improves the prospects for cooperation. Of course, this is not to say that *every* new institutional procedure directly promotes cooperative state behavior, only that, other things being equal, international cooperation is more likely to be found within an institutionalized framework than outside of one. Second, by breaking down the analysis into clear stages, I can also demonstrate how individual institutional elements encourage specific cooperation-inducing behaviors. Third and finally, I can then examine cooperative outcomes more closely to show how they (along with other factors) encourage debates and reforms regarding institutional design.

Why an institutional approach to EU foreign policy cooperation?

The primary outcome to be explained in this study is the progressive development and impact of institutionalized cooperation in foreign policy among EU member states. In general, this cooperation, or policy coordination, requires deliberate, active efforts on the part of states to achieve a certain end. This is particularly true in "mixed motive" situations, where states have incentives both to cooperate and to defect, or in situations (such as EU foreign policy) where it is difficult to determine the costs and benefits of cooperating. To know that cooperation is taking place, we must show that states did not perceive themselves as having identical interests in a given choice situation, yet they still attempted to adjust their foreign policies to accommodate each other (Keohane 1984: 51–52). I provide more specific empirical measures of EU foreign policy cooperation in the next chapter; for the moment, I define such cooperative actions as those which are: (1) undertaken on behalf of all EU states toward non-members, international bodies, or global events or issues; (2) oriented toward a specific goal; (3) made operational with physical activity, such as financing or diplomacy; and (4) undertaken in the context of EPC/CFSP discussions (although the EC can also be involved).[2]

What causes such cooperation? I should first note that cooperation can emerge in the absence of institutional structures, or even in the absence of deliberate efforts to coordinate policy. Even in "Prisoner's Dilemma" type situations explored by realists, where two actors are

---

[2] These are based on my slight revision of criteria found in Ginsberg 1989: Chapter 1.

assumed to be held incommunicado from each other, cooperation can emerge spontaneously through mechanisms such as iteration (Axelrod 1984). Prisoner's Dilemma, however, does not accurately reflect the politics of the EU: it is a highly transparent and multilateral (rather than bilateral) network of states and involves a dense web of policy issues and actors bound by complex institutional mechanisms. Various forms of realism thus generally fall short in attempting to explain cooperation in this setting.

For example, structural (or neo-) realism stresses the international distribution of power, largely defined in material terms, to explain how order can emerge out of the behavior of self-interested actors (Waltz 1979). In this view, such order often results from the presence of a dominant state (hegemon) or set of states engaged in a larger struggle for power. However, although the dynamics of the Cold War rivalry and the security guarantee provided by the US certainly encouraged the initial drive for European integration in the 1950s, EU foreign policy in particular cannot be understood solely by reference to the global balance of power. The US military guarantee undoubtedly created an atmosphere conducive to European cooperation, but the US was still unable to dictate the terms of that cooperation.[3] Nor can fluctuations in US–Soviet rivalry account for the persistence and gradual expansion of EU foreign policy. Cooperation in the EC/EU has taken place under bipolarity (during the Cold War) and unipolarity (if one assumes that the collapse of the Soviet Union in 1991 resulted in a "unipolar moment" dominated by the US). EPC progressed in part because of its usefulness as a third way between the superpowers; it allowed for both a military alliance with the US and a sociopolitical dialogue with the Soviet Union and its successor states. More generally, as critics often observe (Haggard 1991), a single international condition (the relationship between the superpowers) can hardly explain the wide variety of outcomes in world politics, whether conflict or cooperation. Thus, structural realist theory is inadequate to explain the development of foreign policy cooperation in Europe over the past three decades.

Similarly, realist theories involving perceptions of *specific* external threats as a motivating factor for cooperation are not very useful for understanding EU foreign policy (Walt 1988). Major fluctuations in the US–Soviet relationship, for example, are weak predictors of changes in EU foreign policy cooperation: Europe has made specific efforts to cooperate in this domain before and after the demise of the Soviet Union, has not always acquiesced to the US and NATO, and continues to develop its own efforts in this area despite the robustness of NATO. In

---

[3] For one example, see Mastanduno 1988.

short, there has been no systematic relationship between policies of the superpowers and the response of the EU. Even within the EU we cannot explain cooperation by focusing primarily on the behaviors of three regional hegemons (France, Germany, and the UK).[4] These states have not always seen their goals realized, nor have they always taken the lead on every major policy or institutional innovation. The smaller EU states have in fact played more important roles in the development of European foreign policy in terms of its policies and procedural development than a realist would expect. As we shall see, agreements between the big states (or at least between France and Germany) have usually been necessary to *codify* EPC/CFSP institutional changes in the form of a report or treaty, yet the *character* of such changes is usually a product of existing habits and procedures worked out among the officials responsible for EU foreign policy on a daily basis. Most importantly, we have seen the gradual construction of the EU's external capabilities despite the efforts of the US and even of some EU states (such as France and the UK) to resist this process.

In sum, leading versions of realist theory are inadequate to address fully the key questions about EU foreign policy discussed in the introduction to this study: why it persists, its performance record, its relationship to European economic integration, its procedures, and its impact on the domestic politics of its member states.[5] Certainly we must remain attentive to the concern for power and sovereignty that permeates many EPC/CFSP decisions. But we also need to be sensitive to occasions where concerns about power are balanced against competing objectives, or even muted altogether owing to other factors. External forces or pressures such as anarchy, the distribution of power, or hegemonic leadership do not dictate state behavior. Such forces or problems must always be defined before they become objects of action, which requires human choice (or agency). Nor do the largest states within the EU dominate the processes of either cooperation or institution-building, whose rules specifically allow all states to play a leadership role and to veto actions they oppose.

---

[4] This argument is closely related to "alliance dependency" theories, where fear of abandonment or exclusion leads weaker members to support any cooperation advocated by stronger powers. By this reasoning, cooperation is difficult because states must balance the risks of entrapment (being drawn into a conflict because of another state's ambitions) with the risks of abandonment (having no support from others when their own security interests are threatened). Thus the dominant power must be able to raise the costs of non-cooperation (with threats) or lower the costs of cooperation (with payoffs) to produce alliance cohesion with other member states. See Christensen and Snyder 1990.

[5] For an opposing view, see Pijpers 1991.

These problems make the application of mono-causal theories of cooperation, such as realism, to EU foreign policy extremely problematic. Although we should always be sensitive to the role of material power in explaining international cooperation, realism by itself offers no deductive hypotheses, only *post hoc* "explanations" based on general assumptions about national interests.

Liberal theories involving interdependence and institutions attempt to confront these limitations of realist theory. For example, interdependence theories suggest that as security concerns diminish among a set of states, and as issues become increasingly entangled with each other (owing in part to increasing transnational and transgovernmental contacts), then states are more likely to cooperate to manage the costs and benefits of those issues. Complete national autonomy becomes harder to sustain, and states recognize the potential for joint gains in many situations (Keohane and Nye 1977). To the extent that this general tendency toward international interdependence is complemented by an increasing number of regional links and contacts at the European level, it would explain a general convergence of foreign policy interests within Europe. Complex transnational links create common problems and preferences, which induce cooperation among states.

This view provides a key rationale for the persistence and expansion of European foreign policy cooperation and European integration in general. Ginsberg, for example (1989: Chapter 2), finds that most foreign policy actions taken by the EU can be explained by two causal logics: the "regional integration logic" and the "interdependence logic." The regional integration logic involves situations where outside actors make demands on the EU as a result of its efforts to create common policies, primarily in terms of completing the single European market. The EC's Common External Tariff, for example, triggers a response from external actors who in turn require a common response from the EC. According to Ginsberg, this logic explains all but two of the 167 foreign policy actions taken by the EC between 1958 and 1972 (prior to the regular operation of EPC), most of which naturally involved economic issues. The interdependence logic involves international (as opposed to regional) pressures that can encourage a collective response by the EU. This logic became especially relevant to the EC after 1972, when political and economic upheavals involving the Arab-Israeli conflict and the oil crises challenged the EC to find a common external policy.

Yet with many issues a general appreciation of common values or preferences (such as support for democracy and human rights, anti-communism, and a respect for law) masks serious disputes over specific strategies and means – economic, political, or military – to achieve the desired ends. In other words, liberal interdependence theories are somewhat vague on the way these preferences are related or prioritized, and on how they change state policies in specific cases to produce a common response (i.e., cause cooperative actions). Efforts to cooperate can be narrow or comprehensive in scope; they can be weak or strong in their ability to bind state behavior; and they can take the form of "one-shot" deals to long-range plans (Haas 1990). We should be able to explain this variation in the form or nature of cooperation, particularly across issues and over time. To explain cooperation, then, we need to explain choice among competing alternatives; to explain choice, we need to focus on how EU states make collective decisions. Thus, like realism, liberal interdependence theories of cooperation are too indeterminate to understand fully the progressive development of EU foreign policy. A secure environment and a belief in common interests (or a common destiny) are most likely necessary but still insufficient conditions for the increasingly extensive foreign policy cooperation found in the EU.

Given the limits of these general explanations of cooperation, we must take a closer look at the decision-making process within the EU foreign policy system. As Ginsberg notes, a third "self-styled" logic of EU foreign policy action became more prevalent starting in the 1970s, which involved EPC actions (or EPC actions taken in conjunction with the EC):

(Self-styled actions) reflect the EC's *own internal deliberations*, both within the EC bodies themselves and between the member-states and the EC bodies. Self-styled actions reflect the EC's *own sense of mission and interest in the world*. They are not solely dependent on the need to respond to external stimuli but instead are the products of (A) habits of working together; (B) EC and member-state initiatives; and (C) a sense of what Europeans want in foreign policy questions. EPC enables members to reach into all areas of international politics and has served to create an atmosphere conducive to fashioning, since 1974, a foreign policy style that reflects the members' convergent interests in foreign affairs.[6]

As I demonstrate in the next chapter, EU foreign policy actions reflecting the "self-styled logic" began to take place following the creation of EPC. The key point here is that such self-styled actions are driven not only by external forces impinging on the EU, but also by an internal decision-making dynamic increasingly bound by institutionalization. They are the result of EPC/CFSP becoming, over time, much greater than the sum of its parts. EU foreign policy developed its own internal momentum which is not captured by most theories of international cooperation.

---

[6] Ginsberg 1989: 59 (emphasis added).

Institutional change and cooperation: competing paradigms

Theories of institutional development have become increasingly complex and diverse in the past decade. While many realists remain skeptical of the relationship between institutions and cooperation (Grieco 1988; Mearsheimer 1994–95), other theories may shed more light on this question. These include neo-liberal institutionalism (Keohane 1984; Stein 1990), regime theory (Krasner 1983a), and in the specific case of the EU, liberal intergovernmentalism (Moravcsik 1993). These theories generally adopt the realist assumptions of anarchy, state-centrism, and states' concerns with security and cheating, yet they also accept that institutions can serve as bargaining arenas to help states conclude agreements with each other, thus promoting cooperation. Institutions do so by providing opportunities for linking disparate issues into package deals, making side-payments, and by helping states share information about their behaviors. For these theorists, the concern about being cheated by other states is the primary obstacle to relying on institutions to achieve international cooperation,[7] and adherents of this approach tend to focus on economic or environmental cooperation, which invites criticism from realists about the applicability of the theory to "high politics" issues of foreign policy and security.[8]

Although many of these ideas can be applied to an analysis of European foreign policy, and I rely on them in later chapters, the overall approach is still far too narrow. First, as I will discuss in more detail below, it is very difficult to conceive of EU foreign policy as a distinct issue-area of international relations, particularly at its inception in the early 1970s. Regime theory is predicated on convergent expectations regarding the common goals of the institution, yet EU foreign policy cooperation more often than not did not enjoy this convergence of views. It is therefore both a regime for creating common views and actions in an emerging, aspirational issue-area, *and* a "meta-regime" to create additional forms of institutionalized cooperation (such as political dialogues) to handle specific problems. Second, many (though not all) regime theories stress formal obligations and organizations, yet EU foreign policy in its original form (EPC) was an informal, extra-legal arrangement for most of its history, and did not involve organizations to the extent suggested by

[7] This view is not exclusive to international relations, of course. For example, in organized crime and other domains where state authority cannot be relied upon, hostage-taking is a rational way to enforce agreements (Williamson 1983).

[8] In their defense, neo-liberal institutionalists have claimed their theories apply equally to foreign/security and economic issues (Keohane and Martin 1995).

regime theory.[9] Third, regime theory is fairly static in its orientation; it may help explain the particular constellation of forces that led to the creation of an institution (or the "demand" for a regime) but says little about regime development over an extended period of time.[10] Fourth, the heavy neo-liberal focus on reducing transactions-costs, where common interests are predetermined and issues are linked (or side-payments are made) to induce cooperation, does not generally apply to EU foreign policy cooperation. As we shall see, most problems within EPC/CFSP are treated as separate issues and cannot be made into package deals with other EPC/CFSP or EC issues.

Given the limitations of neo-liberalism in explaining institutionalization, I draw upon other approaches in this study. For example, classical liberal theories of institutions (often called "Grotian" perspectives because of their emphasis on law) question many of the fundamental assumptions of realism and hold a more optimistic view of institutionalized international cooperation. For classical liberals, institutions can do more than just act as passive bargaining arenas. Institutions can have an independent effect on world politics, such as providing technical expertise and policy-relevant knowledge. They help bring about the creation of international norms which are then internalized in member states and influence their behavior. In some cases, institutions can develop meaningful autonomy, by supplying new ideas and political leadership to help states reach agreement on potentially contentious issues. Especially in situations where democratic states are highly interdependent, institutionalized cooperation should develop and expand. For some liberals, interests and preferences can even be fundamentally changed by institutionalized interactions among states, thanks to a common respect for law and the harmonization of interests (Young 1989; Sandholtz 1996).

In sum, liberal theories recognize that institutionalized cooperation does not just involve periodic bargaining between unitary, undifferentiated, self-interested actors. Other ways to induce cooperation exist,

---

[9] These points regarding legal obligations and formal organizations are addressed in more detail in Chapters 5 and 6.

[10] Nadelmann (1990: 484–86) does suggest a multistage evolutionary pattern in his study of prohibition regimes, or those which attempt to eradicate certain behaviors (such as piracy and slavery) in international society. These stages involve (1) a pre-regime stage, in which there are no constraints on behavior; (2) the targeting and redefinition of behavior as evil, often by "moral entrepreneurs"; (3) activism by states and non-state actors for the criminalization of the behavior; (4) the use of formal laws and police patrols to control the prohibited behavior; and (5) the reduction or elimination of the prohibited activity. As we shall see, however, these stages are not applicable to the development of European foreign policy cooperation, which increasingly stresses positive action rather than the prohibition of certain behaviors (i.e., positive integration rather than negative integration).

and these can be deliberately encouraged by institutional arrangements. Norms matter for a variety of reasons, and states have some ability to learn and thus change their behavior. However, liberal approaches are largely silent about the sources of norms, how norms change, and why norms develop in some areas but not in others. Liberalism asserts that certain conditions (such as democratic governments, or growing interdependence) favor institutionalized cooperation; however, it stops far short of specifying the precise mechanisms or processes by which institutional development occurs.

The same generally holds true for more recent social constructivist theories of state behavior, which focus on intersubjective ideas, knowledge, and discourse. As critics point out (Checkel 1998), constructivism is vague on the ways by which some ideas achieve dominance or permanence (that is, become *institutionalized*) over others. It also tends to favor structure over agency, in the sense that it treats actors as passive, rule-following entities with little or no capacity to influence their own social environment. More importantly for my purposes, I am attempting to demonstrate cooperation in terms of specific rules and policy changes, which can be documented in the empirical record and, I argue, directly linked to institutional development. Constructivism tends to stress changes in general preferences, interests, or identities, none of which *directly* concerns me here (although I return to this question in the conclusion to this volume).[11] However, constructivism does have the merit of being neither optimistic nor pessimistic about institutions; it thus considers the possibility that institutionalization can have both positive and negative effects on cooperation.[12] This point will become increasingly relevant in the chapters to follow.

Toward a theory of institutionalization

To gain a fuller understanding of the relationship between institutions and cooperation we must move beyond the analysis of *static* institutions

---

[11] Although I do assume a link between changes in preferences and changes in policies, I focus on policy adaptation (i.e., cooperation) because of the methodological problems involved in determining the "actual motivations" of relevant officials from up to fifteen EU states across numerous policy issues over thirty years. Clear evidence of policy coordination is a necessary first step to exploring whether institutionalization changes fundamental national preferences or interests; this study attempts to provide and explain that evidence.

[12] Wendt 1999. Again, this approach stresses general structural conditions (common fate, interdependence, homogeneity of actors, and self-restraint) that apply to EU states and might affect their general propensity to cooperate. However, to explain actual institutional and policy outcomes in the area of EU foreign policy we need to supplement these conditions with more specific factors at work in the EU.

or structures and *single* collective outcomes and consider the cumulative impact of decisions regarding cooperative outcomes and institutional change, or the process of institutionalization. Powerful actors are certainly important in institution-building, as realists argue, but institutions can also constrain those actors and empower others at different stages of institutional development. As we shall see throughout this study, smaller states such as Belgium and the Netherlands have been able to discourage or encourage institutional change in ways that cannot be predicted by an emphasis on material power alone. Thus, European institution-building cannot be wholly explained by examining only history-making intergovernmental deals, such as the Single European Act (Peterson 1995), and EU foreign policy cannot be understood by considering collective actions in isolation from each other, or from the construction of the European Community itself. In other words, we need to consider both the temporal dimension of change (or the key events between each major intergovernmental bargain) and the decision-making locus of change (or the way national, regional, and global processes are reconstituted as policies and procedures at the EU level). This involves "middle-range" theory-building (Merton 1957), where we move from very general propositions about international institutions and cooperation to specific decision-making structures, their mechanisms of change, and the outcomes they produce.

Thus, a primary distinction must be made between "institution" and "institutionalization." In general, institutions are the "rules of the game" of a particular social group, or a set of norms that shape behavior in a social space. They define and condition the choices of individuals (North 1990: 3). Institutionalization is the process by which those norms, or shared standards of behavior, are created and developed. Understanding institutionalization requires us to consider how norms change over time. Although some institutional theories, particularly those derived from examinations of bureaucracies, emphasize the static character of institutional arrangements, institutions which do not exhibit some degree of development or adaptation during their life span are quite rare.[13] For most institutions, change is a constant feature, and rather than simply defining what an institution *is*, we should also attempt to explain what an institution is becoming, or how its norms adapt to each other and to their larger environment over time.

At a minimum, institutionalization means several things, which can serve as a point of departure for the analysis to follow. First and most generally, institutionalization means that certain behaviors of a set of actors persist over time; these actors thus adapt together (though to different

---

[13] For a more extensive examination of this point, see Powell and DiMaggio 1991.

degrees) in the face of internal and external challenges. Institutionalized behavior is thus fairly well bounded, or qualitatively different from its environment. In other words, state behavior conducted within EPC/CFSP is qualitatively different from that in other arenas (such as the EC or NATO) although there may be some similarities.[14] In this way, institutions also help promote stability, even though this stability is not necessarily efficient in terms of relating means to ends (see below). Second, institutionalization also means increasing complexity, in that collective behaviors and choices are more detailed and closely linked, thus applying to more situations. This complexity can be measured in terms of an increase in the number of norms, the clarity of those norms, the change from norms into laws (or formalization), and the bindingness of those norms (i.e., a change from behavioral standards or expectations to behavioral *obligations*). These common behaviors, and the shared meanings on which they are based, create a social space with its own internal dynamism, as norms are preserved, interpreted, and applied in a range of situations, thus both simplifying and complicating collective decision-making depending on the stage of institutional development. There is also likely to be some sense of appropriate roles that actors are expected to play in the process of collective choice (i.e., who leads and when), and often a division of labor involving those roles.

Third, it also means that actors attempt to apply increasingly broad, general criteria in addition to particular norms to make certain decisions; outcomes are not determined exclusively by each set of constraints and opportunities faced by the actors at a given time but are also conditioned by larger principles which apply to all actors in all situations. Decision-making thus becomes more automatic than discretionary as the institution develops (Polsby 1968: 145). Rather than tending to adapt to new circumstances, increasingly institutionalized behavior becomes more instinctive (but not necessarily mechanical). Actors do have a capacity to help redefine and reorient institutions, but this capacity diminishes once institutionalization reaches a certain level of formality and bindingness. This level varies depending on the policy domain and the actors involved, and maintaining a balance between flexibility and stability (or between agency and structure) has been a major hurdle for EU foreign policy considering that it began as a vague and open-ended process, yet also encouraged an improvised, creative style of decision-making. However, these hard-to-reach individual decisions would mean little if they were

---

[14] This is not to say that there are barriers between institutionalized domains. As we shall see later, a key source of institutional change involves functional, social, and political linkages to other institutions.

not preserved and used to help guide state behavior in similar situations later on.

Yet how could this institutionalization occur in a system which was clearly founded on the basis of intergovernmental principles that privileged actors over institutional structures? How did change take place in a system that explicitly controlled any involvement of EC bureaucracies and prevented the establishment of a central EU foreign policy organization for well over a decade? And to what extent could such a weakly institutionalized system actually influence the EU foreign policy cooperation? As we have seen, regime theory may provide some clues in terms of describing the principles, norms, rules, and decision-making procedures that initially define a given issue-area.[15] Similarly, it might be possible to specify the functions of institutions and measure the extent to which any set of cooperative outcomes matches those functions.[16] Yet institutional architects are rarely as far-sighted as these standards seem to require (especially in the area of EU foreign policy), and a description of norms and functions does not by itself explain their emergence, usage, growth, and impact on the actors involved.

Neo-functional theories of integration suggest another process: the logic by which institutionalized cooperation in one area requires cooperation in other domains via "functional spillover" between issue-areas (for example, creating an internal market requires a common external tariff), or via "political spillover" involving the activities of supranational EC actors, chiefly the Commission and the European Court of Justice (Caporaso and Keeler 1995). As we shall see, both of these processes have played important roles in EU foreign policy. EPC was established in part to help protect the economic policies of the EC, which suggests a type of functional spillover (although it is arguable whether economic integration *requires* foreign policy cooperation), and it did involve certain EC organizations, which suggests political spillover. Yet functionalism cannot explain the expansion of EPC into many areas, particularly where the EC has little or no economic interests (such as Central America) or where the attempt to cooperate on foreign policy actually disrupts or interferes with the EC's economic policies (such as South Africa). Functional spillover mechanisms are overwhelmingly directed toward economic policies, where the costs and benefits are easier to measure. Political spillover is similarly limited as an explanatory tool as EC actors have played far

---

[15] This is the standard definition of a regime. See Krasner 1983b: 2.

[16] For example, Bull (1977: 56–57) argues that the function of institutions is to make, communicate, administer, interpret, enforce, legitimize, and protect rules, which themselves must be capable of adaptation to changing needs and circumstances.

smaller roles in EPC/CFSP than in other EC policy areas.[17] The exclusion of the Court in particular has severely limited its institution-building role in EU foreign policy to a mere shadow of the key dispute-resolution role it plays in the EC, which often leads to new rules.[18] Thus we cannot look to spillover processes alone to account for the institutionalization of EU foreign policy cooperation, although they do play a role in the analysis.

In short, existing approaches to international or European institutions, while extremely insightful, address only isolated parts of the question of institutionalization: the role of norms, the functional goals of institutions, and the political role of organizations. Theoretically, we need a way to structure these diverse elements as part of a broader, more general process. Fortunately, a number of relevant insights can be found in the literature on comparative politics.[19] Although there are a number of permutations of this so-called new institutionalism, sociological institutionalism, or historical institutionalism, some common features exist. Together, they provide us with a set of causal mechanisms derived from the environment in which the institution exists and from within the institution itself. It should be stressed at the outset, however, that a focus on institutional processes does not take the place of other important variables in politics: actors, power resources (material or otherwise), and strategies. Rather, an institutional analysis helps to place these variables in context and illustrate the various linkages between them, so that the outcomes with which we are concerned – patterns of institutional change and cooperation – can be better understood (Thelen and Steinmo 1992: 12–13).

Before turning to the specific mechanisms of such change, it will be helpful to review the basic assumptions of the new institutional theory. First, the perspective generally implies bounded rationality, in the sense that while actors may have certain self-serving goals when they first choose to participate in EU foreign policy, they do not have all the information necessary to make optimal decisions, or they have far too much information to process, or they cannot consistently process the information they do have. When actors are uncertain about both defining the issue or problem to be addressed and measuring the costs and benefits involved, processes other than discrete, self-interested calculations about power

---

[17] For more on this point, see Ifestos 1987: Chapter 3; Øhrgaard 1997.

[18] The role of the ECJ in constructing the EC's institutional space is very well documented. For an overview, see Stone Sweet and Brunell 1998.

[19] The following discussion draws upon March and Olsen 1984, 1989; North 1990; Powell and DiMaggio 1991; Steinmo, Thelen, and Longstreth 1992; Finnemore 1996.

and interests may play a role in promoting change. Actors often seek to change institutions, but these information problems prevent a direct calculation of ends and means when attempting institutional change.[20] Moreover, information itself is rarely neutral; it can be manipulated or interpreted for different purposes (March and Olsen 1989: 10).

Second, actors often hold conflicting preferences, or preferences that are not as fixed or ordered as rational-choice theories imply. These preferences or interests – what actors want in a certain social setting – can be shaped by institutions. It is on this key point that the work of the new institutionalists and social constructivists starts to converge: the possibility that interests, and even the identities on which those interests are based, are conditioned by institutional or social structures. Institutions can thus shape the processes of goal selection and the strategies adopted to achieve those goals. This also suggests the possibility of the formation of a distinct polity, as actors reconstitute their behaviors and interests in terms of European norms rather than national ones, although there are certainly overlaps between the two. Identity is not necessarily a zero-sum characteristic, and the nation-state certainly does not have a monopoly on how agents identify themselves. In other words, institutional development and identity change do not require a "transfer" of loyalty to the EU, but only a redefinition (or expansion) of national identity to also include the collectivity symbolized by the EU (Mercer 1995). Thus, although this study is oriented toward explaining *policy* change (i.e., cooperation) rather than *preference* or *identity* change, I am sympathetic to the possibility that increasing participation in the EU project conditions how states define their goals and how they behave in order to achieve those goals.

Third, institutions do not change automatically in response to external or internal pressures. There are lags, contradictions, and gaps between the conditions which helped establish the institution and later circumstances. These dynamics can result in inefficient institutional forms and sub-optimal behavioral outcomes, at least temporarily. They also help stimulate a demand for institutional change. Fourth, institutions exhibit feedback effects, in the sense that today's decisions can influence future behavior, whether actors intended this to happen or not. Although actors often attempt to control institutional change, this is not always possible.

---

[20] As North (1990: 17) notes, "Individuals make choices based on subjectively derived models that diverge among individuals, and the information the actors receive is so incomplete that in most cases these divergent subjective models show no tendency to converge. Only when we understand these modifications in the behavior of the actors can we make sense out of the existence and structure of institutions and explain the direction of institutional change."

Especially in complex policy areas where the costs of institutional change are high, decisions made in one context have long-term consequences (often unexpected consequences) that shape later behavior, even to the point of preventing alternative choices. The effects of decisions made at one point in time constrain future decisions. As cooperation (or the production of common policies) develops, those policies are preserved and future choices are based on those common policies. These "path-dependent" and "lock-in" effects,[21] which effectively limit the capacity of actors to control change, make the temporal dimension of institutions extremely important. One cannot understand the effect of institutional arrangements without comparing behavior at different points in time, preferably over a fairly long period.

In addition to these general assumptions, new institutionalists recognize that certain policy domains or issue-areas invite certain types of political behavior (Evangelista 1989); sociologists make the same point about "organizational fields" (Powell and DiMaggio 1991; Fligstein 1997). The way such fields are originally defined – whether part of a calculated or accidental process – affects the actors who are involved (or excluded) in the collective process, and creates boundaries regarding the appropriate behavior of those actors. The variation among the original EC policy sectors established by the 1957 Treaty of Rome demonstrates the weakness of theories which imply some fundamental agent for institutional change: depending on the policy sector, there are different legislative procedures, different levels of involvement by EC organizations, and different mechanisms to ensure compliance by EC member states (Fligstein and McNichol 1998). The areas most difficult to institutionalize (such as foreign policy cooperation) are those which are extremely sensitive to governments, or those where it is difficult to measure costs and benefits, or those where there are fewer transnational actors whose interests would be directly served by further institutionalization.

To summarize, new institutionalism recognizes that there is no *single* process or agent of institutionalization, just as there is no single path to international cooperation. The trajectory of change varies depending on the policy area, the original agreement to institutionalize cooperation in the policy area and the actors involved in that agreement, and later historical and environmental conditions. Institutional problems often result, and these problems encourage future changes. And since institutional change itself is usually incremental, not revolutionary, it is necessary to analyze

---

[21] More specifically, lock-in effects refer to the difficulty of exiting from an agreed solution, and path-dependency refers to the way small decisions and chance circumstances can, over time, constrain future choices. See North 1990: 94; and Pierson 1993.

small decisions in detail to understand the logic of institutional change (North 1990: 6). This logic can often be described as one of *appropriateness* rather than efficiency, meaning that decisions about institutional change are defined more in terms of existing institutional elements than in terms of finding an optimal fit between means and ends (March and Olsen 1989: 160). Institutions themselves thus provide many clues about the future path of institutional change.

It is possible to go even further along this line of thinking. Historical institutionalism tends to view institutional development in negative terms: institutions take a different path from that intended or expected because states *lacked* the capacity to control them, owing to short time horizons, a prevalence of unanticipated consequences, shifting member state policy preferences, or because EC organizations (chiefly the Commission and the European Court) did not possess enough autonomy to control change (Pierson 1993; Pollack 1997). Yet I argue that institutionalization can involve behavioral change in more positive terms: institutions develop because they have an added-value that states discover in new and unexpected ways. They can develop a power and a legitimacy of their own that make their member states unwilling (not just *unable*) to control or reverse the process. This can be due both to a demonstrated level of efficiency and to the fact that they are embedded within a broader normative, legal, or bureaucratic structure (such as the EU) that also has value for member states. Finally, national policies, preferences, and even identity can be reshaped by institutional cultures in ways that functional approaches to institutions ignore.

Processes of institutionalization

If there is no single mechanism or agent of institutional change, what leads to institutionalization? To be sure, power is often assumed to be the most important factor in explaining change: the most powerful actors tend to get what they want. This argument is behind realist-based intergovernmental theories (where the power and interests of large states determine outcomes) and notions of political spillover developed by regional integration theorists (where powerful EC actors, such as the Commission and European Court, can influence outcomes). These factors do play a role in my analysis. However, since they do not explain everything about institutional change (such as the small-scale innovations created in between intergovernmental summits, or the role of small EU states in European foreign policy cooperation), we must supplement power-based arguments with other theories.

In general, the literature on institutions suggests three additional general logics to explain institutional development.[22] First, a *functional logic* shows that institutional development can help actors achieve goals in the midst of changing circumstances. In other words, to the extent that actors believe that institutional arrangements will help them achieve desired goals, these actors will encourage institutional change. This logic is also behind the functional spillover arguments of regional integration theorists: actors may have to push for institutionalization in one domain to achieve goals in another domain. Second, a *logic of normative appropriateness* is at work here, in the sense that new institutional elements (norms) are often defined in terms of previous ones. Ambiguities, inconsistencies, and contradictions within institutions (and between institutions with similar goals) must constantly be resolved. This leads to the production, clarification, and formalization of other norms, or institutional change. Third, a *sociocultural (or socialization) logic* can emerge, in the sense that actors learn to reorient their attitudes and behavior to an institution's norms as they regularly participate in the system. Actors (particularly ones new to the institution, as occurs during enlargement of the EU) must constantly adjust their own perspective to that of the institution (and vice versa), which adds dynamism to the process of institutional development.

Thus, for the functionalist logic to take precedence, the key question for actors is: will the institution help me achieve goals at an acceptable cost? For the logic of normative appropriateness to dominate, the key question is: to what extent does the institution fit with existing institutions and goals? And the socialization logic comes into play when actors (particularly those who are new to the institution) ask themselves: how do others behave in this social space? A complete explanation of institutional change involves all three elements in addition to conventional notions of power, though often at different stages: some event or episode encourages an evaluation of how to achieve goals, and that evaluation is based on both the existing institutional structure (or set of norms) and the experiences of the actors involved in the institution. Although institutional change can appear to be regressive at times (owing to short-term uncertainties raised by institutional change, normal lag effects resulting from institutional change, and the fact that new rules sometimes displace old ones), these logics allow us to treat institutional change as a cumulative process involving several different internal dynamics. Moreover, these are

---

[22] As noted earlier, Ginsberg (1989: Chapter 2) also discusses three logics to explain EU foreign policy: the integration logic, the interdependence logic, and the self-styled logic. However, these logics provide a rationale for individual EU foreign policy actions, not for institutionalization in general.

all "rational" dynamics, in the sense that actors can ultimately justify the changes on the basis of serving some utility function: the need to solve a common problem, the need to clarify the relationships between increasingly complex rules, and the need to tighten the bonds to one's social group. However, pressures for change intensify, and must eventually be resolved, when actors disagree over *which of these rationales*, if any, should take precedence, and over *what form* the ultimate rule should take based on that rationale.

These arguments about institutional development can tell us a great deal about institutional changes that are not wholly based on power, but what *specific* processes encourage institutionalization? Fundamentally, institutionalization means *change*, and both regime theorists and new institutionalists have suggested a number of change mechanisms located outside of institutional processes, such as broad changes in the socioeconomic or political context; changes in power resources of actors (owing, for example, to economic growth or technology); and crises.[23] These exogenous factors are important for my analysis. For example, it is no accident that "institutional moments" or "critical junctures" in the history of European integration (such as enlargements and Intergovernmental Conferences), where institutional reform is an explicit part of the agenda, are associated with institutional developments in foreign policy cooperation. Changes in the relationship between the superpowers undoubtedly affected foreign policy cooperation in the EU. Similarly, external crises such as the Afghan and Iranian crises of the late 1970s, and the Persian Gulf War and collapse of Yugoslavia in the early 1990s, encouraged serious debates about the means and ends of foreign policy cooperation.

Yet it must be emphasized that major events such as Intergovernmental Conferences usually only codify existing arrangements; they rarely lead to major innovations. And although crises may also stimulate change, they do not by themselves explain choice or the character of change. Actors respond to such events in different ways and draw different lessons from them; these processes can be conditioned in part by institutional arrangements.[24] Thus, it is also necessary to focus on endogenous sources of institutional change (March and Olsen 1989: Chapter 5). The literature on institutions has suggested a number of such internal mechanisms that can induce institutional change, such as:

[23] For an extended discussion, see Krasner 1983b: 10–20; Thelen and Steinmo 1992: 16–18.

[24] For example, during the Suez crisis of 1956, when the US pressured Britain and France to end their war against Egypt, the British "learned" that they should never be on the wrong side of the US, while the French "learned" that they could not always rely on the US for foreign policy support.

1. Bargaining regarding the future course of institutional change.
2. Intendedly rational problem-solving (whether to meet internal goals or handle external problems) to find new solutions to problems; those which are perceived as successful are then preserved as norms.
3. Experiential learning-by-doing as actors adapt to different situations.
4. Imitation, as actors learn from each other and from other institutions.
5. Turnover, which can involve normal bureaucratic turnover within institutions, changes of government, changes of EU presidencies, and when powerful new actors (EC organizations or new EU member states) are introduced into an institution.
6. Policy failures which can lead to a search for new solutions to problems.
7. New policy ideas which have also been identified as sources of change; these can be introduced from the outside or generated within institutions.[25]
8. Internal contradictions and crises (e.g., institutional breakdowns), which of course can be stimulated by external crises and can also induce change.[26]

These change-inducing factors are often related, as we shall see in the chapters that follow. In addition, a key source of institutional change involves the way institutionalized domains relate to each other over time. Institutions rarely exist in isolation from other institutions; the actors, resources, policies, and norms of one institution can affect another. These linkages can be functional, in the sense that when institutions share similar tasks they must coordinate their approaches to those tasks, or social, in the sense that the actors closely involved in several institutions tend to exchange knowledge and expectations among those institutions. As institutions become more embedded in complex networks involving other institutions, they can change through imitation or turnover, as I suggested above. The need to resolve inconsistencies or divisions of labor between institutions also can act as an incentive for change. The interpretation and codification of norms in light of other institutional goals, and norm-generated problems in general, serve as constant stimuli to institutional development. Thus, throughout this study I pay close attention to the relationship between foreign policy cooperation and the development of related domains, particularly the EC.

Summary

In this chapter I defended my choice of an institutional perspective over other leading theories of international cooperation. I also presented some

---

[25] For an extended analysis of this school of thought, see Yee 1996.
[26] This idea is similar to Krasner's (1984) notion of "punctuated equilibrium" in institutional change.

alternative conceptions of international institutions to those offered by dominant theories of international relations. The institution of European foreign policy cooperation was not established like most formal regimes, to be used as a relatively passive forum to make deals over policy. Both cooperation and institutionalization occurred at the same time over a period of years. Agreements reached in EPC/CFSP had value in and of themselves, and they were preserved as a guide to future policy. As this was not always a deliberate, efficient process, I suggested how certain insights based on historical institutionalism might be useful in understanding the complex process of EU foreign and security policy cooperation.

Despite some inefficiencies in parts of the process, as institutions develop they generally make it easier for states to reach decisions and make judgments about the scope, means, ends, duration, effectiveness, and desirability of cooperation. I argued that institutionalization and cooperation are related, dynamic processes, and satisfying explanations of the relationship between them must be sensitive to the way issue-areas or policy domains are defined, and how uncertainty about such definitions affects the process. We must also be open to the ways state preferences can be altered by institutionalized interactions with other states, meaning domestic and international politics are linked in complex ways. Such interaction, in turn, implies that other actors are included in the process besides heads of government and foreign ministers; states act as unitary rational actors only in tightly circumscribed situations. As we shall see throughout this study, the increasing involvement of more state and EU-level officials profoundly influences institutionalized cooperation.

Cooperation, in turn, can involve an array of possible outcomes, from lower order ones (sharing information) to higher order ones (pooling resources for joint action). As these outcomes accumulate over time, they change from effects into causes as actors use them to justify additional institutional changes. This results in a dynamic process that influences future cooperation while also helping to institutionalize it. These observations ultimately call into question many assumptions about international relations based on material power alone. But what kinds of cooperative outcomes actually appear in the historical record of EU foreign policy, and how can they be linked, at least superficially, to empirical evidence of institutional change? And how has the EU foreign policy system in general changed over time since it was created in the early 1970s? These questions are taken up in the next chapter.

2   Institutions and European foreign policy cooperation: the empirical link

The previous chapter argued that institutionalization promotes international cooperation and suggested several general causes of institutionalization, but did not offer precise empirical measurements of either institutionalization or cooperation. This chapter attempts to operationalize these concepts and apply them to the historical record to justify further the merits of an institutional analysis of EPC/CFSP. Although my institutional approach to cooperation is not as parsimonious as theories that focus on single causes (such as the interests of powerful EU member states) or events (such as Intergovernmental Conferences), it has the potential to capture equally important, though subtle, processes concerning the development of EU foreign policy. Institutionalization is often a contentious political process, yet with every major setback the EU has attempted to strengthen its foreign policy procedures to improve the chances of future cooperation. In general, the relationship between institutions and individual foreign policy outcomes will vary over time and across specific foreign policy actions, depending on the costs, states, and EU organizations and policies involved. However, if institutions "matter" we still should at least be able to observe a general intensification and expansion of EU foreign policy cooperation as its institutional mechanisms expand and stabilize.

EPC provides us with an interesting and theoretically useful example of such institutional development, as it began as an informal, extra-legal agreement among EU member states in an ill-defined issue-area. In this domain, many new institutional elements were layered on top of old ones in a series of progressive reforms, so it is possible to examine the effects of each element on cooperation at different stages of institutional development. EU foreign policy also spans more than thirty years of cooperation, ranging from trial and error to formal policymaking, across an expanding array of issues, with an increase in membership from six states to fifteen, accompanied by a closer relationship to EC policies and procedures. Exploring these changes within a common analytical framework should yield insights into the way institutions develop and into the extent to which institutional change affects state behavior (and vice versa). The purpose of this chapter is to establish such a general correlation.

Measuring institutional change

The general hypothesis motivating this study is that institutionalization helps promote greater international cooperation. Conceptualizing this in more explicit terms is far more difficult than it sounds, as there is much disagreement in the literature on how to measure the effectiveness of international institutions.[1] Ideally, we should be able to set down some objective criteria to assess the relationship between two variables systematically: institutional development and EU foreign policy cooperation. As I argued in the previous chapter, however, EU foreign policy involves a dynamic, circular process of institutionalization and cooperation. Thus it is impossible to treat both processes as discrete independent and dependent variables. Still, in the interest of analytical clarity, we should be able to identify stages or progressive changes in institutions, and link them to general changes in outcomes. Although I recognize the existence of feedback loops from cooperative outcomes back to institutionalization, this study begins by treating institutionalization as the independent variable and cooperation as the dependent variable. Since we can pinpoint the precise moment when EU foreign policy was first institutionalized, we can use this as the benchmark to assess later institutional changes and cooperative outcomes. And although both the institutional form of EPC/CFSP and the issue-area itself do not invite the same analytical precision as, say, the establishment of a formal international organization to clean up the environment, we can still specify some fundamental criteria to measure each dimension.

Defining institutionalization

In the literature on European foreign policy cooperation, most analysts implicitly accept that this policy domain has been increasingly institutionalized, yet they do not defend this claim in detail.[2] The most elemental evidence of institutional change is a clearer articulation of the functional goals and behavioral norms of the institution. In the case of EU foreign policy, this involves creating a greater number of norms, clarifying those

---

[1] For an overview, see Young 1992.

[2] For example, in their detailed statistical study of EPC, Schneider and Seybold (1997: 387) argue that EPC "has become more institutionalized over time," but do not explain what this means. This failure to define and measure institutionalization specifically is also true of most studies of EPC/CFSP cited in this volume.

Stage

Stage					
V.					Governance
IV.			Organizations		
III.			Norms		
II.		Information-sharing			
I.	Intergovernmental forum				
	1970		**1973**	**1981 1986–91**	**1993–present**

Figure 2.1 The institutional development of EU foreign policy.

norms in more detail, changing norms from informal customs to formal rules, and bringing EC rules and permanent EC organizations into the process. The clearest expression of the institutional ends–means relationship is that of a *policy process*, which represents a formalized sequence of specific agenda-setting (within the broader goals of the institution), policy/decision-making, policy implementation, evaluation and monitoring/feedback, and (in some cases) some degree of oversight or accountability. In such a process formal rules and organizational roles are laid down as clearly as possible in an effort to achieve the primary goals of the institution. To the extent that this policy process involves binding legal obligations and some independent authority to make rules, it can also be conceived as a system of *governance*.

I argue that this is in fact what was achieved with the Treaty on European Union and its Common Foreign and Security Policy, which in turn raised a new set of institutional issues. Prior to this treaty, however, EPC institutions developed in an ad hoc manner in terms of the norms, rules, and organizations discussed above. To conceptualize this process better, Figure 2.1 graphically illustrates the general timeline during which major new institutional elements of EPC/CFSP were progressively layered on top of existing arrangements.

These stages, including an analysis of the internalization of EPC/CFSP in the domestic politics of EU member states at each stage, provide the structure for later chapters in this study. In the most general terms, through this process of institutionalization, relations among EU states have progressed from the narrow instrumental rationality characterized by intergovernmentalism to a more collective or social rationality characterized by legitimate procedures of governance and corresponding changes in their domestic politics.[3] Before proceeding, however, I must first emphasize that there are no clear divisions between these levels.

---

[3] And to the extent that this system increasingly, and legitimately, binds its participants together and affects their political interests and identity, it could even be conceived as a *polity*, although this possibility is not a primary focus of this study.

Although I argue that each step laid the general foundations for the next step, and each step is associated with an historical event (or "institutional moment"), there was a significant amount of overlap, even inconsistency, between them. In other words, each stage includes some elements of other stages. Still, specific institutional themes or patterns can be discerned at different historical junctures in the evolution of EU foreign policy, each of which has a corresponding impact on cooperation.

Stages of institutionalization

Establishment of the policy domain as an intergovernmental forum
The first step in my analysis of institutionalization involves the original agreement among EU states to cooperate in an issue-area. Although it is possible for cooperation to emerge, and even to develop norms, without an explicit agreement or even communication, institutionalization is far more likely when actors make a conscious, public decision to organize their cooperation, whether this involves a "gentleman's agreement," a treaty, or the creation of a specific organization. The potential for institutional change also depends on the actors who are entitled to participate, the distribution and types of power held by those actors, their interests in establishing institutionalized cooperation, the characteristics of the issue-area or the common problem(s) to be addressed, the environment in which the agreement was reached, and the original norms, if any, used to promote cooperation in that issue-area. In the case of EU foreign policy, the dominant institutional form at its origin was that of an intergovernmental forum for general discussion about global problems.

According to the literature on intergovernmentalism in the EU, this form involves several characteristics.[4] First, it stresses the power, pre-existing preferences, and strategic interaction of individual states. Power is typically measured in material terms, such as the size of a state's armed forces or the strength of its economy. In the EU, this typically means a focus on the economic interests and negotiating strategies of France, Germany, and the UK (Moravcsik 1998). Second, intergovernmentalism stresses the role of government chief executives, or their representatives, in the decision-making process, typically in the European Council of Heads of State and Government or in the Council of (Foreign) Ministers.[5] When decisions of these actors do not require ratification on a regular

---

[4] These are primarily derived from Moravcsik 1991, 1993; Garrett 1992.
[5] Also known as the General Affairs Council or, following the Maastricht Treaty, the Council of the EU. To avoid confusion I favor the term Council of Ministers throughout this study.

basis, as in the case of EU foreign policy, they have even more leeway to make policy. In foreign policy, governments are often acting to provide a non-economic public good which does not impose high costs on specific domestic actors unlike, say, trade policy (Moravcsik 1994). Since these actors do not bear the costs of international cooperation, they are less likely to assert their preferences to chiefs of governments and possibly interfere with, nullify, or complicate an international agreement.

Third, intergovernmentalism, like most functional approaches to cooperation, usually focuses on bargaining: governments "cooperate" in mixed motive situations (where they have incentives to cooperate and to defect) primarily by arranging reciprocal trade-offs among themselves. This usually involves linking issues into package deals or making side-payments to each other, sometimes immediately (specific reciprocity) or at some time in the future (diffuse reciprocity). Further, this bargaining can involve both the broad course of institutional development as well as more prosaic day-to-day decisions about policy, especially where decision-making rules require consensus among all states. In the absence of such bargains, inaction or unilateralism will be the tendency; any European "cooperation" will be ad hoc, informal, and probably reflect the power and interests of the EU's strongest member states, namely France, Germany, and the UK.

Fourth, organizational actors, like rules in general, play a limited role, if any, in many intergovernmental analyses. This chiefly involves helping the negotiators strike or monitor a deal by passively providing information or providing avenues for side-payments for states not immediately ready to agree with a collective decision. Fifth, intergovernmentalism sees cooperation as a simple two-stage process. This involves the formation of national preferences via domestic politics (the first stage), and bargaining between governments over the details of the agreement (the second stage).[6] Sixth and finally, intergovernmentalism often treats each cooperative agreement as a single, closed-end outcome, thus neatly avoiding the potential impacts of policy evaluations and historical context.[7] Previous decisions or policies are assumed to have little or no impact on each bargaining situation beyond the commitments already locked in by earlier bargains. Intergovernmentalism is therefore subject to some path-dependency, but this is both strategic and intentional: governments are

---

[6] The related "two-level games" model (Putnam 1988) brings a third stage (ratification) into the analysis.

[7] As Moravcsik (1993: 473) argues, "From the signing of the Treaty of Rome to the making of Maastricht, the EC has developed through a series of celebrated intergovernmental bargains, each of which set the agenda for an intervening period of consolidation. The most fundamental task facing a theoretical account of European integration is to explain these bargains."

free to treat each act of collective decision as a single deal based on the configuration of their power and interests at the time. In Chapter 3, the origins and functions of these specific elements of EU foreign policy are discussed in more detail.

Information-sharing   Once actors have explicitly agreed to co-operate, even in an intergovernmental forum, they may then begin a discourse about the means and ends of their cooperation. Often, this debate can be an end in itself, in the sense that cooperation can be minimally defined as mere discussions about policy coordination (i.e., "cheap talk") rather than by "results" in terms of specific cooperative policy actions. Yet as this discourse gradually intensifies, it can generate its own dynamics by both facilitating and structuring communication according to common understandings. Thus, although collective behavior can become more ritualized or institution-like in the absence of communication, provided the actors can at least monitor each other's behavior, we can propose that as goal-oriented communication intensifies, the demand for greater structure (i.e., institutionalization) grows and cooperation becomes more likely.

Indeed, many theories of social behavior stress the importance of communication.[8] Where reliable information about motives is lacking, states find it difficult to trust each other. Suspicion about being cheated, not cooperation, is the result.[9] Similarly, the literature on "signaling" shows that states must be able to communicate threats, capabilities, and resolve effectively if they are to have a desired impact on the behavior of other states (Morrow 1994). Knowledge of another state's strategies and capabilities can be used to exploit that state and attain gains for oneself; thus states are tempted to deceive (or at least to outguess) each other.[10] Even in situations which do not involve crises or the threat of war, information is important in promoting stable relations and facilitating bargains among states. For states that do agree to cooperate, institutions that facilitate

---

[8] Even realists concede that part of the problem of anarchy involves the fact that states cannot always know the true capabilities and, more importantly, intentions of other states. Under such conditions, fear and suspicion predominate, and lead actors to concern themselves with power and security. Moreover, even if a state thinks it knows the intentions of others, intentions might change too quickly for a state to react effectively (Mearsheimer 1994–95: 10). This implies that effective, durable signaling or confidence-building mechanisms can help mitigate the effects of anarchy, thus creating an atmosphere conducive to cooperation.

[9] As Waltz (1979: 105) argues, "The impediments to collaboration may not lie in the character and the immediate intention of either party. Instead, the condition of insecurity – at the least, the uncertainty of each about the other's future intentions and actions – works against their cooperation."

[10] For more on this point, see Axelrod 1984: Chapter 2.

sharing information about one's partners can help promote cooperation by at least identifying cheaters. In this view, to the extent that states can communicate credible promises to each other, by virtue of their domestic political processes (transparency) or their external behavior (diplomacy), the chances for cooperation will increase.

Like institutional effects in general, these effects of communication can be conceived along a continuum. At one end, if we can show that institutionalized information-sharing mechanisms at the very least promote trust and confidence among states, making the use of force (or threats to use force) unlikely or unnecessary, then we have started to undermine the realist notion that uncertainty and insecurity are endemic to international relations. If institutions also help identify offenders and allay states' concerns about cheating, as with compliance about trade or arms agreements, then we are moving even closer to the rational-functional (or neo-liberal) approach to institutions. At the other end, if information-sharing generates shared understandings or common knowledge about problems, joint approaches to those problems, and perhaps even a sense of collective identity, then we are much closer to the ideals of classical liberalism and perhaps social constructivism. In the view of these theories, states would be more likely to reject power politics and hard bargaining to embrace other forms of collective action, involving shared leadership, social norms or skills, persuasion, and even partnership/friendship.

Thus, institutionalized structures for information-sharing can dramatically improve the prospects for international cooperation and lay the groundwork for further institutionalization. We can in fact observe several processes concerning information-sharing among the states involved in European foreign policy, mainly through the development of a complex transgovernmental communication network. Paraphrasing Lasswell's (1960: 117) classic formulation of communication, an analysis of this network involves the questions of who shares what information, through which channels, and with what effects. These questions, and their specific institutional mechanisms, are examined in more detail in Chapter 4.

Norm creation and codification   Once communication moves from cheap talk to regular discussions about foreign policy problems and their possible resolution, institutionalization takes on a new dynamic. This dynamic involves the generation of norms, or shared standards of behavior. Intergovernmental information-sharing itself involves norms, of course, but as officials learn to trust each other and develop a shared understanding of what their cooperation actually involves, it becomes possible for them to establish clearer obligations regarding the ends and means of a specific policy domain. Indeed, regular interstate communications often require the coordination of so many actors in so many areas that a resort to norms is almost inevitable. At the very least, the hard-won engineering of consensus about the means and ends of cooperation encourages participants to preserve what has been achieved.

This desire to preserve and reinforce the gains from cooperation is satisfied by creating and codifying norms, and by socializing officials to respect those norms. Socialization is discussed later in this chapter in my examination of domestic politics. For the moment, I argue that information-sharing in EU foreign policy led to a problem-solving culture or style of decision-making, which itself was institutionalized as a set of norms. Where bargaining involves the satisfaction of *self-interests* through trade-offs and incentives, problem-solving involves an appeal to *common interests*, accumulated across time and space, plus the possible use of ostracism or peer-pressure to maintain group discipline. This approach may be more amenable to collective norm-production.[11] Although problem-solving has some inherent weaknesses as an institutional form (Scharpf 1988), it is probably the only way EPC could have proceeded while remaining outside the framework of the European Community.

As numerous definitions of norms and rules exist (March and Olsen 1989: 22), it is necessary to specify their key characteristics clearly if we hope to find them in the empirical record of EPC/CFSP. In general, we can treat them as problem-solving tools or "choice simplification" mechanisms that guide the behavior of actors (Kratochwil 1989). They are not just expectations or constraints (Elster 1989; North 1990), or descriptions of existing ritualized behaviors subject to punishments if violated (Axelrod 1986), but are expressions of what is appropriate or even valued in a given community. In addition, legal scholars often recognize a hierarchy of norms or rules (Kratochwil 1989; Stone 1994); thus it is also possible to classify norms along the dimensions of clarity and bindingness to show that institutional change has been taking place.

Although a number of tacit or unspoken rules exist in any social situation, these provide only a point of departure for my examination of the role of norms in EPC. For one thing, I rely on standards of evidence such that causal factors can be known only by material facts, expressed either in terms of the historical record (such as EPC Reports and EC

---

[11] On "problem-solving" as a style of decision-making, see March and Simon 1958. Of course, this is not to say that EU states make no "deals" in the context of foreign policy cooperation. Compromise and "splitting the difference" always were (and are) key elements of the policy process. Rather, I argue that states in EPC/CFSP attempt to avoid the quid pro quo hard bargaining and complex package deals that regularly occur in the course of EC affairs.

treaties) or by interviews with multiple participants. Thus for the most part I do not concern myself with tacit norms or unspoken rules, which exist only in the minds of EU foreign policy participants. My assumption of bounded rationality discussed in the previous chapter also enables me to ignore whether these actors "really believed" in the efficacy or value of these norms. In addition, actors may not share similar expectations regarding tacit rules, which makes it difficult to make concrete judgments about their effects on behavior. Indeed, tacit rules often persist precisely because of different understandings and the difficulty of formalizing them. Different understandings provide a convenient "escape clause" in situations where the idea of a more binding rule is controversial. However, tacit rules that have become explicit norms, or norms that are produced through other processes (such as negotiation) typically reflect a greater degree of expectation-convergence among actors and we can judge their effects across different situations with far more certainty.

Thus, based on the existing literature on norms, methodological considerations, and the historical record of EPC/CFSP, I find it helpful to distinguish between four types of norms. First, we can observe *informal* (or *uncodified*) *customs*, or the traditions and practices (not just habits) that emerged in day-to-day interactions among EPC/CFSP officials. Again, these norms were often tacit or unspoken but generally understood by all participants. Second, we can examine the codification of these informal customs into explicit, written *norms*, a transition which began to take place during the mid-1970s. Codification is especially necessary when conditions change outside or inside the system (such as when new actors participate or when the arrangement must coordinate with other functionally related institutions, such as the EC). Third, there is evidence of a transition from explicit norms to *rules*, as reflected in EPC/CFSP positions and reports. These rules are expressed as specific rights and obligations applicable to certain situations. Fourth, we can consider the transition from rules into *formal laws* (legal rules), which involve behavioral and legal obligations. Finally, throughout the analysis, I will further distinguish between *procedural* (or constitutive) norms that govern decision-making and institutional change (including rules about future *rule-making*, which approximates *constitution-building* within EU foreign policy; see Stone 1994), and *substantive* (or regulatory) norms that specify the positions and behavioral standards (usually expressed as policy outcomes) of EU states toward the external world. These dynamics involving the creation, influence, and evolution of norms, as well as the role of the ECJ in EU foreign policy, are fully examined in Chapter 5 and then linked to my argument about governance in Chapter 7. Where necessary, I also pay attention to the way these norms encourage sympathetic changes in the domestic politics of EU member states (see below).

Organizations   Behavioral norms are not the only manifestation of institutionalization, although they are the primary focus of this study. The establishment of a permanent organization to administer some policy domain represents an additional degree of institutionalization beyond a decentralized communications network and a set of rules to guide actors. Organizations or agencies are relatively stable groups of officials bound by a common purpose, which often extends to concrete entities with headquarters, staffs, budgets, internal procedures, and other resources that can shape policies or norms (Keohane 1988). In international affairs, the existence of the United Nations, the World Bank, NATO, the agencies of the EC, and a host of other international organizations represents a much higher order of institutionalized cooperation than decentralized multilateral agreements, such as environmental conventions, which must be continually renegotiated to keep up with changes in the circumstances which led to their birth. International organizations are often very costly to establish and even more costly to maintain, yet their existence reaffirms the value states place on the effective management of certain international problems.

Institutionalized behavior that increasingly involves formal organizations or agencies (such as those of the EC) generally changes the propensity for, and characteristics of, international cooperation. At the very least, organizations can provide some institutional memory concerning previous decisions. At the most, the organization itself can become an autonomous actor with influence over both policy innovation and institutional change. Organizations often possess important resources such as knowledge or expertise, and, under certain circumstances, they can develop their own interests concerning international cooperation. When embedded within a complex rule-of-law system like the EU, they can even exert "supranational" influence over policy coordination among their member states, as functional integration theorists argue (Haas 1958).

Thus, to the extent that the EU can be considered a polity, with its own mechanisms of governance (a subject taken up in the next section), we should be able to observe certain behaviors on the part of its permanent organizations and agencies. Bureaucratic politics thus plays a role in my analysis, in terms of the tendency of agencies to worry about their own self-preservation and to enhance their own roles in policymaking.[12]

---

[12] Note that this treatment of agencies as actors in a broader policy process (bureaucratic politics) differs from the classical view of organizational politics, which focuses on the

More specifically, we can analyze the influence of organizations on a policy domain in terms of their formation, environment, goals, structure, and resources (Ness and Brechin 1988). The formation of organizations is not really in question here, since most EC organizations relevant to EU foreign policy existed prior to EPC, giving it a "ready-made" set of bureaucratic actors, chiefly the Commission and the European Parliament, with potential influence (although I do analyze the establishment of the EPC Secretariat and the CFSP Policy Planning and Early Warning Unit). However, the environments, goals, structures, and resources of these organizations are considered in detail in Chapters 6 and 8. I should also note here that the involvement of organizations is not necessarily always efficient in terms of achieving desired outcomes. Bureaucracies can actually complicate or even prevent optimal decision-making; these pathologies may then lead to additional institutional reforms. This possibility is considered throughout my analysis of organizational influence.

Toward governance   The involvement of permanent organizations in a policy domain is a key indicator of institutionalization and can significantly enhance the prospects for international cooperation. Yet the policy domain as an institution will remain limited and incoherent as long as states fail to consider the process of cooperation as a unified whole. Such a policy process would involve setting goals, devising specific policies (or norms) to reach them, implementing such policies, providing the necessary resources to carry out the policies, and establishing some form of policy assessment or oversight to ensure that goals are being met and actors are fulfilling their obligations.

As in domestic political systems, this policy process can be conceived as a form of *governance*, or the authority to make, implement, and enforce rules in a specified domain (Anderson 1995). The EU is the most densely institutionalized network of states ever devised in world politics, and grand theories of integration do not capture many of its most important dynamics. Given this complexity of factors, it is no accident that some have suggested that the most appropriate model of EU decision-making (whether in the EC or EPC/CFSP) may be that of the "garbage can," whereby problems, solutions, actors, and choice opportunities are mixed together in various ways that cannot be predicted or even controlled

---

depoliticization of policy through the use of standard operating procedures and routines. In the organizational model, external stimuli trigger complex, standardized patterns of action without extensive analysis, problem-solving, or the use of discretionary power (March and Olsen 1989: 21). Although EU foreign policy has become increasingly formalized and now allows a greater role for EC organizations, it is not as routinized or standardized as described by general theories of organizational policymaking.

(Richardson 1996). An opposing view, however, argues that the EU is better understood as a supranational polity or quasi-federal state because of its similarity to domestic political processes (in terms of constitutional law, federalism, interest groups, and state structures) rather than international politics (Hix 1994; Risse-Kappen 1996). Some analysts even contend that actors and institutional rules at various levels and during certain policy phases can influence the policy process in ways which make the EU appear to be a form of multilevel governance or even a supranational polity, not merely another regional economic organization (Marks, Hooghe, and Blank 1996; Stone Sweet and Sandholtz 1998a). Normal, day-to-day policymaking in many Community policy domains involves a highly complex set of interest groups, officials, lawyers, and judges at the domestic and EU levels. These domains often involve a redistribution of economic resources, thus prompting attention from the affected parties and, in some cases, a demand for policy or institutional change.

Although it is inappropriate to claim that EU foreign policy is equally subject to the same dynamics behind other EC policy domains (particularly those involving economic integration), there are important similarities.[13] An institutional analysis of EU foreign policy recognizes that, as a policy space becomes more clearly defined, relevant actors attempt to impose discipline on the competing pressures, at least in terms of specifying a policy sequence or process to produce a desired end.[14] This is precisely what happened with EPC/CFSP. I argue that EU foreign policy as an institution does exhibit some elements of governance based on its antecedent institutional developments (under the EPC system), the formal CFSP provisions of the Treaty on European Union (TEU), and decisions made during the first decade of the implementation of the CFSP (including the Treaty of Amsterdam). The specific elements of foreign policy governance are fully discussed in Chapter 7.

Finally, I should note that EU foreign policy is also increasingly institutionally embedded in the broader network of political-economic arrangements already existing in the EU, and the EU itself is nested within more robust multilateral arrangements for cooperation in political and economic affairs (NATO, the WTO, the OSCE, etc.). Since institutions are costly to establish, there is a tendency for agreements to be linked to or subsumed under existing arrangements. This means taking

[13] For a more detailed comparison of issue-areas in the EU, see Stubb 1996.
[14] This approach is similar to the "policy networks" perspective (Peterson 1995). However, we can gain additional analytical leverage by first focusing on how institutions structure those networks (thus determining who gets to act within them), which I describe in terms of a policy process.

into consideration how the CFSP is now functionally related to global multilateralism (UN), Western multilateralism (OECD), Atlantic multilateralism (NATO), and European multilateralism (CSCE, EC, WEU). Interactions or conflicts with these domains affect the institutionalization of EU foreign policy. The CFSP is clearly horizontally linked to other organizations with similar functions, normative goals, and authority. A full analysis of these linkages, and the EU's more general objective of coherence in external relations, is beyond the scope of this study, yet we can make some observations about how the CFSP is institutionally related to the broader post-Cold War multilateral security network in Europe. This aspect of institutional change, as well as other problems concerning governance, is explored in Chapter 8.

Measuring EU foreign policy cooperation

If it is difficult to measure institutional development empirically, there are even more problems with measuring cooperation. Many analyses of cooperation confuse the dependent variable with changes in the independent variable. For example, some analysts use regime "strength" (such as a larger or stricter set of regulations governing some issue-area) as a measure of *cooperation* when this is more effectively understood as a measure of *institutionalization*. To achieve a better conceptualization of the relationship between these processes, I define the dependent variable (cooperation) in fairly strict terms to link it with the independent variable (institutionalization). For example, EPC was established in part to prevent external pressures from creating political conflicts within the EU, so one measure of greater cooperation would be greater stability in the EU, or the absence of war, arms races, serious trade disputes, or other examples of egregious, self-aggrandizing foreign policy behaviors. One might also conceive of EU foreign policy cooperation as a decline in exploitative behavior among EU states: if the EU is indeed cooperating in foreign policy, at the very least its member states might not use external issues to take advantage of each other. This is cooperation defined in negative terms: it exists when states *fail* to act in selfish ways.[15]

However, this is a very limited view of foreign policy cooperation; therefore I do not discuss situations where EU states could have exploited each other over foreign policy issues but neglected to do so. It also could be argued that the goal of preventing foreign policy disputes from interfering with the EC by compartmentalizing them in a new institution clearly

---

[15] Legro (1995) conceptualizes international cooperation in such a manner in his analysis of why Germany and the UK during World War II decided against employing certain methods of warfare, such as chemical weapons.

has been met in view of the continual expansion of European integration since the 1970s despite numerous disagreements, potential and real, over world politics. Instead, I stress specific collective actions or outcomes as my chief empirical indicators of cooperation. Cooperative *behavior* is the primary focus here, and this behavior can be seen in the historical record of EPC/CFSP.

Quantitative indicators of cooperation

To what extent did the institutional changes described above actually encourage greater European foreign policy cooperation, and how can we measure this cooperation in terms of quantitative empirical evidence? One useful distinction can be made between changes in *process*, involving the way EU states interact with each other within EPC/CFSP, and changes in *substantive cooperative outcomes*, which represent specific EPC/CFSP policies. Evidence of procedural change is more subtle and qualitative, making it difficult to summarize here. It involves everything from the messages sent among EU member states to the number of meetings held on EPC/CFSP to the efficiency of reaching decisions. Thus, in keeping with my focus on EU foreign policy expressed as external behavior or actions, for the moment I summarize the evidence concerning the general quantitative expansion of such behavior: specific EPC/CFSP policies since 1970. Distinct changes of process are examined in relevant later chapters.

Since EPC was established we can indeed see a clear expansion of cooperative foreign policy outcomes. EPC was inward-looking during its first decade, as member states tried to establish practical procedures to achieve their ambitions. But positive results of EPC can be seen almost from the beginning. For the purpose of analytical clarity, I present my discussion of quantitative expansion in terms of three sets of factors.

Expansion of actions   The easiest way to demonstrate greater cooperation over time is simply to document the number of actions taken since EPC was established. For these data I rely primarily on Ginsberg's comprehensive listings of EU foreign policy actions.[16] Prior to EPC, European foreign policy cooperation was virtually non-existent. Only

[16] As noted in Chapter 1, these foreign policy actions must be: (1) undertaken on behalf of all EU states toward non-members, international bodies, or global events or issues; (2) oriented toward a specific goal; (3) made operational with physical activity, such as financing or diplomacy; and (4) undertaken in the context of EPC/CFSP discussions (although the EC can also be involved). Adapted from Ginsberg 1989, 1991, plus data from the Official Journal of the EU.

Table 2.1 *EPC actions, and CFSP common positions and joint actions, 1970–95*

1970–74	1975–79	1980–84	1985–89	1990–95
8	7	24	26	94

These data do not include *declarations*, which only express the EU's opinion on an issue.

two major foreign policy actions took place between 1957 (the founding of the EC) and 1970 (the creation of EPC): the imposition of economic sanctions against Rhodesia (1965) and Greece (1967). As Table 2.1 reveals, however, these actions gradually increased in number as EPC developed and was transformed into the CFSP.

During the early years of EPC, explicit actions amounted to only a few each year. The high points during this period came during 1974, when EPC formally established the Euro-Arab Dialogue, responded to the war in Cyprus, began consultations at the UN, permitted the Commission to be involved in most EPC meetings, and established the European Council of Heads of State and Government. Although EPC produced only a modest number of actions in the 1970s, we must keep in mind that during this time EPC was not especially directed toward conducting external actions, and there were no provisions for undertaking such actions within its institutional framework. One could even argue that the actions that EU states managed to take at this time in the absence of explicit arrangements for doing so are a major tribute to the pragmatism and flexibility of EPC, and to the creativity of the diplomats involved. In addition, as EPC progressed, EU states became far more willing to take some foreign policy decisions (such as those involving regional dialogues) in the Community framework rather than under the rubric of EPC. Still, EPC produced explicit external actions on its own and we can see a definite expansion of such actions. The decade after the London Report (1981) particularly resulted in a significant expansion of EPC actions; this expansion was then dwarfed by the number of actions after the CFSP entered into effect in November 1993. We might also note that the growth in actions has also exhibited a greater geographic scope over the past three decades. Since 1970, EPC has rapidly outgrown its original boundaries to encompass policies and relationships in all corners of the globe. The first two major topics discussed at the first EPC ministerial meeting in 1970 concerned Eastern Europe and the Middle East. Both of these topics were later institutionalized within the broader framework of EPC. From there, however, EU foreign policy cooperation rapidly progressed to include relations with Africa, the United States, the rest of the Americas and Europe, and Asia. By the time the CFSP entered into effect in 1993, no geographic region was off-limits to EU foreign policy.

Functional expansion   Similarly, EU foreign policy expanded in terms of the number of functional issues with which it dealt. As the previous discussion of institutional change implies, the EPC agenda was very limited at first. EU states discussed a wide variety of subjects within this setting, but in terms of external EPC actions on specific issues, the member states limited themselves to discussions of a long-term nature, in order to ensure only a common understanding of "great international problems." As with other aspects of EPC, however, its functional tasks were soon clarified in far more detail. EPC thus became oriented toward the formulation of *medium- and long-term common positions* on foreign policy matters. From there its tasks expanded to involve *managing crises*, as in Portugal, Cyprus, Afghanistan, the Falklands, and so on. EPC also became useful in drawn-out efforts to *resolve conflicts*, as in the areas of East–West relations, the Middle East, and Central America. The first major EPC attempt in this area, the Soviet invasion of Afghanistan in 1979, was delayed for months and the policy outcome was quite limited in scope. Yet the 1980s saw many opportunities for EPC to act, and we can use these policies to gauge the development of EPC mechanisms.

In a significant departure from the original EPC agenda, EU states also increasingly considered *security issues* and took several security-related actions. These actions can be defined as "mutual changes in interstate behavior among EU members in order to undertake actions in which the EU deals as a unit with a question that affects its own physical security, the security of a closely related state or group of states, or the security of the international system" (Ginsberg 1989: 57). Such actions have been taken against a number of non-EU states. The EU's participation in the CSCE process also represents security-related cooperation, beginning with EPC's first proposal tabled during the preparatory phases of the process in January 1973. Thanks to this groundwork under EPC, security affairs were explicitly included in the CFSP and helped facilitate the EU's most recent discussions on defense cooperation (although defense is not a major focus of this study).

Instrument expansion   EPC also quickly added to its repertoire of policy tools over the years. Table 2.2 illustrates the expansion of EPC/CFSP policy instruments.

As we see here, EPC possessed only three instruments at first: declarations, démarches, and common approaches to international conferences

Table 2.2 *Year of first use of major EPC/CFSP policy instruments*

1970	Declarations, démarches
1971	Coordination at the UN
1973	Consultations with allies outside the EC (US)
1974	Institutionalized regional political dialogues (Euro-Arab)
1975	Coordination at the CSCE; use of economic tools for EPC
1977	Code of Conduct for EC firms (in South Africa)
1981	Peace plans; endorsement of a military operation by some EC states (Sinai force)
1982	Use of an EC regulation for EPC actions (sanctions against the Soviet Union)
1984	Weapons embargo (Iran and Iraq)
1993	Common positions, joint actions, actions taken in conjunction with the WEU
1998	Common strategies

and organizations. Declarations merely express the EU's opinion on an issue, while démarches are formal presentations of the EU's position on an issue made to representatives of third states and international organizations. Accurate data for the number of EPC démarches do not exist, but it is clear that EU ambassadors to non-EU states made hundreds of such démarches every year, on an increasingly wide range of subjects.[17] The number of EPC declarations made each year expanded as well during the 1980s, ranging from only a few in 1975 to 52 in 1985 to well over 100 in 1995.[18] It is of course possible that the growth in declarations is partly a function of a greater number of events on which to comment, plus the general expansion of the EU's membership (which increases the range of foreign policy issues of concern to EU member states), rather than a function of institutional change alone. However, the other measures of cooperation (quantitative and qualitative) stressed in this volume are not so susceptible to this problem.[19]

[17] An increase in the number of démarches under EPC is confirmed in most of the studies of EPC cited in this volume. Also interviews with former EPC officials, Brussels, 1995–96.

[18] Data from Regelsberger 1993: 278; and the Council of the European Union 1995. Also see Schneider and Seybold 1997: 378–79.

[19] For similar reasons I do not rely on trends in EU voting patterns at the UN, as examined in early studies of EPC (Hurwitz 1975, 1976; Lindemann 1976; Foot 1979; Lindemann 1982). As Nuttall (1992a: 28) observes, cooperation at the UN is much stronger than voting statistics suggest. Resolutions adopted by consensus are usually not included in the vote data, and most resolutions in the UN are adopted by consensus. Also, on a number of votes EU cohesion was undermined by the dissenting behavior of only one state (often France and occasionally Greece), which makes it look as if the EU was more divided than it actually was. Such differences in voting more often than not reflected tactical differences rather than fundamental disagreements over policy. Finally, and perhaps most importantly, voting is not the only manifestation of European cooperation at the UN. Other UN member states, particularly developing and lesser developed states, see the EU as a primary representative of the Western world and as

From this modest start, EPC developed the use of economic and financial aid, and economic and financial sanctions, which typically involved the EC to varying degrees. Policy instruments also expanded to include political dialogues and Association Agreements, embargoes on weapons and other products, anti-terrorism policies, peace plans, and peacekeeping. The budget for EU foreign policy cooperation has steadily expanded as well, and by the 1990s the EU also was laying the groundwork for the use of police or military forces in certain areas. The use of military force in the context of EU foreign policy had long been a taboo subject under EPC, and disagreements about this issue persist, but discussions on this subject are no longer out of place for EU states, even the neutral ones.

Qualitative indicators of cooperation

In addition to the quantitative measures of cooperation discussed above, we can also detect a qualitative change in EPC/CFSP outcomes. Similar to the distinction between rules involving EU states (as a collective) and those involving EC organizations, cooperative outcomes can be distinguished in two basic ways: some are implemented at the national level alone, and others involve some implementation at the EC level (such as economic sanctions). In other words, cooperation as a dependent variable involves the behavior of both *EU member states* (defined as government officials and the permanent bureaucratic officials who support them) and *EC organizations*, who act on behalf of EU member states. Although I touch upon other indirect expressions of cooperation in the domestic politics of EU member states throughout this study (see below), my empirical conceptualization of cooperation primarily involves direct actions of EU states and EC organizations.

These direct actions would involve more positive, proactive behaviors by the EU to address or even solve external political problems.[20] This is the general idea behind the creation of the CFSP, although actions toward this end were taken under EPC as well. Empirically, this desire to influence events would be expressed as a greater variety and complexity of external actions, and possibly more coherence with other external EC policies. However, a far more difficult problem here is measuring

a "privileged interlocutor"; thus EU démarches and backroom discussions can indicate greater cooperation (and more influence on other UN member states) than is possible to measure in quantitative terms, even though it is known to exist (de Schoutheete de Tervarent 1980: 11–18); also interview with a Commission official, Brussels, 1996.

[20] This is also the rationale for studies focused on the "actorness" or "presence" of EPC/CFSP in world politics. For example, see Crawford and Schulze 1990; Rummel 1990; Ginsberg 1999, 2001.

cooperation by the external goals developed in EPC/CFSP. It should be clear that judging cooperation primarily by external measures (i.e., non-EU governments comply with human rights as a result of EU policies) rather than internal ones (the EU manages to reach agreement on human rights issues) would be far beyond the scope of this study. In other words, successful cooperation in terms of this analysis is when EU states take common action on a foreign policy issue, not whether that action achieves its desired ends. The latter is actually a measure of policy effectiveness, not cooperation.

With this caveat in mind, I combine two sets of criteria to measure qualitatively the expansion of EU foreign policy cooperation. The first such criteria, as described by Weiler (1985: 21), involve specifying the rationale for such cooperative actions. Lower-order actions are "reflexive"; they are taken merely to demonstrate some common position for its own sake. "Reactive" foreign policy cooperation involves a response to particular events, usually in the hope of influencing them but primarily to prevent EU member states from acting at odds with each other. "Active" cooperation involves setting goals and the means to achieve them, while anticipating possible responses to common foreign policies (i.e., strategic behavior); this represents the highest form of cooperation. In this sense EU foreign policy has moved from negative integration (protecting the EU from the unilateral foreign policy actions of its member states) to positive integration (acting with a single purpose in world politics to serve common goals).

The second set of criteria involves the collective response of EU member states, ranging from low-cost actions (declarations of common positions), to more substantive actions (such as sanctions) implemented on a national basis alone, and finally, to substantive actions involving both member states and the EC (or delegated to the EC exclusively). EU states have gradually exhibited a greater willingness to use EC resources for EPC/CFSP actions, a willingness that clearly had been absent during the early 1970s. These actions often involve legal obligations as well, and even allow for EC organizations (chiefly the Commission) to implement and monitor the collective actions.[21] These criteria are conceptualized in Table 2.3.

In my view, "greater cooperation" is demonstrated by any movement upward and/or to the right on the matrix. As the matrix indicates, the

---

[21] These categories are closely related to those of Holland (1991a), who distinguishes between declarations, substantive actions, and legal competencies. Similarly, Schneider and Seybold (1997) distinguish between "no action," "weak action," and "strong action." However, their study focuses on EPC declarations rather than many other types of cooperative actions, which limits the scope of their analysis.

Table 2.3 *Qualitatively measuring EU foreign policy cooperation*

	Declarations	National actions	National/EC actions
Active	Moderate cooperation	High cooperation	Highest cooperation
Reactive	Low cooperation	Moderate cooperation	High cooperation
Reflexive	Minimal cooperation	Low cooperation	Moderate cooperation

minimal amount of cooperation for the purposes of this study is when EU states merely issue a declaration following some international event. In most cases, such declarations are not very costly (relative to other co-operative behaviors) and they represent by far the greatest number of cooperative actions taken within EPC/CFSP. The highest level of co-operation is demonstrated by movement upward and to the right: when EU states use EC resources or procedures in the service of active, co-herent, and even strategic, foreign policies. We would hypothesize, then, that a greater degree of institutionalization (as measured in the previous section) should result in more of these types of cooperative actions.

In fact, we can follow these trends historically by tracking several geographic areas that received a great deal of attention by EPC/CFSP to provide some empirical continuity throughout the analysis. If institutions and historical development help foster cooperation, we should see the most change in the areas where EU foreign policy is aggressively pursued, where relations are highly institutionalized, and where policies have had several years to mature. These areas include the Middle East, South Africa, Central/Eastern Europe and the Soviet Union/Russia, Central America, and the US. As always, the chief indicator of success in these areas is not so much that EPC/CFSP "solved" a global political problem, but that it helped produce internal EU cohesion and external cooperative behaviors in a contentious area of foreign policy. Tracking these issues over time is important not only for the way they involved new EU foreign policy tools and resulted in closer links to the EC, but also because they provide vivid examples of changes in the opinions, preferences, and even interests of EU member states as a result of institution-building.

Finally, this brings us to the issue of compliance. It might be possible to judge cooperation in terms of the extent to which EU states actually implement the collective decisions reached in EPC/CFSP. This indeed was a problem during the early years of EPC, when its decisions were implemented on a national basis alone. Although I touch upon this issue, it would be beyond the scope of this study to judge whether all EU states acted in accordance with the hundreds of declarations and decisions reached in EPC/CFSP every year. General trends in compliance are discussed during relevant historical episodes, but I do not use compliance as a general indicator of cooperation. Compliance is only one way to judge the legitimacy and effectiveness of EPC/CFSP rules to promote cooperation.[22] Just as the presence of crime in a society does not automatically discredit a domestic judicial system, deliberate violations of common EU foreign policy norms (which in fact are quite rare) do not invalidate the entire cooperative enterprise. Moreover, since the CFSP entered into effect, many external policies are now implemented and/or funded by EC actors, which reduces the need to examine member state compliance as a major indicator of EU foreign policy cooperation.

Institutionalization, cooperation, and domestic politics

There is one final empirical aspect of institutionalized cooperation to consider. In my discussion of transgovernmental relations above, I implied that EU foreign policy cooperation can involve officials in addition to those at the highest level of decision-making (heads of state and government and their ministers). In fact, it is possible to show that participation in EU foreign policymaking penetrates further into the domestic politics of EU member states. In particular, if high-level governmental officials do not always dominate the policy process, as an intergovernmental perspective assumes, this would create openings for interactions among lower-level state actors, as liberal approaches to cooperation often predict. To the extent that institutions can involve and empower such actors to interact with each other (particularly actors with a professional interest in foreign policy), mutual understanding and cooperation may grow.

In this sense, institutionalized EU foreign policy cooperation (like the EU in general) is perhaps less a process of self-interested, unitary states clashing in an intergovernmental forum than it is the disaggregation and recombination of states into their various functional domains. As cooperation becomes increasingly institutionalized at EU, national, and even sub-national levels, it becomes more difficult to treat the EU, the European Community, and individual member states as separate policy-making systems.[23] State bureaucrats in these forums work on a regular basis with their counterparts in other EU states, at the EU level, and elsewhere in order to devise common solutions to external problems. As these state actors associate with each other in various forums and organize

---

[22] On this point see Chayes and Chayes 1993.
[23] For such a view, see White 2001: 40–41.

their behavior in terms of rules and goals set down at the European level, the governance of EPC/CFSP is enhanced. Yet the involvement and re-combination of these officials are only part of the story. We must also consider the internalization of EPC/CFSP rules and policies in domestic politics, which, in the long run, should create an atmosphere conducive to institutional development and cooperation.

Outside the EU, we know that government officials and societal groups can appeal to international rules and norms to further their interests in the domestic arena (Cortell and Davis 1996), and that international norms can become embedded (or internalized) in the domestic politics and insti-tutions of states, thus affecting debates and choices about foreign policy (Müller 1995). This work shows that domestic sensitivity to international institutions can be described in at least two ways: when domestic actors make reference to international norms during policy debates (whether to advance their own goals or those of the international regime), and when states make more permanent institutional changes (in the form of specific legislation, constitutional changes, or bureaucratic changes) to improve compliance with those norms.

These and other strategies are particularly relevant to our understand-ing of the EU, where analysts have systematically explored the two-way relationship between EU membership and domestic politics or institu-tions (Bulmer 1983; de la Serre 1988). While strong interest-group ac-tivity is generally lacking in the area of EU foreign policy, and the EU does not often set down secondary legislation or regulations for such cooperation (which, among other things, limits the ability of domestic litigants to bring cases before the ECJ), there are other ways that mem-bership in EPC/CFSP can influence foreign policymaking in EU member states. These processes have often been referred to as the "Europeaniza-tion" of domestic politics, defined as "an incremental process reorienting the direction and shape of politics to the degree that (EU) political and economic dynamics become part of the organizational logic of national politics and policy-making" (Ladrech 1994: 69). This approach to coop-eration helps to bridge the gap between functionalist approaches, which privilege the EU level of activity, and intergovernmental approaches, which privilege the interests and capabilities of member states to the exclusion of collective processes. Yet we can draw on them, and on the lit-erature on comparative foreign policymaking, to help understand the way EPC/CFSP membership influences the domestic politics of EU member states, thus promoting both institutionalization and cooperation.

What are the mechanisms of Europeanization in EU foreign policy cooperation? Unlike most socioeconomic EC policy areas, EU foreign policy does not usually involve the adaptation of national legislation in accordance with EPC/CFSP norms. EPC/CFSP decisions are rarely regulatory in nature; even when they do involve EC legislation (as with sanctions or the control of dual-use goods) they do not usually encourage domestic actors to make claims about European laws in national courts the way other EC legislation (such as the single market) does. And the ECJ, like most courts, tends to take a passive stance toward the adjudication of foreign policy, so there are few opportunities (relative to Community affairs) for its decisions to influence foreign policymaking processes in EU member states.

However, EPC/CFSP participation involves other responsibilities (chiefly that of sharing the six-month rotating EU presidency) which strongly encourage member states to adapt at the national level. EU states have also long recognized that their influence in multilateral institutions and negotiations suffers when national positions diverge too far from those reached in EPC/CFSP. Thus, although specific channels or instruments (such as EC regulations, domestic legislation, and court cases) for assessing the impact of the EU on its member states are typically lacking in the realm of foreign policy, in this study I pay close attention to three general processes which are directly related to EPC/CFSP:

(1) Elite socialization, focusing on the diplomats and bureaucrats directly involved in EU foreign policy. This involves three elements: a greater familiarity with each other's positions; greater appreciation of the value of acting together to handle external issues; and acceptance of the idea that it is useful and appropriate for Europe to act as a single unit in world politics.

(2) Sympathetic changes in national bureaucratic structures in order to fulfill the responsibilities of EU foreign policy cooperation. These involve the establishment of permanent officials to handle this policy domain; expansions in the size of national foreign ministries; and a clear reorientation (and in some cases, reorganization as well) of national foreign ministries toward "Europe."

(3) Changes of interpretation of some national constitutions in accordance with EPC/CFSP norms.

Finally, we must also keep in mind a fourth, more general process resulting from the expansion of EU foreign policy: its impact on electoral politics, chiefly in the form of public opinion. In general, I argue that to the extent that the aspirations of EPC/CFSP reach public consciousness, and that public opinion grows in support of those aspirations, governments and other elites should be able to draw on that support when choosing to cooperate and when developing institutions toward that end. Although space prohibits me from undertaking a detailed examination of national attitudes toward EU foreign policy, we can show some general trends as EPC/CFSP developed. And, as usual, all of these processes depend on *time*, meaning that the EU states with the longest history of membership tend to show more evidence of change. These four elements of institutional development are addressed when appropriate throughout the analysis.[24]

Summary

This chapter presented an overview of the empirical terrain of this study: the historical development of EU foreign policy in terms of its institutions and its cooperative outcomes. I attempted to set down, in general but clear terms, what I mean by institutionalization and how we might observe patterns of institutionalization in the historical record in terms of different stages of development. I also presented a more comprehensive definition and measurement of EU foreign policy cooperation than currently exists in the literature on this subject. Finally, I discussed how both of these elements – institutionalization and cooperation – might penetrate into the domestic politics of EU member states and create a political climate more favorable to both processes.

While the examples of cooperation presented here, analyzed individually, might not indicate a major role for EPC/CFSP as an institution, taken together they provide compelling evidence that the system has become far more robust and effective than we might otherwise expect given existing theories of institutions and cooperation. These findings are even more remarkable when one considers how weak and informal the system was in the beginning, and the extent to which some member states worked to keep it that way. However, since a correlation between institutionalization and cooperation does not necessarily mean causation, it is necessary to examine the relationship between these processes in more detail. Before doing so, we need to establish a theoretical and empirical reference point against which both institutional and cooperative change can be measured. This task is undertaken in the next chapter, which describes the intergovernmental origins and early functioning of European foreign policy cooperation.

[24] For an extended discussion of these trends, see Smith 2000.

Part II

The institutionalization of cooperation

3 Origins: intergovernmentalism and European Political Cooperation

As war in the Middle East threatened to erupt during the first week of June 1967, leaders of the Six were settling down into one of their periodic intergovernmental summits only a few hundred miles away in Rome. Although fully aware of the different preferences among EU states regarding this volatile region,[1] and of the apparent intractability of the political problems in the Middle East, Germany suggested the Rome summit might be a rare opportunity for the Europeans to speak with a single voice about the tense situation. However, France, under the leadership of de Gaulle, proposed instead a four-power summit (France, the Soviet Union, the UK, and the US) to discuss a settlement to the conflict, but this offer was rejected by the Americans. This failure on the part of the EU even to attempt coordination on its own during such a major crisis, and the rejection of French leadership, both eased the way for the creation of EPC three years later. As German chancellor Kurt Kiesinger recalled, "I felt ashamed at the Rome summit. Just as the war was on the point of breaking, we could not even agree to talk about it" (Ifestos 1987: 420).

The dynamics of the Rome summit during the 1967 Six-Day War also illustrate three important circumstances facing EU governments as they began to think more seriously about coordinating their foreign policies. First, their positions on important global issues such as the Middle East conflict were clearly, and almost embarrassingly, at odds with each other. Second, the EU lacked any procedures or mechanisms of its own at the time (other than occasional intergovernmental summits) to coordinate such positions. And third, it was not even agreed that the EU was the most appropriate forum for such coordination, as this might stifle the great power ambitions of France and could not include the US or the Soviet Union, the dominant powers at the time.

How the EU managed to overcome these obstacles and establish a rudimentary foreign policy coordination mechanism, chiefly involving

[1] At this time France and Italy supported the Arabs, the Netherlands supported the Israelis, Germany declared itself neutral but tacitly supported the Israelis, and Belgium and Luxembourg expressed their support for the UN and the Atlantic Alliance.

intergovernmental procedures, is the subject of this chapter. This initial focus on EU governments, however, does not mean that intergovernmental theory is the most appropriate analytical tool to explain its performance and development. Although observers are often tempted to apply such theory to EU foreign policy cooperation in light of EPC/CFSP formal decision-making rules (where unanimity tends to govern), I argue that intergovernmentalism must be supplemented with insights from institutional theory to explain fully the expansion and day-to-day functioning of EU foreign policy. Still, in order to explain better how an intergovernmental system became increasingly institutionalized and linked to Community procedures, we first need to understand how the intergovernmental approach influenced the earliest debates surrounding EPC.

As I discussed in the previous chapter, the basic simplifying assumptions of intergovernmentalism – involving self-interested bargaining among high-level government officials with predetermined preferences – appear to offer a neat, parsimonious model to explain complex phenomena. If state preferences are taken as given (or formed by a process distinct from that of strategic interaction), if outcomes are treated as separate deals, and if the focus is on top government officials, then the theory eliminates a great deal of variance which might complicate the explanation. Outcomes are explained largely by determining which state(s) had the most to gain or lose in a bargain, which influences their negotiating position. If most of the assumptions of intergovernmentalism hold true during a certain EU decision-making situation, then it would be a powerful tool to explain specific cooperative outcomes, whether they involve history-making events or normal policymaking. Most important for our purposes, intergovernmentalism should be *most* applicable to situations where negotiations are in fact dominated by governments to the exclusion of domestic influences and EC actors, and where institutional arrangements are weak or non-existent. These attributes perfectly describe EPC in its early years.

Indeed, the characteristics of EU foreign policy both in terms of its boundaries as an issue-area and in terms of its formal institutional structure have led many analysts to explain it through the use of general intergovernmental models (Bodenheimer 1967; Wallace 1983a; Pijpers 1991; Øhrgaard 1997) or similar theories of two-level games (Bulmer 1991). On the basis of day-to-day policymaking, EPC could easily have been an informal bargaining arena, where deals were worked out behind the scenes between major players. Chiefs of government and their representatives had the authority to decide the issues and options that could be discussed within EPC. Their monopoly over agenda-setting and the general secrecy of the entire process, both domestically and at the EU level, insulated them in at least three ways: from domestic pressure about issues taken up within EPC, from criticism about the performance of EPC, and from ideas concerning the institutional development of EPC and its relationship to the EC. Thus an intergovernmental or two-level games approach, where chiefs of government make collective policy in between the "game boards" of domestic and international politics, seems especially appropriate for analyzing EPC, especially during its formative years. To evaluate this claim thoroughly, the rest of this chapter explores the origins, institutional structure, and early performance of EPC through the conceptual lens of intergovernmental theory.

EPC: the origins

The "pre-history" of EPC has been recounted in a number of excellent studies (Allen and Wallace 1982; Ifestos 1987; Nuttall 1992a); I do not attempt to repeat their efforts in detail here. Instead my purpose is to frame the debate over European foreign policy cooperation in terms of institutional arrangements to understand why EPC took the weak form it did with the Luxembourg Report of 1970, and how it performed during its first years in operation. However, to appreciate the achievement represented by the Luxembourg Report fully, we need to consider the long series of debates that preceded it. In this sense, the discussions leading up to the Luxembourg Report are highly instructive about the way EU member states tend to define collective problems and devise institutional mechanisms to address those problems. To this day, the earliest postwar debates over the means and ends of political integration and cooperation in Europe still condition discussions about how to create formal institutional mechanisms for these purposes. These differences are still best described as "a tension between those who wanted a concert of sovereign nations expressing coordinated views on foreign policy questions, and those who wanted a common foreign policy as the expression of a European Union" (Nuttall 1992a: 2). Although EU states have slightly varied their positions on this question over the years, in general the smaller states (Belgium, Italy, Luxembourg, and the Netherlands) in the 1960s tended to fear any mechanisms for foreign policy cooperation that fell outside the original Treaty of Rome,[2] which could too easily be dominated by France and Germany (and the UK, once it joined), and which could damage relations with the US and NATO.

[2] The Treaty of Rome linked the European Coal and Steel Community, the European Atomic Community, and the European Economic Community. Following common usage, I refer to these communities collectively as the European Community, or EC, when the narrative requires.

The French, however, persisted in efforts to achieve an independent voice in world politics for the EU, but such efforts had to be pursued only on their terms. However, in one of the great ironies of European integration, French plans for a European Defense Community (EDC, or the "Pleven Plan"), embedded in a "European Political Community" modeled along EC lines, failed on August 29, 1954 after an unusual coalition of socialists and Gaullists in the French Assembly refused to ratify them.[3] The EDC, encouraged in part by the US as a mechanism to permit German rearmament in the face of the Korean War, was very ambitious. It was intended to enhance peace within Europe through military integration, to defend Western Europe against the Soviet threat, and to help Europe build itself up as a "third power" to prevent the dominance of the US and the Soviet Union in world politics (Jopp 1997: 153). If the plan succeeded, French leadership of European political integration would be assured as Germany was in no position to contest French aims and the UK was not yet a member of the EU.

As a result of the EDC failure, and instead of a defense community closely linked to the EU, the UK extended the membership of its nascent Western European Union (WEU) project to include Germany and Italy. For the moment, it seemed that political integration and foreign/security policy cooperation were set aside as European institution-building focused on NATO, the European Communities, and, to a much lesser extent, the WEU. At the same time, the French, under President de Gaulle, were frustrated in their attempts to create a framework for political cooperation among themselves, the Americans, and the British. De Gaulle's proposal for a three-power directorate was quickly opposed by Washington and London,[4] leading him to focus his efforts on Germany and other EU states.[5] Here the French suggested that EU governments hold informal quarterly meetings of their foreign ministers to discuss foreign policy issues, and agreement to do so was reached at Strasbourg in November 1959. Defense matters were avoided in these meetings, and the talks were primarily oriented toward European, not Atlantic, concerns.

Despite its limitations and the as-yet unresolved relationship with the US, this modest agreement provided the intergovernmental embryo of the Luxembourg Report a decade later. There also was broad recognition that efforts to integrate Europe economically would affect political relations as well. In fact, even at this time, some observers (influenced by realism)

---

[3] On the EDC see Fursdon 1980; the French vote is examined in Kanter 1970.

[4] This directorate would have made "joint decisions in all political questions affecting global security . . . and would draw up and, if necessary, implement strategic action plans, especially as regards the use of nuclear weapons" (Grosser 1980: 304).

[5] For details, see Menon, Forster, and Wallace 1992.

suggested that economic integration could cause "reverse spillover" in political relations, leading to European disunity rather than unity. Given the American security guarantee for Europe, and the growing view that the use of military force between EU states was no longer a viable policy option, Europeans would be free to pursue their own national interests at the expense of economic integration.[6] However, as will be seen later in this study, EPC originally was intended to prevent such disunity and it proved extremely successful in achieving this goal.

Still, discussions in this Strasbourg framework rarely led to coordinated action, as we might expect of such an untried, barely institutionalized forum. During their first series of quarterly meetings, EU foreign ministers discussed key issues such as the 1960 Congo crisis, but they did nothing concrete about this or any other issue. The limitations of this consultation mechanism led de Gaulle to seek and win the support of German chancellor Konrad Adenauer for his proposals concerning a political union largely based on intergovernmental summits supported by a permanent political secretariat in Paris. However, small EU states, led by the Dutch, continued to oppose any "Political Committee" or permanent secretariat, particularly one dominated by France and/or Germany, if such an organization threatened to undermine the existing EC organizations or procedures which had taken so much effort to establish, and which were still somewhat fragile.

Instead, ideas for a loose intergovernmental procedure to support political integration, one which enjoyed no permanent organizational support, were developed. Toward this end, France called for a conference of EU heads of state and government (and foreign ministers) in Paris on February 10–11, 1961. At this first conference, participants explicitly agreed to "discover suitable means of organizing closer political cooperation" as a basis for "a progressively developing union" among the Six. The vehicle for this effort was a study commission led by Danish foreign minister Christian Fouchet, which made a series of proposals (the so-called "Fouchet Plans") centered on the idea of a new "council of heads of state or government" with powers to "harmonize, coordinate, and unify the foreign, economic, cultural, and defense policies of the Six" (Allen and Wallace 1982). Once again the small EU states, this time led by Belgium, blocked the proposals. Although the Fouchet Plans were revised and reconsidered in their details, EU states still could not seem to reconcile the general impasse between intergovernmental and supranational visions of political cooperation. At the same time, the US and the UK,

---

[6] Hoffman (1965, 1966) has been a leading proponent of this view. His skepticism has persisted after the Maastricht Treaty and the CFSP; see Hoffman 2000.

in de Gaulle's view, were unfairly dominating all defense issues through the Atlantic alliance, which led him to veto the UK's application for EU membership and to pursue closer Franco-German cooperation instead.[7]

The instrument for this cooperation was the Franco-German Treaty of Cooperation (Elysée Treaty) of January 22, 1963, which established twice-yearly meetings of French and German heads of government and quarterly meetings of foreign ministers to promote cooperation in foreign policy, defense, and culture.[8] But Germany required a concession for including defense issues in this Treaty: it insisted that the Treaty include an explicit reference to cooperation in the framework of the Atlantic alliance. The way Germany effectively blocked a wholly independent European defense policy while affirming its commitment to the EU in general, and to the Franco-German partnership in particular, has since become a constant theme in the story of European foreign policy. However, despite Germany's reservations, the Elysée Treaty was successful in improving Franco-German cooperation, and its functioning provided some useful lessons during the formative years of EPC ten years later. Still, as France could find no support in Europe for a defense policy more independent of the Atlantic alliance, and the French were not yet willing to consider any form of foreign policy cooperation that excluded defense issues, European foreign policy beyond the Franco-German relationship stalled for the rest of the decade.[9] In addition, the defense provisions of the Elysée Treaty were never implemented and France pulled out of NATO's integrated command structure in 1965 in order to pursue its own course in this area.

The idea of institutionalized foreign policy cooperation gained new momentum only a few years later, when events exogenous to the conduct of foreign policy led EU governments to rethink their attitudes. In particular, the growing prospect of the first enlargement of the EU in the late 1960s, and the beginning of the final stage of the Common Market project, led the EU heads of government to agree "to study the possibility of gradually tightening their political links through methods and procedures relevant to their experiences and circumstances."[10] Yet the

---

[7] For a more detailed analysis of the Fouchet problems, see Bodenheimer 1967: 27–40.

[8] Italy was to have been included in this initiative but the Italians felt they would have been dominated by the other two larger states. For details on this Treaty, see Wallace 1986.

[9] Of course, most EU states had some form of institutionalized bilateral contacts with other EU states and with non-EU states. These usually involved regular intergovernmental summits, and some (such as the British–German relationship) involved political or defense issues. However, these relationships were not as central to the creation of EPC as the Franco-German partnership, thus I do not analyze them here.

[10] Decided at a meeting in May 1967 to celebrate the tenth anniversary of the Treaty of Rome; see Johnston 1994: 5.

gap between these ambitions and the actual level of policy coordination among EU states seemed wider than ever before when the EU failed even to discuss the Six-Day War only a month later. It was not until de Gaulle left office in April 1969 that a new debate about institutionalized EU foreign policy cooperation could begin, as France became more eager to reach agreement on other pressing issues, such as securing permanent financing for the Common Agricultural Policy, which greatly benefited French farmers. At The Hague summit on December 2, 1969, EU heads of government or state finally declared they were ready to pave the way "for a united Europe capable of assuming its responsibilities in the world of tomorrow and of making a contribution commensurate with its tradition and its mission." Toward this end, EU foreign ministers were directed to "study the best way of achieving progress in the matter of political unification, within the context of enlargement."[11] In other words, foreign ministers were not directed to create institutions for foreign policy cooperation, only to consider the matter of "political unification," a term not defined in the instructions.

The EU foreign ministers in turn passed on their instructions to the Political Directors of the Six foreign ministries. These officials, not the EU foreign ministers, largely drafted the Luxembourg (or Davignon) Report,[12] which created European Political Cooperation (de la Serre and Defarges 1983). According to one participant in the negotiations, the legacy of the failed EDC and of the failed Fouchet Plans weighed heavily on the deliberations.[13] The negotiators did not want to reopen those dead-end debates and they were determined to find some way of satisfying both intergovernmental and supranational visions of "political unification." In addition, they were aware that enlargement might create a division between old and new member states, and the admission of another major nuclear power and permanent UN Security Council member (the UK), with its own vast network of foreign relationships (including a "special relationship" with the US) and a great capacity for independent action in foreign affairs, threatened to undermine what little political cohesion among the Six already existed. Moreover, French leadership was in short supply with the political unrest in that country in the aftermath of de Gaulle's exit from office. Germany, as well, was not yet ready to assume

---

[11] Unless otherwise noted, quotes from summits, EPC reports, and documents come from the documents collection *European Political Cooperation*, 5th ed. (Bonn: Press and Information Service of the Federal Republic of Germany, 1988). The Hague summit quotes are on p. 14.

[12] Official title: "The First Report of the Foreign Ministers to the Heads of State and Government of the Member States of the European Community, 27 October 1970." Hereafter "Luxembourg Report."

[13] Interview with a Luxembourg Report negotiator, 1996.

more leadership in the EU and take charge of the negotiations, while the US was still generally hostile to the idea of a more politically independent EU and did not play a constructive role in the debate.

Yet EPC *was* successfully established in this difficult political climate, mainly because opportunities for self-interested bargaining existed at the time. Although the Luxembourg Report committee was headed by a Belgian, Etienne Davignon, all participants were aware of the need to satisfy French concerns. France still hoped that European political unification could be used to formulate a policy more independent of the US, but it also required that EPC be kept intergovernmental, which meant that the Commission and the European Parliament (EP) had to be kept on a tight leash or, better still, excluded from the matter entirely. Germany and the Netherlands essentially gave in to these demands in exchange for the enlargement of the EU.[14] EPC thus succeeded because it avoided the problems that had doomed the first two attempts at cooperation: it was neither supranational/federal (like the EDC) nor wholly intergovernmental and separate from the EC (like the Fouchet Plans) (Nuttall 1992a: 30). In the end, the Luxembourg Report indeed had something for everyone: the UK used it to show its commitment to greater Europe as a new member of the EU; France used it to maintain an element of government control over the process of European integration and to distinguish European (e.g., French) policies from those of the US; and Germany thought it could be a way to promote *Ostpolitik* and help bridge the gap between East and West, while possibly making a more active German foreign policy more acceptable to its EU partners. Finally, the smaller states appreciated how the enlargement of the EU might ultimately help dilute the influence of France and Germany.[15]

However, although EPC's framework was intergovernmental, many participants (especially the smaller states) also expected EPC and the EC to become linked over time. In Belgium, for example, the government attempted to sell the plan to the national parliament (even though it did not require ratification) by emphasizing that the EC and EPC would eventually be brought closer together. As the Belgian foreign minister argued: "The [Luxembourg] Report viewed the Community as the kernel of European development; relations would be established with the [European] Parliament and the Commission . . . The perspectives of the

---

[14] In the words of Dutch foreign minister Joseph Luns, "For several years now the Netherlands has considered that should Great Britain join the Common Market it would be necessary to accept in Europe political cooperation more or less reflecting the views outlined in the second Fouchet Plan." Cited in Johnston 1994: 7.

[15] On the compromises of the Luxembourg Report, see Allen and Wallace 1982: 27–29.

Davignon [Luxembourg] Report are not the same [as the Fouchet Plan] and its underlying philosophy is clearly distinct."[16]

In addition, although most EU states found something in EPC they could support, it is not quite proper to speak of a clear demand for foreign policy cooperation among them at this time. Above all, EPC appeared to be a weak commitment to placate France in order to get on with pressing EU business after the shameful impasse of the 1960s. EU member states essentially agreed to disagree on the means and ends of EPC, and on its relationship to the EC. Especially during the economic difficulties of the times, and in light of perceptions of American inattentiveness (if not hostility) to European problems in the context of the Vietnam War, all EU member states recognized that radically different national foreign policy positions could harm the EC, its policies, and relations between its members and between it and the outside world. The prospect of the EU's first enlargement greatly intensified these concerns and thus provided the key institutional moment that resulted in the creation of EPC.

The institutional structure of EPC

The modest provisions of the Luxembourg Report revealed little of the nearly two decades of heated debate which had preceded it, but they clearly reflected the EU's acceptance of the intergovernmental vision of political unification. Most obviously, EPC was provided with a bare minimum of institutional support. Indeed, in view of the origins, original structure, and goals of EPC, it is probably an exaggeration to consider it as an institution or even as a specific issue-area. Since member states agreed only on the need for some small, even symbolic, measure of foreign policy coordination, the institutional structure of EPC reflected the fact that governments would dominate and define any such coordination and that it would be separate from EC policies and procedures. Small EU states which wanted EPC to be subject to the same supranational processes of the EC were seduced with the hopes that EPC would eventually be integrated into the Community; large states which opposed this (chiefly France and the UK) were confident they could prevent excessive or unwanted involvement by the Community. Germany and the Netherlands became the most vocal opponents of a rigid distinction between EPC and EC affairs, as did the EP, but in the beginning these actors had to accept the views of France and the UK.

---

[16] Cited in Franck 1983: 89.

With the Luxembourg Report, then, EPC was endorsed by the EU foreign ministers to achieve an indeterminate set of ends, in parallel with the goals of the existing EC treaties:

(1) To ensure, through regular exchanges of information and consultations, a better mutual understanding on the great international problems.
(2) To strengthen their solidarity by promoting the harmonization of their views, the coordination of their positions, and where it appears possible or desirable, common actions.[17]

Under this framework, EU foreign ministers were to meet at least twice a year to discuss "great international problems," a phrase vague enough "to promise everything or nothing," according to some observers (Allen and Wallace 1982: 25). If a "grave crisis or matter of particular urgency" arose, a meeting of foreign ministers could be convened between the biannual colloquies.[18] The idea of a *common* foreign policy, mentioned in previous proposals in this area, was conspicuously omitted in the Luxembourg Report. The possibility of discussing defense issues was avoided as well, which placated the EU states fearful of interfering with NATO (such as Denmark, Germany, the Netherlands, and the UK) and the new neutral EU member state, Ireland.

Moreover, instead of specifying (or even suggesting) appropriate topics for discussion, the Report referred only to "cooperation in the sphere of foreign policy."[19] By agreeing to "consult on all questions of foreign policy" during these summits,[20] EU states held hopes of at least determining common interests and, if possible, coordinating their foreign policy positions and taking common actions. However, there were no specific decision-making mechanisms for producing such positions and actions, and the actual institutional innovations of the Luxembourg Report were few. Directly below the level of foreign ministers, coordination was to be achieved through regular meetings of a *Political Committee* composed of national Political Directors from member state foreign ministries. In the UK the role of a Political Director had to be created for EPC; this was one small early example of the impact of EPC on the domestic political systems of its member states. The Political Committee was to meet at least four times a year to prepare ministerial meetings and to carry out tasks delegated to them by the foreign ministers. It was also permitted

---

[17] Luxembourg Report, Part II, Section 1. This Report is also known as the Davignon Report (and EPC was also known as the Davignon Procedure), after Viscount Etienne Davignon, the Belgian Political Director who chaired the meeting of the committee which created EPC.
[18] Luxembourg Report, Part II, Section 2.
[19] Luxembourg Report, Part II.   [20] Luxembourg Report, Part II, Section 4.

to set up working groups to consider specific problems, but the Luxembourg Report did not indicate what problems should be considered or how such working groups should be staffed and organized. Finally, the Report recommended that each foreign ministry designate a liaison official to manage EPC on a daily basis in the absence of a secretariat. Although the Luxembourg Report did not designate them as such, these officials later became known as "European Correspondents."

In addition to its spare institutional structure and focus on national foreign ministries, the Luxembourg Report was also noteworthy for the way it limited the involvement of EC procedures and organizations in EPC. As we shall see in Chapter 6, the European Commission, which enjoys the right to initiate all EC legislation, clearly was marginalized in EPC. It could be "invited to make known its views" only if the work of the foreign ministers in EPC affected the activities of the EC.[21] However, in the hopes of giving a "democratic character" to EPC, the Luxembourg Report explicitly recognized the political legitimacy of the EC by instituting an informal "biannual colloquy" between EU foreign ministers and members of the EP. The president in office of the EU was also directed to prepare an annual progress report on EPC and to communicate this report to the EP. These provisions gave the appearance that EPC had some popular legitimacy beyond the wishes of EU governments.[22] They also would soon make the EP a vocal advocate of policy and institutional changes in EPC/CFSP. The same cannot be said for the European Court of Justice (ECJ), however, which is not mentioned at all in the Luxembourg Report. Nor does the Report provide any other adjudication or dispute resolution mechanisms to take the place of the ECJ. It is probably safe to say that a tacit understanding among the Report's negotiators made them feel it was unnecessary to consider the legal ramifications of EPC, since it was not a treaty and would not come under the supranational provisions of the Community.[23] It is also highly unlikely that the negotiators would have reached agreement on the Report had they attempted to frame their discussions in terms of legal obligations.

The Luxembourg Report did, however, include provisions for further institutional change, a pattern which has persisted in most agreements concerning EU foreign policy. EU foreign ministers agreed to "pursue their study on the best way of achieving progress in the field of political unification," and to produce a second report on the subject only two years after the Luxembourg Report entered into effect. This report

---

[21] Luxembourg Report, Part II, Section 5. [22] Luxembourg Report, Part II, Section 6.
[23] Interview with a Luxembourg Report negotiator, Brussels, 1996.

would assess the results of EPC, consider methods for improving the mechanism, and search for other fields where such cooperation could be extended. The study was also expected to take into account related developments in the Community. Toward this end the foreign ministers directed the Political Committee to prepare summary reports on EPC at the end of each biannual ministerial meeting.[24] With this key provision for self-monitoring and evaluation the seeds for additional institutional change, in the form of the 1972 Paris summit and the 1973 Copenhagen Report, were thus sown.

Finally, the concluding section (Part IV) of the Luxembourg Report mentioned the "correlation" between EC and EPC activities in order to clarify the obligations of membership in EC/EPC to the applicant countries at the time (Denmark, Ireland, Norway, and the UK). The Report specified that the applicant countries were expected to adhere to the EPC procedures it outlined once they became full members of the EC. This was hardly a demanding obligation, considering how loose and vague EPC procedures were at the time. Still, this requirement is novel in that EPC existed entirely outside the framework of the Community and was not a treaty; thus EPC participation could have been rejected by the applicant states. This did not happen, of course (excepting Norway's rejection of EC/EPC membership), and the Report helpfully provided ways to facilitate participation in EPC by the applicants as "observers" prior to their full accession to the Community.[25] This effort also reflects two important, and fundamental, early norms of foreign policy cooperation: that the EC and EPC, despite their distinct rules, were considered two means to a single end (European integration), and that all new EU member states must agree to participate in both of these institutions of integration.

The main features of EPC under the provisions of the Luxembourg Report are summarized in Table 3.1. These elements provide a reference point against which we can measure future changes in the system.

As an institution to promote cooperation, the Luxembourg Report is probably far more noteworthy for what it omitted. As Morrow (among others) has argued (1994), effective institutions must solve at least four problems: sanctions, monitoring, the distribution of benefits, and the sharing of information. EPC involved almost none of these elements at first; only the provision to hold meetings to consult on foreign policy could possibly be seen as a mechanism to share information. EPC also

[24] Luxembourg Report, Part III.

[25] The formal Act of Accession was signed on January 22, 1972; the applicant states were permitted full participation in EPC discussions at every level after that point (Allen and Wallace 1982: 25).

Table 3.1 *EPC according to the Luxembourg Report (October 1970)*

Component	Actors and functions
Intergovernmental direction	EU foreign ministers meet at least twice a year.
	EU presidency chairs EPC meetings and provides administrative support as needed.
	Crisis procedures initiated by EU presidency if necessary.
Transgovernmental support	Political Committee: preparation of ministerial meetings. Meets at least four times a year.
	European Correspondents: liaison between capitals.
	Working groups: geographical/functional analyses for EPC.
Linkages with the EC	Commission invited to make known its views on EPC.
	Biannual colloquy with EP Political Committee, and annual report on progress on EPC.
Obligations	States consult on all questions of foreign policy.

was not linked to the EC, not supported by any permanent institution or bureaucracy (although one was considered during the Luxembourg Report negotiations), and not even negotiated nor ratified as a treaty. Its agreements were rarely open to public scrutiny or approval, public opinion was unaware or uninterested in EPC, and there were no access points to relevant policymakers.[26] EPC also had no permanent budget, finances, or staff for many years; no fixed meeting place; no secretariat-general or other chief official; and no designated subjects to form a starting point for discussions. It had no compliance standards, record-keeping system, legal obligations, or enforcement mechanisms to speak of, and it formally required little more than a pledge (not a legal obligation) among EU states to consult with each other and to coordinate their foreign policies if possible.[27] It was little more than "a private club, operated by diplomats for diplomats" (Nuttall 1992a: 11), subject to the goodwill of its members, run strictly by consensus, and largely closed to outside scrutiny.

Additionally, EPC's administrative infrastructure was centered in the foreign ministries of its member states, and did not include other ministries involved in EC affairs (agriculture, finance, interior, and so on). The "low politics" of EC affairs was handled by the economics or EC section in most foreign ministries (notably those of France and Germany, among others); EPC was "high politics" handled by the political section. Finally, EPC's three most important founding documents between 1970

[26] As Hill noted (1983a: 188) after ten years of EPC, "public opinion within the member states [was] sadly ill-informed about and remote from EPC."

[27] This description is broadly based on Wessels 1982; Wallace 1983a; Ginsberg 1989; Nuttall 1992a; and author interviews with former EPC officials, Brussels, 1995–96.

and 1981 (the Luxembourg, Copenhagen, and London Reports) did not have treaty status and were not submitted to national parliaments for ratification. In short, for states which preferred to cooperate informally, EPC exhibited all the requisite characteristics: states avoided explicit, formal, visible pledges; their agreements were not ratified; they could quickly change or renegotiate their commitments according to circumstances; and they could use and develop (or abolish) the system as quickly or as slowly as they desired.[28] Indeed, if EU states had insisted on defining explicit policy goals or a firm end point to the process (such as political integration or union), the system would never have left the negotiating table.

In the end, the Luxembourg Report depended on a rare confluence of events during the late 1960s. In particular, external factors helped create an environment conducive to the intergovernmental bargain that resulted in EPC. These factors include the change of government in France, the failure of the EU to respond to a major external crisis (the Six-Day War), and the EU's first enlargement. Although these developments suggest a rational logic behind the creation of EPC, the key catalyst was French insistence on some form of political integration as their price for supporting enlargement. What they got, however, was hardly an ambitious, innovative approach to political integration: EPC was largely based on the Franco-German Elysée Treaty. However, French power or leadership does not wholly explain the final form of EPC, in particular its initial exclusion from the EC and the taboo against discussing defense issues. To explain these characteristics, we need to pay attention to the diplomats who actually negotiated the Luxembourg Report, and to the role of smaller EU states, if only for their ability to block certain French proposals (such as an EPC secretariat based in Paris, a *directoire* of large EU states, or the more general "intergovernmentalization" of the EU itself). Thus, we can see even at this early stage the important roles played by all four logics of institutionalization discussed in this volume: power (the leadership of France), functional (bargaining), appropriateness (changes in a related institution, the EC), and socialization (negotiators who copied and expanded certain elements of the Elysée Treaty). This is not to say, however, that intergovernmentalism is an entirely inappropriate theory. It does help explain the formation of EPC on the basis of a significant bargain in EU history, and it may be useful for explaining single episodes of cooperation. Yet it does leave out of the process many important factors which are better captured, over time, by an institutionalist (but not necessarily

---

[28] On the basic characteristics of an informal agreement to cooperate, see Lipson 1991: 501.

supranational institutionalist) perspective. Above all, intergovernmentalism does not explain how EPC changed over time, to become "less than
supranational but more than intergovernmental" (Wessels 1982: 15).

More specifically, the real issue here is the extent to which the Luxembourg Report encouraged substantial European foreign policy cooperation and acted as a catalyst for additional institutional change, particularly
in light of the assumptions of intergovernmental theory noted earlier in
this volume. I take up these questions in the rest of this chapter.

The early performance of European
Political Cooperation

This section assesses EU foreign policy cooperation in terms of changes
in the way EU states conducted their relations with each other (procedural changes) and in terms of specific collective outcomes (substantive
changes). This is more than a theoretical distinction; as we shall see in
Chapter 5, EU states themselves evaluated EPC in terms of intra-group
relations and substantive EPC policies or decisions. In other words, discussions about procedure were always closely linked to those of substance.
Especially when EPC deliberations or policies involved any element of
economic policy, this invariably led to further debates about the proper
role of the EC in that policy (Wallace and Allen 1977). Still, while recognizing that procedures and substance were closely linked, we can make
some tentative judgments about the relative performance of these two
elements of EPC. I begin with procedural changes.

Procedural changes

To what extent did EPC help modify the general conduct of foreign policy
among EU states? I began this chapter by suggesting that intergovernmental theories should be most relevant in situations where institutions do
not exist, or exist only in a weak form. Although the utility of the intergovernmental model in understanding the EPC process diminished over
the years, in the beginning it was not very far off the mark. To help organize my assessment of changes of process in EPC, I focus on two major
areas: developments at each level of collective action (governmental or
ministerial, at the Political Committee/European Correspondent level,
and at the level of working groups), and the growth of linkages between
business conducted in EPC and that conducted in the Community.

At the ministerial level, the first task was to set the agenda of EPC.
After all the heated debates surrounding the Luxembourg Report, its
architects were not encouraged at its prospects. It could not even be

assumed that regular meetings actually would take place. With such a weak institutional structure, EPC inevitably developed on a trial-and-error, case-by-case basis. As Nuttall put it (1992a: 4), "There was no grand design [of EPC]; rather the way in which EPC reacted to events determined the type of organization it became." He further notes the absence of ground rules and the climate of uncertainty surrounding that first meeting of foreign ministers in Munich on November 19, 1970, barely a month after the adoption of the Luxembourg Report:

> The Ministers had never met before in that format; they were not certain what they were supposed to achieve nor in what conventions they would be operating; there had been some preparatory work for the meeting, but not the full-blown, professional preparation of the agenda which the Political Committee was to develop in later years. The setting of the agenda was by no means self-evident. (Nuttall 1992a: 55)

Also, and as intergovernmentalism might predict, the first two major topics discussed in this doubtful setting (the Middle East and East–West relations) generally reflected the interests of the more powerful states within EPC: France and Germany. These important early initiatives will be explored in more detail below.

While efforts at the level of foreign ministers were fairly tentative, the Political Committee rapidly became a driving force behind EPC. Meeting on a regular basis in the capital of the country holding the EU presidency, this group enjoyed the benefits of regular consultation on foreign affairs. EPC generally allowed foreign ministries (particularly the Political Directors) to play a much stronger role, although perhaps indirectly, in European affairs than before, after having been marginalized by other domestic ministries involved in EC business. As Hill put it:

> EPC is good for foreign ministries, and foreign ministries good for EPC . . . Accordingly, the Foreign Ministry in every country (with the possible exceptions of France and Greece) has become a powerful internal lobby for the benefits of common external policies, on the grounds of both international effectiveness and the stimulus given to general cooperation within the Community. (Hill 1983a: 189)

Indeed, EPC participants at this level recall a high degree of eagerness and enthusiasm when the project was started.[29] In addition to the possibility of influencing European policy, one also should not dismiss a natural bureaucratic tendency to expand an agency's functions and status. For example, in France, EPC was "warmly welcomed" by the Political Directorate of the Quai d'Orsay, according to de la Serre and Defarges; thus

---

[29] Interviews with EPC participants, Brussels, 1995–96.

"EPC made it possible for this directorate to participate in the construction of Europe" after having been overshadowed in Community affairs by the Economic Directorate of the French foreign ministry (de la Serre and Defarges 1983: 62). In Italy, the establishment of EPC "marked the beginning of a new moment of glory" for the Political Affairs Directorate (Bonvicini 1983: 74). Finally, EPC in general allowed foreign ministries/Political Directors to reassert themselves as the primary "gatekeepers" between national policies and international cooperation, an important function that had been increasingly threatened by the growth of the EC (Allen and Wallace 1982: 29).

Since membership of the Political Committee was fairly stable, it quickly began to develop its own *esprit de corps*. According to EPC insiders, the atmosphere in the Committee was "friendly, almost casual," quite unlike the "stiff formality" of the EC's own COREPER, which prepared meetings concerning EC business for the Council of Ministers.[30] This body also had the authority to forge consensus and compromises, which could then be defended to governments back home. With this very positive atmosphere, the group began to meet more often than the four times a year mandated by the Luxembourg Report; in fact, it met nine times during 1972.[31] Similarly, the European Correspondents also threw themselves into EPC; in addition to liaison, their tasks included handling EPC procedural matters, organizing the EPC dossiers within their respective foreign ministries, preparing the draft conclusions for ministerial and Political Committee meetings, and managing the EPC aspects of the rotating EU presidency. However, while the Correspondents were important for bridging the gap between economic and political directorates in foreign ministries, they became neither a "mobile secretariat" nor a true working group (Bonvicini 1982: 38). The problems involved in managing this gap without a permanent organization would create pressures for institutional change as the agenda of EPC expanded.

Instead, most analytical and preparatory work in EPC took place in the working groups organized around substantive policy areas. In the first two years after the Luxembourg Report, fully twenty EPC working groups were established, a remarkable display of organizational energy for such an untried framework. These groups dealt with geographic regions (Africa, Asia, the Mediterranean, the Middle East, Latin America, and Eastern Europe), substantive issues (the CSCE, the UN, and the UN-disarmament process), and particular functions (heads of protocol, heads

---

[30] Nuttall 1992a: 17. Also interviews with EPC participants, Brussels, 1995–96.
[31] "Results Obtained from European Political Cooperation on Foreign Policy," annex to the Copenhagen Report, July 23, 1973.

of communications, and senior civil servants from justice ministries, who dealt with legal cooperation). Working groups reported to the Political Committee and operated on the basis of a mandate from the Committee; however, they quickly adopted the practice of exchanging views under the heading of "other business," which allowed EPC to expand quietly into new areas not specified by the Political Committee (da Fonseca-Wollheim 1981: 4–5). The groups were usually staffed at the level of heads of department, and they met a bit more often during each EU presidency than groups at higher levels in EPC. Until 1986, when they moved to the new EPC Secretariat after the Single European Act, the working groups met in national capitals as a self-contained traveling EPC administration.

The main function of the working groups was to exchange information and arrive at common analyses, then identify and recommend options to the Political Committee. Working groups could not take decisions themselves, however, as they did not have the authority to make compromises at that level. Instead, an informal practice soon developed whereby proceedings of working groups were summarized in an "oral report," which was actually written. The report was drafted by each EU presidency, and did not require a consensus to approve it. In addition, working groups demonstrated "a natural tendency to turn themselves into management committees for the execution of policy," which somewhat undermined both the Political Directors and the Commission (Nuttall 1988: 108, 1992a: 16–18). Even in this loose framework, disputes over the division of labor among these actors, whether actual or potential, were a key feature of EU foreign policy from the start and have remained a point of contention ever since. Such disputes also created pressures for new rules to govern this increasingly complex system.

Finally, in terms of linkages between EPC and the EC, the external economic and political relations of the EC were superficially compartmentalized. At this time, EPC's provisions suggested dominance by governments and the exclusion of the EC's actors and procedures. EPC had different ground rules, working methods, policy issues, legal foundations, instruments for action, timetables, venues for meetings, and even working languages (English and French only below ministerial level), which together created a new EPC political culture. The division between those domains was sacrosanct for several member states, such as France, to the consternation of others (Germany and the Netherlands in particular).[32] In the beginning, governments went to absurd lengths (such as changing meeting places when discussions of EC affairs gave way to EPC matters)

---

[32] The Danes were an exception to this tendency, proposing instead that foreign policy cooperation be subject to the national parliaments rather than governments, keeping in line with their constitutional provisions for foreign policymaking.

to emphasize that EC and EPC procedures were separate. In one notorious episode in November 1973, this distinction even led EU foreign ministers to fly from Copenhagen to Brussels on the same day to emphasize a shift from the EC agenda to the EPC agenda (Wallace 1983a: 381). Terminology was also important here: in EPC, foreign ministers met as the "Conference of Foreign Ministers of the EEC Countries"; in the EC, they met as the "Council of Ministers." Political Directors in national capitals also had little or no contact with COREPER in Brussels, although they certainly were accustomed to multilateral cooperation in other forums like NATO.[33]

To some extent, then, the French were successful in maintaining the separation between the EC and EPC at this early stage, as there was not yet enough consensus to permit the Commission a greater role in this domain than that specified by the Luxembourg Report. Nor was the Commission willing to lobby for a more active role in EPC at this time. However, EU states could not escape the fact that some discussion of global economic issues would be inevitable in EPC, and that the Commission should be involved on a more consistent basis than formally allowed in the Luxembourg Report. For example, the CSCE process and the general discussion of East–West relations were stimulated by the fact that individual trade policies of EU states toward Eastern Europe were due to end by December 31, 1972, when trade was to become an exclusive EC competency. As trade policy is a key tool in foreign relations, this deadline provided a convenient procedural reason for the EC to formulate a common approach to the East in both economic and political terms (Nuttall 1992a: 58). Thus the Commission was reluctantly permitted to participate in certain meetings concerning East–West relations and what came to be the Euro-Arab Dialogue. EPC also held its regular colloquies with the EP, and it made the required annual report to the Parliament on progress toward political unification. After two years, another informal procedure was added whereby the EU presidency informed the EP Political Committee ahead of time as to the upcoming topics for discussion. This allowed the EP to prepare itself better to ask questions about EPC, which eventually led to an enhanced change of views between the two entities. Yet parliamentary involvement in EPC at this early stage, in terms of either policy substance or institutional reform, was still severely limited.

To summarize, even though EPC was supposed to be an informal, flexible system, dominated by member states and kept separate from the

---

[33] Wallace and Allen 1977: 231. COREPER is the Committee of Permanent Representatives (i.e., member state ambassadors) to the EU. The separation between the Political Committee and COREPER would persist for nearly twenty years.

EC, we can observe some small violations of these intergovernmental provisions even in the beginning. The institutionalization of the mechanism began as soon as skilled national officials began meeting within the framework of EPC on a regular basis. Three developments in EPC are important at this point.

First and most generally, these officials quickly looked to the EC model to organize their work on foreign policy. In other words,

> the character of political cooperation as it developed came to resemble closely that of policy-making in many areas within the competencies of the Treaties. The Political Committee, like COREPER, prepared the agenda for ministerial meetings; like COREPER and the Commission, it spawned subcommittees and working groups on specific topics. Although political cooperation was not constrained by the legal framework of the Treaties, its working methods were similar to the process of *concertation* used to coordinate other areas of policy not yet subsumed to the authority of the Commission. (Wallace and Allen 1977: 232)

Although EPC was far more confidential than other areas of *concertation*, this tendency to imitate policymaking in other EC areas reflects a key insight of institutional theory: since innovation is often costly (especially when it fails), institutions tend toward isomorphism or imitation. This tendency is perhaps most pronounced in situations of high uncertainty where the environment is complex and changing. Actors rarely devise international institutions out of thin air; they look to existing models to organize their behavior in new areas. For EPC, the Community became that model. This early procedural imitation – and a more general recognition that both the EC and EPC served European integration – helped bring the two domains closer together over time despite the intergovernmental intentions behind the Luxembourg Report.

Second, and far more importantly, governments (in the form of chief executives or foreign ministers) did not dominate EPC, nor did its key officials (Political Directors and European Correspondents) use EPC as a forum for bargaining over policy. Indeed, here bargaining appears to be the exception, not the rule. Even in the beginning, the EPC system was not considered a forum for making side-payments, threatening sanctions, or linking issues into broad package deals. Such deals, of course, regularly occur in other EC policy sectors or during intergovernmental conferences, but they did not take place in EPC. Thus we cannot consider EPC as a mechanism to solve incomplete contracting problems so that states could further their own interests by trading favors. EU member states simply were not that ambitious, and they likely viewed EPC as a mere talking shop (at least at first) rather than a real policymaking forum. According to most accounts of the EPC process cited in this volume, and according to numerous interviews with participants, it was most inappropriate to use overt hard-bargaining tactics to make policy in EPC. Its officials honestly attempted to avoid power politics and stark confrontations during EPC discussions. They seemed genuinely willing, by virtue of their status as both professional foreign policy experts and participants in the construction of "Europe," to attempt to forge a consensus about common European interests based on the strength of argument alone.[34] As a result, it is problematic to rely exclusively on intergovernmental theory to explain EPC even at its early stages because of this theory's primary focus on grand bargains at the expense of day-to-day policymaking. Most history-making reforms of the EU are controlled by governments and require treaty revision, but normal policymaking is conducted in a variety of arenas that also deserve our attention (Peterson 1995). As I shall explain further in Chapters 4 and 5, through the use of informal then formal institutional mechanisms EPC clearly tended towards a "problem-solving," not bargaining, style of decision-making. Even during difficult discussions over the imposition of sanctions for political ends, officials usually avoided bargaining.[35]

Third, it is also necessary to look beyond written instruments and examine the informal customs and procedures that encourage cooperation. In fact, right from the beginning EPC started to develop beyond the spare provisions outlined in the Luxembourg Report. Meetings were held more frequently than required, other transgovernmental links were established to improve the mechanism, new norms were devised to improve its functioning, and EPC's responsibilities soon involved higher stakes and new issues. For example, where working groups were not established, other meetings of national experts took place on issues such as cooperation in the event of national disasters. Ambassadors of the Nine in the capitals of EU states began to discuss foreign policy issues of particular interest to them, and each of their embassies appointed a diplomat whose duty was to maintain contact with the foreign ministry in the country of residence on matters concerning European foreign policy. In another

---

[34] For an extended discussion of the role of argument in collective decision-making, see Risse 2000.

[35] Interviews with former EPC officials, Brussels, 1996. Conversely, Martin (1992) has argued that EU states did make a bargain on at least one occasion: the Falkland Islands crisis. Nuttall (among others) rejects this interpretation: "It is going too far to suggest that a link between the price decisions [on annual EC agricultural prices] and the Falklands sanctions was ever established, but it is certainly the case that the climate of sympathy for the United Kingdom which had been created by the Argentinian invasion was in the process of being dissipated by the feeling that in the eyes of Whitehall Community solidarity was a one-way street" (Nuttall 1992: 212). I shall return to this episode in Chapter 5.

important change, EPC also gradually replaced the Western European Union as the key forum where EU states could coordinate their positions at the UN General Assembly, the UN Economic and Social Council, and the UN Food and Agricultural Organization.[36] And since the EPC agenda was not set down in the Luxembourg Report, nor was it affected by domestic interest groups, national officials had a fair amount of lee-way regarding the types of issues they could discuss, even if no specific action or decision on those issues was forthcoming. The privileged status of foreign ministries in EPC, combined with the initial tendency toward problem-solving and the first tentative links between EPC and the EC, would fundamentally affect the institutionalization of European foreign policy.

Substantive EPC outcomes

As the previous discussion indicates, the first few years of EPC were pre-occupied by the familiarization of EU member states with each other's views on foreign policy, by debates over procedural matters, and, to a lesser extent, by discussions about the appropriate ends of EPC. Thus at this stage we would not expect any drastic expansion of EPC in terms of its agenda or its policy tools. Yet the agenda at the first meeting was fairly substantial considering the uncertainty surrounding the establish-ment of EPC. Items discussed at the first meeting involved aid to Pak-istan, relations between Cuba and the US, the representation of China in international financial institutions, the political aspects of the Mutual and Balanced Force Reduction talks (MBFR), and the future role of the Council of Europe. To deal with this last question, the Nine agreed to strengthen their coordination at the Council of Europe headquarters in Strasbourg (Nuttall 1992a: 69), and we can also see that a question of security (the MBFR talks) was tentatively broached even at the first meet-ing although this would prove a contentious issue for years to come. EPC also began moves toward a common policy in the Mediterranean, though with very limited results. Suggestions for a conference of the Mediter-ranean non-aligned countries and links with CSCE talks did not go very far. However, EPC did manage to establish a Mediterranean working group by early 1972. At this time it was charged with conducting only a series of geographical studies (Ginsberg 1989: Chapter 5).

EPC also had very few policy tools at its disposal at this time, so we cannot evaluate its performance in terms of specific external actions.

---

[36] "Results Obtained from European Political Cooperation on Foreign Policy," annex to the Copenhagen Report, July 23, 1973.

Informal coordination at the UN began in 1971, but the fact that the Federal Republic of Germany was not a full member of the UN until September 1973 prevented more substantial efforts along these lines. Also discouraging (but not unexpected) was the fact that no major EPC declarations were produced between 1970 and 1973. Finally, above all there was no chance of using EC instruments or competencies to support EPC at this time; such actions could not even be considered. Thus, the only real external expressions of EPC at the time were occasional diplomatic démarches in third countries (i.e., non-EU member states) or international organizations; these were carried out by the ambassador of the state holding the EU presidency. Again, most EPC efforts at this time were directed toward internal cohesion rather than external action.

The Cold War and the overwhelming dominance of NATO in European security affairs during these years probably created an incentive to avoid even the appearance of undermining the Atlantic alliance vis-à-vis the Soviet Union. Since the EC was focused on creating institutions related to commercial matters at this point, the political uses of such institutions could be only a peripheral concern. Given EPC's lack of firm leadership, policy tools, and compliance mechanisms, outcomes were as modest as we would expect. France dominated the emerging Euro-Arab discussions, and Germany pushed for talks regarding East–West relations as part of its move toward *Ostpolitik*. But these modest results and the difficult early years of EPC also stimulated EU states to think about institutional changes that might improve the effectiveness of EPC. A pattern of reform developed whereby problems were identified, options were suggested, and solutions were established informally and became customs. These customs then found their way into formal EPC reports and treaties. In addition, the rotating EU presidency gave smaller states a fairly equal role in the process, which invested EPC with a certain competitive dynamic as states took their turn at leading it. This tendency also challenges the idea that larger states dominated EPC, and the overall performance of the system is still quite remarkable when one considers that EPC was still little more than a gentleman's agreement at the time, with no legal basis at all.

A closer look at the Middle East and East–West relations, EPC's first major topics between November 1970 and July 1973, illustrates some of these early dynamics. With the Euro-Arab Dialogue, EPC's struggle for a common approach to the Middle East must be considered in the context of broader EU attempts to unify its stance toward a number of difficult but related issues in this region: energy policy, relations with former colonies, international development, industrial policy, EU–US relations, and Arab-Israeli violence. When EC/EPC made the first serious attempts to address the problems of this region collectively, the complexity of the problems was matched only by the vast dissimilarity of EU member state positions. As we saw earlier, the EU was unable even to discuss the Six-Day War in 1967 not only because of dissimilarities in member state positions but because of a general feeling that it was inappropriate for an economic organization to take a common foreign policy position.

Yet at the very first EPC meeting in Munich the foreign ministers managed to agree to produce a joint paper on the Middle East. Toward this end, the second EPC ministerial meeting in May 1971 devoted an entire day to the subject (Allen 1982: 73). Despite the profound disagreements between pro-Arab and pro-Israeli EU states, EPC managed to approve a joint paper on key issues in this region on May 13, 1971. These involved the question of refugees, the proposed demilitarized zones on the border between Israel and Egypt, what forces should be deployed there, and the terribly difficult question of Jerusalem (Nuttall 1992a: 68). Although this position statement, the "Schumann document," innocuously called for a "just peace" in the Middle East and approved UN Security Council Resolution 242,[37] it was a clear step forward for EPC solidarity considering the EU's embarrassing inactivity after the 1967 war, and called for Israel's withdrawal to its 1967 borders (among other provisions). However, in a slight blow to the fragile EPC process, the document was soon leaked to the media even though it was not supposed to be made public, in deference to the wishes of Germany, Italy, and the Netherlands. The resulting uproar in Israel and Europe, particularly in Germany, undoubtedly revealed the risks that EU states assumed by virtue of their participation in EPC, even though common position statements had no legal force and EU states assumed they could strictly control the secrecy of the process. German foreign minister Walter Scheel, for example, had to quickly disavow the significance of the Schumann document, declaring it was only a "working document."[38]

Intergovernmentalism also dominated in the response of the EU foreign ministers to a memorandum from the European Commission calling for consultations with the Middle East countries, if only to protect the EU's vital energy supplies. The Commission also recommended providing EC aid for the economic and social development of the energy-exporting states in exchange for guarantees on oil prices and supplies (European Commission 1972). These proposals were to form the basis

---

[37] UN Security Council Resolution on the Situation in the Middle East, November 22, 1967. Among other things, this resolution calls for Israel to withdraw its forces from territories it occupied during the 1967 war and notes the need to solve the refugee (i.e., Palestinian) problem in the Middle East.

[38] For details on this early stage, see Allen 1978; Artner 1980; Allen 1982.

of the Euro-Arab Dialogue, but at the time no action was taken. And although the Middle East was discussed in the framework of EPC, and a working group of Middle East experts was established, EPC produced no more public statements until after the October 1973 Arab-Israeli War and the crippling oil crisis that followed (Allen 1978: 325). By this time, however, EU states were already considering another set of EPC institutional reforms; these will be examined in the next chapter.

EPC actions to improve Europe's position between the superpowers were considerably more successful than those directed toward the Middle East. In the beginning, these efforts took place within the framework of the Conference on Security and Cooperation in Europe. Formal CSCE negotiations were to begin in November 1972, giving EPC exactly two years to develop a coordinated approach to this issue. By most accounts, it was very successful in adopting a unified approach to what previously had been a series of uncoordinated bilateral discussions on East–West relations. This approach involved seven major areas for action: principles of international law (or "Basket I" of the final CSCE document), military security, matters concerning economics, science, technology, and the environment ("Basket II"), humanitarian questions ("Basket III"), information exchange, culture and education, and Mediterranean questions (von Groll 1982: 60–63). Here we can see the early tendency toward breaking down complex problems into functional issue-areas, if only to determine the division of labor between the EC and EPC. The most comprehensive of these efforts were explicitly linked to other relevant policies and institutions from the beginning, quickly demonstrating EPC's capacity to tie together disparate issues into single packages before attempting any resolution. Areas of Community competency were especially important given EPC's immaturity. These involved the relationship of Eastern European states to the EC, the possibility for improved cooperation between the two halves of Europe, the role of the UN Economic Commission for Europe in East–West relations, and an assessment of Eastern bloc positions concerning the CSCE (including the question of EC trade "discrimination" toward the East). Accordingly, the EU set up its own "mixed" working group within EPC in May 1971, known as the ad hoc CSCE working group. This consisted of the "normal" CSCE working group plus representatives from the Commission. Procedures were then established to determine the CSCE questions to be considered by each group. The activities of these groups will be considered in the next chapter as they began after the next phase of EPC institutional reform (September 1973 to July 1975).

These two areas were the only ones EPC could address in any substantial way during the first several years of meetings. Any collective policy toward the US was risky given the generally apprehensive attitude of the Americans toward the EU (and EPC) at the time. The EU's expansion from six to nine member states, the growth of a European free trade area, the increasing number of EC Association Agreements with less-developed countries, and other EC external policies helped to put the US on the defensive (Kohler 1982: 84–85). Feelings of ill will between the US and the EU further intensified because of the Vietnam War and President Nixon's abrupt decision in August 1971 to refuse to redeem US dollars for gold at a fixed price, thus abdicating US responsibility for the international monetary system. Regarding EPC in particular, the US was almost hostile toward it during these years. The suspicion that France (and possibly other EU states) hoped to use EPC as a mechanism to pursue a foreign policy which was more independent from that of the US made European foreign policy a highly antagonistic subject for Nixon and his secretary of state, Henry Kissinger. These difficulties ultimately resulted in the collapse of Kissinger's "Atlantic Charter" concept for US–EU cooperation by the end of 1973. While the Europeans appreciated the need for a more comprehensive approach to the Atlantic relationship, they were also extremely sensitive to the idea of playing only a support role for US policies. This failure to forge a common vision for transatlantic cooperation, while understandable at the time, nonetheless allowed EPC to develop on its own as a means to promote European independence in world politics, although common European approaches to South Africa, Central America, and other key areas were not even on the horizon at this early date.

To conclude, although these results were probably far beyond what most observers expected of EPC, it was still hard to escape the image of a "gentlemen's dining club," as Wallace and Allen put it (1977: 237), based on the recollections of one EPC participant: "So we meet, eat well, and exchange views; and if we disagree, then *tant pis* [too bad], we will return to the question when we meet again." Yet this should not lead one to treat EPC as an intergovernmental bargaining system or mere talking shop. EPC in fact was conceived as a novel, different form of intergovernmental policy coordination. It was intended to be a forum for an exchange of views, not for crude bargaining. If states discovered a common interest during discussions they could act in common, but there was neither an obligation to do so, nor provisions for trading favors to forge a common action. Also, unlike the EC, EPC did not possess its own resources to implement such an action; these were to be supplied (at first) by individual EU states. A more sophisticated view of policymaking than that of intergovernmental bargaining suggests that the system demonstrated a paradox of institutional strength: although EPC was an informal, decentralized, non-coercive institution, and did not enjoy strong public support or interest, it resulted in an expansion of foreign policy cooperation and ultimately changed the way EU states defined and pursued their national interests. As Wessels once argued (1982: 15), intergovernmentalism quickly became a limited tool for analyzing EPC because of the system's "multi-diplomatic structure, socialization processes, reliability, continuity, and its *de facto* binding character." These factors suggest that other analytical devices beyond intergovernmentalism must be employed to understand fully the performance of EPC and its growth into the CFSP.

4 Information-sharing and the transgovernmental EPC network

Given the vague provisions of the Luxembourg Report it rapidly became clear that EPC's participants would have to improvise their cooperation. As we have seen, although senior government officials played a leading role during EPC's formative years, even then the system involved an embryonic lower-level infrastructure – the Political Committee, European Correspondents, and working groups – to assist foreign ministers with foreign policy coordination. Fundamentally, EPC at this time was little more than a system of "regular exchanges of information and consultation" on "great international problems,"[1] primarily involving periodic summits among EU member governments. This aspect of European foreign policy reflects one of the most fundamental functions of institutions: information-sharing. As May (1984) has pointed out, perspective-taking alone cannot always enable actors to predict each other's behaviors, and predictable behavior is the essence of cooperation. In a world of uncertainty regarding the behavior of states, institutional mechanisms that make it easier for states to communicate with each other are highly valued.[2]

The cooperation-inducing effects of regular communication can vary, ranging from confidence-building (at a minimum) to providing a shared understanding of, and potential solutions to, certain problems (at a maximum). However, there can be an enormous amount of variation regarding the ends and means of communication. With respect to EU foreign policy, I stress four aspects of communication: the actors involved, the types of information they share, the channels through which this information is shared, and the effects of that communication on cooperation and institution-building. As these elements develop over time, and as

---

[1] Quotes from the "First Report of the Foreign Ministers to the Heads of State and Government of the Member States of the European Community of 27 October 1970" (Luxembourg or Davignon Report), Part II.

[2] In this chapter I use the terms "information," "information-sharing," and "communication" interchangeably.

communication intensifies, institutionalized cooperation should change as well.

Concerning the actors, we should first note a distinction between senior government officials and lower-level diplomats and technical experts. To the extent that diplomats and technical experts are able to develop their own transgovernmental relationships in a policy domain or institutionalized space, the prospects for international cooperation may improve. The idea that technical experts in international organizations can exert considerable influence over policy has a long history in functional theories of integration (Haas 1964; Mitrany 1966), but we need not assume at this point that such expertise is confined to non-state (i.e., EC) actors like the Commission. Specialists within and across states can be mobilized in the service of a common European goal, and the regular involvement of these officials in EU foreign policy helps provide the enterprise with a greater sense of permanence and substance. Disaggregating states in this way thus alerts us to the behavioral dynamics that can be missed by assuming that states single-mindedly devise and pursue fixed, ordered foreign policy preferences.

Concerning the information itself, states obviously communicate many things to each other: preferences, intentions, ideas, fears, demands, requests, threats, analyses, intelligence, scientific knowledge, and so on. However, we can at least suggest a distinction between information necessary to demonstrate *compliance* with agreements, which often involves domestic processes, such as transparency, in states who are parties to the agreement, and information necessary to establish a *common view* of, and potential solution to, problems, which involves making principled arguments about the collective enterprise itself.[3] In this sense communication evolves from a negative-preventative purpose (confidence-building through the communication of information regarding intentions) toward a more positive-affirmative purpose (common analyses, understandings, and purposive action, or problem-solving). Thus, to the extent that states can agree on the policy-relevant content of information (such as the causes of and solutions to external political problems), the prospects for institutionalized cooperation will be enhanced.

This brings us to the primary channels through which information is shared. Periodic intergovernmental summits are one possibility, and this mechanism is often employed in the EU. Yet students of transnational and transgovernmental relations have long argued that links or networks between technical experts, interest groups, businesses, diplomats, or other

---

[3] For a similar distinction between information about compliance and information about regime effectiveness, see Mitchell 1998. For a more general discussion about the role of debate in international relations, see Risse 2000.

actors can play an important role in determining cooperative outcomes.[4] These links are likely to emerge in dense, complex issue-areas, especially those already institutionalized. Transnational groups can mobilize in support of, or opposition to, an agreement between states (or its implementation), which can affect the final product. Transgovernmental links can also be important, in the sense that meetings, phone calls, e-mails and other communications between governments and bureaucrats encourage cooperation and institutional change. In EU foreign policy, these dynamics can be seen in the relationships among foreign policy officials at all levels in a number of arenas: among EU member states, with EC organizations, in third countries, and in international organizations and conferences.

Finally, what effects of information-sharing are directly relevant to international cooperation? Here we need to stress the interaction of the three elements above (actors, types of information, and the channels of communication) in the service of a single goal: the engineering of consensus around a common reference point, the EU. Together, these elements help prevent the "noise" or confusion that might result from sharing information in an unstructured or ad hoc way. Thus, in this chapter I discuss five direct effects of information-sharing that encouraged foreign policy cooperation among EU states. These include: confidence-building; defining European foreign policy as an issue-area; producing common views and analyses about international problems; evaluating the performance of European foreign policy in terms of outcomes and institutional development; and the regular generation of norms in this domain, which takes institutional development to the next level.[5]

These various aspects of information-sharing, particularly in the context of the transgovernmental EPC infrastructure created by the Copenhagen Report of 1973, are examined in the rest of this chapter. As in the previous chapter, I focus on both changes of procedure (or EPC institutions) and changes of substance (EPC policy outcomes). I argue that the EPC's communication mechanisms were deliberately structured to produce consensus, and not only to further national interests. EPC's dense transgovernmental infrastructure helped prevent, or at least restrain, a

---

[4] For early treatments, see Huntington 1973; Keohane and Nye 1974. More recent work can be found in Risse-Kappen 1995a.

[5] There are of course some caveats to these arguments. Involving too many lower-level officials could easily introduce confusion and disarray into the system. Also, institutionalized communications can become too complex to promote cooperation if some centralization is not pursued in the face of expansion. Finally, the misperception of communication is always possible, as is outright deception, and I cannot delve into the psychological or cognitive factors behind these behaviors. I only assume that EPC officials used their communication system primarily in the way it was intended: to enhance cooperation.

head-on clash of foreign policy interests among EU states, and it eventually promoted the harmonization of views with the goal of solving common problems, not defending national interests. Many of these mechanisms and processes were not ordained by EU governments; they were based on the habits and customs of EPC diplomats themselves. Still, their eventual appearance in EPC reports as legitimate, effective, collective procedures gives us a convenient point of departure for making judgments about the causes and effects of institutionalized communication.

Information-sharing in EPC: the mechanisms

After EPC entered into effect in late 1970 under the terms of the Luxembourg Report, EU governments wasted little time before attempting to improve the mechanism. The Luxembourg Report had included its own self-monitoring component, in the form of a provision to present a second report on EPC to discuss "progress in the field of political unification" and to "deal with improvement of cooperation in foreign policy matters and with the search for other fields where progress might be achieved."[6] November 1972 had been set as a deadline for preparing a second study on these questions, and work toward this end began almost as soon as the Luxembourg Report entered into effect.

The context of change

This second round of institution-building was more of an effort to deal with the unfinished business of the Luxembourg Report rather than an attempt at institutional innovation. Many of the same external factors behind the Luxembourg Report came into play at this time: the unresolved problem of political union, the pressing issue of economic and monetary union, institutional questions related to enlargement, conflicts in the Middle East, tensions in EC–US relations, and other matters. These issues led EU states to consider another summit conference to build on the achievements at The Hague in 1969. However, France was not yet willing to give up the idea of having member states guide the course of European political integration, ideally through the use of consensual decision-making and the establishment of a political secretariat based in Paris. Germany and several smaller EU states continued to resist this plan, and the impasse prevented any significant changes to EPC for the moment. To complicate matters, the Dutch expressed their desire for closer ties between the EC and EPC in a memorandum submitted to

---

[6] Luxembourg Report, Part III, Sections 1 and 2.

their EU partners in preparation for the Paris summit; the Belgians expected such links as well. Neither of these states wanted to institutionalize EPC further without stronger links between it and the EC.

As a result, during the Paris summit of October 19–20, 1972, EU heads of state and government reaffirmed their intention to proceed with the integration of Europe, including the goal of transforming "the whole complex of their relations into a European Union" by the end of the decade. Part of this goal, which of course went unfulfilled, included making some reforms to EPC. However, beyond the usual rhetoric of improving and intensifying their foreign policy cooperation, participants at the summit could agree upon only two formal institutional changes: to increase the number of EPC ministerial meetings from two to four per year, and to make one of the aims of EPC the formulation of medium- and long-term common positions where possible. Both of these "reforms" largely reflected behavior that already had been taking place within EPC. Still, and despite disagreements over more substantial changes, at Paris the EU's foreign ministers were directed to produce a report by June 30, 1973 on methods of improving EPC in accordance with the Luxembourg Report. EC organizations were also required to draw up a report on "European Union" by the end of 1975 for submission to an intergovernmental conference.[7] Dutch concerns about EC–EPC links delayed the publication of what became known as the Copenhagen Report in July 1973, but ultimately, this effort failed to tighten the formal linkage between the EC and EPC. In the end, EPC was still officially considered "distinct from and additional to the activities of the institutions of the European Community."[8]

The Copenhagen Report reaffirmed the goals of the Luxembourg Report and praised the EPC mechanism. Significantly, after only three years of EPC, the foreign ministers could refer to the "reflex of coordination" that the mechanism encouraged among states, meaning that they had adopted the habit of automatic consultation on important foreign policy positions. According to the ministers, thanks to this reflex, a new "collegiate sense in Europe is becoming a real force in international relations." This "coordination reflex" has since become one of the most important rules and terms in the vocabulary of European foreign policy. The ministers also cited the "flexibility and effectiveness" of EPC,

---

[7] "Statement of the Conference of the Heads of State and Government of the Member States of the European Community" (Paris, October 21, 1972). Also known as the "Paris Communiqué."

[8] "Second Report of the Foreign Ministers to the Heads of State and Government of the Member States of the European Community of 23 July 1973" (hereafter "Copenhagen Report"), Part II, Article 12a.

claiming it represented a "new procedure in international relations and an original European contribution to the technique at arriving at concerted action." They also noted that "this habit of working together has enabled the procedure for concerted action to become more widespread wherever common action or common consideration seemed desirable."[9] But how could these efforts be improved without subordinating EPC to the EC or creating a permanent EPC secretariat?

The institutional mechanisms

The vague wording of the Copenhagen Report reflected persistent disagreements over the means and ends of European foreign policy. As intergovernmental theory might predict, any institutional change taking place in this climate, where another grand bargain was unlikely so soon after the last one, would likely be minimal, uncontroversial, and low-cost. Thus, the Report included and slightly built upon the enhancements mentioned in the Paris Communiqué, adding the formulation of medium and long-term positions to the original Luxembourg Report goal of EPC consultation. This innocuous provision took EPC a step further by attempting to enhance the coordination of national positions with a common European view in specific cases. In addition, the Report codified a new norm for EPC: that member states must not take up final positions on major foreign policy issues without prior consultation with their EU partners. However, the establishment of a permanent secretariat for political integration in general or EPC in particular would have to wait, and provisions for medium- and long-term foreign policy planning (as suggested by the Italians) ultimately were rejected.

The other, less substantial, institutional mechanisms of the Copenhagen Report can be considered in terms of *innovations* which were new to EPC and in terms of *changes* to existing procedures. By "innovation" I mean the first appearance of the mechanism in an EPC written report (or treaty), even though most such innovations in the history of EU foreign policy have merely reflected existing informal habits and customs (in other words, improvisation). The specific procedural changes to the provisions set down in the Luxembourg Report are summarized in Table 4.1.

As we can see, most changes to EPC at this time were incremental. Links to EC organizations like the Commission and the EP were only slightly enhanced in the Copenhagen Report.[10] The Netherlands and

[9] Copenhagen Report, Part I.

[10] Also note that while the Commission president participated in the Copenhagen summit thanks to the precedent set at the 1972 Paris summit, he did not attend the first afternoon's discussions on the future of EPC (Johnston 1994: 18, fn. 33).

Table 4.1 *EPC according to the Copenhagen Report (July 1973)*
Major changes since the Luxembourg Report appear in **boldface**.

Component	Actors and functions
Intergovernmental direction	EU foreign ministers meet at least **four times** a year.
	EU presidency state chairs meetings, provides administrative support as needed, and **oversees implementation of conclusions**.
	Crisis procedures initiated by EU presidency if necessary.
Transgovernmental support	Political Committee: preparation of ministerial meetings.
	Meets as frequently as its work requires.
	European Correspondents: liaison between capitals, **monitoring of EPC**.
	Working groups: geographical/functional analyses for EPC.
	Chairmen of working groups allowed more flexibility to ensure continuity of their work.
	EU embassies: consultation on EPC matters in capitals of member states, in third countries, and in delegations to international conferences and organizations.
	COREU: encrypted telex network to share information.
	Other administrative support to be provided to the presidency state as needed.
Linkages with the EC	Commission invited to make known its views on EPC.
	Colloquy **four times a year** with European Parliament Political Committee, and annual report on progress on EPC.
	Council of Foreign Ministers informed through COREPER about EPC conclusions which might impact on the work of the EC.
	Ministers able to use EPC to prepare studies on political aspects of problems under examination in the EC.
Obligations	States consult on all questions of foreign policy.
	Formulation of medium- and long-term common positions.
	General rule not to take up final positions without consultation with EPC partners.

Belgium had wanted to involve the Commission more, and to bring the EP into the EPC process as well. In defiance of the larger EU states, both of these states successfully pressed for the consideration of EP questions in EPC and a doubling of the colloquies held with the EP (Pijpers 1983: 173). Also, the Commission representative could now be invited to participate in EPC discussions at all levels, from the working groups upwards. However, the Copenhagen Report did not include a bureaucracy to administer EPC, although the question of a permanent secretariat was raised during the discussions. Instead, administrative assistance could be provided to the state holding the EU presidency by other member states (rather than the EC) and only for specific tasks on a temporary basis.

Yet the Copenhagen Report also expanded and codified two major transgovernmental procedures in EPC, which provide the analytical focus of this chapter.[11] First, the embassies of the Nine in the capitals of the EU member states and abroad were formally recognized as important participants in the implementation of EPC. Embassies of the Nine in the EU capitals could receive information about EPC and be consulted on specific subjects in two ways: (1) at the seat of the presidency at the request of the Political Committee, the presidency, or another member state; or (2) in another capital at the request of the foreign ministry. One staff official of each embassy was to be entrusted with "ensuring the necessary contacts with the foreign ministry of their country of residence within the framework of EPC." Embassies in third countries and the permanent representatives to international organizations were formally brought into the system as well. They were to be provided with information about EPC and invited to make common reports if necessary. EU member state delegations to major international organizations were directed to "regularly consider matters together and, on the basis of instructions received, seek common positions in regard to important questions dealt with by those organizations."[12]

Second, the Copenhagen Report established the unique *Correspondance Européenne* (or COREU) encrypted telex network to help with information-sharing in EPC.[13] The COREU system became one of the most important and innovative mechanisms in the development of European foreign policy. EU states had sent telexes to each other before, of course, but such messages were usually conveyed on a sporadic, bilateral basis (Nuttall 1992a: 4). This often held up the process of decision-making as EU states still could not agree to establish any permanent organization to oversee the EPC process. Instead, the COREU system would be used to communicate simultaneously with all other EU states (and eventually the Commission and EPC Secretariat as well) about issues of concern to EPC. Virtually all levels of national foreign ministries, from the foreign minister to desk officers, could make use of the system and thus contribute to deliberations. The COREU system was administered by the Communications and Materials Branch of the Dutch Ministry

[11] The Copenhagen summit also approved a document entitled "The European Identity," an early effort to give some substantive direction to EPC. It will be considered in the next chapter, which focuses on the norms and rules of European foreign policy.

[12] Copenhagen Report, Part II, Sections 6–7.

[13] Copenhagen Report, Part II, Section 9.

for Foreign Affairs, and its operating costs were split equally among EU states, making it the only permanent, collectively financed manifestation of European foreign policy until 1986. It began operating in late 1973 during the first Danish EU presidency (Nuttall 1992a: 23–24).

The European Council and EPC

Before turning to a performance evaluation of EPC following the Copenhagen Report, we must digress for a moment to consider the role of the European Council. In addition to the Copenhagen Report negotiations, EU heads of state/government were also working at the time (under pressure from France) to consolidate their authority over the entire EC/EPC structure. Despite the failure of the EDC, France still had not given up the idea of using regular intergovernmental summits to give direction to European integration in general and to advance political unification in particular. These efforts were often curbed by the smaller EU states, who consistently resisted the use of intergovernmental summitry for fear it might disrupt (if not completely eclipse) the process of supranational Community-building.

However, once these states had finally agreed to an intergovernmental form of EPC, the door was opened to the establishment of another intergovernmental "institution" which had an unclear function and a dubious legal identity relative to EC procedures: the European Council. As a result, in December 1974 the "European Council of (EU) Heads of State and Government" began to meet regularly in high-profile summits to consider both EPC and EC issues. Although the French preferred to limit participation in the European Council to heads of state and government, the smaller EU states insisted that foreign ministers and the Commission president be included as well (Bulmer and Wessels 1987: 33). The European Council, which never became an EC body,[14] was to be the dominant intergovernmental "umbrella" under which all EC/EPC business was eventually conducted and given direction. Among other functions, the summits were supposed to set EPC guidelines, make declarations on European foreign policy issues, coordinate EC/EPC policies, and solve disputes when they clashed (Bulmer 1985; Bulmer and Wessels 1987; Johnston 1994). Although the European Council as such is not mentioned in the Copenhagen Report, this body was increasingly institutionalized and its role in European foreign policy was formalized with the Treaty on European Union, as we shall see in later chapters.

---

[14] As we shall see in later chapters, the European Council is mentioned in the Single European Act and the Treaty on European Union, but is not part of the original legal structure of the EC as set down by the Treaty of Rome.

For the moment, we can note that under the terms of the 1973 Copenhagen Report, EPC still largely appeared to be an intergovernmental, informal system, with weak institutional links to the EC. And with the creation of the European Council only a year later, EU heads of state and government appeared to have consolidated their authority over both the EC and EPC. They provided general direction for both structures and took up decisions that were too important or controversial for the Commission or EPC. European Council summits also were supposed to provide the main link between the EC and EPC and provide general political direction for both. Summitry was viewed as a safer, more flexible, and appropriate approach to these important issues, and it provided regular occasions for EU governments to hold informal discussions, or "fireside chats," concerning international politics. As Bulmer and Wessels note (1987: 122–23), "Both EPC and the European Council eschew a constitutional approach to European Union, preferring the less rule-bound pragmatic approach of intergovernmentalism." They rightly argue that this summitry has two general effects on EU foreign policy: it intensifies work at regular intervals (i.e., during the preparatory phase of a summit), and it symbolically upgrades the status of certain declarations by virtue of their association with the heads of EU governments.

However, for most of the history of EU foreign policy, the European Council has not provided much central direction. First, it simply does not meet often enough (only twice a year, and usually for only a day and a half) to give much substantial input to EPC/CFSP. With subsequent enlargements to the EU, it now takes well over two hours for a *tour de table* so that everyone's views can be heard on an issue; this limits serious discussion on many issues. Second, when the European Council does meet it is almost always preoccupied with Community problems, not foreign policy.[15] Bulmer and Wessels are emphatic about this point: "The substantive contribution of the government heads to EPC has been less important. From the 1969 summit onwards the government heads have restricted themselves in large measure to confirming developments or statements which had already been prepared by foreign ministers and their officials."[16] Nor does the European Council concern itself with

[15] In fact, there have been occasions when the European Council's attention to EC problems completely overshadowed progress on foreign policy issues. This happened, for example, at the Athens European Council of December 1983 (and again in Brussels, 1984), where the bitter debate over the UK's request for a budgetary rebate from the EC led participants to refrain from their usual practice of reiterating EPC declarations (Johnston 1994: 107). Bulmer also notes (1985: 101, fn. 19) that an EPC statement on the Turkish-Cypriot secession, already prepared, was not issued at the Athens European Council.

[16] Bulmer and Wessels 1987: 123. They also argue that European Council summits merely "rubber stamp" foreign policy documents produced beforehand. Nuttall also argues

questions of procedural changes to either the EC or EPC, although such matters are occasionally discussed (Bulmer and Wessels 1987: 70–72). The same pattern has generally continued,[17] while insiders have referred to this process as the "pre-cooking" of EPC texts for approval by EU governments.[18] There have been, however, several important occasions during which the European Council was able to break deadlocks, as we shall see in later chapters. Still, the transgovernmental EPC/CFSP network, not the European Council, has been the driving force behind most day-to-day matters of EU foreign policy. How this came to pass is discussed in the rest of this chapter.

The effects of communication on EPC processes and outcomes

By late 1973, then, EPC had established regular consultations among EU foreign ministers, supported by a dense transgovernmental communications network, loosely overseen by the European Council and marginally linked to the Commission and the European Parliament. To what extent did this system encourage foreign policy cooperation? And what pressures for additional institutional changes, if any, resulted from that cooperation? I begin with a discussion of the effects of these procedures on relations among EU states, then turn to the expression of EPC in terms of substantive external policies.

Procedural changes

Given the limited involvement of the European Council in EPC, and the preparation of ministerial meetings by the Political Committee, the new transgovernmental communication links among EU foreign ministries, embassies, and delegations provided key opportunities for policy harmonization at lower levels in between the less-frequent ministerial meetings. This is where the real momentum for the growth of EPC can be found after 1973: within the system itself. In fact, it is not going too far to suggest that a unique culture of EU foreign policy cooperation was encouraged

(1992a: 14) that only rarely has the European Council given direction to EPC or played "an important role in an EPC question, one example being the Venice Declaration of 1980."

[17] As Johnston notes (1994: 104), "Normally, preliminary discussions [in the Political Committee] prepare political issues almost to the point of agreement before they come to the European Council." Also, "It is rare that prolonged discussion takes place or that [foreign policy] texts undergo significant alteration [by foreign ministers]. The same is usually true for heads of government."

[18] Interviews with Commission and COREPER officials, Brussels, 1995–96.

Table 4.2 *Growth in the number of COREU telexes on EPC, 1974–94*

Year	Number
1974–82	4,800 (avg.)*
1985	5,400
1986	9,800
1990	7,548
1991	10,184
1992	11,394
1993	11,714
1994	12,699†

* This is the more conservative estimate from Wessel 1982: 2. Rummel (1982: 152) puts the figure at 8,000 COREUs per year by 1982.
† Institut für Europäische Politik (Bonn), *CFSP Forum* 1 (1995): 8. It is difficult to evaluate more recent data on the annual number of COREUs for two reasons: the 1995 enlargement of the EU is most likely the cause of any major increase in COREUs beyond 12,000 a year, and the advent of e-mail in the European Union may have supplemented the use of the COREU system. My purpose here is to show the central importance of institutionalized communications during the formative years of EPC, and the COREU data clearly reflect that finding.

by regular intergovernmental and transgovernmental communications.[19] For example, cohesion in the group of European Correspondents became especially close over the years, and many personal friendships were forged within it. With their common bureaucratic roles, *esprit de corps*, and devotion to a new policy system that privileged their input, European Correspondents and their counterparts in other states (and in the Commission) made common analyses of problems rather than bargained on behalf of their governments.[20] The same dynamic could be observed among the working groups during their hundreds of meetings each year.

Beyond these countless meetings below the ministerial level, bureaucratic officials rapidly made use of the communications mechanisms provided by the Copenhagen Report. As Table 4.2 reveals, the number of COREUs quickly mushroomed to thousands per year, and the system enabled points of view to be shared between all member states

[19] By "culture" I simply mean the collective ideas, beliefs, values, and assumptions regarding foreign policy held by EPC participants. However, culture is not central to my argument, which focuses instead on how these general ideas or values are translated into specific collective behaviors through the use of norms and rules. Thus I do not elaborate the concept any further in this study.

[20] The transgovernmental component of EU foreign policy is described in detail in Wallace 1982 and Nuttall 1992a: 14–25. Also interviews with EPC/CFSP officials, Brussels, 1995–96.

(and eventually the Commission and EPC Secretariat) within a matter of hours. Part of this growth, of course, reflects the enlargements of the EU in 1981 and 1986, but most of it is due to more consultations about external events and an expanded EPC agenda. In addition to this quantitative change, officials familiar with the system also acknowledge a *qualitative* change in the subject matter of COREUs over the years, with more security and military matters being discussed via telex (such as arms control or East–West issues) than in the beginning.[21] Moreover, COREUs were not exchanged on a *quid pro quo* basis (as often occurs when governments share sensitive intelligence information bilaterally). They were generally broadcast to all other participants in EPC to invite a response. As Nuttall (1992a: 24) reflects, the thousands of COREUs sent each year serve "as a perpetual reminder of EPC to all those over whose desks COREUs pass." This open, multilateral information-sharing also encouraged coalitions that were unusually fluid, changing as the problem demanded and cutting across issues and regions, rather than hardening into blocs of states with dominant shared interests or forming permanent cleavages (Hill 1983a: 196).

Other institutionalized transgovernmental relationships established by the Copenhagen Report influenced the system as well. EU officials coordinated their EC/EPC efforts in EU capitals and in third countries with monthly meetings between EU ambassadors and the heads of the respective EU delegations. EU ambassadors prepared joint reports (which was not always desired by EU member states), shared information, and made policy recommendations to more senior foreign ministry officials back home. They also conducted common démarches in third countries, held common debates with high representatives of third countries, and cooperated during crisis situations without much guidance from EU capitals. Frequently missions of large EU states acted on behalf of small EU members who had limited representation in the developing world. Especially when small or remote states were the object of action, links between missions became a vital "back door channel" for cooperating in foreign policy. This was occasionally resented by foreign ministers and by the Political Committee; the French even attempted to put a halt to such activity during the 1980s.[22] Despite these concerns, the EPC correspondents of EU

---

[21] Interviews with member state foreign ministry officials and COREPER officials, Brussels, 1995–96. Also note that interview subjects often mentioned the importance of the COREU system with no prompting by the author.

[22] Also, in at least one case (policy toward South Africa) the EU ambassadors to that country were invited back to Brussels as a group to help EPC develop its anti-apartheid policies. Interview with a Commission official, Brussels, 1996.

embassies regularly liaised with the foreign ministries of each EU capital, helping to intensify the policy coordination.

How did all of this activity influence its participants? There is no doubt that the growing volume of information shared in this transgovernmental network made a powerful impression on EPC practitioners. Indeed, considering EPC's impact not only on behaviors but on attitudes as well, this institutionalized interaction is frequently described in terms of elite socialization,[23] although it probably is not as intensive as that which occurs in Community institutions, such as COREPER.[24] Between the personal links reinforced through constant phone calls or meetings, and the rapid growth of the COREU system, EPC participants were gradually able to establish a body of understandings, procedures, and policies that gave substance to EPC. Participants in the EPC process often recall its "club-like" atmosphere; it provided many opportunities for stimulating discussions, and then common actions, concerning world politics.[25] As Nuttall (1997a: 3) recalls the atmosphere from personal experience:

The success of EPC came through socialization. All participants in EPC attest to the beneficial effect of the club atmosphere in bringing points of view closer together and making concessions easier . . . For socialization to work, however, you had to socialize. Meetings were important, but so were lunches and dinners and agreeable little excursions, and the atmosphere depended on light procedures and not too many participants.

Even rotations of personnel between domestic and foreign ministries (first common in Italy) became more acceptable to other EU states by the late 1970s in order to understand the international dimensions of EU membership better. These activities were employed to make EPC less like a series of periodic summits (as with many intergovernmental forums) and more like a decentralized but highly institutionalized framework for policy coordination. This helped to erode the monopoly that government

---

[23] Elite socialization plays a central role in the analyses of individual EU member states in Manners and Whitman 2000; also see Smith 2000. Similarly, Weiler and Wessels (1988) have argued that the most appropriate theory to explain EPC is the "consociational model," where a "cartel" of elites regularly cooperates to preserve functionality and stability in a policy domain.

[24] Galloway 1995: 217. On elite socialization in COREPER, see Lewis 1998.

[25] Interviews with officials from national foreign ministries and with Commission and COREPER officials, 1995–96. Also, many EPC participants demonstrated common career patterns, which probably contributed to the socialization process. They were usually specialists in European, EC, or NATO affairs and followed common paths to advancement through similar posts. Hill and Wallace (1979: 56–57, 66) argue that even in the UK, the enthusiasm for EPC and reorientation to it were aided by the fact that "important elements in the career diplomatic service were increasingly convinced that EPC was the way of the future and were determined to make it work, with a will that was not perhaps quite so evident in (EC policy) areas like harmonization or fishing."

officials held over EPC while reorienting all EPC participants toward Europe. In the words of former British foreign minister Douglas Hurd (1981: 383):

Since I first joined the Foreign Office in 1952 the biggest change of diplomatic method stems from European Political Cooperation. In 1952 it was broadly speaking with the Americans only that we shared information and assessments; policy-making was a national preserve. Now in some areas of diplomacy our policy is formed wholly within a European context, and in no area is the European influence completely absent. The flow of information between the foreign ministries of the Ten is formidable.

This is a telling statement, considering Hurd's thirty years of diplomatic experience at the time and the UK's supposed attitude of "Euroskepticism." Through their regular communications, EU states attempted to coordinate their positions on the most detailed subjects, such as the terms on which they granted visas to artists from a country they did not recognize (da Fonseca-Wollheim 1981: 5). Moreover, this socialization did not depend on the influence of a dominant EU member state, as realist-based hegemonic theories suggest (Ikenberry and Kupchan 1990). It became far more collegial over the years, as another British official described the process:

The practice of EPC . . . has made European foreign policy coordination second-nature. There's no doubt about it. I mean, when I joined the office in the late seventies, people did not give a toss for Europeans. You didn't think about speaking to "Europe," you thought about speaking to French and Germans and things, and to close allies. You didn't speak about, you know, consulting "colleagues"; it was basically national foreign policy first, and consulting European colleagues second. Now there is, I think, a reflex action [toward consultation].[26]

In other words, participants changed their attitudes not only regarding each other's foreign policy positions, but also about each other as interlocutors, even seeing them as partners or colleagues in a common enterprise. This involved "thinking out loud" about problems and appropriate collective polices, not a mere one-to-one exchange of information. This is a key change from the way diplomacy is normally conducted in other forums (as in trade negotiations, for example), and it shows that EPC enabled EU states to form collective positions without having to resort to intergovernmental bargaining. Indeed, intergovernmental summits are often confrontational. They are viewed as public battles, dramatized in the press in terms of winners and losers.[27] EPC avoided such

[26] Interview with a British foreign ministry official, London, 1995.
[27] For example, see the analysis by Putnam and Bayne (1987) of the Group of Seven (G-7) summits.

confrontations by channeling diplomacy away from the spotlight into other arenas where collective solutions could be found among professional diplomats and technical experts, who came to view each other as co-workers or colleagues, not adversaries.

Beyond the general socialization effects of EPC information-sharing, I argue that the transgovernmental EPC network had five more specific effects on European foreign policy cooperation.[28] First, at a minimum, information-sharing was a *confidence-building measure*. It reduced the likelihood that EU states would be caught off-guard by each other's foreign policies. One participant (von der Gablentz 1979: 691) recalls that:

The intense system of Community briefings and the constant exchange of views on all levels have created a high degree of predictability of the partners' behavior on which everyone has learned to rely ... EPC has become an efficient confidence-building measure among Community partners in the field of foreign policy and an important educational process for something like 5,000 diplomats in nine foreign services.[29]

According to other EPC insiders, "There are no longer any surprises" (in foreign policy), and "we all know each other's minds."[30] Or as another participant noted, "For diplomats it's not the end result that counts, but the atmosphere and the sense of mutual understanding" (Wallace and Allen 1977: 232). Encouraging openness and trust was the most basic function of EPC, and here it succeeded brilliantly.

Second, information-sharing helped *define European foreign policy as an issue-area or policy domain*. Since the Luxembourg Report was so open-ended about the "great international problems" EPC was supposed to address, EU states gradually learned what activities and topics were appropriate in that forum, as opposed to being handled on a purely national basis. In the words of one long-time participant, a "European dimension" was built into policy issues which previously had been almost exclusively based on national considerations (de Schoutheete de Tervarent 1980: 118). Some of these issues were established by the European Council;

---

[28] I should make clear that I am not arguing that EU foreign policy officials transferred their loyalties to the collective enterprise, as Haas (1961: 366) once suggested of the process of political integration. Supporting such a claim would require a far more systematic and extensive study of the mind-set of EPC/CFSP participants than I can offer here, although I suspect such a change has occurred among some officials (for a similar argument, see Wessels 1982: 13).

[29] This attitude was reflected in personal interviews with other EPC/CFSP participants, Brussels, 1995–96.

[30] Quoted in Allen and Wallace 1982: 29. They also note that one EU member state representative to London in 1973 complained that, thanks to EPC, the desk officer on Vietnam in the British Foreign and Commonwealth Office was better informed than he was about his home foreign ministry's thinking on Southeast Asia.

most, however, emerged at lower levels of contact between those involved in foreign policy on a regular basis. As Hill and Wallace put it (1996: 6):

From the perspective of a diplomat in the foreign ministry of a member state, styles of operating and communication have been transformed. The COREU telex network, EPC working groups, joint declarations, joint reporting, even the beginnings of staff exchanges among foreign ministries and shared embassies: all these have moved the conduct of national foreign policy away from the old nation-state national sovereignty model towards a collective endeavor, a form of high-level networking with transformationalist effects and even more potential.

Third, within the bounds of these appropriate issues and problems (which expanded over the years), information-sharing within EPC helped *produce common viewpoints and analyses*.[31] EPC explicitly encouraged the search for joint gains and common perceptions of problems, and a distinct *communauté de vue* on foreign policy issues emerged. In other words, transgovernmental relations were structured here to produce consensus, not for the more self-interested purpose of exploiting divisions in other member states' domestic politics, as some analysts of two-level games have argued (Knopf 1993). Personalities and tenure of office mattered of course, as did the commitment to develop a new system for common objectives, but thanks to the general tendency toward information-sharing and consultation, officials also felt more committed to the EPC *communauté de vue* since they had been closely involved in its articulation. Through the organization of its working groups and other mechanisms described in this chapter, EPC divided external problems into geographic and functional compartments. The idea was that common analyses of problems encouraged common solutions; such collective behavior is at odds with much of the bargaining-based literature on the role of information in international cooperation under anarchy.

Fourth, information-sharing had an *evaluative component*, in that EU states discussed not only the performance of EPC in specific areas, but also its overall development and effectiveness as an institution. European foreign policy cooperation raised expectations among EU member states, and both positive and negative results fed back into the system through these communication channels. Together, these aspects of institutionalized information-sharing helped drive the process forward and change national foreign policymaking styles despite the absence of central authority or a permanent bureaucracy. As a result, "officials with less than twenty years' experience of national diplomatic service have grown up entirely within the context of European Political Cooperation, taking as given the

---

[31] Similarly, regime theorists include "principles" in their analyses, which are defined as "beliefs of fact, causation, and rectitude" (Krasner 1983b: 2).

exchange of confidential information not only about third countries but about their own governments' intentions and domestic constraints" (Hill and Wallace 1996: 11–12).

Fifth and finally, information-sharing helped increase the demand for additional *norms and rules of behavior* to address common foreign policy problems, and to aid in the day-to-day management of EPC. This aspect of institutionalization is taken up in the next chapter.

Beyond these effects of institutionalized communication, EPC continued to break down the desired distinction between EPC and EC affairs. The way EPC began to imitate Community policymaking structures (institutional isomorphism) was mentioned in the previous chapter. After the Copenhagen Report, the sheer density and complexity of the transgovernmental EPC network provided many opportunities for officials to discuss EC and EPC issues together, despite the wishes of some member governments (such as France) to prevent this. Diplomats in the missions of EU member states to third countries (and their local interlocutors) rarely if ever observed the formal distinction between EPC and the EC, and they could hardly be forced to do so by their foreign ministries. Similarly, EC organizations could not be forced to treat foreign policy cooperation and economic integration as wholly separate domains. Finally, in EU capitals, discussions about the connection between the EC and EPC took place at first on an informal basis at all levels from the working groups upwards; this practice was gradually endorsed by successive EPC reports.[32] Even EU foreign ministers had their own institutionalized opportunities to discuss EPC and EC affairs together, primarily through their informal and secret "Gymnich-type" meetings (named after the Schloss Gymnich near Bonn where the first was one held in 1974; see below).

To be sure, several other factors were involved in the early breakdown of the barrier between EC and EPC affairs. Most notably, a decisive change in French policy took place after Giscard d'Estaing won the French presidency on May 9, 1974 following the death of Georges Pompidou. Giscard clearly was more "pro-EC" than both de Gaulle and Pompidou, and his new foreign minister, Jean Sauvergnargues, said he saw no harm in linking the EC with EPC issues (Allen and Wallace 1982: 30). Although it still had the atmosphere of an informal club, some logistical support for EPC was necessary and all EU states (especially small ones) were aware of the need to preserve traditional EC procedures. Without a permanent staff to manage EPC and keep it separate from the EC, the creation of a transgovernmental infrastructure was an acceptable, low-cost alternative, but it was still a major step in the institutionalization of EU foreign

---

[32] Interviews with former EPC officials, Brussels, 1996.

policy cooperation. While the specific norms and rules of EPC eventually emerged through a sometimes painful process of trial and error, few EU states could object to the seemingly harmless lower-level links between their professional bureaucrats and diplomats.

Substantive EPC outcomes

As EPC was still emerging in the mid-1970s, the changes of process discussed above probably were far more important to the development of EU foreign policy than any substantive external policies. Like the Luxembourg Report before it, the Copenhagen Report was in effect for roughly three years before further efforts were taken to enhance EPC (the Tindemans Report of January 1976, which is considered in the next chapter). Yet even in the few years between the Copenhagen and Tindemans Reports we can observe two important substantive developments in European foreign policy.

First, the immediate years after the Copenhagen Report saw the emergence of a new EPC policy tool: *institutionalized regional political dialogues*. The first use of this tool involved the Arab states, and its provisions will be discussed below. At this point it need only be recognized that the Copenhagen Report did not provide any guidelines for such dialogues, other than to promote the formulation of medium- and long-term common positions. Yet events in the Middle East in 1973 prompted EU states to put their relations with the Arab states on a firmer footing and the outcome ultimately set a precedent for dialogues with other third parties. Second, EPC made its first experiments with *crisis management*, another exogenous functional rationale for institutional change.[33] These efforts involved the EU's responses to the 1973 October War, which broke out soon after the Copenhagen Report was finalized, the Portuguese Revolution of April 1974, the July 1974 Cyprus coup, and the execution of Basque terrorists in Spain in late 1975, which the EU was unable to prevent. The results were mixed, but in each case the EU learned a new and different lesson about the limits of EPC and the importance of closer linkages to EC procedures. The October War will be considered below in the broader context of EU–Middle East relations; for the moment I review the most important lessons from the other three crises.

---

[33] EPC documents do not clearly define the term "crisis"; this was always a case-by-case political decision. However, for the purposes of analytical clarity, we can define crises as situations where participants believe that: (1) the stakes are high and involve a threat to basic values or interests; (2) the probability of violence is high; and (3) there is a finite time limit for a response. Often an element of surprise is involved as well (Winn 1996: Chapter 1).

The Portuguese issue was raised by the Dutch at an EPC meeting on June 10, 1974, but it resulted in only a weak statement hoping for democracy in Portugal and offering support to foster social and economic development for the Portuguese. However, an EPC Southern European working group was created and charged with the task of considering the issue in more detail. Further action on this question stalled for over a year primarily because of French objections about taking more decisive measures in the context of EPC. In an important precedent, EU foreign ministers finally agreed on October 7, 1975 to provide financial aid to Portugal in the amount of 150 million units of account drawn on the European Investment Bank (EIB), and to open discussions on the improvement of the EC's existing trade agreement with Portugal (which had entered into effect in January 1973). In addition to this first use of an EC competency as a political tool since the creation of EPC (an action which took place in the context of both EPC and EC procedures; see Chapter 5),[34] the EIB loan is also notable for the active involvement of the Commission as a neutral diplomatic link between the Portuguese regime and the EU since national channels were subject to politicization by domestic actors.

In Cyprus, the UK was in a key position given its role in providing security for the island, and the British indeed attempted to make use of EPC by encouraging negotiations between the Greeks and the Turks. Toward this end, EPC rapidly produced a statement supporting the "independence and territorial integrity" of the island and opposing "any intervention or interference" tending to put those goals in question. This position was communicated to the Cyprus government and to Athens and Ankara through the French EU presidency.[35] The warning of course did not prevent Turkish intervention, but all three countries involved enjoyed Association Agreements with the EC and they were keenly sensitive to the disruption of these agreements. Although the EC did not make an explicit threat to break its Association Agreements with Cyprus, Greece, or Turkey, the EU's collective diplomacy through EPC (and its cooperation with the US through a new mechanism; see below) helped to encourage a temporary cease-fire on July 23, 1974 (Nuttall 1992a: 120). The EU

[34] Van Praag 1982a: 98. This is not to say that EPC directed or instructed the EC to take action with the loan and trade agreement (such provisions did not exist at the time), only that discussions on the issue took place in both forums. In the end, it was the EC that took action on the issue, and Nuttall argues (1992a: 125) that in fact the EIB loan "ran roughshod" over usual EC procedures in the way it was agreed (under pressure from the European Council). EPC would have to wait for several years before it was able to use EC resources for its own ends; this development is considered in the next chapter.

[35] "Communiqué by the Nine Governments on the Situation in Cyprus" (Paris, July 16, 1974).

also abandoned its neutral position regarding disputes between Greece and Turkey (especially as Greece announced its intention to join the EU after the fall of the colonels on July 24), indicating that it was ready to take sides on political issues despite its desire to maintain good relations with both countries.[36] However, EPC was still reluctant to use EC measures (such as breaking Association Agreements) for its own ends; this attitude would diminish in the next few years. Moreover, once the Turks invaded the island, EPC found it increasingly difficult to maintain a unified stance. The EU gradually backed off from the crisis, content to play the passive role of an "adviser" while the UN and the US took the lead from that point on.[37] However, as we shall see in Chapter 6, while EPC found it difficult to respond, the Commission attempted to use the pending negotiations of the second stage of the EC's Association Agreement with Cyprus as a bargaining chip.

The limitations of EPC, particularly in terms of giving so much discretion to the EU presidency, also were highlighted during the Spanish crisis. Rather than calling for face-to-face meetings among EU diplomats to react to the pending executions of five Basques in September 1975, the Italian EU presidency relied primarily on the COREU system to forge a common EPC position (Nuttall 1997b: 29). This approach was more time-consuming, and it was not until three days before the executions took place (September 27) that EPC agreed to the principle of a joint action on the issue. A position was finally worked out among the EU's foreign ministers at the UN; this too was weak as it only appealed to Spain's sense of mercy and did not condemn the Spanish justice system or threaten stronger measures on the part of the EU. As in the Portuguese crisis, the Dutch (and the Danes) called for such action, but it was held up until the last minute primarily because of French objections. Even then, action within EPC was timid, as seven out of nine EU states failed to coordinate the withdrawal of their ambassadors to Spain, thus weakening the collective impact of the gesture. They also failed to coordinate the *return* of their ambassadors, yet another reasonable suggestion of the Dutch and Danes. And once again, the Commission (with much support from the EP) took the lead in proposing more concrete joint action on the issue, first in the form of a protest on the day of the executions,

[36] The Greek coup in 1967 had led to a partial "freezing" of its Association Agreement with the EC, but this situation did not change as a result of the Cyprus coup (van Praag 1982a).

[37] Van Praag 1982a: 100. Hill (1992: 140) notes that unlike the Portuguese situation, the Cyprus invasion was not perceived as a crisis by the EU. However, given the military ramifications of the Cyprus episode, and compared to most other long-term issues considered in EPC, the Cyprus case can be considered a crisis for the purposes of this study.

followed by a statement that the Commission could not proceed with negotiations concerning commercial relations with Spain. The Council of
Ministers somewhat reluctantly endorsed this decision in the face of divisions between the "moralists" (such as Denmark and the Netherlands)
and the "pragmatists" (such as France, Germany, and the UK), but at
least the EC was able to signify its displeasure with the Spanish government through a tangible political action (van Praag 1982a: 102–103).

These difficulties clearly can be attributed to a general lack of collective political will, but institutional limitations also played a major part.
There were no planning capabilities for EPC, no firm procedures for crisis management or even a clear definition of a crisis in EPC texts,[38] no
procedures to use EC tools for EPC/political ends, and no real definitions
of common interests or values (such as support for democracy or human
rights) on which to base joint action.[39] As intergovernmental theory ex-
pects, the Commission was unable to play a stronger role in EPC because
several EU states, who were also opposed to the idea of using any EC resources for external political ends, objected. Still, during all three crises
there was a clear resort to EC instruments (the EIB loan for Portugal;
the agreement to develop an Association Agreement with Cyprus; and
the postponement of trade talks with Spain), though in a tenuous way,[40]
with consistent involvement by the Commission even at this early stage,
despite the lack of concrete provisions for such actions in EPC reports.
Finally, EPC saw the active use of common declarations and démarches in
all cases, indicating the general acceptance of these policy tools (although
these were somewhat limited during the Spanish crisis). Thus, although
EPC was not yet robust enough to take an active, independent role, particularly where military forces were involved, it can still be considered a
success in that policy differences during these crises were at least partly
moderated by EPC, while diplomatic efforts were largely channeled into
common and productive (rather than self-interested and counterproduc-
tive) deliberations. These results clearly demonstrated EPC's usefulness
as a confidence-building mechanism and its potential as a tool for crisis management, both of which would encourage additional institutional
change.

---

[38] Under the terms of the Luxembourg Report (Part II, Section 2), "Should a grave crisis or
matter of particular urgency arise, extraordinary consultations will be arranged between
the governments of member states. The chairman [EU presidency] will get in touch with
his colleagues in order to determine the best way of ensuring such consultation."

[39] For similar arguments see van Praag 1982a: 104–108; Nuttall 1997b: 29.

[40] Van Praag (1982a: 108) notes that even in the difficult cases of Portugal, Cyprus, and
Spain, "Despite the jealousies that exist within the separate structures there is scope
for EPC policy to be executed with Community instruments, having been transmitted
across the increasingly sophisticated, if still largely *ad hoc*, coordination network."

Beyond these key developments, the post-Copenhagen Report period saw changes to other substantive EPC policies. In the Middle East, EPC was compelled to take the first concrete steps toward the Euro-Arab Dialogue very soon after the Copenhagen Report was announced. During the 1973 October War in the Middle East, France once again attempted to take the lead in handling the crisis. Unlike in 1967, however, the French now called for a collective *European* response to the war rather than attempting to coordinate a great power summit outside the EU. Still, the prospects for European cooperation seemed even less promising than they had been during the 1967 war, given the failed attempt by the EU to maintain a coordinated response to the 1973 oil embargo. This failure resulted in different treatment for EU states under the Arab oil embargo and provoked serious Franco-German divisions over American proposals for an oil consumers' cartel.[41] The resulting Copenhagen summit of the Nine in December caused the EU even more embarrassment when four Arab foreign ministers showed up uninvited and requested a more structured relationship between the Arab states and the EU.[42] This bold external request stimulated the preparations for what was to become the Euro-Arab Dialogue. Finally, institutional problems compounded the political ones: there were no provisions in the EC/EPC for any regional or group-to-group dialogue, except perhaps for the EC's limited Association Agreements and the Yaoundé/Lomé conventions, which were strictly confined to economic issues (and the Yaoundé/Lomé conventions were further confined to developing countries).

Yet the EU took a bold leap of faith on the issue. In doing so it not only created a new policy tool but also institutionalized one of the most important norms of EU foreign policy: promoting regional cooperation or integration along EU lines in other troubled areas of the world. In this case, an EPC foreign ministers' meeting in Brussels in March 1974 resulted in a threefold plan of action to deal with the Arabs. This involved opening contacts with the twenty member states of the Arab League, the establishment of a number of joint Euro-Arab working groups, and plans for a conference of EU–Arab foreign ministers. This plan was immediately thrown into confusion when Henry Kissinger angrily accused the Europeans of endangering his diplomatic efforts in the Middle East. It was not until the Europeans and the Americans resolved their differences over the question of Atlantic consultation in mid-1974 (with yet another

[41] The Netherlands (like the US) was completely embargoed, France and the UK were viewed as "friendly" by the Arabs and received normal supplies of oil, and the other Six were threatened with phased reductions of 5 percent per month.

[42] Lieber (1976: 18) suggests that the UK and France actually invited the Arabs to Copenhagen.

informal institutional arrangement; see below) that EPC could proceed with the Euro-Arab Dialogue.

Perhaps inevitably, the Dialogue developed by virtue of the fact that the most divisive problems, and the ones which had prompted it, were left off the table at first. These involved the war in the Middle East and oil prices/supplies. In what would become a common pattern for European foreign policy, discussions on the issue started by emphasizing commonalities rather than differences. However, although EU states agreed that economic and development issues would be stressed (suggesting the Community as the appropriate forum for consultation), the problems of the region were explosive enough to warrant the use of EPC (rather than the EC) for conducting the Euro-Arab Dialogue. This unusual decision to have EPC handle issues that should have been an EC competency laid the foundations for an increasing institutional fusion of the two domains. This took place only within the context of EU–Arab relations at first, but later involved other important external relationships of the EU. This fusion is taken up in more detail in Chapter 6; for the moment, it need only be stressed that the structure of the Euro-Arab Dialogue (initially involving a General Commission and seven joint working groups, most of which involved EC competencies) encouraged a much closer working relationship between the EC and EPC than some Europeans, mainly the French, preferred.

The Dialogue is also significant for the way it affected EPC itself, in particular the way leadership and responsibility for European foreign policy are shared among EU states through the institution of the EU presidency. The Dialogue began with a very rocky start when the Arabs demanded observer status for the Palestine Liberation Organization (PLO) at the General Commission during Ireland's first EU presidency in the first half of 1975. Under what became known as the "Dublin formula," the Dialogue was able to proceed after Irish foreign minister Garret FitzGerald convinced both sides to allow the working groups to begin their discussions even though the General Commission was held up, then to structure the Dialogue on the basis of *regional* (rather than national) delegations. This formula enabled the Europeans to put off for several years the terribly difficult question of bestowing diplomatic recognition on the PLO, while allowing the players to hold the first session of the General Commission in May 1976 (Al-Mani 1983; Allen and Pijpers 1984). This meeting will be considered in the next chapter in the context of related moves toward rule-making in EPC.

The impact of the Copenhagen Report on EPC's consideration of East–West relations coincided with the second stage of the CSCE meetings in Geneva, from September 1973 to July 1975. Here the transgovernmental network of working groups was the most complex, with up to fifteen special committees of the Nine meeting on a regular basis. Between this institutional EC–EPC linkage and the incredible density of the preparatory network, the EU achieved a very high degree of coordination during the talks leading up to the Helsinki Final Act in August 1975. The EU's consensus position regarding the CSCE process was expressed in a key declaration of the European Council on July 17, 1975.[43] In fact, coordination here was so successful that EPC's Political Committee agreed to continue its cooperation on CSCE matters after the conference, primarily by commenting on the long text of the Final Act. CSCE working groups and sub-working groups were mobilized toward this end, preparing their commentary through the summer of 1976. Both EU states and the Commission were closely involved in this massive project, which produced a text of about 450 pages. During this time as well, the Nine established a permanent group in Geneva to handle relations between the CSCE and the UN Economic Commission in Europe following the Final Act. However, according to von Gröll (1982: 65), it was not entirely clear whether this group was part of EPC or part of the EC's own Committee of Permanent Representatives. The confusion reflected the growing difficulty of compartmentalizing the EU's external relations into economic (EC) and political (EPC) affairs, especially with issues as broad and complex as the CSCE process. This Geneva group was perhaps the only permanent organizational manifestation of EPC (other than the COREU system) until the EPC Secretariat was established in 1986, and it represented Europe's continued commitment to its most visible and successful foreign policy at the time.

EPC also attempted to move beyond its newly institutionalized policies concerning the Middle East and East–West relations in the period following the Copenhagen Report. One major priority concerned the United States. By seeming to vacillate between ignorance and a divide-and-conquer strategy toward Europe (which often left France at odds with the rest of the EU), the US had seriously complicated the EPC discussions surrounding the Paris summit and Copenhagen Report. After EPC decided to proceed with the Euro-Arab Dialogue, where Kissinger was pushing his own solution to the problems in the Middle East, the Europeans felt that something had to be done to stop the US from complaining about every new attempt to improve political cohesion in Europe. The response was formulated in a new EPC institutional device, the "Gymnich-type" meetings among EU foreign ministers. These meetings

---

[43] "Statement by the Second European Council on the United Nations and the CSCE" (Brussels, July 17, 1975).

are held over the weekend in some pleasant place so that EU foreign ministers can informally discuss whatever they want. Supporting officials are not invited, no formal decisions are taken, and no official record is kept, but EC and EPC topics are always discussed together at these meetings (Nuttall 1992a: 15).

The first such meeting on April 20–21, 1974 helped to break the stalemate between France and its eight EU partners over relations with the US. In one of EPC's most important decisions, the so-called "Gymnich formula,"[44] the Nine established the principle of periodic consultations with allied or friendly countries, starting with the US. In announcing this policy on June 10–11, 1974, German foreign minister Hans Dietrich Genscher called it a "gentlemen's agreement" designed to promote "smooth and pragmatic" consultations with the US (Nuttall 1992a: 91). Genscher and Kissinger met on June 11 as well, and Kissinger announced afterward that they had reached full agreement on the idea of regular consultations. He also ceased his objections to the European efforts in the Middle East (Kohler 1982: fn. 9). This new informal but clearly institutionalized procedure led to a continuous dialogue with the US on foreign policy problems, and helped overcome America's opposition to EPC. Instituted at the Ottawa summit later in 1974, the agreement undoubtedly paved the way for the Euro-Arab Dialogue, and proved very useful during the Cyprus crisis, allowing the EU and the US to coordinate their policies.

With the raised stature of EPC under the Copenhagen Report, EU governments also began to turn their attention to the situation in South Africa. However, national policies toward this country continued to dominate until the Portuguese revolution in 1974 and its subsequent impact on Portugal's colonial relationships in Africa and elsewhere. Although this event focused world attention on the African situation, the EU still was unable to act in concert under the EPC mechanism. For example, the EU could not even complete its coordination of the recognition of the MPLA government in Angola when the French decided to act ahead of their EPC partners. EPC did not produce its first real declaration until February 23, 1976, when it finally condemned the policy of apartheid in South Africa.[45] EPC was also unable to follow up this statement at the UN later that year, when the EU's three larger states (France, Germany, and the UK) voted against a series of UN resolutions calling for embargoes on investment, trade, and arms, and the end of sporting contacts

---

[44] The name derives from the fact that the agreement to consult with allies was made during a Gymnich-type meeting of EU foreign ministers.

[45] EC Foreign Ministers, "Statement on the Situation in Southern Africa" (Luxembourg, February 23, 1976).

with South Africa. The EPC moralists (Denmark, Ireland, the Netherlands, and to a lesser extent, Italy) chose to support the measures (van
Praag 1982b). Rhetoric remained the EU's rule regarding South Africa
for the time being, until EPC took its first steps toward a more active
policy. These steps will be considered in the next chapter.

Finally, the immediate post-Copenhagen Report years saw the first
formal EC contact with Central America.[46] This involved a visit by
Sir Christopher Soames, then vice-president of the Commission, to the
headquarters of the Central American Common Market (CACM) in
Guatemala City in 1975. Soames met with the economic ministers of
Costa Rica, El Salvador, Guatemala, Honduras, and Nicaragua, and with
the secretary-general of the CACM.[47] Prior to this visit, the EU had dis-
played very little interest in Latin America. Economic links were under-
developed, and there was still some sensitivity to the Monroe Doctrine,
America's long-standing, and controversial, expression of dominance in
this increasingly troubled region. Only France was willing to challenge
the US predilection for asserting itself in the Western Hemisphere; this
defiance took the form of French arms sales to Cuba and their vote against
the US in the UN Security Council after the US invaded the Dominican
Republic in 1965 (Hertogs 1985: 69–70). While most EU states were still
content to take a back-seat role to the US in the region, the Soames visit
opened the door to a common European policy here. Economic decline,
increasing debt, fears of US interference, and growing political instability
made the states of the region far more receptive to European overtures.
The real turning point came only a few years afterward, with the downfall
of the Somoza dictatorship, the installation of the Sandanista regime in
Nicaragua, and the civil war in El Salvador (Duran 1988). These events
helped to "internationalize" what had been a regional crisis, thus stimulating the involvement of the Europeans. This case and those mentioned
above will be revisited in later chapters as we delve deeper into the institutional expansion of EU foreign policy.

---

[46] Limited contacts between the EC and Central America had taken place in 1968 and
1971; these focused on complaints by Central America about protectionism in the Community and did not achieve significant results.
[47] *EC Bulletin* 9 (1975): 64.

5   Norms, rules, and laws in European foreign policy

The Luxembourg and Copenhagen Reports clearly laid the foundations for intensive information-sharing about foreign policy among EU member states. Yet we can say much more about the relationship between institutionalized communication and international cooperation than those who view cooperation as one-shot deals or quid pro quo contracts. When patterns of communication persist and become increasingly complex and dense, whether by accident or design, the demand for common standards of behavior may grow as actors continue to engage one another. The emergence of these standards, or norms, takes collective behavior to a higher level of institutionalization by translating general values or ideas into specific behavior patterns. In the case of EU foreign policy, norms helped EPC progress from a passive forum or talking shop to a more active, collective, foreign policymaking mechanism. This occurred despite the fact that EU governments continued to claim the right to maintain their sovereignty and flexibility over foreign policy and often rejected the formal legalization of their cooperation in this domain.

The specific processes involved in this transition are the subject of this chapter. As I proposed in Chapter 2, norm development can be conceived in terms of several steps: (1) the emergence of *informal (uncodified) customs,* or the (often unspoken) traditions and practices that emerged in day-to-day interactions among EPC officials; (2) the codification or ordering of these informal customs into explicit, written *norms*; (3) the transition from explicit norms to *rules* (rights and obligations), as reflected in EPC reports; and (4) the transition from rules into *formal laws* (legal rules), which involve behavioral and legal obligations.

The notion of customary law is particularly important to EU foreign policy since EPC was not a treaty until 1986. Customs can ripen into international law when three conditions are present: the customs or practices are fairly uniform, they persist over a period of time, and they are observed on the basis of *opinio juris*. That is, actors must believe, or at least act as if, the customs are legally binding even if they never formally agreed to them as such. These customs can be imposed, negotiated, or emerge in a spontaneous fashion, as with markets or rules of language (Axelrod 1986; March and Olsen 1989; Nadelmann 1990; Legro 1997). Since EPC customs were not imposed by a hegemonic state or other authoritative actor (such as the European Court of Justice), were codified on the basis on consensus, and did not ordinarily involve bargains among the actors involved, I argue that most innovation (or norm-creation) took place in the transgovernmental communications network and depended on the culture of problem-solving described in the previous chapter. More specifically, we can identify three general types of norm-creation that took place within EPC. These are (1) rituals or habits; (2) trial and error adaptation; and (3) imitation (or institutional isomorphism). In addition, the institutional logics of functionality and appropriateness are both relevant here: actors may rely on instrumental rationality when they devise a new norm to solve a problem, but these new norms often must also conform to, or at least respect, the existing institutional framework that governs the problem domain. The key point is that the normative response to any external or internal stimulus also strongly depends on the fit of a proposed norm within the existing collective decision-making system.

How a norm is created also conditions its influence on social actors. Imposed and negotiated norms generally reflect other incentives (in the form of coercion or reciprocal favorable treatment) rather than possess some inherent power or legitimacy of their own. However, when norms are spontaneously generated by voluntaristic actors, even in the context of debate or argument, they can acquire some measure of legitimacy which encourages compliance on this basis alone. As norms reduce uncertainties about behavior among a given set of actors, actors will support such norms to the extent that stable patterns of interaction help them solve problems (functional logic), reinforce existing norms (appropriateness logic), or maintain valued social relationships (socialization logic).[1] Once a norm has matured into a rule or law over time, violation of it can result in internal psychological discomfort and external embarrassment among actors even in the absence of some authority to impose compliance through punishments (Axelrod 1986; North 1990). When made public, such norms can also encourage "rhetorical entrapment" since actors must live up to the norm or risk shame or serious damage to their reputations, which can, in turn, erode their political power (Schimmelfennig 2001). Thus, even without explicit compliance or sanctioning mechanisms, and even without codification in a treaty or reinforcement by a court, norms can acquire enough legitimacy to influence state behavior. This legitimacy

---

[1] These dynamics also involve the issue of coherence, which is explored further in Chapter 8.

clarifies the rights and duties of the members of a social group (or polity, in the case of the EU), and involves a change from an instrumental, regulatory conception of institutions to a more deontological view, in the sense that they frame standards of behavior in terms of obligations, duties, or moral purpose.

This argument is further supported by the notion "soft law," or "rules of conduct which, in principle, have no legally binding force but which nevertheless may have practical effects."[2] Dehousse and Weiler (1991) have argued that a "sociological" view of such soft laws makes them legal when actors increasingly justify their behavior in terms of norms (even when defecting), and that EPC could be understood as a system of soft law until it was codified as "hard law" with the Single European Act (SEA). Also, the fact that sovereignty in EPC was pooled or ceded to a center (the EU presidency supported by the transgovernmental network) created the impression that it had legal personality, although EPC was of course neither a state nor an international organization (Lodge 1989). Viewing norms as standards about what is valued rather than as mere expectations, constraints, or habits invests them with a higher moral purpose, from which we get our respect for law.[3] In short, while norms can be used, in a narrow functional manner, to stop undesirable activity and to encourage desirable activity, they also represent common aspirations, values, and moral goals in line with the logics of appropriateness or socialization (Kindleberger 1986). These symbolic purposes of norms are clearly reflected in the history of European integration, and this is no less true with EU foreign policy.

Thus, to the extent that EU foreign policy norms persist over time, are clearly defined, are linked to previous norms, mature into legally binding obligations, are used as points of reference for future norms, and are internalized in EU member states through socialization processes, they have been institutionalized and are likely to influence state behavior. Moreover, to the extent that EPC norms are related to EC treaties and case law, and are endorsed or interpreted by the EC's supranational organizations (chiefly the European Court of Justice), they have also been *legalized*.[4] These ideas form the structure of this chapter. In the next section, I focus on the development and effects of *procedural or constitutive*

---

[2] This definition is found in Snyder 1993, cited in Cram 1997: 4.

[3] For example, tacit rules, as existed between the superpowers (in the form of precedents, traditions, recurring patterns of behavior, and lessons from history), may have created *expectations* about behavior (Keal 1983; Gaddis 1986) but they were not necessarily viewed as *obligations*. Also note that the regime literature defines norms in terms of expectations.

[4] By "legalization" I mean that EPC norms have been (1) explicitly clarified as rules (usually by written expression); (2) codified, or ordered, in relation to other rules in that setting and in related settings; and (3) invested with the status of law, which involves legal

norms on European foreign policy during the period surrounding the 1981 London Report, the primary focus of this chapter. Of particular importance was the increasing tendency for EPC decisions to be tied to the EC's own legal, treaty-based procedures, even though, as Wessels once observed (1982: 14–15), "discussions about legal questions which aimed to avoid or produce precedents rarely occurred in EPC." Following my discussion of EPC's major procedural norms, I examine the development and effects of *substantive or regulatory* norms on European foreign policy. Finally, although I analyze these sets of norms separately, it should be stressed that the distinction between procedural and substantive norms is not a sharp one; it is more of a conceptual distinction than an empirical one. Institution-building (through procedures) and cooperation (through substantive policies) interact with each other and it is not always possible to specify which process is taking precedence. Still, it should be noted that EPC officials themselves found it useful to distinguish their norms explicitly in two ways (procedural and substantive) to help clarify their associated obligations. As we shall see, they clearly observed a difference between the general "rules of game" for EPC decision-making and the more specific policy requirements in certain geographic or functional areas.

Procedural norms of European foreign policy

Conceptualizing the role of norms in EU foreign policy cooperation is a difficult task. Given the inherent sensitivity of the issue-area and EPC's informal nature, norms took time to develop and arduous debates took place whenever any actor attempted to formalize them.[5] As the legalization of EPC was such a contentious topic, the system did not even gain treaty status until 1986 with the SEA. Indeed, EPC would not have been created at all if EU states had deliberately attempted to impose legal rules on themselves. In the words of one former EPC participant, "The first decade and a half of [European] Political Cooperation [was] marked by extreme conservatism in the drafting of theoretical papers and bold innovation on the ground" (Nuttall 1992a: 54).

Since theoretical debates over formal rules were more spirited and intensive than those concerning substantive policy questions, one of the most trenchant criticisms of EPC was that its procedures were emphasized over its substance (Wallace and Allen 1977). Indeed, EPC's

---

(i.e., formal and justiciable) rights and obligations toward other actors. Such legalization imposes new demands on actors as they continue to institutionalize a social space; this argument is developed in more detail in Smith 2001a.

[5] Interviews with former EPC participants, Brussels, 1995–96.

procedures at first *were* its substance; they were more important in and of themselves (primarily for internal confidence-building) rather than for their utility in attaining some desired external policy goal. The heated debates over how to articulate EPC in terms of rights and obligations reflect the extent to which norms rely upon common meanings or discourse (Kratochwil 1989: 5–6). The search for a specific vocabulary on which to base EPC's rules was in fact often highly problematic, as general terms such as "common foreign policy," "obligations," "security affairs," "defense," and so on were long prohibited. Additionally, for some states (such as Denmark and Ireland) debates over procedure were as difficult as those over substance because of the thorny domestic constitutional issues they raised; thus they were avoided as much as possible. As another observer once remarked, "Pragmatism is one of the main features governing political cooperation. The fixing of rules and procedures in official texts before they have proven their usefulness is alien to EPC procedure" (Regelsberger 1991: 163). However, once EPC procedures were established, even informally, EU states generally supported their "correct" use on good faith, even if they did not agree with specific policies.[6] This became especially important as EPC norms and procedures increasingly overlapped with those of the EC, and vice versa.

The emergence and effects of procedural EPC norms

The period between 1977 and 1986 is the most important for our analysis of the production of EPC procedural norms, although such norms were of course established before and after this time period. After the 1973 Copenhagen Report, EPC resulted in only one more public codification of its procedures (the 1981 London Report) until it was legalized with the SEA in 1986. The London Report is the focus of this chapter; the SEA is the subject of Chapter 6. And although several EC organizations had produced reports on the idea of "European Union" by the mid-1970s,[7] which involved a common foreign policy, these did not provoke summit-level intergovernmental agreements about EPC similar to the Luxembourg and Copenhagen Reports.

For example, the Tindemans Report on European Union of January 1976 proposed an end to the distinction between the ministerial meetings of the EC and those of EPC, although EPC could maintain its Political

---

[6] Interviews with various EPC/CFSP officials in the Commission, COREPER, and EU member state foreign ministries, 1995–96.

[7] The Commission's views can be found in the *EC Bulletin*, supplement 5/75. For the views of the European Parliament, the European Court of Justice, and the Economic and Social Committee, see the *EC Bulletin*, Supplement 9/75.

Committee structure to prepare EPC ministerial meetings. Like informed observers in the Commission, Leo Tindemans (the prime minister of Belgium) thought EPC at that time was better equipped to react rather than act; in response to this deficiency, he argued that EPC's procedures needed to be substantially enhanced. His report also proposed the establishment of an *obligation* to arrive at a common decision, which would move EPC from the coordination of national positions toward a true *common* foreign policy governed by laws. To promote such a policy, the minority would be encouraged (if not required) to adapt to the majority view (Tindemans 1976). However, the Tindemans Report ultimately was rejected because of these drastic proposals, although, as we shall see, many of its provisions appeared in later EU foreign policy texts (Ifestos 1987: 192–99; Bulmer and Wessels 1987: 86–87).

With the summit-level codification process stalled by the mid-1970s,[8] we must for the moment focus on the informal customs that matured into written norms during behind-the-scenes discussions among EPC participants. In particular, I focus on three customs which later developed into explicit norms: *confidentiality*, *consensus*, and *consultation*. I also discuss two tacit norms (or unspoken rules) which remained as such during the entire history of EPC/CFSP: the notion of *domaines réservés*, and the prohibition against hard bargaining.

First, EPC discussions were private; states could not use information shared during the meetings to embarrass or blame other states. Communication and trust were the foundations of the system; the norm of secrecy undoubtedly encouraged confidence among EU states since they typically did not have to fear public politicization of sensitive issues, embarrassment at failure, or that information shared would be used against them. Second, EU states adopted a general rule to consult with each other before adopting final positions of their own so that EPC was given a chance to build consensus. This norm was intimately linked to EPC's communications network: little progress toward cooperation could be made if states merely used the system to express rigid foreign policy positions to each other. With this norm, a "true consultation reflex" emerged, so that EU member states were rarely willing to "jeopardize present commitments to consult before adopting formal positions or launching national initiatives on important international questions of mutual concern" (de Bassompierre 1988: 49). Failure to respect this rule could have adverse consequences for EU states; this fact is clearly reflected in British

---

[8] One minor exception to this argument is that the administrative practices of the European Council were further institutionalized with the London Declaration of 1977 (reproduced in the *EC Bulletin*, No. 6 (1977).

foreign minister Douglas Hurd's remark that "perhaps one reason why these unilateral efforts now usually come to nothing is precisely that they are unilateral" (Hurd 1981: 389). Moreover, these institutionalized consultations directly led to more substantive norms, which are considered below. Third, EPC discussions were also conducted with unanimity; any state could block a discussion of a sensitive matter with little or no justification. There were no provisions for voting or weighting of votes as in regular Community affairs.[9] This was not necessarily a paralyzing rule, as one might assume of a consensual system. Officials did not always resort to the lowest common denominator position or habitually threaten the veto, but instead tended toward compromise and a median position in the hopes of finding a solution (Nuttall 1992a: 12).[10]

The consensus norm is closely related to the two most important tacit norms or unspoken rules: the notion of *domaines réservés* and the prohibition against bargaining. First, concerning *domaines réservés*, EU states generally avoided discussing issues that were viewed as extremely sensitive by one or more of their partners. Unsurprisingly, consensus was more easily maintained by respecting these *domaines réservés*. These included unilateral problems between member states (such as Northern Ireland), bilateral "special relationships" whereby one EU state was expected to take the lead on an issue or could prevent disruption of the status quo (such as colonial relationships), and crises with military consequences affecting one or more partners (such as Africa). For a long time, these situations were outside the scope of EPC, except at the direct initiative of the EU state(s) claiming the *domaine réservé* (Franck 1983: 100–102). Thanks to this understanding, substantive norms in EPC were more easily defined in terms of what subjects were off-limits rather than what issues could be discussed, although this norm came under pressure (and the *domaine réservés* contracted) as EPC developed and its ambitions grew. When these common positions were made public and embedded within a larger normative structure, it became increasingly difficult for EU states to request special treatment on an issue (i.e., rhetorical entrapment).

The second tacit norm was mentioned in the previous chapter; it involves the prohibition against outright bargaining in EU foreign policy. Such deal-making regularly occurs in normal EC business, of course, yet the activities of technical experts in EPC working groups produced a culture of problem-solving with regards to foreign policy issues. These

---

[9] This situation changed slightly with the Treaty on European Union, as we shall see in Chapter 7.

[10] Interviews with EPC/CFSP participants generally confirmed this finding; Brussels, 1995–96.

experts attempted to find common viewpoints and solutions without haggling across issues or attempting to purchase support by offering incentives. Again, this is not to say that "splitting the difference" or making compromises on areas of disagreement did not occur,[11] only that, thanks to this unwritten rule, EU foreign policy officials have always understood that the hard-bargaining approach to EPC is inappropriate. Of course, this was true only of decisions about procedural customs and the substance of foreign policy; bargaining among EU heads of state or government about codifying the general institutional form of EU foreign policy as a treaty did take place during major Intergovernmental Conferences.

In addition to these five norms, many others emerged to improve the day-to-day functioning of EPC. Although these were not formally codified for many years, and they were usually "enforced" through intra-group politics of reputation and persuasion rather than by reference to legal obligations or sanctions, nonetheless a peculiar set of unwritten laws emerged during EPC discussions according to ministers, diplomats, bureaucrats, and scholars familiar with the system.[12] Most of these supplementary procedural norms were codified as EPC customs in the short period following the rejection of the Tindemans Report. Although they had agreed not to "communitarize" their foreign policy cooperation for the moment, EPC members also realized that consistency of the policy process would be difficult in a system with no central bureaucracy and with rotating directors (the EU presidencies) every six months. Thus, in 1976 Denmark suggested the idea of the *coutumier* ("custom"), a compilation of all formal and informal working procedures which became the "bible of EPC" for European Correspondents in foreign ministries. This was done primarily to smooth transitions between EU presidencies in the absence of a permanent secretariat (Haagerup and Thune 1983: 110). EPC customs that found their way into the *coutumier* (or the *acquis politique*, in accord with the *acquis communautaire* of EC procedures) became a kind of "EPC common law," and were subsequently referred to, when appropriate, by each state holding the EU presidency. EPC officials thus established, preserved, and applied their own normative precedents in foreign policy without the involvement of the European Court.

In fact, thanks to the *coutumier* procedures, long before the SEA many began to suggest that the informal, extra-legal arrangements worked out between governments in EPC were sufficiently constraining to be

[11] The EC's practice of "splitting the difference" as an alternative to lowest-common-denominator bargaining is discussed in Haas 1961: 369.

[12] In addition to the insider recollections of de Schoutheete de Tervarent (1980) and Nuttall (1992a), see von der Gablentz 1979; da Fonseca-Wollheim 1981; Hurd 1981, 1994. Also interviews with former EPC participants, Brussels, 1995–96.

considered *legally* binding. As early as 1977, ten years before the SEA, Belgian foreign minister Henri Simonet told the EP that in EPC "a kind of law of custom has emerged . . . which naturally does not envisage any sanctions but which has nevertheless taken on the character of a recognized rule which can be occasionally broken but whose existence one still recognizes."[13] Others have argued that even without formal codification, the reports and practices of EPC "could well have come to form a beginning of customary European law as far as applied in practice, as implementation pursued consistently would have provided validity by precedent" (Lak 1989: 282). The fact that EPC officials acted as if these rules were legal (*opinio juris vel necessitatis*, or sense of legal obligation) and followed them more or less consistently over time meets the three basic criteria for customary international law (Dehousse and Weiler 1991: 123).[14] In any event, the *coutumier* was also significant because it represented an effort to write down, and thus make more permanent, what had been the unwritten norms of EPC. With this taboo broken, and with the disappointments of EPC's response to the Iran and Afghanistan crises between 1979 and 1980, EU member states entered the next major stage in EPC's institutional development: the 1981 London Report.

The London Report on EPC

The London Report was agreed during the British EU presidency, and was intended to offer practical improvements to EPC without necessarily making the process more supranational. Suggestions toward this end came in the form of speeches by Douglas Hurd and Lord Carrington, on two separate occasions in 1980. They stressed three areas for improvement to EPC: an improved consultation mechanism for emergencies or crises; a permanent, small secretariat to help administrate EPC; and the need for EU member states to make a stronger political commitment to EPC. While the proposals received a guarded reception at first, support gradually increased on the continent, particularly with the Soviet invasion of Afghanistan in December 1979, which shocked the world. In the few months after the invasion, Germany, Italy, and France expressed

---

[13] Cited in de Schoutheete de Tervarent 1980: 49.

[14] The "guidelines" set down by the European Council on EC/EPC starting in the mid-1970s similarly raised legal problems, since it too was not an EC body. However, some have argued that there is nothing in the EC treaties that prevents heads of EU governments from meeting as the Council of Ministers. This possibility was later codified in the Amsterdam and Nice Treaties, using the language "The Council (of Ministers), meeting in the composition of heads of state or government." The European Council was given a legal basis under the terms of the SEA, but like EPC it is not subject to the jurisdiction of the European Court of Justice (Bulmer and Wessels 1987: 78; Johnston 1994: 15).

their readiness to institutionalize EPC further. Germany and Italy were particularly creative, working together throughout 1981 to develop the idea of European union, which inevitably involved the strengthening of European foreign policy and, if necessary, treaty changes (Ifestos 1987: 285).

These efforts, which led to the "Solemn Declaration on European Union," and a draft of the SEA (see Chapter 6) sparked a wide-ranging debate on European institutional questions. This debate lasted several years; in the meantime, EU foreign ministers had managed to agree to the third report on EPC, the London Report, in October 1981. Although the discussions around this time involved the usual disagreements about the role of security affairs in EPC, fears among small states about an inter-governmental EPC dominated by the larger states, and reluctance for the moment to codify EPC's procedural changes in the form of a treaty, the London Report included several enhancements to EPC's structure while still keeping the mechanism at arm's length from the EC. The foreign ministers expressed their conviction that, while much had been achieved, the Ten were "still far from playing a role in the world appropriate to their combined influence." This declaration revealed a major change in emphasis in EPC: from a mere coordination mechanism to an instrument for asserting the EU's interests in global affairs (or from negative to positive integration). To address this perceived deficiency in the performance of EPC, EU states agreed that changes in the coordination of foreign policy should be instituted in order to "shape events and not merely react to them."[15] These changes are summarized in Table 5.1.

As EU states still refused to provide a permanent organization for EPC, or to delegate more responsibility to the Commission, the London Report instead focused on expanding the role of the EU presidency. It became more central as EPC's main contact with outsiders, which reduced the importance of bilateral "special relationships" in some cases (Wallace and Edwards 1976; de Schoutheete de Tervarent 1988). Unique among most regional economic organizations, the EC has "legal personality,"[16] or the formal capacity to enter into international legal agreements.[17] EPC,

---

[15] "Report on European Political Cooperation Issued by the Foreign Ministers of the Ten on 13 October 1981" (London Report), Part I.

[16] Articles 210 and 211 of the EC Treaty, Article 184 of the Euratom Treaty, and Article 6 of the European Coal and Steel Community invest these bodies with legal personality (rights and obligations) under international law. In general, the Commission embodies this personality when it negotiates agreements on behalf of these bodies.

[17] The term "agreements" includes treaties, conventions, understandings, declarations, protocols, exchanges of notes, and any other such instruments used by the EC to enter into a relationship with other entities subject to international law. See the ECJ Opinion 1/75 of November 11, 1975, *European Court Reports* 1355.

Table 5.1 *EPC according to the London Report (October 1981)*
Major changes since the Copenhagen Report appear in **boldface**.

Component	Actors and functions
Intergovernmental direction	EU foreign ministers meet at least four times a year. **Such meetings will focus on taking decisions for future action.**
	EU presidency state chairs meetings, **represents EPC abroad**, oversees implementation of conclusions.
	Procedures for EPC / third country contacts via EU presidency or Troika.*
	Informal "Gymnich" meetings of EU foreign ministers.
	Crisis procedures for ministerial meetings, Political Committee, heads of mission in third countries.
Transgovernmental support	Political Committee: preparation of ministerial meetings, **long-term studies.**
	European Correspondents: liaison between capitals.
	Working groups: geographical/functional analyses for EPC, including **potential crisis areas.**
	EU embassies: consultation on EPC matters in capitals of EU member states, in third countries, and in delegations to international conferences and organizations.
	COREU: encrypted telex network to share information.
	Other administrative support to be provided to the presidency state as needed.
	Joint reports from EU heads of mission in third countries at the request of the Political Committee or on their own initiative.
	Regular meetings among heads of mission within the capitals of the Ten.
	Administrative support for EU presidency by officials seconded from preceding and succeeding EU presidencies.
EC involvement	Commission **fully associated with EPC at all levels.**
	Colloquy four times a year with European Parliament Political Committee, and annual report on progress on EPC. **EU presidency answers EP questions about EPC and makes speeches to the EP. Informal meetings with the EP. President of the European Council also makes speeches to the EP.**
	Council informed through COREPER about EPC conclusions which might impact on the work of the EC.
	EPC meetings can be held on the occasion of EC ministerial meetings.
	Ministers able to use EPC to prepare studies on political aspects of problems under examination in the EC.

(cont.)

Table 5.1 (*cont.*)

Component	Actors and functions
Obligations	States consult on all questions of foreign policy. Formulation of medium- and long-term common positions.
	General rule not to take up final positions without consultation with EPC partners.
	Possible to discuss in EPC certain foreign policy questions bearing on the political aspects of security.
	EPC declarations must be called to the attention of third states by the local representative of the Ten.
	States must preserve the confidentiality of EPC.

* The "Troika" consists of the current, immediately past, and immediately following holders of the EU presidency.

however, possessed no such right, thus it was necessary to invest the EU presidency with the responsibility for representing EPC. Yet the fact that EPC (and later, the CFSP; see Chapter 8) never enjoyed legal personality prevented it from entering into legal agreements on behalf of the EU, a problem which demanded greater legal creativity as EPC expanded. The rotating EU presidency also encouraged a healthy spirit of competition while building a foundation of trust among EU states, which is elemental to problem-solving. Given the inherent secrecy of EPC deliberations, the EU presidency is perhaps the most important forum where public shaming of a state can occur if it fails to manage this role well.[18] Each EU presidency is closely watched by other EU states, which involves demonstration, reputation, and socialization effects. EU states cannot expect to use the presidency for their own ends if they wish to appear successful in the eyes of their EU partners; in this role they must take the lead in devising, articulating, and representing the EU's common foreign policy position in a number of diplomatic settings. EU member states thus learned how to evaluate and imitate successful EU presidencies, helping to advance new procedural norms of European foreign policy.

In addition to norms regarding the EU presidency, the coordination of positions became a rule in organizations and conferences, while EU states which were also members of the UN Security Council were required to take account of EPC positions in that forum and to inform

---

[18] As Wallace notes (1983b: 5), "Reputations are strengthened or damaged by the conduct of each presidency, both the personal reputations of the ministers and the political directors concerned and the overall image of the effectiveness or ineffectiveness of their government machine and its ability (or inability) to raise its horizons beyond the pursuit of immediate national interests."

their EU partners about its deliberations. This did not always take place of course, but as Wessels observed (1982), complaints about not conforming to these general procedures were rare.[19] Similarly, EPC was intended to produce medium- and long-term positions; however, by the late 1970s, EPC members had come to the conclusion that the limited crisis procedures (*consultations d'urgence*) suggested in the Luxembourg Report needed improvement. Although EPC's ability to handle crises was a weak spot,[20] its performance in this area did improve compared to its first decade of operation. Consider that during the May 1978 rebellion against Mobutu Sese Seko in Zaire, Belgium and France could not agree, and barely even considered, to undertake joint humanitarian operations or a rescue mission for the tens of thousands of French and Belgian citizens in that country.[21] At this time, EPC crisis decision-making involved only information-sharing, not joint action. The same thing happened during the Iran and Afghanistan crises, during which EU states could not easily agree upon a collective response. EPC did agree to impose mild sanctions on Iran after the 1979 hostage crisis, but only on a national basis and only after a long period of hesitation. Ultimately, the delay and limited response produced much ill will between the US and Europe.

As a result of these embarrassments, EPC's crisis procedures were slightly enhanced in the London Report of 1981. This helped ease the way toward the use of EC sanctions during the Poland crisis of 1981–82. The clearest example of improved procedures involved the 1982 Falkland Islands crisis, when the UK mobilized the rest of the EU in support of its decision to adopt sanctions against Argentina.[22] This resulted in a formal Council Regulation to suspend imports into the EC of all products from Argentina.[23] In addition to this ability of EPC to act decisively during a crisis, the Falklands episode is also notable for the fact that a clear security/defense issue was brought onto the EPC agenda for the first time (see below). Other practical working procedures, such as the protocol of EPC meetings, are too detailed to be mentioned here and they are not very important to the overall development of EPC. Rules involving the role of permanent organizations in EPC are covered in the next chapter.

---

[19] Wessels (1982) cites two examples: when France recognized Angola without consulting its EU partners, and when Denmark voted in the UN to condemn West Germany, France, and the UK for arms sales to South Africa, it was made clear in subsequent EPC meetings that such actions were perceived as deviant by the rest of the EU.

[20] For more on this point, see van Praag 1982a; Hill 1992; Anderson 1992; and Edwards 1992.

[21] Instead, Belgium, France, Germany, the UK, and the US assisted on a national basis (Franck 1983).

[22] On the Falklands crisis, see Edwards 1984; Martin 1992; and Stavridis and Hill 1996.

[23] Council Regulation 877/82.

EPC norms and EC laws

As the cases above suggest, one of the more important aspects of the growth of European foreign policy procedural norms involved situations where EPC participants decided, sometimes with great difficulty, to use EC economic competencies for EPC ends.[24] Such decisions inevitably threatened to "contaminate" EPC's informal norms with the EC's own, and far more complex, legal rules. These norms deserve special attention, as they allowed greater interaction between the two domains and promoted the general legalization of European foreign policy. At first, politically motivated EC sanctions were imposed on only a national basis, as happened with the imposition of sanctions against Rhodesia and Greece in the 1960s, rare pre-EPC examples of EU foreign policy cooperation. After EPC entered into effect, EU governments eventually agreed to invoke EC procedures symbolically, as necessary. However, the rigid distinction between the "high politics" of EPC and the "low politics" of the EC began to disappear as foreign ministers considered how EC resources or procedures could give more weight to EPC actions, which in the late 1970s still tended toward hollow declarations on many subjects (Holland 1991a). More specifically, when EPC decisions affected an EC competency, the invoking of certain EC treaty articles automatically made EPC a more rule-based and "Community-sensitive" regime than usual practice warranted. As Lak observes (1989: 283), the "interaction rules" of the SEA constituted the most "legal" of its EPC provisions given the language used, in part because these rules made Commission involvement in EPC mandatory (see Chapter 6).

This process of EC/EPC interaction ran both ways. As I discussed in Chapter 4, decisions in the EC, not EPC, first showed the potential importance of EC competencies to EU foreign policy during the 1974–75 Portuguese crisis, when the EU struggled to back up its political declarations with some type of concrete action. In this case, Article 130 concerning the European Investment Bank was reinterpreted in order to make its funds available for a political action, a decision not taken in EPC but rather in the EC. This also involved the appropriation of some Community funds in addition to national funds, which helped to speed up the disbursement.[25] And as noted above, during the 1979 Iran hostage crisis

---

[24] By "competency" I mean legal jurisdiction (i.e., the legal power to act) over EC treaty objectives and other goals that have been delegated by EU member states to the EU/EC (Macleod, Henry, and Hyett 1996: 38–39).

[25] The loan involved a 3 percent interest rebate to be paid by the EC budget, which avoided the necessity of the rebate being entered (and then approved) in the national budgets of the Nine (van Praag 1982a: 98).

Table 5.2 *EC rules invoked in the context of EPC*

Article 113	Empowers the Commission to recommend to the Council of Ministers when accords with third states are needed. The Council then directs the Commission to open and conduct negotiations (typically for economic policies).
Article 223	Protects EC members from the disclosure of information (such as that concerning national arms industries) which may damage their security. It effectively allows such industries to be exempt from the requirements of Europe's common market.
Article 224	Calls for member states to consult to prevent the functioning of the common market from being disrupted from serious internal or international disturbances, such as war.
Article 228	Empowers the Commission to negotiate accords with third states and international bodies.
Article 229	Empowers the Commission to ensure the maintenance of relations with international bodies (such as the UN and GATT) and their specialized organs.
Article 238	Permits the EC to conclude accords with a third state, a union of states, or an international organization. Such accords may involve reciprocal rights and obligations, common action, and special procedures.

I use the original Treaty of Rome article numbers through Chapter 7 of this study to maintain historical continuity. These were renumbered with the Treaty of Amsterdam in 1997, the focus of Chapter 8.

EC sanctions were discussed, but they were rejected in favor of national action. Since then, several articles of the Rome Treaty have been invoked (more than one article in some cases; see the South Africa example below) in the context of EPC discussions. Articles 113, 223, 224, 228, 229, and 238 were particularly relevant for EPC.

Articles 113 and 228 were often cited when EC and EPC actions were taken parallel to each other and decided with their separate procedures. Article 113 (the common commercial policy) was later invoked to provide a makeshift legal basis for an EPC decision to use EC tools, although there were some doubts as to whether Article 113 could be legally used for political ends. After much heated debate over procedure in the 1980s (provoked by the Iran and Afghanistan crises), Article 113 EC legislation which referred to "discussions in the context of EPC" became standard practice for sanctions; this opened the door to other "interactive" EC/EPC external political actions and the production of "dualist" EC/EPC case law (see below). This was done as much for the sake of functional efficiency as it was to respect appropriate (that is, legal) EC competencies, as EU states grew to realize it would be difficult to ensure compliance with EPC economic measures without EC regulations and the monitoring of member state behavior by the Commission. Eventually, a 1989 EC regulation on controlling weapons-grade chemicals finally provided an acceptable legal formula for EPC/EC procedures to be combined in a single text.[26] These procedural innovations greatly reduced the amount of time it took for EC sanctions to be used; one need only compare the speed of EPC/EC sanctions against the Soviet Union after its invasion of Afghanistan in 1979 (well over a month) with that of sanctions against Iraq in 1990 after its invasion of Kuwait (less than a week).

However, EU states during the time of the London Report still generally preferred to use their economic resources for "soft" political ends (such as the Euro-Arab Dialogue and the CSCE process) rather than for "hard" politics in crisis situations or those with a military/security character. EU foreign ministers still dominated EPC, of course, and at no time did EU governments seriously entertain the involvement of defense ministers within the context of EPC. This would have taken EPC much further down the path toward defense cooperation than several EU states preferred at the time.[27] Similarly, in October 1978 the French instituted informal talks among EU justice ministers about cooperation in criminal cases in an attempt to create *a European judicial space*. However, in June 1980 the Dutch refused to sign a draft treaty to this effect since these efforts were not based on the Rome Treaty but would have been linked to the EC's own legal culture.[28]

EPC norms and the European Court of Justice

These challenges involving the formal (that is, treaty-based rather than custom-based) legalization of EPC at this time are also reflected in the way EU governments effectively kept their foreign policy cooperation outside the jurisdiction of the European Court of Justice (ECJ). As we shall see in the next chapter, while EU governments were somewhat able to accept greater involvement in EPC of the Commission (for the sake of efficiency) and the EP (for the sake of democratic legitimacy), they have long been particularly adverse to the formal "judicialization" of diplomatic processes. EU governments learned their lesson the hard way from

---

[26] Council Regulation (EEC) No. 428/89 of February 20, 1989, OJ L 50/1/1989 (see Nuttall 1992a: 199–207).

[27] The EP first suggested regular meetings of EU defense ministers in 1978, in part to discuss arms sales, procurement, and related matters. This idea was soundly rejected by EU member states. See the draft report for the EP Political Affairs Committee, *PE 78/344 revised*, p. 35 (cited in Hill 1983a: 202, fn.). Member state defense ministers would not be permitted to meet within the EU for another twenty years.

[28] de Schoutheete de Tervarent 1980: 135–37. Talks among EU justice ministers later become part of the EU's third pillar, Justice and Home Affairs cooperation.

several landmark ECJ cases on external relations in the 1970s. One such decision set an important precedent stating that the EC had a right to engage in international affairs wherever it had internal competencies under the Treaty of Rome; another affirmed that all matters of international trade in goods were an exclusive Community competency.[29] The ECJ also ruled that the EC had competency to participate in the establishment of international organizations and to be a member of such organizations.[30] EU states thus found that since the Court does not have a specific policy jurisdiction its rulings could not be predicted or controlled by them. For its part, the Court (like many national courts) is largely a passive actor in foreign policy, given the lack of opportunities for EU states, firms, or citizens to press for litigation in this domain (unlike with many EC policies, typically under Article 177 of the Rome Treaty). Combined with the Court's own unwillingness to demand a greater role in EPC, the result is the absence of a substantial body of EC/EPC case law, although several important rulings helped bridge the legal gap between the EC and EPC. This involves the development of so-called "parallel powers," or "dualist case law," which involves EC competencies (usually Article 113, the common commercial policy).

Also, since EPC did not enjoy legal personality under international law in the same way that the EC does, the years surrounding the London Report saw a proliferation of "mixed agreements" which involved the Commission (representing the EC) and EU member states (representing EPC) as signatories.[31] Although this notion of shared competency (which actually represents shared *sovereignty*) may raise confusion in terms of *international* law, the mixed agreements derived from this principle represent only one of at least five situations where shared competencies are compatible with *Community* law and thus become part of its own legal order.[32] As we shall see in the next chapter, all of the "Europe Agreements" reached with Central and Eastern Europe in the late 1980s were mixed agreements. These pacts represented EPC's increasing capacity to

[29] See *ERTA, EC Commission* v. *EC Council*, Case 22/70 (1971); also Opinion 1/75 of November 11, 1975, *European Court Reports* 1355, and Opinion 1/78 of October 4, 1979, *European Court Reports* 2871.

[30] Opinion 1/76 (1977), *European Court Reports* 741, 756.

[31] Note that the idea of "mixed agreements" is not confined to, and did not originate with, linkages between the EC and EPC. Other agreements involving the EC and individual EU member states as signatories exist.

[32] According to Macleod, Hendry, and Hyett (1996: 63–64), the other four situations are: where shared competencies stem from a treaty article conferring power on the EC; where the EC has potential competence which it has not exercised; where the EC competence arises from the existence of internal rules that set minimum EC standards; and in other areas (such as the protection of intellectual property) where EC and member state competencies (or rights) can coexist without either displacing the other.

overcome its weak standing in international law (compared to that of the EC) while at the same time preserving the central role of EU states in the practice of EPC. In addition, thanks to several other ECJ rulings,[33] the provisions of these and other such "Association Agreements" may have direct effect over EU states (like normal EC legislation), and the councils or committees established by such agreements may be able to produce legally binding decisions (i.e., they can makes their own rules) if the agreement so specifies, even in the absence of corresponding EC legislation.[34] Like the ECJ rulings noted above, these developments suggest a far greater potential for legal-constitutional (and even supranational) processes to affect European foreign policy than one might otherwise expect of EPC's treaty-based provisions.[35] Still, the involvement of the Court itself should not be overemphasized, as none of these decisions directly imposed on the decision-making processes of EPC; at best they merely made EU states recognize the relevance, legitimacy, effectiveness, and even supremacy of EC rules during their EPC deliberations. Moreover, EU states took deliberate steps to insulate themselves in EPC from the actions of the ECJ, as we shall see in later chapters.

Substantive European foreign policy norms

The procedural norms discussed above were intended to help EU states improve their understanding of each other, forge common foreign policy positions, and, if possible, take joint action on important issues in world politics. Such positions and actions comprise the substantive (or regulatory) norms of EPC; they helped define and orient "Europe" as a collective entity toward the outside world. These EPC norms or policy orientations emerged in much the same way as the procedural norms: through constant interaction, debate, and trial-and-error learning. This process often involved linking new substantive policies to previous ones, and defining such policies in terms of the more general statements of EPC's goals as reflected in the Luxembourg, Copenhagen, and London Reports (among other sources, such as declarations of the European Council). These processes are also important because they challenge

---

[33] Case 181/73 R. & V. Haegman v. Belgian State (1974), European Court Reports 449; and Case C-192/89, S. Z. Sevince v. Staatssecretaris van Justitie (1990), European Court Reports 3461.

[34] This finding is also consistent with international legal practice concerning the councils or commissions established by international treaties. It now appears to extend even to certain decisions of the European Council, whether formally ratified by member states or not. See Curtin and van Ooik 1994; McGoldrick 1997: 183–84.

[35] For more details, see Pescatore 1979; Govaere and Eeckhout 1992; Cheyne 1994; Sack 1995.

realist-based views of cooperation, which stress the continuity of power and interests and the dominance of security concerns over all other considerations. Although EU states clearly had (and still have) individual national positions when EPC was formed, and they often act to protect their positions, this situation gradually changed as EPC expanded into new territory. Over time, EPC's policy agenda became far more coherent and extensive, and included many issues which cannot be reduced to concerns about security. This can be seen by an examination of its substantive norms, which reflected an increasing degree of cooperation and a contraction of the *domaines réservés*. In the previous chapter, this cooperation was largely described in terms of "negative integration": EPC was used to eliminate barriers of uncertainty or mistrust among EU states in foreign policy. Around the time of the London Report, however, we start to see more manifestations of "positive integration," ranging from common positions, to joint actions implemented on a national basis, then finally to joint actions involving EC resources and competencies.

The emergence and effects of substantive EPC norms

This section focuses on EPC policies or actions designed to serve certain collective goals or interests of EU member states. Since there was no formally institutionalized representation of European political interests apart from those of member states, it may be tempting to consider EPC's substantive policies or norms as the sum of its members' interests. Any EPC policy would reflect a "lowest-common-denominator" consensual position, which had often been forged by the state holding the rotating EU presidency. As we saw above, however, this was not necessarily the case. Instead, EPC involved a constant process of collective interest definition which extended beyond the original common EU foreign policy positions. Once established, these interests accumulated and they were increasingly used as reference points by EU member states. To be sure, respect for EPC procedures was greater than that for substantive EPC policies, but in neither case could the norms associated with these processes be understood as mere lowest-common-denominator, minimally cooperative decisions. In addition, EPC's attempts to forge substantive policies on various subjects proved to be useful experiments for two reasons. First, each attempt helped to clarify, codify, and express what had been Europe's collective position regarding foreign affairs up to that point. Second, the heated debates surrounding these attempts clearly indicated that high profile Intergovernmental Conferences were perhaps not the best way to determine what EPC stood for; instead, regular position statements on current issues forged by EPC insiders came to represent the substantive content of EU foreign policy. The grand statements made by EU governments during summit conferences rarely involved much more than announcing basic ideas or values with which most liberal democratic states could agree.

The EU's first post-EPC attempt to specify European interests, the "Document on the European Identity" of December 1973, clearly illustrates this point. This document was intended to help define a set of general principles to guide the EU's external relations and future development. Not surprisingly, it stressed broad themes and common values such as interdependence, representative democracy, the rule of law, social justice, and human rights. Among other things, EU states also pledged to continue their experiment in foreign policy cooperation, expand their network of relationships, and transform "the whole complex of their relations into a European Union by the end of the present decade." All of these principles were subject to redefinition in the future, in the context of developing a "genuinely European foreign policy."[36]

Although the grand aims of this document, such as creating a European Union by the end of the 1970s, fell short at the time, EPC did make progress in specific areas. In the absence of agreement at the summit level, and with the exclusion of EC organizations such as the Commission and the Court, this growing body of substantive EPC policies was codified in much the same way as the codification of EPC procedural norms. In particular, at the initiative of the first British EU presidency in 1977, EPC participants decided to compile their substantive EPC texts from each presidency into a permanent *recueil* ("collection"; see Wessels 1982: 6; Nuttall 1992a: 147). Although the *recueil* expanded in unforeseen ways over the years, EPC was first and foremost a defensive measure to protect the EC. As such, it could be considered in terms of negative integration, or even as a "regime of common aversion."[37] In other words, EU member states generally agreed on the need to shield the still-evolving EU from unilateral foreign policy actions of its own members. This "damage-limitation" function has been continually recognized since the Luxembourg Report; it also justified the role of the Commission to give its views on how EPC might affect the EC (see Chapter 6). EU states gradually realized that radically independent or selfish foreign policies threatened to disrupt their hard-won efforts regarding economic integration.

[36] "Document on the European Identity Published by the Nine Foreign Ministers," (Copenhagen, December 14, 1973).

[37] On regimes of common aversion, see Stein 1983: 125–27. The role of EPC as a means to protect the EC is described in detail in Bonvicini 1982.

Beyond this general damage-limitation norm, many other positions and actions emerged to form EPC's own *communauté de vue* on important foreign policy questions. Although the expansion, clarification, and codification of these substantive EPC norms was difficult, it still occurred and helped bring Europe closer to a state of positive integration, or even political union. It is impossible to discuss all of them here; instead they might be classified as sets of collective values or policy orientations surrounding a geographic and/or functional domain. At first, EPC typically emphasized long-term goals with third countries or regions closest to the EU (hence the CSCE and the Euro-Arab Dialogue). In line with the aims of the "Document on the European Identity," these plans generally emphasized progressive conflict resolution as opposed to crisis management. In part to distinguish itself from US foreign policy positions, EPC declarations on these issues showed what behaviors or principles, if followed by outside interlocutors, would result in a favorable response from the EU.

For example, EPC's substantive policies in the Middle East by the late 1970s affirmed that peace in the region depended on Israel's withdrawal from the occupied territories, defended the recognition of the rights of the Palestinian people, and perhaps most controversially, argued that the Palestine Liberation Organization should represent the Palestinians in all international peace efforts.[38] This laid the groundwork for the most comprehensive EU policy statement regarding the Middle East: the 1980 Venice Declaration. This was perhaps the most important (but still rare) contribution to EPC by the European Council, where the Middle East was a favorite topic for discussion (Wallace 1983a: 395). The Declaration supported the right of all states in the region, including Israel, to exist within secure frontiers and affirmed the right of the Palestinian people to self-determination.[39] To reconcile these seemingly contradictory goals, the Ten also confirmed their hopes for an international peace conference on the issue, rather than the more piecemeal solution offered by the US at the time, which involved only Israel and Egypt. Moreover, the EU followed up these political statements with more EC economic aid to the territories occupied by Israel since 1967, a clear example of enhanced consistency between EC competencies and European foreign policy.

A desire to distinguish EPC from America was also reflected in Europe's substantive policies concerning the CSCE process. Here the EU placed East–West security relations within a broader framework that

[38] See the "Communiqué Issued after the First Meeting of the General Committee of the Euro-Arab Dialogue" (Luxembourg, May 20, 1976).

[39] "Declaration by the 17th European Council on the Euro-Arab Dialogue, Lebanon, Afghanistan, and the Situation in the Middle East" (Venice, June 12/13, 1980), or the "Venice Declaration."

also included arms reductions, human rights, and strengthening mutual trust and understanding. This approach, often criticized by the US during the Reagan era, was especially tested following the 1979 Soviet invasion of Afghanistan, which directly violated two fundamental Helsinki principles: restraint from the use of force in foreign policy and respect for the right of people to equality and self-determination. Despite Soviet obstinacy and continued violations of human rights, the Ten pressed their solution in the form of a two-part conference involving the UN and the CSCE. This was to take place in the context of a gradual expansion of rights and freedoms within the Soviet bloc.[40]

The evolution of EPC's policy toward South Africa offers some additional lessons regarding the evolution of substantive norms. The EU expressed its total dedication to the dismantling of apartheid through peaceful means, and to replacing it with a democratic, non-racial system of government. As usual, EPC's first statement on this issue was fairly weak; it merely condemned apartheid and stressed opposition to racial discrimination. The EU did, however, state that it would do everything possible to promote democratic majority rule and non-racial government for the peoples of South Africa.[41] Following this opening, in a series of increasingly bold statements, the EU stressed that the state of emergency in South Africa must be lifted, that all political prisoners must be freed, and that the ban on political parties must be lifted. To encourage a more uniform approach to this issue, in 1977 the EU instituted a novel policy tool, the "Code of Conduct for Community Companies with Interests in South Africa."[42] Although the Code was implemented on a national basis, it was an important step forward for EPC substantive norms since it linked a general common interest (protection of human rights) to a clear foreign policy orientation (anti-apartheid) supported by specific behavioral standards (involving EU governments and their countries' firms in South Africa). When this action did not bring about the desired reforms, the EU progressively added stronger measures to its policy through the 1980s. These included both restrictive measures and more positive inducements, plus a reinforcement of the Code of Conduct.[43]

[40] EC Foreign Ministers, "CSCE: Opening Statement on Behalf of the Ten" (Madrid, October 27, 1981).

[41] EC Foreign Ministers, "Statement by the Foreign Ministers on the Situation in Africa" (London, April 18, 1977).

[42] The Code is mentioned in the "Report on European Union Submitted by the Nine Foreign Ministers to the 9th European Council" (Brussels, December 5/6, 1977). Also see the Irish EU presidency's "Press Statement by the Council Presidency (Ireland) on the Code of Conduct in South Africa" (November 20, 1984).

[43] See the "Code of Conduct for Companies from the EC with Subsidiaries, Branches, or Representation in South Africa as Revised by the Ministers for Foreign Affairs of the Ten Countries of the European Community and Spain and Portugal" (Brussels, November 19, 1985).

EPC's South African policy is also noteworthy because of its increased relationship to the EC. Here, EPC actions eventually involved EC tools and procedures after much debate, showing the growing ability of EU states to bridge the legal gap between the EC and EPC. In South Africa, EPC was used as far more than a coordination instrument (unlike in the Middle East), and the use of EC instruments for political ends in South Africa expanded in new ways between 1977 and the end of the apartheid regime in 1991. Over a period nearly spanning the history of EPC itself, actions against apartheid ranged from diplomatic démarches, to EPC declarations, the original Code of Conduct (1977–84), the joint initiatives of 1985, regional funds, the first use of European Coal and Steel Community rules as an EPC tool to partially ban imports of steel and iron in 1986, and finally, restrictions on certain new investments and imports of Krugerrands.[44] In particular, EPC/EC interaction over South Africa eventually led to a Council Regulation, a Council Decision, and an ECSC decision.[45]

EPC's Central America initiative also reflected its emerging ability to back up principled declarations with more specific policy orientations and substantive behavioral norms. In this case, the EU expressed its support to achieve peace in the region in accordance with the Contadora Group's[46] objectives of September 9, 1983, which expressed the belief that a solution must emerge from the region itself (and not be imposed from the outside; i.e., by the US) and must guarantee peace, democracy, and respect for human rights.[47] In addition to the institutionalization of an annual political dialogue with the region, beginning with an historic meeting in San José, Costa Rica, on September 28/29, 1984,[48] EPC's efforts were later enhanced with several Community-based trade and economic assistance agreements to encourage regional integration.[49] In particular, the EC gave the states of the Central American Common

[44] On South Africa, see van Praag 1982b; Holland 1987, 1988, 1995a, 1995b, 1997b.

[45] EC Regulation 3302/86 prohibiting the import of Krugerrands; EC Decision 86/517 prohibiting new investments in South Africa; and ECSC Decision 86/459 prohibiting certain iron and steel imports (Holland 1988; Nuttall 1992a: 263–64).

[46] Colombia, Mexico, Panama, and Venezuela.

[47] These principles are outlined in the "Conclusions of the 26th European Council on the Solemn Declaration on European Union, Poland, the CSCE Follow-Up Meeting, the Middle East, and Central America" (Stuttgart, June 17–19, 1983).

[48] From the "Joint Communiqué of the Conference of Foreign Ministers between the European Community and its Member States, Portugal, Spain, the States of Central America and the Contadora States" (San José, Costa Rica, September 28/29, 1984).

[49] See the "Joint Political Communiqué of the Luxembourg Ministerial Conference on Political Dialogue and Economic Cooperation Between the Countries of the European Community, Spain, and Portugal, and the Countries of Central America and of Contadora" (Luxembourg, November 11/12, 1984); and the "Statement by the Twelve on the Meeting of the Foreign Ministers of the Contadora Group" (Caraballeda, Venezuela, January 20, 1986).

Market (CACM),[50] plus Panama, a five-year non-preferential economic agreement. It was based on Articles 113 and 235 of the EC Treaty, making it binding on EU states and subject to interpretation by the European Court of Justice (Coignez 1992: 105).

In addition, where the political dialogue was negotiated by the EU presidency, the economic agreement was negotiated by the Commission (on the basis of a mandate from the Council of Ministers); thus, both the Central American and South African initiatives especially reaffirmed Europe's ability to achieve greater consistency in its external relations, and also brought the Commission closer to EPC (see Chapter 6). Finally, the political agreement represented a precedent for rule-setting in the sense that it was the first time that a political dialogue had been initiated by a formal act, the "Final Act of 1985." This represented the highest expression of political support by the EU, although it was not legally binding in terms of international law in the same way that the EC's economic agreement with the CACM had been (Nuttall 1986: 328). Still, the Central American initiative was notable for three reasons: First, no EU state had significant interests, economic or political, in the region so as to push for EPC action for unilateral reasons.[51] Indeed, for many EU states the rule was unabashed indifference toward Central America. Second, by becoming involved here, the EU directly confronted two long-standing principles of US foreign policy: the Monroe Doctrine and American desires to keep communism out of the Western Hemisphere. By generally agreeing that problems with communist insurgents should not be considered an East–West conflict but rather reflected more fundamental socioeconomic inequalities, the EU provided a welcome economic-based solution to America's use of military instruments. Third, it is important because the Central Americans themselves turned toward the EU precisely because they wished to escape from US dominance and interference.[52] The EU eschewed a military solution and presented itself as a non-ideological, civilian power with the best interests of the Central American states in mind, a posture that made the Europeans increasingly attractive in the region (Smith 1995).

Beyond the policies mentioned above, many other discussions in the framework of EPC enabled EU states to bridge previously divisive cleavages over a number of specific issues, increasingly in line with the general

---

[50] Costa Rica, El Salvador, Guatemala, Honduras, and Nicaragua.

[51] Also note that EPC's Central American initiative began ten years before Portugal and Spain joined the EU, the two states that shared stronger interests in the region than other EU states because of their historical ties.

[52] The same might be said of the EU–Mexico Free Trade Agreement, negotiated in the 1990s.

principles (human rights, democracy, rule of law, etc.) discussed above. These issues include North–South conflicts, the question of ending colonialism while promoting development, the debate between justice and human rights versus economics and strategy, and many specific cleavages over tactics (such as rewards versus punishments). The collective positions that emerged from these debates were eventually codified in EPC reports and treaties as substantive norms. They also laid the foundation for more substantive common positions and joint actions under the CFSP, as we shall see in Chapter 7.

EPC and European security

The area of security deserves special mention, as it constituted one of the most important *domaines réservés* of several EU states for a variety of reasons. The memory of the failed attempts regarding the European Defense Community made most EU states unwilling to provoke directly a new debate over the issue. A number of EU states felt such discussions should be handled by NATO, and/or they thought that the Community's external reach should be strictly limited to economic, and if necessary, "soft" political affairs, such as human rights. A desire to respect the views of neutral European states, whether EU members or not, further complicated this question. Even though Article 224 of the Rome Treaty obliged EU member states to consult each other when considering any unilateral action on security issues which may impact on the functioning of the EC, such questions were rarely the object of intensive discussion in EPC during its first decade. However, the CSCE process represented a major step toward the inclusion of more security issues on the EPC agenda, as did certain aspects of Middle East affairs involving the security of Europe's oil supplies.

With these positive experiences, and after the negative experiences of the Iran and Afghanistan crises where EU states could not easily agree on collective action, the time came to codify what understandings had been achieved in security affairs. The 1981 London Report finally admitted the necessity of discussing in EPC "foreign policy questions bearing on the political aspects of security,"[53] which clearly helped to undermine the security taboo, although this final wording still reflected Irish concerns about the potential for military/defense affairs to be incorporated into EPC. This decision was quickly implemented, and in May 1981 the Gymnich meeting of the Ten in Venlo included discussion of the political aspects of European security for the first time (Pijpers 1983: 176). The

[53] London Report, Part I.

European Council also showed an increasing tendency to discuss security issues during this period, often during dinner or fireside chats afterwards. Topics included relations between superpowers, Afghanistan, the NATO "double-track" decision on Euro-missiles, and internal conflicts in non-member states (such as Cyprus, Turkey, Spain, Portugal, Africa, and Central/South America; see Bulmer and Wessels 1987: 65–66). Several working groups at the expert level also began to discuss terrorism inside and outside of EPC by the mid-1970s. This eventually resulted in the creation in 1976 of a much weaker (than EPC) intergovernmental framework known as "Trevi" (Hill 1988b). Since Trevi, unlike EPC, was not made part of the SEA and overlapped with other complex domestic legal issues (such as crime and immigration),[54] it developed on an alternative track from EU foreign policy (though one closely linked to the EC) and eventually led to the creation of the "Third Pillar" of the EU: Justice and Home Affairs. Thus, only its external dimensions will be considered in the rest of this study.

Two other topics exemplify EPC's growing attention to security affairs: military/defense-related issues and non-proliferation. Regarding defense, although it took a long time for EPC to make progress in this area, gradually the taboo against discussing military matters was broken. As we might expect, EPC generally concentrated on the use of sanctions (with corresponding EC competencies) rather than military deployments, to support its emerging security and defense policy. For example, Article 113 was applied in the cases of the Iran hostage crisis and the Soviet Union's invasion of Afghanistan, while Article 224 was applied in the Falklands Islands conflict.[55] The Falklands case was particularly noteworthy, as it was the first time that territory claimed by an EU member state was attacked with military force. Although several EU states expressed reservations about British policy in this area, and two EU states (Denmark and Ireland) bowed out of the sanctions regime once the crisis turned into war, most observers (and certainly the Argentinians) were surprised at how quickly the EU threw its support behind the UK in the form of political statements and economic sanctions. And, as I have noted elsewhere, they apparently did this without reverting to a bargain involving EC agricultural prices and the use of sanctions.[56] Yet most overt military crises were still hard to handle in EPC as member states diverged over the means and ends of defense policy (and defense ministers of course

[54] Also note that Article 220 of the Rome Treaty provides for negotiations among EU states on a number of civil law questions (Freestone 1985).
[55] For details, see Holland 1991a.
[56] Edwards 1984; and Stavridis and Hill 1996. For the bargaining-based hypothesis, see Martin 1992.

were not permitted to meet in Council or EPC). This disagreement directly led to the "reactivation" of the Western European Union (WEU) in 1984 as only a quasi-defense arm of the EU (since Denmark, Ireland, and Greece were not WEU members), and it increasingly challenged the ability of EPC to handle the rapid changes in the Soviet Union in the late 1980s.[57] However, the WEU did provide the EU with a "ready-made" defense-related institution (albeit a very weak one) to graft onto the CFSP in 1991, as we shall see in Chapter 7.

Concerning EU non-proliferation policies, EPC began to play a central role in governing increasingly complex developments in nuclear technology. While EU states clearly (if reluctantly) recognized their dependence on the US nuclear umbrella,[58] they also initiated their own efforts to halt the proliferation of nuclear weapons in accordance with the Nuclear Non-Proliferation Treaty (NPT). This is perhaps the one area where a common security problem encouraged EU states to pursue a common foreign policy, as they all more or less exhibited a common sensitivity to the threat of nuclear proliferation on the EU's southern flank. Although they disagreed on several issues regarding nuclear technology, EU states managed to confront many of these questions within the framework of EPC, and they created a number of substantive rules governing such questions. To a large extent, these efforts replaced the Commission's own legal authority in nuclear matters (by virtue of its role in the European Atomic Energy Community, or Euratom).[59]

The EU's disputes (chiefly between France and the Commission) over the proliferation of nuclear weapons outside the EU led to a novel solution: putting the entire issue under the control of EPC, rather than the EC. This rare example of "competency transference" from the EC to EPC led the Dutch and British in 1981 to encourage the successful creation of an EPC working group on nuclear non-proliferation, which eventually managed to set down explicit rules about transfers of nuclear technology.[60] As Müller notes (1992: 195), this act was a watershed in the evolution of EPC for three reasons: first, it represented a major breach

---

[57] On the reactivation of the WEU, see Duke 1996; and Jopp 1997.

[58] For example, the "Document on the European Identity" notes that EU states who are members of the Atlantic alliance "consider that in the present circumstances there is no alternative to the security provided by the nuclear weapons of the United States and by the presence of North American forces in Europe."

[59] Euratom is one of the few original EC policy areas of the Rome Treaty where cooperation within the Community remained almost completely stagnant. Rather than nurture a Europe-wide nuclear-energy industry, Euratom did little more than handle non-commercial tasks such as materials testing and nuclear safety experiments.

[60] This was the "Statement by the Ten on Non-Proliferation" (Brussels, November 20, 1984).

of the taboo against discussing security matters in EPC; second, the continuous discussion of the issue "almost automatically led the group to discussions of an ever wider area connected to its core mandate; and socialized national bureaucrats to think about proliferation in terms of coordinated policy"; and third, since EPC was controlled by EU foreign ministries, they were able to enmesh themselves in national decision-making on non-proliferation policy. Thanks to their involvement in EPC, EU foreign ministries thus usurped some of the authority of other relevant national authorities, such as atomic energy commissions, economics and energy ministries, defense ministries, technology ministries, and so on. However, EU states remained sharply divided over the idea of a Comprehensive Test Ban Treaty and the issue of international plutonium storage. Thus, the next stage of progress on this issue came around the time of the SEA; it will be considered in Chapter 6.

In sum, and except for overt military policies, EPC thus quietly and persistently fostered a major expansion and codification of the EU's foreign affairs agenda, in both geographic and functional terms, and a simultaneous contraction of the *domaines réservés*. The veto was used less frequently; even when it was attempted, the system rarely "gave up" on important matters. Officials simply wore each other down with arguments until previously taboo subjects were treated as appropriate topics for discussion. In this manner the scope of EPC steadily expanded, so that virtually no subject was completely off-limits by the time of the Treaty on European Union. Moreover, under the terms of the Greece accession to the EU in 1981, new member states were required to accept EPC procedures when joining the EU, a condition later made part of the SEA.[61] Finally, this expansion of EPC's procedural and substantive norms helped to institutionalize the involvement of EC organizations in EU foreign policy, a topic explored in the next chapter.

[61] Greece's accession to the EC/EPC is discussed in Nuttall 1992a: 173–74.

6   Organizations and European foreign policy

Once EPC began generating its own norms and rules in the late 1970s, the stage was set for a far more comprehensive approach to EU foreign policy cooperation a decade later: the CFSP. Before examining the CFSP, however, we must digress for a moment to consider the role of permanent organizations in EU foreign policy. These organizations comprise budgets, professional staffs, buildings and facilities, unique policy goals, and a host of other features which affect both policy performance and institutionalization. As I noted in Chapter 3, although the Luxembourg Report briefly acknowledged the Commission and the European Parliament (EP) as supporting players in EPC, most EU states generally preferred EPC to remain a decentralized system dominated by national governments. Their strong preference for intergovernmental foreign policy cooperation created a barrier to both the involvement of existing EC organizations and the creation of any permanent organization to administer EPC.

However, this barrier gradually broke down and EC organizations began to affect the development of European foreign policy cooperation.[1] Organizations that have achieved some level of permanency, legitimacy, and competent authority are more likely to influence the policy process, thus increasing the prospects for cooperative outcomes and institutional growth. Organizations have the capacity for coordinated, purposive action; as their permanent staffs are established, as their institutional memory develops in a particular policy area, and as policy norms are preserved and followed by these organizations, cooperative outcomes will be affected. This may be especially true when organizations become involved in decentralized systems such as EPC. Here, EU states faced a dilemma: bargaining over outcomes was not an option, consensus and equality among EU states were especially prized, and governments genuinely hoped that they could share the burden of administering EPC

---

[1] In this and subsequent chapters I use the terms "organization," "bureaucracy," and "agency" interchangeably to refer to the permanent organizations involved in European foreign policy.

(through the mechanism of six-month rotating presidencies) despite vast differences in their experience and capabilities. These conflicting factors became increasingly strained with the expansion of Europe's foreign policy agenda, leading EU states to allow a greater role for EC organizations in the process.

At the same time, EC organizations (chiefly the Commission) were gradually developing their own interests and capabilities in the realm of external political relations, making them more valuable actors in the EPC process. These two streams of activity gradually came together so that EC organizations were able to develop a more independent influence on state behavior, by providing policy-relevant information, implementing policy, and reinforcing practices over time, not just acting as a passive channel for the sharing of information between states. Greater involvement of EC organizations in EPC also raised new institutional conflicts and questions that required reconciliation. When these roles were legally codified, as with the Single European Act (or SEA, the subject of this chapter), or enhanced, as with the Treaty on European Union (or TEU, the subject of the next chapter), the EU's institutional apparatus for foreign policy reached a new status, with corresponding effects on policy outcomes.

Before turning to the specific organizations involved in EU foreign policy, we should note several general points about the opportunities and limitations faced by those actors in this domain. One important factor is that the *environment* within which these actors operate is extremely fluid and complex. Foreign policy in general requires a steady attention and adaptation to constantly changing external circumstances, making it difficult for organizations (or any other actors) to adopt a rigid set of standard operating procedures applicable to different situations. EU foreign policy in particular is fairly decentralized (compared to the Community method of policymaking), decision-making procedures are not as routinized as in domestic polities (or in other EC policy domains), and overall guidance regularly shifts among the major players (EU states) in the form of rotating presidencies. Although these characteristics often make it difficult to discern a systematic, consistent role for EC actors in foreign policy, the system permits such actors to make effective use of access points, windows of opportunity, and inherent uncertainties in the process. Once these openings are exploited and "locked in" as precedents (or norms) for future behavior, it becomes difficult for member states to shut EC actors out again.[2]

We should also note that the *goals* of EC actors are often described as "pro-integrationist," which enhances their stature in the integration

---

[2] On these lock-in and feedback effects, see North 1990: 7.

project (as theories of bureaucratic politics suggest) but also puts them at risk if, in the view of EU member states, they exceed their authority or capabilities (Ross 1995: 14). Pollack (1998) calls this a "competence-maximizing" agenda, while Garrett and Tsebelis (1996: 280) argue that the preferences of the Commission and the EP are more extreme than any other actor since their very existence depends on the preservation of the EU. More specifically, EC organizations are primarily concerned with proposing, implementing, and monitoring compliance with EU-wide legislation. They are the agents to whom the principals (EU states) delegate authority to carry out these common goals. Although the principals have a number of administrative and oversight mechanisms at their disposal to control the agents, under certain conditions these mechanisms falter. Such conditions include the complexity of the issue-area, conflicting interests of the principals, the priority of some EU policies over national ones, and the high costs of monitoring or sanctioning the behavior of EC organizations (Pollack 1997). EU foreign policy involves all of these conditions, and they may permit EC actors a greater role in the foreign policy process than EU member states might otherwise prefer or expect.

The use of such principal-agent models helps us avoid two extreme views of organizations: one where such actors have virtually no influence (intergovernmentalism as an ideal type), and one where they can act as "runaway bureaucracies" against the desires of their creators (supranational institutionalism as an ideal type). Although the line between "influence" and "autonomy" can be hard to discern, we can still rely on some of the insights of principal-agent analysis. However, applying this model to European foreign policy involves certain qualifications, for three reasons. First, EU states did not formally delegate authority to EC agencies until the TEU; before that, EC agencies provided input to EPC on only a limited basis. Although the Commission and Parliament were mentioned in EPC reports, the language was vague enough to ensure that, on a practical basis, member states could include or exclude these organizations as they saw fit. Second, at no point did they establish a powerful, central bureaucracy for EPC. Member states could agree on only a small secretariat; this decision was not even reached until the system had been operating for sixteen years. Third, not all EC organizations themselves wanted a greater role in EPC. The Commission often was (and is) far more concerned about protecting its place in Community affairs than with extending its reach in EPC, and (as we saw in the previous chapter) the European Court of Justice (ECJ) did not attempt to revolutionize EU foreign policy with a series of path-breaking legal decisions on EPC. Only the EP has consistently attempted to expand its influence in EU foreign policy, a goal it has met with modest success.

The rest of this chapter explores the role of EC organizations in EPC in more detail. I first provide some general historical context on this subject, leading up to the codification of EC organizational roles with the SEA in 1986. As the ECJ was covered in the previous chapter, in later sections of this chapter I explain the changing roles of three other permanent organizations in EPC: the Commission, the EPC Secretariat, and the European Parliament.[3] These changes led to a greater role for EC organizations in the CFSP under the terms of the Maastricht Treaty, as we shall see in the next chapter.

Organizations and EPC: from the London Report to the Single European Act

While outside observers may still argue about the impact of EC actors on state sovereignty in certain policy areas, EU member governments are certainly convinced about the power of the Community's bureaucratic machinery. This conviction is clearly reflected in the bitter ideological disputes over the extent to which EC organizations should be included in certain policy domains, particularly those involving foreign affairs. Not surprisingly, then, considering the sensitivity and open-ended nature of EPC as an issue-area, member states have continually argued about a clear definition – as reflected in EPC reports or treaties – of the role of EC actors in this domain. For the same reasons most EU states also resisted the establishment of any permanent bureaucracy for EPC during most of its history.

However, as EPC began to expand, EU governments realized that their cooperation would become more consistent, if not efficient, if they could draw upon some resources of the EC. This realization came about via three general processes. First, in the face of growing political and economic interdependence it became increasingly impossible for the EU to formulate coherent external policies while insisting that EPC and EC procedures be kept separate. Second, on a more practical level it became difficult to coordinate regularly the logistics of two sets of procedures as the EC's own external relations expanded into new areas. Particularly when the EU began to create complex politico-economic package deals with other regions of vital importance to it, or during crisis situations where time was at a premium, ministers and diplomats realized they simply could not afford to duplicate their efforts in order to maintain an artificial, ideological distinction between the EC and EPC. Finally, as

---

[3] Also, I generally stress institutionalized organizational roles in my analysis of EPC, not individual personalities (such as Commissioners).

the only formal organizations involved in both EC and EPC on a regular basis, the Commission and the EP acted to take advantage of openings in the EC–EPC policy processes and play more important roles than might be inferred by the dry language of EPC reports.[4] At first this activity could be defined in negative terms (i.e., stressing the damage-limitation function of EPC); the Commission could act only to help prevent EPC from interfering with Community procedures and policies. Later this involvement took on a more positive character, as when the Commission or EP pushed for more coherent or ambitious policies than EU member states may have desired. Still, in terms of codifying these activities in formal EPC reports, there were enough differences of opinion to prevent any consistent role for EC actors within EPC, as we have seen in previous chapters. Given these problems of interpretation it was not until 1986–87 that Title III of the SEA legalized EU foreign policy cooperation as a treaty for the first time. Even this document did not resolve debates over certain aspects of the EPC policy process (and its very legality vis-à-vis the EC), which had to be addressed with the TEU. These general issues regarding the SEA will be examined in the rest of this section; the specific reforms concerning EC organizations in EPC will be discussed later in the chapter.

EPC and the Single European Act

The origins of the SEA's provisions on EPC can be found in the 1983 Stuttgart Declaration, which attempted to take the provisions of the London Report a step further.[5] After much heated discussion over basic terminology (reflecting a sensitivity to the binding nature of Title III), EU member states were still referred to as "High Contracting Parties" (not EC members) in the SEA, emphasizing the *de jure* intergovernmental character of EPC. According to Title I of the SEA, the EC was still based on the EC treaties; EPC was still based on its various reports and the "practices gradually established among the member states" (the *coutumier*). The SEA also referred to "cooperation in the sphere of foreign policy" (EPC) in the hopes of forming "a European foreign policy" rather than stating the goal of a *common* foreign policy. There also was no

---

[4] Of course, the Committee of Permanent Representatives (COREPER) to the EU and the Secretariat-General of the Council of Ministers have permanent bureaucratic staffs of their own and could be treated as organizational actors. However, their roles in EU foreign policy were not formally enhanced until the TEU (see Chapter 7).

[5] For example, see the "Document on the European Identity Published by the Nine Foreign Ministers" (Copenhagen, December 14, 1973) and the "Solemn Declaration on European Union" (Stuttgart Declaration, June 19, 1983).

Table 6.1 *EPC according to the Single European Act (February 1986)*

Major changes since the London Report appear in **boldface.**

Component	Actors and functions
Intergovernmental direction	**The European Council (heads of state and government, plus the president of the Commission) meets at least twice a year.**
	EU foreign ministers meet at least four times a year. Such meetings will focus on taking decisions for future action.
	EU presidency state chairs meetings, represents EPC abroad, oversees implementation of conclusions, **and initiates action.**
	Procedures for EPC/third country contacts via EU presidency or Troika.
	Informal "Gymnich" meetings of EU foreign ministers.
	Crisis procedures for ministerial meetings, Political Committee, and heads of mission in third countries.
Transgovernmental support	Political Committee: preparation of ministerial meetings, long-term studies.
	European Correspondents: liaison between capitals, **monitoring implementation of EPC.**
	Working groups: geographical/functional analyses for EPC, including potential crisis areas.
	EU embassies: consultation on EPC matters in capitals of member states, in third countries, and in delegations to international conferences and organizations.
	COREU: encrypted telex network to share information.
	Establishment of EPC Secretariat based in Brussels, to work under the authority of the EU presidency.
	Joint reports from EU heads of mission in third countries at the request of the Political Committee or on their own initiative.
	Regular meetings among heads of mission within the capitals of the Ten.
	Administrative support for EU presidency by officials seconded from preceding and succeeding EU presidencies (the Troika).
	Other administrative support to be provided to the EU presidency as needed.
EC involvement	Commission fully associated with the proceedings of EPC.
	Colloquy four times a year with EP Political Committee, and annual report on progress on EPC. EU presidency answers EP questions about EPC and makes speeches to the EP. Informal meetings with the EP. President of the European Council also makes speeches to the EP.
	Council informed through COREPER about EPC conclusions which might impact the work of the EC.
	EPC meetings can be held on the occasion of EC ministerial meetings.
	Ministers able to use EPC to prepare studies on political aspects of problems under examination in the EC.

Table 6.1 (*cont.*)

Component	Actors and functions
	External EC policies and EPC policies must be consistent. The EU presidency and the Commission shall ensure such consistency.
	European Court of Justice excluded from EPC.
Obligations	States consult on all questions of foreign policy.
	Formulation of medium and long-term common positions.
	Implementation of joint actions.
	General rule not to take up final positions without consultation with EPC partners.
	Possible to discuss in EPC certain foreign policy questions bearing on the political aspects of security. **Coordination of positions bearing on the political and economic aspects of security.**
	Possibility of political dialogues with third countries and with regional groupings, as necessary.
	General rule to avoid any action or position which impairs the EU's effectiveness as a cohesive force in international relations or within international organizations.
	General rule to refrain from impeding the formation of a consensus and the joint action which it could produce.
	General rule that in international institutions where not all EU states participate (i.e., the UN Security Council), those EU states which do participate shall take account of EPC positions.
	EPC declarations must be called to the attention of third states by the local representative of the Ten.
	States must preserve the confidentiality of EPC.

stated obligation to achieve common positions, only that member states should "endeavor" to achieve this end.[6]

Despite these limitations, the SEA did include the most complex provisions on foreign policy cooperation since EPC was created, involving the intergovernmental, transgovernmental, and rule-governed aspects of the system. The SEA's major provisions on foreign policy are summarized in Table 6.1.

Three aspects of the SEA are especially important to EU foreign policy. First, it slightly reinforced the intergovernmental character of EPC,

---

[6] Article 30.1 and Article 30.2(d), SEA. Wallace (1983b: 6) argues that a general commitment to a "common foreign policy" was acceptable as an unspecific aim to all member states (except Denmark) by 1980, but this goal was watered down in the SEA.

particularly by codifying the composition and role of the European Council along the lines of what had been set down in the Solemn Declaration
on European Union. Its tasks would involve defining the guidelines for
integration in general and advocating particular policies; initiating cooperation in new areas; assuring the consistency of EPC and EC policies;
and issuing declarations on foreign relations. These tasks imply policy
monitoring as well (Bulmer and Wessels 1987: 76–80), although the European Council still does not have the resources to carry out this function
effectively. Although it was made legal with the SEA, the European Council was not mentioned in the section on the EC and would remain linked
to, but legally separate from, the EC (like EPC itself). In addition, EU
foreign ministers' EPC meetings in Brussels and Luxembourg could now
be held in tandem with the General Affairs Council (GAC) of the EC,
another small challenge to the procedural distinction between EC and
EPC affairs. As the same (foreign) ministers attended both sets of meetings, EPC business was discussed at both monthly GAC meetings and
EPC summits by the 1980s (Nuttall 1992a: 14–15).

Second, the EPC transgovernmental network was slightly enhanced.
Recognizing the need for stronger links between the EC and EPC, the
SEA negotiators considered that the Political Committee could be moved
permanently to Brussels. The Political Directors themselves had second
thoughts; they did not want the press to invade their privacy and they
wanted to maintain their separation from the EC.[7] Instead, the SEA
merely provided that the European Correspondents could help monitor
the implementation of EPC. The immediate years after the SEA also saw
a rapid increase of COREUs and the creation of six new working groups
(bringing the total to twenty-five) to handle EPC's greater responsibilities. The working groups also increased the frequency of their meetings
and began to meet in Brussels (rather than in the capitals of each EU presidency) after the SEA, which intensified the consultation and brought it
slightly closer to the EC's machinery.[8]

Third, the SEA codified a number of EPC customs as legal rules or
"general obligations" in the wording of Title III. Above all, the SEA required that external EC and EPC policies must be *consistent*, a direct extension of the damage-limitation function of EPC discussed in Chapter 5.
Thus, for the first time, these two unconnected policy domains were tied
together and made legally binding on EU member states. Action in one
domain had to support action in the other, and the EU presidency and

---

[7] Interview with a Commission official, Brussels, 1996.
[8] On the enhanced activities of EPC working groups after the SEA see Regelsberger 1993:
273–74.

the Commission were directed to make sure EC/EPC consistency was sought and maintained (Articles 30.3–30.5, SEA).[9] This provision meant that, at least in external relations, EPC and the EC should not be distinguished from each other (Coignez 1992). The SEA also codified the use of regional political dialogues and EPC joint actions, two existing customary instruments whose codification also helped link the EC and EPC, and which led to greater involvement of EC actors in foreign policy (see below). Finally, after more heated debate against the backdrop of renewed US–Soviet tension during the early 1980s, the SEA included a reference to cooperation on the "political and economic aspects of security" within the framework of EPC, a slight advancement of its formal agenda.[10]

In sum, EPC was not formally "communitarized" with the SEA; it largely codified existing practices in an attempt to clarify and preserve what had already been achieved. But the SEA did create stronger legal obligations than had ever existed under EPC, strongly reinforcing the effects of legalization discussed in the previous chapter. The SEA provision that parties shall "endeavor" to formulate a European foreign policy created an obligation to act in good faith, a recognized concept in international law.[11] The SEA also enhanced the overall stability and acceptability of the EPC process by combining the institutional instruments of both EPC/EC. As Dehousse and Weiler observed (1991: 130–36), the total separation of the two (legal) systems (of EPC and the EC) had become untenable; because of the progress they achieved in the EC, EU member states effectively abdicated part of their autonomy as EPC partners. The real problem was the lack of effective adjudication or enforcement mechanisms in EPC, not the lack of specific legal obligations (of course, these problems exist in many other international agreements). The SEA also officially excluded any differentiated participation in EC/EPC, which would have an effect on future enlargements. Prospective member states (Portugal and Spain at the time) would have to accept the obligations of EC and EPC membership in tandem, just as Greece had.

One setback to the legal expansion of EPC under the SEA involved Article 31, which prevented ECJ involvement in EPC legal

---

[9] Also note that the preamble to the SEA stressed the need for Europe "to aim at speaking ever increasingly with one voice and to act with consistency and solidarity in order more effectively to protect its common interests."

[10] Article 30.6, SEA. Recall that the 1981 London Report had allowed discussion of only the political aspects of security.

[11] Also note that the Irish Supreme Court ruled that the EPC provisions in the SEA were legally binding, which required a constitutional amendment to change Irish neutrality, and the Danes had a similar problem with the SEA (and later with the Treaty on European Union).

controversies. This provision effectively codified the long-standing under-standing among EU states to prevent the "judicialization" of their non-EC diplomacy, as we saw in the previous chapter. However, Article 32 explicitly prohibited EPC procedures from adversely affecting those of the EC. Violations of this provision could have been brought before the ECJ, but this did not happen as EU states wished to preserve EPC's con-sensual decision-making and, more importantly, they did not want to give the Court an opening in EPC that it could exploit. In addition, the Com-mission was excluded from suing on the direct basis of EPC, although it theoretically could have sued if EU states attempted to circumvent EC procedures with an EPC action. On the whole, then, the opportunities for using the ECJ to advance the legal standing of EPC were still very cir-cumscribed. However, the way EU states deliberately excluded the ECJ from EPC lends much credence to the view that they truly respect the Court's unpredictable, distinct power to advance integration further than they would like. As we shall see in the next two chapters, although this fear was expressed again in the Treaty on European Union, EU states are finding it increasingly difficult to develop a common foreign policy without reference to the EC's own comprehensive body of legal rules.

Despite the exclusion of the ECJ in the SEA's provisions on EPC, the SEA did establish a new administrative organization for EPC and did cod-ify a number of norms involving the relationship of EC organizations to European foreign policy.[12] These subjects are examined in the rest of this chapter, beginning with a discussion of the most powerful organizational actor involved in EU foreign policy: the European Commission.

The Commission and European foreign policy

One of the Commission's most important supranational functions in-volves external representation and negotiation, chiefly in the context of international trade negotiations and, less frequently, enlargements of the EU. In these domains the Commission now generally enjoys a fairly high degree of autonomy (compared to its role in EU foreign policy), although this was not always so. Indeed, efforts by the Commission, under Presi-dent Hallstein, to gain a greater role in external negotiations were once a major source of irritation for Charles de Gaulle. Sir Roy Denman recalls that when he was a British trade official in Geneva in the 1960s, "a Com-mission representative would sometimes turn up for negotiations, flanked

---

[12] These include procedural changes to EPC made at a post-SEA meeting and subsequently codified at Maastricht; see the "Decision of 28 February 1986, Adopted by Ministers, Meeting in the Framework of European Political Cooperation, on the Occasion of the Signing of the Single European Act," *EPC Bulletin*, 1986, Doc. 86/090.

by French and German officials, who appeared to have him under a kind of house arrest" (cited in Buchan 1993: 13). This attitude eventually changed, and the Commission has gradually exploited its treaty-based authority in a number of economically oriented areas of EU external relations, such as the common commercial policy, agricultural and technical matters, the common fisheries policy, development policy, enlargement negotiations, environmental policy, and even competition (or anti-trust) policy.

The expansion of the Commission's role in EPC was far more controversial, as revealed in the relevant provisions of EPC reports and the SEA. The privileged role of foreign ministries in EPC tended to strengthen them against the Commission in this domain. The Commission also was feared as an actor within EPC by many states (chiefly France); it had little or no diplomatic status or experience, and it might also encourage the "communitarization" of EPC. As an issue-area, EPC also was not very conducive to the kind of power the Commission has been especially adept at mobilizing: generating support for European policies among businesses and other interest groups, as through the use of Commission-sponsored public–private forums. Likewise, the Commission was highly suspicious of the way both EPC and the European Council could reduce its own authority in EC affairs and contaminate the Community method with intergovernmentalism. Moreover, it was more preoccupied with preserving its existing powers under the Treaty of Rome rather than with risking its reputation and limited resources to extend its influence into areas where it enjoyed no real legal authority.[13] However, this situation gradually changed, even in the face of many obstacles. How did this happen?

The evolution of Commission involvement in EPC

As Chapter 3 noted, EPC's architects in the 1970s did recognize the need to invite the Commission "to make known its views" to EPC in the event the activities of EPC affected the EC. Given this very limited formal mandate in EPC, practices here changed according to the issue at hand and the attitudes of the EU presidency and, to a lesser extent, the Political Committee. During EPC's early years, the Commission's role first involved providing advice on the economic implications of EPC initiatives, chiefly to help reinforce the damage-limitation norm of European foreign policy. At first it could be invited to EPC discussions as an observer or source of expertise on the EC, as with the CSCE and Euro-Arab

---

[13] Interviews with Commission officials, Brussels, 1995–96.

Dialogue working groups on economic cooperation. The early years of the Euro-Arab Dialogue also saw the development of an informal new institution, the "bicephalous presidency" (consisting of representatives from the Commission and the EU presidency), to help share external representation and policy coordination (Allen 1978). Similarly, the fact that trade policy for Eastern Europe was taken over by the EC at the beginning of 1973 provided the Commission with a convenient procedural excuse to be consulted on CSCE issues, and it attempted to make the most of this opening (Bonvicini 1982: 39–40).

Still, compared to the situation today, the Commission's influence in EPC was severely limited during these years. Several EU governments viewed the Commission as the "virus of integration" and wanted to isolate it completely from EPC. Commission officials from the period recall their humiliating treatment in EPC discussions; in some cases, they were admitted to EPC meetings only when specific points relevant to the EC were on the table, then were quickly ushered out. The Commission representative participated as a member of the EU presidency's delegation,[14] and even when admitted, the presidency could often decide whether the Commission representative could be allowed to speak at all. In most cases, the Commission representative could attend EPC meetings only with the consent of all EU member states, which was not always possible to achieve. Finally, the Commission was not even formally linked to the COREU network until 1982, although it was occasionally supplied with COREUs by "EC-friendly" diplomats.[15] According to EPC insiders, smaller EU states (often Belgium, Luxembourg, and the Netherlands) were especially generous in providing the Commission with EPC information that other EU states had wanted to keep from it.[16]

The Commission's "second-class" status in EPC during the years prior to the London Report is succinctly recalled by Simon Nuttall (1988: 104–105), the Commission's representative to EPC in the 1980s:

The Commission was excluded from whole areas of EPC and from certain types of activity. Only on rare occasions was the Commission invited to meetings of the Middle East working group and never to those of the working group on UN disarmament. It was excluded from all activities of the European Correspondents, including the all-important luncheon after the meetings of the Political

---

[14] Based on an EU foreign ministers meeting of September 10–11, 1973, to decide how to represent EC/EPC at the CSCE talks. This formula generally held until the SEA (Nuttall 1992a: 111).

[15] Prior to 1982 the Commission had to send COREUs through the Belgian foreign ministry, which happened only rarely.

[16] Interviews with Commission and EU member state foreign ministry officials, Brussels, 1995–96.

Committee at which the draft conclusions are discussed, and the Commission's representative in the Political Committee was invited to the Political Directors' luncheons but not their dinners, presumably on the grounds that in diplomatic circles secrets are revealed only after dark.

Yet by the late 1970s the Commission was seen as a valuable, regular participant in EPC discussions, even though it did not enjoy the same powers it possessed in EC affairs. Indeed, the expanding role of the Commission in EPC represents one of the most notable institutional changes in European foreign policy. Part of the reason for this change was the Commission's very positive involvement in the preparatory committee for the European Security Conference (CSCE). This also marked the first time that a major non-EU state – the Soviet Union – openly accepted the Commission's institutionalized involvement in a diplomatic process.[17] In addition, the arrival of President Giscard d'Estaing of France saw a more flexible approach to EU affairs, which included an expanded role for the Commission. Previously, the French had been a major obstacle to such a role. In fact, the British, Dutch, and Germans began suggesting common external representation for EPC/EC in the mid-1970s, but French opposition held this up until the TEU. Even after French resistance began to crumble, they still argued against Commission involvement because of its "leakiness" (Wallace and Allen 1977: 232), which violated one of EPC's most basic principles. Finally, with no permanent secretariat for EPC yet, the expanding foreign policy agenda necessitated the involvement of the Commission to provide some bureaucratic consistency, even if only in an informal way (Bonvicini 1982: 37).

The Commission's involvement in EPC was slightly expanded and codified with the 1981 London Report. This was mainly due to the influence of François Mitterrand and his foreign minister, Claude Cheysson, a former Commissioner who had witnessed the Commission's exclusion from EPC firsthand. The French change of attitude was expressed at a Gymnich-type meeting on September 5–6, 1981, where they finally withdrew their objections to full Commission participation in EPC at all levels (Nuttall 1992a: 177). Thus, according to Part II, Section 12 of this report, EU member states "attach importance to the Commission of the European Communities *being fully associated with Political Cooperation at all levels*" (emphasis added). This convoluted language – "attach importance" – reflected the considerable rancor among some member states regarding the full inclusion of the Commission in EPC. Although the French change of attitude was key, the Commission clearly was not supposed to have any new powers (a major concern of Denmark), and

---

[17] Interview with a Commission official, Brussels, 1996.

it has been suggested that the Commission was actually brought closer to EPC in part to prevent it from becoming a "loose cannon" in EU foreign policy.[18] Another concern was the preservation of confidentiality, and the Commission was required to show how it would handle sensitive information in EPC. This was deemed not to be a major problem for the Commission,[19] and the immediate years following the London Report saw the Commission's association with EPC at all levels, from the European Council to EPC ministerial meetings to the all-important EPC working groups.

Later, a Gymnich-type meeting in April 1983 decided that the Commission could be allowed to represent EPC in the Troika framework. The SEA then gave the Commission its first legitimate, codified responsibility (shared with the presidency) in EPC: ensuring that consistency of the EU's external relations was sought and maintained (Article 30.5). This took the Commission beyond mere "association" while helping to limit further the *de jure* intergovernmental character of EPC.[20] Finally, under Article 30.9, the Commission was to intensify cooperation between its representatives accredited to third countries and to international organizations. These provisions gave the Commission a status in EPC much closer to that of EU member states, a far cry from what it had experienced during the formative years of EPC.

Structure and resources

Before turning to explicit examples of the Commission's increasing involvement in EPC, we must keep in mind three basic facts about its post-EPC structure and resources since I cannot fully explore the Commission's complex internal dynamics. First, even in EC affairs, where it dominates the legislative process, the Commission has its share of organizational or bureaucratic problems, such as inadequate resources, bureaucratic inertia, turf battles, internal divisions, a lack of coherence or strategic action, irregular or ineffective leadership, and even corruption. The key point is that despite these limitations, and despite more general fears about protecting their sovereignty, EU member states still thought it beneficial to include the Commission in certain aspects of EPC. How and why this happened is the focus of the rest of this section, and I will

---

[18] Interview with a Commission official, Brussels, 1996.
[19] According to Nuttall (1988: 105), "If there have been leaks, they have not come from the Commission."
[20] In an earlier draft of the SEA, EU states had considered sharing the responsibility for consistency among the Commission and Twelve, but this was rejected as unworkable (Nuttall 1988: 109).

address the Commission's internal problems only where they impact on EU foreign policy.

Second, the Commission has gradually adapted itself to cope with the increased workload of EU foreign relations. During the EPC era, this generally involved Directorate-General I (or DG-I) for external relations (with industrialized countries) and DG-VIII for relations with developing countries, with some input from other Directorates as necessary.[21] In 1977, the Commission established its own small but permanent office to handle EPC affairs,[22] where no more than a handful of Commission officials dealt with EPC on a full-time basis. Also at this time some Commission staff began to be attached to the foreign embassies of EU states holding the EU presidency. The Commission also saw an expansion of its staff in Brussels and overseas, from 50 representations in third countries by the late 1970s to over 100 representations by the late 1980s, plus more Commission delegations to international conferences and organizations. However, coordination and information-sharing among the various DGs (particularly DG-I and DG-VIII) involved in foreign policy developed slowly and with some difficulty.[23] As we shall see in Chapters 7 and 8, the Commission made serious attempts to overcome this organizational confusion after the TEU. Similarly, the creation of a system for ensuring the secrecy of sensitive documents took some time, which damaged the Commission's reputation among some EU member states (Hill and Wallace 1979: 50–52).

Third, the Commission worked beyond organizational changes to actually improve its understanding of, and participation in, EPC. It established its own internal telex and cipher system to improve security and communications, and instituted a system of rotation between its various Directorates so that relevant personnel could gain experience abroad. The Commission also attempted to set down its own understanding of EPC in an internal document,[24] not an easy task considering the proliferation of unwritten rules in EPC. By the time of the SEA, the Commission had institutionalized its own internal procedures for coordinating EPC and EC affairs and representing itself in EPC, mainly involving the president of

---

[21] The Commission dispensed with numerical designations of its Directorates after the Treaty of Amsterdam. To maintain historical continuity, I use these numbers until Chapter 7.

[22] Known as "Relations with Intergovernmental Cooperation of Member States." Interview with a Commission official, Brussels, 1996.

[23] Interviews with Commission officials, Brussels, 1995–96. Also note that these two competencies (external relations and development) also comprise DG-E in the Secretariat-General of the Council of Ministers, which may have reinforced the competition between them.

[24] This document is da Fonseca-Wollheim 1981.

the Commission, the Commission Secretariat-General, DG-I, and DG-VIII. These links with EPC were generally structured along the same transgovernmental lines – hierarchical and functional – as those of EU member states. As a result, the Commission usually managed to find a coherent EPC policy position, not least because "it is always the same officials who work on political cooperation. This reinforces their ability to influence the Political Committee and those working groups charged with the formulation of a common policy on a specific issue" (Bonvicini 1982: 37). Only the TEU prompted a far more comprehensive reorganization and expansion of the Commission, in part to handle the transition from EPC to the CFSP. This subject is taken up in the next chapter. In the rest of this section, I examine several major areas of Commission influence in EU foreign policy, particularly after the London Report and the SEA.

The Commission's influence in EPC

At least six areas of Commission influence in EPC can be discerned, some of which also apply to the Commission's activities in external economic relations and other EC business. Throughout the discussion it should be stressed that the Commission's involvement also strongly depended on the attitude and capabilities of the state holding the EU presidency, which could vary widely. As an intergovernmentalist might expect, larger EU states (particularly France) preferred to minimize the Commission's influence, while the smaller EU states (particularly Belgium and Luxembourg) appreciated the support of the Commission in EU foreign policy.

First, the mere fact that the Commission, a complex, permanent organization possessing policy-relevant technical expertise, was linked to EPC, a decentralized system, meant that European foreign policy could enjoy some degree of *institutional memory* beyond the periodic compilations of EPC discussed in the previous chapter (the *recueil* and the *coutumier*). As EU states required sixteen years to agree finally to a permanent secretariat to help administer EPC (see below), the Commission provided a quick, "ready-made" alternative to establishing a new organization for EPC. At the very least, then, the Commission's position between the EC and EPC had a general stabilizing effect on the EU's external relations, which somewhat compensated for the lack of continuous attention by the European Council and other EU intergovernmental forums.

Second, in keeping with its function as a bridge between the EC and EPC, the Commission acted as a *source of information and expertise*, particularly regarding the economic implications of EPC. This of course was the Commission's most fundamental, widely recognized role in EPC, as most EU states (particularly the smaller ones) were concerned that EPC might, at best, act counter to Community policies and, at worst, contaminate the EC with intergovernmental procedures. The Commission was their chief ally against these potential detriments. As we have seen, this general advisory capacity justified the Commission's inclusion in the earliest EPC initiatives, the Euro-Arab Dialogue and the CSCE process, where it acted at the working group level (at first) on the economic aspects of each initiative.

The Commission also became an alternative resource when departments in foreign ministries neglected to share information with each other, or when foreign ministries did not share information with other ministries involved in EC affairs (owing to, for example, bureaucratic rivalries or time constraints). It was especially helpful in filling the information gap between states' foreign ministries and their economics (or EU affairs) ministries/departments, and the information gap in Brussels between COREPER and EPC officials when EC tools were being considered since the Commission's representative was often the only person to participate in both meetings. This role (shared with the EU presidency) was legally codified with the SEA provision to ensure the "consistency" of EC and EPC policies. The advent of the single European market also increased the opportunities for the Commission to inform EPC about EC concerns.[25] Nuttall recalls this resulted in a "shared perception" that EC and EPC activities could be made to work together, and he notes few "glaring cases" of inconsistency, if any; as "the vast majority of EC policies do not have direct foreign policy implications, and much of the work done in EPC does not impinge on that of the Community" (Nuttall 1988: 108–109). Similarly, Regelsberger argues (1993: 284–85) that the key requirement of consistency was "widely fulfilled" after the SEA, as reflected in her analysis of various EPC declarations and actions.

Third, the Commission became more active as an informal *policy entrepreneur* or *agenda-setter* of its own, even though it did not enjoy in EPC the same exclusive "right of initiative" it held in the EC.[26] Still, the Commission was in a unique position to move beyond *informing* EPC participants about EC considerations to *defining* external political issues in economic terms (and vice versa) and *suggesting* possible courses of action. According to one observer, when asked for help when the Council of Ministers needed to define whether a problem was mainly political (involving EPC/Political Committee) or economic (involving the EC/COREPER),

---

[25] EPC's Political Committee, for example, was often quite ignorant in terms of EC competencies and their legal basis. Interviews with Commission and COREPER officials, Brussels, 1995–96.

[26] For an expanded discussion of this role, see Nugent 1995.

the "Commission tends to defend COREPER, if only because it is a Community institution."[27] Moreover, the Commission's independent status vis-à-vis other EU states put it in a strong position to mediate among competing views of policy, very similar to the role it plays in EC affairs.

This change of emphasis took some time to achieve; at first, the Commission was wary of using information received in EPC to further its own ends because of concerns about being shut out of the process, and usually was excluded from the informal working dinners where most EPC matters were discussed.[28] Thus, we see little evidence of strong Commission advocacy for particular EPC policies in the 1970s, except in the context of the Euro-Arab Dialogue and the CSCE process, and the Commission did not emerge as a true EPC policy entrepreneur until some time after the London Report (Bonvicini 1982: 43). However, the Commission often acted within its own sphere of competence to support external political goals, such as by granting or withholding economic aid or manipulating trade or Association Agreements. As we saw in Chapter 4, the Commission refused to proceed with the EC's new Mediterranean policy regarding Spain because of that country's execution of five Basques in 1975. Although this was not a case of the Commission acting within EPC, it demonstrates the Commission's ability, even at this stage, to influence (even embarrass) EPC through indirect methods. The Spanish case also illustrates the Commission's function as a mediator for policy compromises, in this case between the Netherlands and Denmark, who wanted a stronger response, and France, Germany, and the UK, who wanted to step lightly in the interest of not harming relations between Spain and the Nine (van Praag 1982a: 101–103). In other cases, such as Poland, the Falklands, Central America, and South Africa, the Commission was explicitly directed by EPC to draw up suitable policy proposals for the use of economic aid and/or sanctions for political ends.

Fourth, the Commission's status as an *external representative* or *negotiator* gradually grew in EPC, since its representative was usually the only permanent dialogue partner on the European side thanks to the EU's rotating presidency system. The Commission's authority expanded even more when economic issues became part of the talks, as we have seen with the Euro-Arab Dialogue and CSCE talks. In other cases, a Commission representative was attached to EU state missions to third countries and delegations to international organizations, as the Commission enjoyed

---

[27] Bonvicini 1982: 40. This tendency was also confirmed by interviews with officials inside and outside the Commission, Brussels, 1995–96.

[28] As the EP Political Committee (1977) put it, "The Commission believes that on account of its position as a guest at political cooperation meetings, information received there should be used with discretion."

few independent delegations of its own at the time. Where the Commission did have delegations, its representative usually participated in meetings of EU ambassadors, both for EC matters and EPC. The ambassador of the state holding the EU presidency could decide on such Commission participation, and usually followed what his or her government wanted at the time (Bonvicini 1982: 38–39). The Commission's external network is now more extensive than that of many EU member states, particularly in the African, Caribbean, and Pacific countries, where only a small number of EU member states are represented (Nuttall 1988: 107).

Moreover, the Commission was increasingly lobbied by outside actors (such as the US) to undertake EPC initiatives. To outsiders, such Commission involvement gave the impression of true coherence between EPC and EC representation. The Commission's role in negotiating accession agreements also provided it with a way to use political criteria to make its decisions, as when it persuaded Spain to sign the Nuclear Non-Proliferation Treaty in the context of its accession to the EU (Müller 1992: 198). It could even be argued that Commission involvement in EPC in third countries was greater than that in Brussels, thanks to the tendency for EU diplomats abroad to generally ignore the distinction between EC and EPC that was maintained in Brussels.[29] This distinction was further eroded in the 1980s with the proliferation of regional dialogues used to enhance cohesion between the EC and EPC, with the Commission playing the central role. The rationale behind these dialogues was primarily political, though not in all cases (such as with the ACP or EFTA[30] states), and the Commission's experience of the Euro-Arab Dialogue was an important precedent for its close involvement in dialogues with Central America, the Association of Southeast Asian Nations (ASEAN), and the Gulf Cooperation Council (Nuttall 1988: 111). By the time of the comprehensive "Europe Agreements" with Central and Eastern European countries, the Troika was abandoned in favor of joint Commission/EU presidency representation (the "bicephalous" or "tandem" presidency), a significant procedural change compared to prior dialogues (Nuttall 1992a: 293). With the collapse of the Soviet Union, the EU also created more limited "Partnership and Cooperation Agreements" to handle relations with former Soviet states (see Chapter 7), which similarly privileged the role of the Commission.

Fifth, the Commission also emerged as an *agent for policy implementation and monitoring* by the 1980s. Indeed, since EPC was implemented on a

---

[29] Interviews with Commission officials, Brussels, 1996.

[30] European Free Trade Association. Dialogue between the EC and EFTA was initiated in 1984 (the "Luxembourg process").

national basis at first, the Commission's role was that of a monitor, so the two areas can be considered together. Here, on the one hand, the Commission had to gain the trust of EU member states and look for practical opportunities to make a contribution to EPC, and on the other hand, it had to protect its key role in EC affairs by warning EU states not to usurp Community competencies. The Commission is the leading authority on the use of EC instruments for EPC ends, and it was charged with monitoring state behavior when EC/EPC "mixed agreements" (such as the control of dual-use goods for political ends) were established.

For example, during the 1979 Iran hostage crisis, the Commission became involved (under Article 225) to prevent sanctions decided under EPC from adversely affecting the Common Market. In other cases, proposals made by the Commission inevitably led to their implementation by the Commission, thus enhancing its role. In South Africa, the implementation and oversight of the 1985 package of measures were primarily the responsibility of the Commission (which had proposed many of those measures; Holland 1988: 117–18). A number of ad hoc oversight and administrative procedures were devised in this area, mainly within the scope of EPC, largely because of the Commission's role as an initiator and executor of the EC budget. This role was limited, however, because funds were lacking and the Commission did not enjoy the right to monitor the oil embargo, potentially one of the more powerful weapons in that sanctions package. The extraordinary decision taken in 1989 to make the EC, and the Commission in particular, the primary coordinator for the distribution of Western aid to Central and Eastern Europe also greatly strengthened the status of the Commission in foreign policy, although this decision was reached outside the EPC framework. It also helped lay the groundwork for even more involvement following the TEU.

Sixth and finally, the Commission emerged as a strong *advocate of institutional change* regarding European integration. It plays this role within the EU, by respecting, defending, and extending the Community's competencies in foreign policy, and outside the EU, by acting as an example of successful regional cooperation or integration, one of EPC's most important substantive norms. Regarding its internal role, the Commission had urged combining the political and economic aspects of the Intergovernmental Conference that led to the SEA (although the Milan European Council of June 28–29, 1985 had the opposite idea).[31] And while numerous other factors (such as perceptions of policy failure, crises, changes of government, and grand bargains) also helped encourage institutional reforms in EPC, the Commission helps to focus, synthesize, and expand

[31] See the "Commission Opinion of 22 July 1985" regarding its thinking on EPC.

pro-integration opinions in Europe. In this way, the Commission can easily fill an ideas vacuum when EU states are unwilling or unable to do so. The Commission played this role very effectively in its proposals for replacing EPC with the CFSP, as we shall see in Chapter 7.

Regarding its external role, the Commission provides an example of successful regional cooperation, a clear (and deliberate) product of the regional dialogues mentioned above. If EC organizations generally share an interest in "more Europe," they must also share an interest in exporting Europe's cooperative ideals to other regions of the world, an important form of the EU's "soft power." The Commission embodies a broad aspiration toward regional integration (of an *institutionalized* nature) which it stresses whenever it can. In fact, the Commission "tries to manipulate the financial component of group-to-group dialogue in such a way as to promote intra-regional cooperation" (Nuttall 1990: 146), as with the Lomé III convention. The Commission is often at its best in regional dialogues, since it largely represents the EU as a civilian power, which characterizes most regional groupings. And although eleven of twelve EU member states in the 1980s were members of NATO, it is remarkable that the EU was seen as standing alone from superpower rivalry, even though it tends to support the West. This perception is a peculiar consequence of the EU's institutional and normative structure, which is perceived by outsiders "to stand apart from the policies of its members either separately or collectively in other fora (NATO, WEU). Since this perception is apparently not dependent on the specific policies adopted by the Community it must arise from its institutional nature as an integrationist regional grouping" (Nuttall 1990: 144). Thus, the fact that the EU had no military arm for most of its history is important, but to the extent that the Commission embodies this institutionalized, interregional, civilian form of cooperation, it matters a great deal. The general stability of its policies (compared to those of EU member states) and its sensitivity to the developing world are also important in distinguishing the EU from other global actors.

Finally, we should note that EPC affected the Commission as well. It was increasingly expected to consider a more comprehensive approach to problems of democracy, stability, and development rather than view them only in economic terms. The Commission's willingness to confront more security-related issues, such as crises and non-proliferation, was also significantly enhanced by its experience in EPC. Although its position clearly expanded in this domain, the Commission's autonomy had severe limits at this time, which always rested on the evolving attitudes and goodwill of EU member states. The holder of the EU presidency in particular largely controlled the Commission's influence in EPC. However, the Commission's position has improved markedly since the late 1980s and the TEU, as we shall see in the next chapter.

The EPC Secretariat

As I noted in Chapter 3, the Italians and the Germans proposed an EPC Secretariat in December 1971, while Georges Pompidou and Willy Brandt further agreed on the principle at a meeting in Paris in February 1972. The British agreed to it as well later that year (Franck 1983: 89). Yet France wanted to locate the Secretariat in Paris, while a majority opposed this idea and argued that, if a Secretariat was necessary, it should be located in Brussels. There was further disagreement (as usual) over whether the Secretariat should be linked to existing EC structures or established outside of them. This difference of opinion prevented the establishment of a formal administrative body for EPC for nearly two decades, although the delay also helped encourage the development of other alternatives to aid the administration of EPC, such as the COREU network, the Troika system, and the increased involvement of the Commission.

Origins, structure, resources

Yet the rapid expansion of the EPC agenda, the increased burden placed on the EU presidency by such an agenda, and the limitation felt by small EU states when they held the presidency led to some important informal changes. In particular, the Secretariat had its roots in the informal practice of sharing some of the burden of the EU presidency among members of the Troika. In 1977 EU states quietly adopted the practice of seconding a few of their junior officials to the next EU presidency state as a support team to assist with the transition. This practice of lending diplomats was formalized in the London Report and it became especially useful to help maintain EU/EPC contacts with Turkey after the accession of Greece to the EU. It also helped educate officials about the national foreign ministries of their EPC partners and the functioning of the EPC network.[32]

Over the next several years an intense debate raged over whether to create a permanent Secretariat to do the preparatory work for EPC business and to help reduce the load on the EU presidency, which now requires (among other tasks) the organization and chairing of dozens of meetings among hundreds of participants over a six-month period. The creation

---

[32] London Report, Section 10; also see Nuttall 1990: 19–20.

of an EPC working group of policy planners under the German EU presidency in 1983 helped, but the question of a Secretariat was not firmly resolved until the SEA in 1986. At this time, France finally accepted that the Secretariat would serve EPC, not the European Council, and it gave up its long-held insistence that any EPC Secretariat must be based in Paris. The Secretariat idea posed an especially difficult problem for small EU states: they often needed administrative help during their EU presidencies, but were still wary of any permanent EPC (i.e., intergovernmental) organization and were reluctant to rely too heavily on the larger EU states. Given all these concerns, British and Italian proposals for a "minimalist" EPC Secretariat finally prevailed.

Thus, the Secretariat's tasks at first were administrative and organizational, it was based in Brussels, and it was supposed to serve the EU presidency (or the Political Committee). As the SEA negotiators could not agree to the Secretariat's functions at the time, a decision on this matter had to wait until a later Council meeting of EU foreign ministers. This decision specified the organization and functions of the EPC Secretariat,[33] which included:

1. Assisting the EU presidency in the organization of EPC meetings, including the preparation and circulation of documents and the drawing up of minutes.
2. Working with the European Correspondents Group.
3. Assisting the chairmen of the working groups.
4. Assisting the EU presidency in the preparation of texts to be published on behalf of the member states, including replies to parliamentary questions.
5. Maintaining the EPC archives.
6. Preserving the rules governing EPC.
7. Assisting the EU presidency in its contacts with third countries.
8. Organizing on its premises all working party meetings and, if necessary, meetings of the ministers and the Political Committee.

In terms of structure and resources, the Secretariat consisted of only seventeen people at first: five diplomatic officials plus a Head, supported by a small administrative staff. All were seconded from national foreign ministries, and were responsible for specific policy dossiers (geographic and functional). The Secretariat was not nearly as strong as Franco-German proposals had suggested, with no budget or authority of its own. Nor was it involved in political dialogues or actions. The Secretariat was

---

[33] See the "Decision of 28 February 1986 by EC Foreign Ministers Meeting in the Framework of European Political Cooperation on the Occasion of the Signing of the Single European Act," *EPC Bulletin*, 1986, Doc 86/090.

entirely dependent on the EU presidency, which paid a symbolic fee of one ECU to the Council for the EPC Secretariat in recognition of services it provides (da Costa Pereira 1988: 86). The daily operation of the Secretariat was paid by the EC via the Council budget, while staff salaries were paid by national administrations (the EU presidency). And although the Secretariat was located in the Council's Secretariat building, it was clearly isolated from the rest of the Council Secretariat by doors with special locks on them.

The Head of the Secretariat was appointed jointly by member states and served a three-year term. The choice of its first head, Giovanni Januzzi (a former deputy Political Director in the Italian foreign ministry), was made by "accidental consensus," as da Costa Pereira put it, since the larger EU states could not find support for their own candidates. Five other civil servants served for two and half years, thus covering five to six EU presidencies and providing a greater degree of bureaucratic consistency. The terms were staggered so that a new diplomat came in every six months with each new EU presidency, and "although in a sense they do form a 'European team,' they are still attached to their respective civil services, albeit in a different hierarchy" (da Costa Pereira 1988: 87). And although the Secretariat was linked to the COREU system and could participate in EPC deliberations, its own information resources depended on the goodwill of EU member states. There also were no formal, institutionalized links with EC actors, although informal contacts were maintained.[34] But the Secretariat permitted EPC working group meetings to be held at the site of the Secretariat in Brussels (in the Council's Charlemagne building), rather than rotating among EU presidency states. Also, there were few real barriers to contact between EPC participants; lines of communication crossed both horizontally (among the EU presidency/Troika, the Secretariat, and national foreign ministries) and vertically (among the Political Committee, European Correspondents, and working groups).

The performance of the EPC Secretariat

As these functions suggest, the Secretariat most certainly did not enjoy the same resources or autonomy as did the Commission. Still, according to insiders and observers, it generally performed its limited functions very well. These involved providing all translation for EPC and maintaining the all-important "suitcase" of documents (the *recueil* and *coutumier*) relevant to EPC. More so than the Commission, then, it was the guardian of

---

[34] Interview with a Commission official, Brussels, 1996.

EPC orthodoxy as the repository of all EPC documents and by virtue of its preparation of answers to questions about EPC asked by the EP. It also housed a stable, independent core of archives (unfortunately, one not yet open to the public or scholars), so EPC documents could be used more effectively and consistently. In addition, the organization of meetings during each EU presidency was handled almost exclusively by the Secretariat, except on questions of protocol. While the EU presidency still set the EPC agenda, the Secretariat organized it. The Secretariat also engaged in some limited conceptual work, such as drafting texts and preparing speeches for the EU presidency.

The most intense relationships in the Secretariat were those with EPC working groups, partly because working group meetings were held at the Secretariat. One Secretariat official always participated in working groups involving dialogues with a regional grouping, giving that official a *de facto* role in external representation. In fact, von Jagow has argued (1990: 196) that "the political dialogue with regional groupings could not be conducted" without the Secretariat, which highlights the rapid growth in its importance. In other relationships with third countries the Secretariat acted as a broker in formulating common texts, and helped to maintain contacts with third countries in general. Liaison with the EP was also important, as the EU presidency usually attached little importance to the task. This is an important example of how the influence of one EC actor (the EP) and one institutional role (the EU presidency) helped justify the creation of another organization (the Secretariat) to draft replies to EP questions and to ensure consistency among them between rotating EU presidencies. The Head of the Secretariat also regularly appeared before the EP's relevant committees to discuss EPC issues, acting as EPC's *de facto* spokesperson in those settings (da Costa Pereira 1988: 93–100). The Secretariat also helped manage the transition between EU presidencies, an increasingly important task with the enlargement of the EU in 1986, the growing number of items on the EPC agenda, and the proliferation of regional dialogues in the EC/EPC throughout the 1980s.

However, beyond these useful administrative functions, it is difficult to point to a significant, independent role for the EPC Secretariat in any single case of EPC decision-making, particularly relative to the Commission. It had no decision-making powers or policy resources of its own, and the Head of the Secretariat did not emerge as an influential neutral broker as his autonomy always depended on the holder of the EU presidency. Still, the advent of the EPC Secretariat was important for three more basic reasons: first, its *symbolic effect*, in that it represented the breakdown of resistance to a permanent organization for EPC of any kind; second, its *permanence effect*, as a central repository for EPC documents and activities, which became more consistent over time; and third, its *socialization effect*, in the sense that it helped national diplomats work together, trust each other, search for a common European view on external problems, and express that view to the EP and the outside world. On the negative side, it is possible that the Secretariat competed to some extent with other EPC participants, such as the European Correspondents in national capitals and even the Commission (Regelsberger 1993: 277). As a result of such concerns, the Secretariat was only slightly enhanced by the TEU and brought closer to the EC as part of the EU's single institutional structure, as we shall see in the next chapter.

Outside looking in? The European Parliament and foreign policy

The Commission, and to a far lesser extent the EPC Secretariat, were the two organizations most directly involved in EPC. Two other EC actors did not enjoy the same status in EPC. One, the ECJ, was discussed in the previous chapter; it possessed the potential for more authority in EPC but often lacked the opportunities and will to exercise such authority. The other, the EP, strongly pushed for more involvement but lacked the power to assert itself in EPC. However, the EP deserves some attention at this point, if only because its role in EU foreign policy became an object of interest with the Treaty on European Union, the subject of Chapter 7.

Resources and influence of the EP

It should first be kept in mind that one cannot consider the EP's role in EPC without noting that it is subject to the same problems of democratic control of foreign policy confronted by national legislatures. Foreign and security policy are often considered special domains, ones dominated by executive bodies or officials. Most national parliaments have a limited number of tools at their disposal to influence foreign policy directly: questions, motions of no confidence, budgetary authority, fact-finding missions, investigations, treaty ratification, and approval of certain political appointments. While the EP possesses some of these powers, and although the Commission and EP often side with each other in debates over EPC, there has always been an inherent tension between the EP and the Council of Ministers, just as in domestic political systems where the legislature does not have direct control over the executive.[35]

---

[35] For more comprehensive discussions, see Schmuck 1991; Judge, Earnshaw, and Cowan 1994; and Corbett, Jacobs, and Shackleton 1995. This discussion also relies on interviews with EP officials in Brussels, 1995–96.

Also, the flexibility and secrecy required of foreign policy make parliamentary scrutiny especially difficult. Finally, the EP has struggled for years with its own legitimacy and authority within the EU as a whole, which are far more important to it than its specific role in EU foreign policy.

Thus, it is not surprising that the EP played a very limited role in EPC, especially during the early years. In general, its chief function was to provide a veil of democratic legitimacy to a very secret, non-legal process (particularly after the first direct elections to the EP in 1979). Like the Commission, the EP was only briefly mentioned in the Luxembourg and Copenhagen Reports on EPC and did not enjoy any significant involvement here except for occasional colloquies each year. The SEA further codified several existing practices regarding the EP, mainly that the Parliament's views were supposed to be taken into consideration in EPC. The EP could pose written and oral questions to the EU presidency about EPC and the presidency was required to forward EPC texts to the EP and to reply to major EP resolutions on which the Parliament requests its comments. Lodge (1988) reports that these resolutions were examined by relevant EPC working groups and did occasionally have some impact on their deliberations.

Despite its lack of more substantial EPC powers, or perhaps because of this lack, the EP became noted for taking often controversial positions on international issues, mainly with regard to human rights. In fact, after the SEA the EU presidency also was informally required to report to the EP on activities regarding human rights. According to Neunreither (1990: 170), the EP is far more likely than the Commission or the Council of Ministers to politicize the EU's external relations; he notes that as early as 1967 "it was the Parliament which insisted against a hesitant Commission and a more than reluctant Council that the Association Agreement with Greece should either be canceled or at least frozen when the colonels took over and parliamentary democracy was abolished." In this sense, the EP viewed itself as the "conscience" of the EU (and EPC) and tabled many questions on foreign affairs (more than 500 a year; most of which involved human rights issues), which EPC had to answer. In fact, reports on EPC were prepared by the EP even before it was requested to do this by the SEA.

Although the EP lacks the capacity to initiate EPC actions, it has been able to amend decisions to suit itself. One favorite tool is to increase or decrease economic aid in light of political goals, as happened with South Africa in the mid-1980s. The EP also was the only EC organization to comment adversely on the implementation of the Code of Conduct in South Africa, which it did in 1983. It also called for the Commission to draft annual analyses of the Code.[36] The EP was also the only EC actor to display any interest in monitoring the economic sanctions against South Africa (although it lacked the capacity to punish violators), as the Commission was not willing to antagonize the pro- and anti-sanctions factions in the EU. Thus, the EP's External Relations Committee monitored the negative measures, while its Development and Cooperation Committee covered the positive measures (Holland 1988: 42–43). Another favorite ploy was to delay negotiations with third countries, particularly for violations of human rights. Most importantly, the *assent procedure* (Article 238) of the SEA explicitly gives the EP the right to approve the EC's Association and Accession Agreements[37] (the EP also sought, but was not given, the same powers concerning trade and cooperation agreements). Although EU states may not have desired it, the assent procedure has been extended to include the EP's approval of renewals, additions, and amendments to Association Agreements, including financial protocols, which take place on a regular basis. In the first eighteen months after the SEA entered into effect, the EP invoked the assent procedure thirty-one times.[38]

With the assent procedure in place, and with the episode involving Greece in 1967 as a precedent, Association Agreements have since been held up by the EP, such as those with Turkey and Israel in 1987–88. In addition, the Luns-Westerterp procedure (also codified by the SEA)[39] requires that the EP be informed prior to, and consulted after, all external negotiations. However, there is no evidence of the EP using this procedure to affect substantially the Commission's negotiating position in the immediate years after the SEA. This situation changed after the TEU, as we shall see later.

More than any other EC actor, the EP also tends to ignore the distinction between EC and EPC/CFSP affairs, acting as a forceful advocate of greater consistency between the two systems. Here the EP does have a number of other indirect tools at its disposal which could affect EU foreign policy, but only in limited ways. These include hearings, investigations, fact-finding missions, and parliamentary delegations. For example, after a series of scandals involving German nuclear and chemical exports,

---

[36] In particular, the EP's report on the Code criticized its supervision by the Council of Ministers as "totally inadequate" (European Parliament 1982).

[37] The assent procedure requires the EP's approval by the majority of more than 50 percent of all its members for Association Agreements and treaties of adhesion. There is no time limit on the procedure, so the EP can hold up an agreement indefinitely.

[38] These cases involved protocols with Algeria, Egypt, Jordan, Lebanon, Tunisia, and Yugoslavia, all of which were approved with large margins.

[39] On the origins of this procedure, which dates to the "Luns procedure" of 1964, see Corbett, Jacobs, and Shackleton 1995: 213–15.

the EP led an investigation and its report on the issue asked for greater attention to non-proliferation and requested Euratom to submit regular reports on its safeguards activities (Müller 1992: 199). Delegations are a particular interest of the EP, in that they often help to stimulate regional integration elsewhere, a major foreign policy concern of the EU. By 1990, the EP's parliamentary delegations, involving anywhere from eight to twenty-six members of the EP (MEPs) for each one, included those for countries/regions in Europe, North Africa/Middle East, the Americas, and Asia/Australia, plus international organizations (the UN). It is beyond the scope of this chapter to assess the long-term influence of the EP's external delegations, but we should be aware that its potential exists (Neunreither 1990). Also, in the years prior to the Maastricht Treaty, the EP became increasingly belligerent during EPC question time when it was not satisfied with the EU presidency's answers. During one debate in January 1990, an MEP complained that "the Council has a duty to answer the question, and so far it has not done so . . . [the minister] will not give an answer." Another MEP charged that "the Council never answers questions properly."[40] Here the rule of confidentiality in EPC often conflicted with the EP's right to ask questions about it, a well-known problem in any democratic political system.

Finally, although it enjoyed no autonomous role in policymaking under EPC, the EP has perhaps been more effective in pushing for procedural changes in foreign policy by consistently opposing a rigid distinction between EPC and EC business. It was especially annoyed at the way foreign ministers, while holding the EU presidency, initially refused to discuss with the full EP "matters which do not fall within the competence of the Council" (i.e., EPC).[41] The EP has continually attempted to "extend its competence and its representative role to this new area of collaboration, and maintained a continual feeling that [European] Political Cooperation represented a threat to the Communities" (Wallace and Allen 1977: 231). The EP pushed for an EPC Secretariat as early as 1974 and formally asked for EPC reports in 1977.[42] It also was the first to push for EU action on security (for example, by adopting reports on security, creating a security and disarmament subcommittee, and developing links with the WEU Assembly) and called for improved crisis-management procedures for EPC. Both of these reforms found their way into the London Report in 1981 (European Parliament 1981). The EP's comprehensive "Draft

[40] Debates of the European Parliament, 3–3894/64–68 (December 12, 1989) and 3–385/61–63 (January 16, 1990), cited in Dinan 1991: 405.
[41] Debates of the European Parliament, *Official Journal of the European Communities*, July 9, 1974, p. 89.
[42] See the European Parliament 1977.

Treaty on European Union" directly led to the SEA and its improved EPC procedures (Corbett 1989; Elles 1990). The EP also has consistently called for more supranationalization of EU foreign policy (and EC) decision-making, for more democratic control of foreign policy, and for more involvement in EU affairs by the Commission.

To varying degrees, these concerns were addressed in the SEA and in the TEU, as we shall see in the next chapter. Yet this grudging acceptance by EU member states of the EP's influence in external relations is slightly puzzling when one considers that, for most of EPC's history, European citizens knew or cared little about it, or indeed, about the Parliament itself. Since there was little domestic pressure for such involvement, part of the explanation must involve a realization by EU states that their collective foreign policy activities must show some sensitivity to democratic legitimacy, and to the EP's key role in providing that legitimacy, to be compatible with other principles of European integration. This is an entirely appropriate development if one accepts the logic of normative appropriateness discussed in previous chapters. Whether this norm enables the EP to change from a passive to active participant in EU foreign policy, and expands to other domains (such as defense policy), are still open questions.

To conclude this chapter, we should note that the expanding participation of EC actors in EPC involves all four logics of institutionalization discussed in this volume. In terms of the logic of raw power derived from legal competencies and physical resources, the Commission is positioned to play a leading role in EU foreign policy relative to other organizations involved in European integration. But this ability is always conditioned by new opportunities involving the functional logic, in terms of satisfying a need to improve the general effectiveness and consistency of EU foreign policy. This is where the Commission (and to a much lesser extent, the Secretariat) can exploit its authority and resources to full effect. The logic of appropriateness also comes into play, particularly in the way EPC rules about EC actors had to respect the basic norms of the EC, regardless of the actual effectiveness of those actors. Thus, concerns about openness and democratic legitimacy, which are fundamental rules in the European polity, allowed the EP at least to comment on EPC right from the beginning. As the locus of all economic policy, the Commission also enjoyed a window of opportunity any time an EPC initiative involved economic issues or instruments. Finally, the logic of socialization played a role here as well, particularly in terms of turnover (changes of government in France) and in the collusion between the Commission and "Community-friendly" governments (particularly when they held the EU presidency), which allowed for more intensive EPC–Commission interactions than were officially permitted by EPC reports. This socialization logic is also reflected in the more general tendency for EU diplomats and ambassadors in third countries, during their day-to-day activities, to ignore the rigid EC–EPC distinction set down by EU member state governments.

However, it should again be emphasized that, for most of the history of EPC, the involvement of EC actors and the EPC Secretariat was far less important than the initial intergovernmental bargain over EPC, the transgovernmental EPC network, and the codification of EPC norms described in previous chapters. But the limited involvement of EC actors described in this chapter clearly set the stage for more profound institutional change at Maastricht. This involved an attempt to replace the pragmatic, informal EPC system with a formal CFSP, expressly linked to the policies, organizations, and procedures of the Community. The CFSP thus represents a much higher degree of institutionalization in this domain, in the sense that it begins to approach a formal system of *governance* for European foreign policy, a major departure from the informal system created by the Luxembourg Report twenty years before. This important transition is explored in the next chapter.

7   Toward governance: the Common Foreign and Security Policy

The SEA represented a significant step forward for European foreign policy, yet the EU, like much of the world, was caught off-guard by the momentous events of 1989–91, beginning with the fall of the Berlin Wall and ending with the disintegration of the Soviet Union and Yugoslavia. There is no doubt these exogenous changes prompted major reforms in a number of institutions, including NATO, the EU, the WEU, and the CSCE, and helped create entirely new ones, such as the European Bank for Reconstruction and Development (Keohane, Nye, and Hoffman 1993). However, it is also clear that the specific institutional reforms of EU foreign policy resulting from these events largely reflected endogenous, path-dependent processes. Rather than a decisive break with the past, the CFSP represented a natural, logical progression by both clarifying what had been achieved through EPC and building only a few truly innovative goals and procedures onto that mechanism. Virtually all elements of EPC described in previous chapters were affected, and they clearly laid the foundation for the CFSP at Maastricht.

Yet a closer examination of both the treaty-based provisions of the CFSP and its early performance suggests that European foreign policy has in fact reached a new level of institutionalization. In particular, we can describe this evolution as moves toward a system of *governance*, broadly defined for the moment as the authority to make, implement, and enforce rules in a specified policy domain. As Allen once put it (1998: 48), the EU is now trying to reproduce foreign policy governance without an actual government. Is this even possible, and what institutional problems does it raise? This chapter and the next attempt to address these questions. I argue that, although this process is quite incomplete, there is no escaping the fact that the CFSP is not a passive, decentralized forum the way EPC was structured. The many horizontal linkages that gave substance to foreign policy cooperation in the past have been deliberately reconfigured into a policy process involving more *vertical* authority, ranging from the European Council level down to the foreign policymaking structures of EU member states. And although there are still a number of gaps and conflicting competencies in the CFSP (as in other EU policy domains), which I address in Chapter 8, it is still a step forward compared to EPC.

Thus, under the TEU, the governance of the CFSP now involves four major elements. First and most generally, it involves a much greater *coherence of the policy sector and rationalization of the policy process*, far beyond what had existed under EPC. This change can be described in terms of the definition of the CFSP itself, its linkages to the policies, organizations, and procedures of the EU's first pillar (the EC), and its practical operation. Second, the CFSP is *legally binding on EU member states*, which includes compliance mechanisms. Third, the CFSP includes several *authoritative decision-making rules*, in the form of qualified majority voting (QMV). Although the procedures are somewhat convoluted, and they are not applicable across the entire range of CFSP activities, their inclusion in the TEU clearly represents a breach of the long-standing taboo against supranational decision-making procedures for EU foreign policy. Fourth and finally, the TEU provides a *greater degree of autonomy for EC organizational actors* in European foreign policy. As we shall see, part of this autonomy derives from explicit delegation to EC actors, part of it involves greater linkages between those actors and other aspects of the CFSP process, and part of it is a result of EC actors attempting to involve themselves in the CFSP process beyond the wishes of EU member states.

Having already explored the emergence and effects of individual elements of EU foreign policy (intergovernmentalism, transgovernmentalism, normative structures, and organizations), the task of this chapter is to put the pieces back together again and assess the system as a whole. Throughout the discussion, it must be emphasized that the CFSP should always be considered part of an ongoing, evolutionary process of institution-building, based as it was on EPC and some informal practices that had grown up between the SEA and the TEU. In other words, the process of institutional change did not end at Maastricht; this Treaty merely raised new expectations and created new pressures for reform, thus setting the stage for the 1996–97 Intergovernmental Conference (IGC) of the EU, which is examined in the next chapter. In the present chapter, I concentrate on the emergence and performance of the CFSP under Maastricht.

The Treaty on European Union

As the TEU is the single most important event in European foreign policy since the founding of EPC, we need to place the institutional debate in the context of the times. Although there was a clear improvement in the performance of EPC after the SEA, only two years after the Act entered into effect, Europe was confronted with an unprecedented set of challenges. EU states clearly felt EPC needed improvement to cope with the number of foreign policy problems surrounding democratic revolutions in Eastern Europe and the growing difficulties in the Soviet Union and elsewhere. Not surprisingly, the EU was overshadowed by discussions between the superpowers during these years. However, slightly more embarrassing was the fact that EPC did not even play a supporting role in coordinating EU policy concerning these events. The unification of Germany was largely negotiated among the four occupying powers and East/West Germany in the "2 + 4" framework, despite the dramatic implications this might have for the Community (Jarausch 1994: Chapter 8). German unification was neither considered nor negotiated as an enlargement of the EU; instead, West Germany "absorbed" East Germany according to the terms set down in the 2 + 4 talks. And as we saw in Chapter 6, the EC won a major responsibility as the coordinator of all Western aid to Eastern Europe in 1989, a decision that took place in the margins of EPC. The massive migrations from East to West that occurred in the midst of these events also helped to accelerate the reform process, and eventually facilitated the "third pillar" of the EU, cooperation in Justice and Home Affairs.

In the midst of these challenges, several EU member states began fielding proposals for institutional reforms in a number of policy domains. Following a Belgian memorandum[1] on political union (which was strongly supported by the EP), the European Council in Dublin (June 25/26, 1990) formally decided to convene an IGC on political union to coincide with the IGC on economic and monetary union (EMU) that had already been scheduled by the Strasbourg European Council in December 1989. A letter jointly authored by Chancellor Kohl of Germany and President Mitterrand of France was submitted to their EU counterparts just prior to this IGC; among other things, it clearly confirmed their willingness to discuss provisions for greater foreign policy coordination as part of the talks on political union. Mitterrand hoped to constrain the new Germany in a more comprehensive European political structure, and Kohl was eager to bolster his EU-integrationist credentials with other EU states. This loose bargain in the face of EU expansion was not unlike the creation of EPC under French leadership in anticipation of British accession to the EU twenty years before. Moreover, both France and Germany (and the rest of the EU) appreciated the general need to transform the reactive nature of EPC into a more proactive cooperative mechanism.

---

[1] *Europe Documents*, No. 1608, March 29, 1990.

Two aspects of these talks deserve special attention. On the one hand, the TEU reflected the key role of certain states (France, Germany, and the UK) in defining the broad outlines of the new structure for foreign and security policy cooperation. These actors, often negotiating in the European Council,[2] resolved a number of key issues surrounding the new CFSP: its relationship to the EC in the new "tri-pillar" EU structure, its decision-making procedures, and its mention of defense matters. Deadlocks over these issues (particularly security and defense) were broken in part by external events, namely the Persian Gulf War and the eruption of civil war in Yugoslavia. Crises in general have been a particular deficiency of EPC,[3] and the lack of a coordinated EPC security policy during these events was felt throughout the EU. They also revealed the continued possibility of serious security and defense problems in the post-Cold War era, and exposed deficiencies in the ability of EPC to influence the foreign policies of its most powerful member states. Germany's unilateral recognition of Slovenia and Croatia in December 1991, which took place during the final Maastricht negotiations, was particularly offensive to those who wanted the EU to take a unified stand on the issue of Yugoslavia (Crawford 1996). Moreover, US reluctance to get involved in Yugoslavia, and NATO's own self-imposed taboo against such involvement, further led the Europeans to believe that they would have to be more responsible for their own security in the post-Cold War era. Within the EC itself, the advent of the Single European Market and the growing possibility of EMU suggested that Europe would have more foreign interests but lacked the institutional resources to protect those interests. Finally, the growing challenge of aiding the Central and Eastern European countries also encouraged a serious debate on how to prevent the dilution of the EC's supranational institutions and policies.

On the other hand, however, the particular details of the CFSP demonstrate the extent to which small states and EC organizations helped to provide momentum, broker compromises, and most importantly, supply the key details regarding the specifics of the new CFSP. Following their initial letter, Kohl and Mitterrand actually contributed very little to the discussion about what the CFSP should involve. The result was an array of proposed institutional reforms that probably caused more confusion than rational debate; these began to coalesce during the Irish and Italian EU presidencies of 1990. The outbreak of the Persian Gulf crisis in August 1990, and EPC's quick response in the form of a declaration of

---

[2] On the enhanced role of the European Council at this time, see Johnston 1994: Chapter 5.

[3] For post-SEA analyses, see Nuttall 1992b; Wood 1993.

condemnation and economic sanctions, helped to raise the profile of the security question in the discussions. This did not extend, however, to the idea of fully integrating the CFSP into the EC (as suggested in a Dutch proposal of September 1991), which was opposed by France, Denmark, Greece, Portugal, and the UK.

As a result, the negotiators took the path of least resistance by adopting incremental rather than revolutionary reforms, much like the entire history of EPC. Indeed, the CFSP as finally agreed in December 1991 is almost an exact duplicate of the provisions put forth by the Commission over a year before, in its official submission to the IGC on political union (Commission of the European Communities 1990). The EP as well had called for greater foreign policy cooperation in a resolution issued just before (March 14, 1990) the Belgian memorandum (Corbett 1992; Baun 1995–96). The general rationalization of the process of EU foreign policy is due in large part to the input of these actors; they attempted to fill in the gaps regarding the CFSP that had been neglected by the main IGC negotiators, who tended (for nine out of twelve states) during the later stages of talks to be the personal representatives of the EU foreign ministers, not the more informed Political Directors (i.e., Political Committee).[4] However, it is not possible to explore here the various aspects of political union discussed in the context of the IGC, such as reforming the voting weights of EU states in Council or developing common electoral rules. Instead, I focus on the ways in which the Maastricht Treaty replaced EPC with a formal and potentially more robust CFSP under its Title V. The new CFSP was to be the second pillar of the tri-pillar European Union along with the first pillar (the EC) and the third pillar (Justice and Home Affairs).

The Common Foreign and Security Policy

With so many issues left unresolved during the Maastricht negotiations, the CFSP provided only a broad framework, rather than a blueprint, for future cooperation in this area. It was the product of numerous bargains and compromises made over several years. Under these circumstances, the CFSP also represented a complex mix of intergovernmental and supranational elements, involving enhancements and extensions of institutional mechanisms that had developed under EPC. Although the TEU was, in the end, a disappointment to those who wanted a more

---

[4] The Political Directors had generally drafted the SEA provisions on EPC. For more details on the CFSP negotiations, see de Schoutheete de Tervarent 1997; Nuttall 2001: Chapter 5.

Table 7.1 *The CFSP Policy process under Maastricht (major provisions only)*

Policy stage	Relevant actors
Agenda-setting: defining general principles/areas for the CFSP	European Council of Heads of State/Government (includes a member of the Commission)
Decision-making regarding specific CFSP policies	Council of Ministers and Commission (supported by COREU, Political Committee, European Correspondents, working groups, CFSP Secretariat, COREPER)
Implementing common positions and joint actions (includes external representation)	EU presidency, Council of Ministers, Commission, plus EP and the WEU. Involves qualified majority voting in some cases
Funding of the CFSP	Member states and the EC (Commission and EP)
Performance evaluation in terms of coherence (EC/CFSP) and compliance	Council of Ministers, Commission, Political Committee
Democratic oversight (limited)	EP

"communitarized" foreign policy, it clearly established the CFSP as a formally institutionalized European policy sector, despite claims to the contrary regarding its intergovernmental provisions. It is not necessary to review here every single TEU provision concerning the CFSP; instead, in this section I describe them in terms of the four components of governance noted above: the rationalization of the policy process, the establishment of binding legal obligations, the use of authoritative decision-making rules, and the enhanced autonomy of EC organizations. In addition, I stress major changes, not continuity, as compared to EPC.

The CFSP as a rational policy process

The CFSP's provisions under Maastricht were somewhat convoluted thanks to the lingering disagreements and negotiations described above, yet they did involve a sequence of stages and a delegation of responsibilities to govern EU foreign policy. These are summarized in Table 7.1.

The CFSP's policy process was a marked improvement to EPC, whose provisions for cooperative actions were extremely circumscribed.[5] First, the TEU specified a number of broad agenda-setting aims of the CFSP

---

[5] For more detailed examinations of specific CFSP provisions, see Nuttall 1993; Edwards and Nuttall 1994; Regelsberger 1997; Ginsberg 1997a; Holland 1997a; Cameron 1998; Soetendorp 1999.

within the EU's single institutional framework (Article J.1.2).[6] The Preamble, Article B, and Article J.4.1 also asserted that one of the objectives of the Union was to assert its identity on the international scene, which could include more cooperation in defense matters. The explicit mention of defense was one of the most hotly contested and significant provisions of the CFSP on account of opposition from Denmark, Ireland, the Netherlands, Portugal, and the UK. Their reluctant acceptance of this provision reflected the changed external circumstances surrounding the negotiation of the TEU. However, since these states still could not agree to a merger of the WEU and the EU at this time, a declaration attached to the TEU[7] further reiterated the WEU's commitment to strengthen itself as the defense arm of the EU (which satisfied the French) *and* as the European pillar of the Atlantic alliance (which satisfied the British and the Americans). Both decisions satisfied the Germans, long caught between the ambitions of France and the effectiveness of NATO.

Second, concerning decision-making, the CFSP clarified the use of common positions and joint actions in addition to the normal consultations, declarations, and démarches established under EPC (Articles J.2.1 and J.6). These took the place of normal EC legal instruments (under Article 189) and were loosely based on intergovernmental practices developed under the EPC regime.[8] Common positions are expressed through the conformity of national positions and through coordination at international organizations and conferences (Articles J.2.2 and J.2.3). Joint actions (Article J.3) are more complex; they involve more decision-making procedures and often require the use of EC financial resources (see below). Both were defined according to specific decision-making procedures by EU foreign ministers acting in the Council of Ministers[9] (with input from the Commission) rather than on behalf of EU member states (as "High Contracting Parties" under EPC). Thus, unlike EPC, which largely involved consultations, the CFSP was designed to produce *regular foreign policy outputs.*

---

[6] These include: safeguarding the common values, fundamental interests, and independence of the EU; strengthening the security of the EU and its members in all ways; preserving peace and strengthening international security; promoting international cooperation; and developing and consolidating democracy, the rule of law, and respect for human rights and fundamental freedoms.

[7] "Declaration on Western European Union," signed by members of the EU and WEU, and attached to the TEU.

[8] Article 30.2(a), SEA.

[9] The EC Council of Ministers is actually known as the "Council of the EU" now; however, to avoid confusion I refer to it by its previous name.

Third, policy implementation and external representation were similar to decision-making since they were a joint responsibility of two actors: the EU presidency and the Commission. However, like EPC, the EU still does not enjoy legal personality under the terms of international law; thus, its intergovernmental pillars (the CFSP and Justice and Home Affairs) could not conclude international agreements on their own (unlike the EC). This omission created some unusual institutional improvisation in external negotiations, as we shall see in Chapter 8. Instead, under Article J.5, the holder of the EU presidency (rather than the Commission alone, as in EC affairs) represented the Union under the CFSP, implemented its policies, and expressed its positions in international organizations and conferences. It could be assisted by the Troika and the Commission in these tasks. In addition, the WEU was directed to "elaborate and implement" any decisions and actions of the Union that have defense implications (Article J.4).

Fourth, the CFSP policy process also includes the provision of adequate resources to implement its decisions, if necessary. Article J.11 distinguished between "administrative" and "operational" expenditure for the CFSP. Administrative expenditure for the CFSP was to be charged to the budget of the EC, which necessarily involved a greater role for EC actors (see below). Operational expenditure could be charged to the EC budget with a unanimous decision of the Council of Ministers, making it subject to the usual Community budgetary procedures, or it could be charged to EU member states in accordance with a GNP scale.[10] As we saw in previous chapters, finance was not even covered under EPC, which expected contributions to collective actions to be made on a national basis (and there were no formal provisions to codify this expectation). EPC generally used Community resources in a limited, ad hoc way, with no consistency, planning, or oversight. The CFSP clearly changed that practice. Also, the WEU Declaration attached to the TEU generally implied that the CFSP would be able to draw upon the expertise and resources of the WEU in areas involving defense.

Fifth, evaluation and compliance were covered at many levels. While the European Council oversaw the entire tri-pillar structure of the EU (Article D), both the Council of Ministers and the Commission were responsible for ensuring the unity, coherence, and effectiveness of the EU's external activities in terms of security, economic, and development policies (Articles C and J.8). The Council of Ministers was further charged

---

[10] In other words, an EU member state's contribution to a CFSP action is the same proportion as that of its GNP compared to the GNP of the entire EU. *European Report*, No. 1958, June 15, 1994.

with ensuring that EU member states complied with the principles of the CFSP (Article J.1.4). Below this level, and as under EPC, diplomatic and consular missions and Commission delegations in third countries and in international organizations and conferences were directed to ensure that common positions and joint actions were complied with and implemented (Article J.6). Finally, the Political Committee was required to monitor the implementation of CFSP policies, though without prejudice to the responsibilities of the EU presidency and the Commission (Article J.8.5).

Sixth and finally, the TEU provided for some small measure of democratic accountability over the CFSP beyond the provisions already discussed. The importance of democracy to the functioning of the EU's institutions was mentioned in the Preamble to the TEU, and the development of democracy was listed as a general objective of the CFSP. More specifically, the EP was the primary EU forum in which democratic accountability over the CFSP was to be exercised. Under Article J.7, the EU presidency was to consult with the EP and ensure that the views of the Parliament were duly taken into consideration. The EP was to be regularly informed by the EU presidency and the Commission about the development of the CFSP. Finally, as under EPC, the EP could ask questions of the Council, make recommendations, and hold an annual debate on the implementation of the CFSP.

Binding legal norms in the CFSP

The second element of governance concerns the extent to which the CFSP imposed binding legal obligations on EU member states. There is no doubt that it does in terms of international law since the TEU was ratified as a treaty, and certain of its provisions are subject to adjudication by the ECJ (although the ECJ is excluded from jurisdiction over the CFSP in and of itself; see below).[11] The obligatory nature of the CFSP can be inferred from several TEU provisions. In the first place, Articles C and E basically established that the CFSP was part of the single institutional structure of the EU, even though EC organizations operated according to different rules in the EC and the CFSP. The Treaty also replaced the "High Contracting Parties" language of EPC in the SEA with terminology that conformed to existing EC usage. Although EC and CFSP procedures still varied, there was no more practical distinction between EC policy and the CFSP (the SEA, of course, had maintained such a distinction). Rather than special EPC ministerial meetings, the Council

---

[11] For more on this issue, see Eaton 1994; Macleod, Henry, and Hyett 1996: Chapter 24.

of (Foreign) Ministers dealt with all EU policy issues regardless of the pillar (the EC, the CFSP, or JHA) from which they originated. This fact alone stimulated several important debates over institutional matters in the CFSP (and other pillars), as we shall see below and in the next chapter.

In addition, the TEU demanded a stronger commitment to common policies than did EPC. Article J.1.4 required that EU member states "*shall support* the Union's external and security policy actively and unreservedly in a spirit of mutual solidarity" and they "*shall refrain* from any action which is contrary to the interests of the Union or likely to impair its effectiveness as a cohesive force in international relations." Further, Article J.2 asserted that EU member states "*shall inform and consult* one another," that they "*shall ensure* that their national positions conform to the common positions of the CFSP," and that they "*shall coordinate their action* in international organizations and at international conferences" (emphasis added).[12] These obligations were mandatory, even without clearly specified provisions for their enforcement. And according to the rules of procedure (Article 17) of the Council of Ministers, CFSP common positions took the form of a formal legal act of the Council of Ministers, making them legally binding on EU states.[13] Finally, the specific terminology of a *Common* Foreign and Security Policy reflected a higher-order obligation than the notion of consulting or cooperating in foreign policy (as under EPC). It represented the EU's aspirations as an international organization and global actor, not the mere coordination of individual national foreign policy goals.

Authoritative CFSP decision-making rules

Closely related to the TEU's legal obligations are the detailed decision-making rules to be used in the formulation of CFSP joint actions. Beyond the provisions already noted, the CFSP's decision-making rules permitted CFSP joint actions to be initiated and/or implemented by QMV in Council (Article J.3; this included funding decisions). Maastricht provided that the initial decision for CFSP action must be unanimous, but that later stages (such as the means, duration, and procedures for implementation or financing) could be subject to QMV. As with the CFSP provisions on defense, the inclusion of QMV rules in this pillar was a

---

[12] Compare this language to Article 30.2(d) of the SEA: "The High Contracting Parties shall *endeavor* to avoid any action or position which impairs their effectiveness as a cohesive force" (emphasis added).

[13] That is, they are published in the *Official Journal of EC Legislation*, rather than in the *Official Journal of Communications*. See Galloway 1995: 214.

major departure from EPC practice. However, the actual procedure for turning a European Council policy guideline into a specific CFSP joint action was extremely convoluted. The TEU actually created a decision-making system consisting of up to five veto points in the CFSP, where a member state(s) could block, or at least delay, a foreign policy decision. These veto points included:

1) General European Council guidelines/conclusions for CFSP priority areas (unanimity; Articles D, J.3.1, and J.8.1/J.8.2).
2) Specific Council of Ministers positions/actions for the CFSP (unanimity; Article J.3.1).
3) Council decision to define further decisions (scope, objectives, duration, means, procedures and conditions for implementation, funding) which could be taken by QMV (unanimity; Article J.3.2).
4) Council decision to charge CFSP "operational" funds to the EC budget (unanimity; Article J.11.2) rather than to member states.
5) Final QMV decisions adopted after following the above procedures, with the further proviso that such decisions be taken by a minimum of eight EU member states (Article J.3.2).

Maastricht imposed additional limitations (such as Article J.3.6) to these rules that served as escape clauses and allowed varying degrees of member state compliance to CFSP decisions. When one also considers the role of working groups, Political Directors, and COREPER in the CFSP (see below), it is clear that the system set up so many levels of decision-making that decisive action in the CFSP would be very difficult. In addition to these complex rules, if the joint action involved defense matters, then QMV did not apply at all and unanimity was the standard rule in this domain (Article J.4.3). Together, these rules clearly inhibited the application of supranational procedures to the CFSP. They also, however, represented a far more sophisticated exposition of this rule than had ever occurred under EPC, and for that reason alone they should be singled out as key reforms.

Enhanced autonomy of EC organizations

Finally, the CFSP provided for a greater degree of autonomy on the part of EC organizations. Part of this autonomy derives from explicit TEU provisions, while other aspects can be inferred from more complex linkages between EC actors and other elements of the CFSP policy process. Part of this autonomy is also a result of EC actors simply attempting to involve themselves in the CFSP process after the mechanism was implemented, as we shall see below.

For example, the Commission, under the aggressive leadership of Jacques Delors during the Maastricht period, saw several of its desires for institutional reform incorporated into the TEU. Although the TEU did not go as far as the Commission preferred (such as by granting it an exclusive right of initiative in the CFSP), its stature in the policy process has improved in the areas of agenda-setting, decision-making, implementation, funding, and compliance/evaluation. And while the Commission did not enjoy with EU member states the right to veto decisions, it could no longer be excluded from a CFSP policy matter, even those extending to security and defense matters. We also should note here that this new authority in the CFSP prompted a number of internal changes in the Commission during the ratification of Maastricht; together, these constituted the most important reorganization for foreign policy in the Commission's history.

In fact, the Commission endured two internal reorganizations and hired more foreign advisers during the first two years of the CFSP in the hopes of creating a "Unified External Service." By 1996 it had a network of 127 foreign delegations, with 729 staff in Brussels and 2,452 overseas. According to some estimates, this represented the fifth largest diplomatic service in Europe.[14] Before the departure of the outgoing Delors Commission presidency, a new Directorate-General, DG-IA, was created to handle all EU external political relations (including the CFSP) under a single Commissioner.[15] DG-IA provoked criticisms inside and outside the Commission, and it also competed to a certain extent with the Secretariat-General of the Council. In response, the new Jacques Santer Commission in early 1995 reorganized the external relations portfolios along geographic lines, with each external relations Commissioner controlling both economic and political relations for his/her geographic area. Unlike the original form of DG-IA, this new hybrid form reflected the Commission's long-standing insistence that the economic and political functions of external relations were inseparably linked. And although it did not enjoy as many resources as other DGs in the Commission (such as those dealing with economic affairs), DG-IA represented a substantial expansion of capabilities compared to the handful of Commission officials who regularly handled EPC affairs. Also, the fact that a single Commissioner (Hans van den Broek) was appointed to oversee the CFSP regularly provided an opportunity for the Commission to raise its profile in this domain. Commission President Santer also institutionalized a number of internal Commission procedures to improve coordination with the CFSP.

---

[14] Nuttall 1996; Cameron 1998: 63. Also interviews with Commission officials from DG-IA and from the cabinets of individual Commissioners, Brussels, 1995–96.

[15] Interviews with several Commission officials in DG-IA, Brussels. For more details on these changes, see Allen and Smith 1994: 68; Nuttall 1995: 3–4.

Maastricht also anticipated a small change in the EPC Secretariat,[16] which previously was at the disposal of the state holding the rotating presidency. Soon after the TEU entered into effect the EPC Secretariat was permanently attached to the Council of Ministers and directed to serve it as well, not just the EU presidency alone. The political functions of the CFSP and the existing external economic functions of the EC were established as two departments under a single director-general in the Council Secretariat General, and the Secretariat's staff was increased. The new CFSP Secretariat was an improvement over the previous EPC unit, with about twenty-seven permanent staff by the mid-1990s (one official from each member state following the 1995 enlargement and nearly an equal number of Council officials, plus secretarial support). These officials are mostly experts from foreign ministries; other staff are added during each EU presidency as necessary. Its main tasks generally continued the trend established by the EPC Secretariat. However, beyond its greater size and its directive to serve the CFSP (rather than the EU presidency), the new location of the CFSP Secretariat is symbolically important: as an arm of the Council Secretariat General it became a *Community* institution, making it a central administrative resource for the constantly changing number of officials (from EU member states and EC organizations) involved with the CFSP, directly or indirectly.

Although a strengthened role for the EP in the CFSP could have enhanced the "political union" goal of the TEU, it gained no notable new powers; the TEU largely preserved most of the EPC provisions of the SEA where the EP was concerned. Its most important external relations power, the assent procedure[17] was preserved from the SEA and it typically lies outside the domain of the CFSP (Articles 237 and 238). However, the TEU extended this procedure somewhat; now the EP could approve all important international agreements[18] and those related to Article 113, the Common Commercial Policy. For all other agreements the EP must be consulted, but with the derogation from normal practice that the Council of Ministers may set a deadline for the EP's opinion. Indirectly, however, the TEU provided for a role for the EP in the CFSP funding process, as the rules above indicate. CFSP administrative funds could be charged to the EC budget, giving the EP a say over the matter

---

[16] Declaration No. 28, TEU, "On Practical Arrangements in the Field of the Common Foreign and Security Policy."

[17] The EP's right to approve accession and Association Agreements and their renewals.

[18] These are defined as any agreement establishing a specific institutional framework, or having important implications for the EC budget, or requiring the amendment of EC legislation pursuant to the new co-decision procedure established by the TEU (under Article 189b), which applies to about one-quarter of all EC legislation.

(Article 209). If CFSP operational funds were charged to the EC budget the EP also had the right to be involved, as it must approve all non-compulsory spending (Article 203). As we shall see in the next chapter, the EP quickly acted to clarify the use of these powers.

Finally, the ECJ is mentioned in the TEU, but its role in the CFSP process largely followed the tradition set down under EPC. Under Article L the ECJ was formally prevented from having jurisdiction over the CFSP. This provision was further qualified by Article M, which provided that nothing in the TEU shall affect the treaties amending the EC (other than the amendments provided for in the TEU). In other words, CFSP activities could not be used to modify or undermine Community competencies. This means that the ECJ "can and must police the borderline between the Community pillar and the CFSP."[19] In addition, the ECJ now had the ability to impose fines on states that did not comply with its rulings in the first pillar (Article 171.2); this provision possibly could be extended to the CFSP to ensure compliance with certain actions.[20] Some CFSP (and JHA) competencies, such as sanctions, export controls, customs, and visa/asylum policy, clearly overlapped with those of the EC and might eventually require review by the ECJ, which is legally bound to protect the *Community's* legal order, not that of the CFSP (or JHA).

However, as McGoldrick notes (1997: 149), "no member state or institution can bring an action before the ECJ concerning compliance with obligations under CFSP, or the validity of a CFSP instrument. Rather, it is the Council's responsibility (Article J.1.4) at a political level to ensure that the obligations of support and solidarity under CFSP are complied with." Moreover, this would not violate Article 219 of the EC Treaty (which gives the ECJ jurisdiction over EC affairs) since it would not concern the interpretation or application of the EC Treaty but rather the Maastricht Treaty. Such an action is unlikely, however, as it would violate more powerful norms of secrecy and consensus within the CFSP. Still, these limitations concerning the formal role of the ECJ have not prevented the codification of some informal CFSP practices, as we shall see in the next chapter.

In sum, then, although some elements of intergovernmentalism were preserved (mainly the role of the European Council and the limits on

---

[19] Eaton 1994: 221. Weiler also has noted (1993: 55) that the ECJ is able to police its own exclusion from the CFSP based on the language of the TEU, arguing that "the attempt to exclude the Court of Justice from the CFSP and Justice and Home Affairs *in toto* is doomed."

[20] Also note that, in an early CFSP procedural decision (Council Decision 94/308/CFSP), the EC Court of Auditors was invited to audit non-Community expenditures, such as those of the CFSP.

decision-making by QMV), many other aspects of the CFSP policy process justify the use of the term "governance," though not necessarily *supranational* governance, to describe the functioning of the CFSP, at least in terms of its formal treaty provisions. The extent to which the notion of governance affected the *practice* of the CFSP in the mid-1990s is considered in the rest of this chapter.

Institutional performance: the CFSP in action

The CFSP, along with the rest of the Maastricht Treaty, entered into force in November 1993 following a delayed ratification process. Between November 1993 and June 1996, the start of the next major stage of institutional reform (covered in Chapter 8), the CFSP produced a number of common positions and joint actions on a variety of subjects. These activities provide the raw material for my analysis of CFSP performance. As in previous chapters, I distinguish between changes of procedure and changes of substance, both of which have been extensively analyzed by scholars,[21] EU member states (Reflection Group 1995: 39–49; Council of the European Union 1995: Part V), and EC organizations such as the Commission (High Level Group of Experts on the CFSP 1995–96; Commission of the European Communities 1995 and 1996) and the EP (1995). Although the general consensus is that the CFSP clearly has a mixed record of successes and setbacks and thus did not live up to its promise, the primary question here is the extent to which institutional reforms have improved the prospects for EU foreign policy cooperation, as compared to EPC. I argue that, although it has exhibited a number of limitations, the CFSP did in fact enhance the EU's external relations capabilities (i.e., improve cooperation). I begin with an analysis of the performance of the CFSP's general procedural elements before turning to substantive policy outcomes.

Procedural performance: the CFSP policy process

There is no doubt that the CFSP generated a great deal more cooperative activity as compared to EPC. Much of this involved information-sharing, using many of EPC's existing transgovernmental mechanisms. Meetings at all levels and in all forums increased considerably during the

---

[21] For example, see Ginsberg 1994 and 1995; Regelsberger and Wessels 1996; Gordon 1997–98; Forster and Wallace, 1997; Anderson 1998; Smith 1998b; Peterson and Sjursen 1998.

negotiations and implementation of the Maastricht Treaty.[22] The number of COREU telexes also rapidly grew from 7,548 in 1990 to 12,699 in 1994.[23] The advent of e-mail among EU states and EU organizations also undoubtedly contributed to information-sharing on less-sensitive matters, although it is impossible to document the number of such messages. Together, these activities constituted a continuing transition from the previous EPC network toward what one participant termed "CFSP society."[24]

To appreciate the full procedural impact of the CFSP, we can examine each stage of the policy process noted in the previous section. Concerning agenda-setting, the European Council rapidly performed its limited functions here, even before the CFSP entered into effect. At Maastricht, negotiators could not agree on a set of "essential European interests" to be served by the CFSP, although foreign ministers previously had attempted to create such a list at a meeting in Asolo, Italy, in October 1990 (the so-called "Asolo list"; de Schoutheete de Tervarent 1997: 49). Instead, the Lisbon European Council (June 26/27, 1992) approved a report by the EU foreign ministers on the likely development of the CFSP (EU Foreign Ministers 1992). This report identified certain "factors determining important common interests"[25] and the specific objectives to be taken into consideration when adopting a CFSP joint action. These objectives included:

* Strengthening democratic principles and institutions, and respect for minority and human rights;
* Promoting regional political stability and contributing to the creation of political and/or economic frameworks that encourage regional cooperation or moves toward regional or sub-regional cooperation;
* Contributing to the prevention and settlement of conflicts;
* Contributing to more effective international coordination in dealing with emergency situations;
* Strengthening existing cooperation in issues of international interest such as the fight against arms proliferation, terrorism, and traffic in illicit drugs;
* Promoting and supporting good government.

---

[22] Interviews with Commission, COREPER, and EU member state foreign ministry officials, Brussels, 1995–96. Also see Regelsberger 1997.
[23] Figures from *CFSP Forum*, No. 1 (Bonn: Institut für Europäische Politik, 1994), p. 1; and *CFSP Forum*, No. 1 (Bonn: Institut für Europäische Politik, 1995), p. 8.
[24] Interview with a Commission official, Brussels, 1996.
[25] These factors are: geographical proximity of a given region or country; an important interest in the political and economic stability of a region or country; and the existence of threats to the security interests of the EU.

Based on these factors, the European Council explicitly defined a number of specific geographical and functional areas open to joint action in the CFSP.[26] When the CFSP entered into effect in November 1993, several of these areas became the objects of the first CFSP joint actions.[27] European Councils in 1992 and 1993 also set out issues in the security field which could be suitable for joint actions. Considering the heated debates that surrounded even the mention of security issues under EPC, the fact that the European Council was able to set down fairly detailed objectives in this area marks a major breakthrough for the CFSP. These efforts will be explored further below. Still, as under EPC, the European Council does not devote much attention to the day-to-day implementation of CFSP policies because of the reasons discussed in Chapter 4.[28] The European Council primarily helps ensure that all EU policy, particularly in the second and third pillars, seems wholly subordinate to the dictates of EU member governments, not EC organizations. Additional limitations regarding the role of the European Council can be seen as we examine other stages of the policy process.

For example, during CFSP decision-making, most policy proposals involve the Council of Ministers, with support from its Secretariat, the Commission, the Political Committee, and COREPER. Declarations have continued as under EPC and have increased in number, now averaging about two or three per week. Common positions and joint actions involve more complicated decisions, and there was some confusion as to the practical differences between these instruments.[29] As we shall see below, the Council initiated a number of CFSP positions and actions related to the agenda previously set down by the European Council. These were considerably more elaborate than the ad hoc decisions produced under the EPC system. Although the CFSP followed most of these procedures when undertaking common positions and joint actions, EU states could not manage to utilize the convoluted QMV decision-making rules. The

---

[26] These areas included Central and Eastern Europe, the Maghreb and the Middle East, and several security issues (CSCE, disarmament and arms control in Europe, nuclear non-proliferation, and controlling the transfer of arms technology to third countries). See the EU Foreign Ministers 1992.

[27] These first CFSP actions included the Stability Pact in Central and Eastern Europe, support for the Middle East and Yugoslavia peace processes, and support for transitions to democracy in South Africa and Russia. See the EU Heads of State and Government 1993.

[28] The limited role of the European Council in day-to-day CFSP decision-making was confirmed in numerous interviews with CFSP officials. Also see Johnston 1994: Chapter 5.

[29] Interviews with CFSP Secretariat and Commission officials, Brussels, 1996. Also see Galloway 1995: 214–15.

way the EU was able to "bend the rules" to improve the coherence of the CFSP is discussed in the next chapter.

A related problem here is that the Commission was not very aggressive in initiating CFSP policies. Of course, it shares this right with fifteen member states, so it cannot be expected to be the only or even the primary source of initiatives. This shared responsibility, and the fact that "initiating" a CFSP joint action is far more complex and delicate than initiating EC legislation, led the Commission to pursue its strategy of embedding CFSP issues in broader sets of EC agreements or policies rather than instigate stand-alone CFSP actions.[30] The Commission also senses member states' fear of precedent-setting, and has tried to develop a "critical mass" of precedents and experience in the CFSP to serve as a foundation for future foreign policies.[31] This is especially crucial when economic instruments besides aid and joint action financing are involved (i.e., sanctions or Association Agreements), since they affect the EU's internal market and its external economic relations. The overlap between all EU policy domains and the enlargement process also requires the Commission to embed foreign policy questions within a broader vision of the EU's future. However, the Commission is still somewhat wary of involvement in security issues and, of course, it was further preoccupied with a number of internal changes to help its implementation of CFSP decisions, as we have already seen. Yet all policy initiatives ultimately require an advocate, and the Commission is the only actor in the EU who can play this role on a consistent basis.

Policy implementation and representation have been more successful than the application of QMV procedures to CFSP decision-making. I cover this aspect of the CFSP in more detail in my discussion of specific actions below. For the moment, it should be noted that the TEU was necessarily vague on the specific division of labor between the two main actors charged with representation/implementation: the EU presidency and the Commission. Arrangements for their respective roles were generally worked out on a case-by-case basis. In some cases, this involved the use of ad hoc external representatives with temporary mandates for particular areas and problems (such as Bosnia, Cyprus, Mostar, the Middle East, and the Great Lakes region of Africa).

Another controversy concerning implementation (in addition to the aforementioned decision-making problems) involves the provision of

---

[30] Exceptions include EU involvement in Rwanda (against the resistance of the French), EU participation in the Korean Energy Development Organization, an initiative on demining war-torn areas, and a joint action on renegotiating the Nuclear Non-Proliferation Treaty. Interviews with Commission officials in DG-IA, Brussels, 1995.

[31] Interviews with Commission officials in DG-IA, Brussels, 1995.

adequate material resources for the CFSP, which will be covered in more detail below. Since the Commission still lacks tangible resources for influencing the CFSP (compared to some EU member states), it has been far more creative in the way it makes its administration of external funding (such as the huge PHARE and TACIS programs)[32] and its negotiation or implementation of external agreements subject to political criteria, even though some member states oppose this power.[33] For those CFSP positions and actions which have not involved financing, there have been clear success stories (such as the renewal of the Nuclear Non-Proliferation Treaty and the Stability Pact in Central and Eastern Europe). With the Stability Pact, for example, the EU presidency and the Commission jointly represented the EU; its success demonstrates the vitality of the "bicephalous" or "tandem" presidency (mentioned in Chapter 6) in cases where representation by the presidency or the Commission alone is not politically feasible. These examples will be revisited below, while far more complex institutional problems surrounding implementation, such as legal personality, are covered in the next chapter.

Substantive performance: CFSP common positions and joint actions

Although the CFSP record since 1993 in terms of changes of process is somewhat mixed, with clear improvements and informal innovations frustrated by lingering deficiencies and ideological disputes, the fact is that the CFSP did lead to a rapid expansion of the EU's foreign policy activities. As we might expect given their low costs, declarations are still the most common CFSP instrument. While they are often derided as weak mechanisms, it can also be argued that "through such open expression of the *acquis politique* the [EU] fifteen can and do exercise influence on the behavior and policy of other governments, as the reactions of the addressees of declarations, démarches, and other diplomatic means demonstrate" (Regelsberger and Wessels 1996: 38). The CFSP record in terms of positions and actions is somewhat more modest than the TEU's architects may have hoped, yet quite a large number of the post-TEU positions/actions shared three important features: their subject matter was extremely wide-ranging compared to EPC (indicating the contraction or even disappearance of *domaines réservés*), they were more explicitly tied to other external policies of the EU (i.e., greater coherence), and the joint

---

[32] PHARE is the "Poland-Hungary Assistance for Recovering Economies" program. TACIS is "Technical Assistance to the Commonwealth of Independent States."

[33] For example, the Commission held up the interim Partnership and Cooperation Agreement with Russia because of the violence in Chechnya, an improper use of the Commission's authority in the view of some member states.

actions in particular often drew upon the resources and capabilities of the Community.

The official record shows that a total of twenty-seven common positions were taken between November 1993 and June 1996, the start of the IGC that led to the Amsterdam Treaty.[34] These common positions involved ex-Yugoslavia (ten positions); Ukraine; Haiti (two positions); Nigeria (three positions); Rwanda; Sudan; Libya; Burundi (two positions); Angola; blinding laser weapons; biological and toxic weapons (fourth review conference); East Timor; the creation of an emergency travel document for EU nationals; and plans for the rescue of EU diplomatic missions.[35] Nearly an equal number of CFSP joint actions have been taken; twenty-nine during the time period under consideration. Again, most were related to the situation in ex-Yugoslavia (twelve actions). Others involved South Africa; an envoy for the Great Lakes region of Africa; the Stability Pact with Central/Eastern Europe (two actions); the Middle East peace process (three actions); preparation for renewal of the Nuclear Non-Proliferation Treaty; observation of Russian elections; action against anti-personnel landmines (two actions); the Korean Peninsula Energy Development Organization (KEDO); and controls on dual-use technology (five actions).

The rest of this section briefly surveys some of the more important common positions and joint actions during the first three years of the CFSP, from its beginning in November 1993 to the start of formal IGC negotiations in June 1996. As in previous chapters, I focus on specific geographic/functional areas addressed by the CFSP. I do not attempt here a detailed examination of all CFSP positions and actions; instead, I cover those whose implementation provides key lessons concerning the relationship between institutional reforms and cooperation. Three areas in particular deserve close attention: the former Yugoslavia, South Africa, and relations with Central and Eastern Europe and the former Soviet Union. A more detailed analysis of the CFSP's activities in security is provided in the last major section of this chapter.

As the record shows, the most comprehensive CFSP activity involved the former Yugoslavia. The EU's difficulties here have often been cited as a major deficiency of the CFSP, as it failed to use its economic leverage over Yugoslavia effectively before it broke up, failed to coordinate its recognition of the separate republics when dissolution seemed imminent,

---

[34] Note that where the record shows multiple CFSP positions or actions for a single issue (such as Yugoslavia), most were merely modifications, clarifications, or extensions of previous decisions.

[35] This last position was not published in the Official Journal (in June 1996) due to Danish reservations; see below on security issues.

and then failed to stop the violence following dissolution.[36] Although these criticisms are well deserved, it is somewhat unfair to judge the CFSP by its performance in this area alone. First, it is arguable that no state or institution, within Europe or without, acted decisively and effectively at the time. The collapse of Yugoslavia was a major challenge not only to the EU but also to the UN, the OSCE, NATO, and their member states. Consensus among all of these actors was lacking, even among states who possessed the political will to intervene at the crucial early stages of Yugoslavia's dissolution. Second, it should be kept in mind that the CFSP was not explicitly designed for stopping nationalist violence on the scale that took place in the Balkans. Like EPC before it, the CFSP is primarily devoted to long-term conflict resolution with diplomatic and economic tools, not quick crisis management using military means. Even if the EU had decided to intervene by force at an early stage (with or without the help of the US), it is not certain that such an act would have prevented civil war. Third, the CFSP did not even enter into effect until November 1993, by which time the problem may have escalated beyond the control of any single actor. Even if the TEU had been ratified before then, it is questionable whether implementation of the CFSP would have taken place so immediately and efficiently. A number of issues concerning the implementation of CFSP joint actions (external representation, funding, and oversight) had to be resolved first. Fourth, the EU clearly has learned from the Balkans case, largely in the form of several institutional changes that will be discussed further in Chapter 8.

These comments do not exonerate the EU from its limited impact in the Balkans; they are only intended to place the evaluation of the CFSP in the proper context. Although military force through NATO ultimately ended the violence here (for the time being), the EU in fact devoted a great deal of attention to the region, and the CFSP clearly facilitated these efforts beyond what was typical under EPC. Through its common positions, the CFSP imposed various sanctions and instituted an arms embargo against the former Yugoslavia. Through its joint actions, the CFSP provided aid to Bosnia-Herzegovina and supported the electoral process in the region, and took over the administration of the city of Mostar. This last action saw the first involvement of the WEU in a CFSP activity, although this was not a formal CFSP joint action as set down by Article J.4.2 (see Chapter 8). Through these decisions, the EU/CFSP clearly proved that it was capable of behaving as an independent "action organization" with its own goals rather than as a passive "framework" organization (like the UN, OSCE, Council of Europe, or NATO's Partnership for Peace) that

---

[36] On these problems, see Woodward 1995; Crawford 1996.

primarily reflects the goals of its most powerful member states (Hill 1998: 35). In the long run, these patient efforts involving state–civil society relations, market development, legal systems, and democratization are likely to prove as valuable to troubled regions as military intervention,[37] particularly as the US often seems unwilling to engage in what it calls costly "nation-building" exercises.

The second major area confronted by the CFSP during its first few months of operation concerned South Africa. These efforts involved a transition from working against apartheid (as under EPC) to helping to improve new democratic institutions and economic development in South Africa (Holland 1995a, 1995b, 1997b). Toward these ends, the Commission began producing policy option papers on this issue as early as 1992, and an outline of the EPC-CFSP policy transition was set down during the Danish presidency in June 1993. After rescinding the Code of Conduct and the 1985 sanctions against South Africa (involving nuclear and military cooperation and the exchange of military attachés) in late 1993, the EU implemented a series of positive actions to assist the new government. These included dispatching a team of 450 officials to help with elections. The activities of this group went far beyond mere elections monitoring,[38] and the Commission (chiefly DG-IA) was fully responsible for coordinating these activities. Its successful involvement here showed much potential for implementing future CFSP joint actions.

Thus, following this first joint action, the EU began a more extensive effort to integrate the former pariah state into the global community. A Commission delegation was established in Pretoria in December 1993, and it became the central contact between the EU and the local government. This was a major change compared to EPC, when relations were conducted through EU member states with embassies in South Africa.[39] In April 1994 the Council adopted a Commission proposal for stronger relations with South Africa; the new framework involved trade and economic cooperation, a political dialogue (where the EU placed its usual emphasis on human rights, democracy, the rule of law, and social justice), and development cooperation. Through these strands of activities involving the EC and CFSP, the EU showed more coherence and uniformity of its policy toward South Africa than ever before. Holland's detailed assessment (1995b: 566) of this policy deserves quoting at length:

[37] For more detailed evaluations, see Edwards 1992 and 1997; Nuttall 1994; Kintis 1997.

[38] For a description of their activities, see Holland (1995b), who also asserts (pp. 563–64) that in terms of "observer days," the EU was perhaps the major player compared to the UN.

[39] Though the Commission did have a small, non-accredited "European Commission Technical Coordination Office" in South Africa, which handled the 1985–86 Special Program and development assistance.

From both the European and South African perspectives, the joint action has been an almost unqualified success . . . [T]hrough the joint action a comprehensive approach was adopted rather than segregated incrementalism. Coordinating the various policy sectors (development, trade, election-monitoring, etc.) together under a single initiative (the joint action), while difficult and possibly time-consuming, had led by the end of 1994 to a compatible and comprehensive policy mix that was regionally sensitive as well as of direct benefit to South Africa.

The South African experiment ultimately "improved the effectiveness of European policy" and confirmed the Commission's enhanced status in this domain, as it "fully utilized its power of initiative and was the leading player throughout 1993–94 in structuring the Union's contemporary policy, fulfilling a role of at least *primus inter pares*" (Holland 1995b: 566). Thus, the EU's comprehensive approach to South Africa and the activities of EC actors such as the Commission strongly indicate an enhanced capability for EU foreign policy as compared to EPC.

The third major area involved CFSP actions toward the former communist world, where the EU hoped to apply its most fundamental ordering principles: democracy, the rule of law, market economics, and respect for human rights. These principles were enshrined in the primary framework for these relations, the Europe Agreements with the Central and Eastern European countries (CEEC), which were dominated by the Community, not EPC.[40] The most prominent CFSP action here was the "Stability Pact" with the CEEC (also known as the Balladur Plan, after the French prime minister who first proposed it; Ueta 1997). Although greeted with a great degree of skepticism at first (from inside and outside the EU),[41] the Pact created a framework of preventative diplomacy to help head off conflicts over borders and ethnic minorities, a major concern given the situation in Yugoslavia. The Pact clearly fostered productive discussions on a number of sensitive topics: the consolidation of borders, the EU's changing relationship with the CSCE (the original forum for airing concerns over borders and minorities), and the possibility of helping to secure the East without extending formal defense guarantees.[42] The entire exercise also encouraged a more general debate over the

---

[40] For details, see Lippert 1997.

[41] On this point, Rummel argues (1996: 56–57) that one of the French motivations behind the Pact was to prevent Central and Eastern Europe from becoming a German *domaine réservé*.

[42] In particular, the major Pact conferences (Paris, May 26–27, 1994; and Paris, March 20–21, 1995) covered regional trans-border cooperation, questions relating to minorities, cultural cooperation, economic cooperation and administrative training, and environmental problems.

conditions for future membership of the EU, a main concern for most states involved in the talks. As noted above, the Commission's regular participation in both the CFSP and the EU enlargement process gave it a highly privileged position in these discussions.

The Pact involved the EC in other novel ways. First, it showed the efficacy of the "bicephalous" (or tandem) presidency approach to external negotiations.[43] Second, although the Pact did not involve its own finances to any substantial degree, it drew upon PHARE funds for a large number of small-scale projects. Through the end of 1995, 870 million ECU (MECU) were devoted to Stability Pact projects, and the Commission was charged with implementing the funds and preparing a final report on their use (European Commission 1995b). In the end, the Pact produced an extraordinary number (47) of agreements between interested countries and EU states, and an even greater number (76) of agreements between the interested countries themselves. Of special importance were the two "good neighbor" agreements between Hungary and Romania and Hungary and Slovakia. The OSCE took over the Pact following the conclusion of the CFSP joint action at the final Paris conference on March 20/21, 1995 (Schneider 1997; Long 1997). Considering the current state of peaceful relations among these states, the Pact must be considered a success from the EU's point of view.[44]

Actions involving Russia and the Commonwealth of Independent States (CIS) proceeded along similar lines, although they were far more modest and less of a priority than those involving the CEEC. Still, one of the very first CFSP joint actions involved elections-monitoring in Russia. According to Commission insiders, this was the first real "test case" (and a successful one, in their view) of their ability to devise, implement, and fund *independently* a CFSP joint action with Commission resources.[45] Later, the CFSP common position on Ukraine effectively used EC funds and Commission expertise to help pay for the closure of part of the Chernobyl nuclear reactor (Peterson 1998: 6). The Commission also showed its willingness to make Partnership and Cooperation Agreements (and their Interim Agreements) subject to political criteria; these agreements also are closely linked to EC activities. And although the EU/CFSP can be criticized for not producing a more comprehensive, long-term strategy toward Russia and the CIS at the time (as it did with the CEEC),[46] these direct efforts to engage these countries are still far more extensive,

---

[43] Interviews with Commission DG-IA officials, Brussels, 1996.

[44] McManus (1998: 128–29) is somewhat more critical about the reception of the Stability Pact among CEECs.

[45] Interviews with Commission officials in DG-IA, Brussels, 1996.

[46] For such a critical view, see Allen 1997.

forward-looking, and coherent than those applied under the EPC system. In addition, the question of common strategies for the CFSP was addressed later, as we shall see in Chapter 8.

Beyond these three major areas, the CFSP acted in a number of other areas beyond what had been achieved in EPC. The CFSP worked to revitalize the Euro-Arab Dialogue, which was now included within a broader Mediterranean framework (Barbé and Izquierdo: 1997). When violence broke out in the West Bank in 1996, the EU added 20 MECU to its aid budget for Palestine and, in doing so, gave the Commission considerable autonomy to negotiate a new trade agreement with the Palestinians (Peterson 1998: 15). The CFSP devoted attention to other African and Caribbean countries (such as Angola, Burundi, Haiti, Nigeria, Rwanda, and the Sudan) in its concern with the developing world. This also involved appointing an EU representative to the Great Lakes region of Africa to help prevent conflicts and improve relations (Keatinge 1997). Finally, political dialogues were extended to several other countries beyond those already mentioned, such as Japan and the US (Monar 1997a, 1997b).

The new Dialogue with the US was particularly noteworthy. Although it did not involve a separate CFSP joint action, EU–US relations were institutionalized in a far more complex "New Transatlantic Agenda" involving a "Joint Action Plan" to address the economic, social, and political dimensions of transatlantic cooperation. This was the most comprehensive statement of EU–US relations ever, growing out of the EC–US Transatlantic Declaration negotiated in 1990. Although the parts of the Action Plan were not uniformly implemented, the whole concept is much more substantial than the incoherent, ad hoc approach to EU–US relations that had taken place in the past.[47] Equally importantly, the Dialogue (and the new CFSP in general) also invited more attention on the part of US officials in Brussels, who began to recognize the potential of the EU as a global actor despite its difficulties in the Balkans. The Dialogue also was strongly influenced by negotiations between the US, the Commission, and the Spanish EU presidency; intensive collusion between these actors helped to sell the idea to those EU states (such as France) who were extremely suspicious of it.[48] The advent of the Dialogue was one of the more positive accomplishments of the CFSP during a time when the US and the EU were often at odds with each other over problems

---

[47] For more on the New Transatlantic Agenda, see Ginsberg 1997b and 1998; Krenzler and Schomaker 1996; Philippart and Winand 2001.

[48] Interviews with Commission, COREPER, and US mission to the EU officials, Brussels, 1996.

involving the institutional architecture of Atlantic security and more parochial issues (such as trade disputes and the Helms–Burton Act).[49]

The CFSP, security, and the WEU

As noted above, European Councils in 1992 (Lisbon; Edinburgh) and 1993 (Brussels) set out specific issues in the security field that could be suitable for joint actions.[50] Considering the extent to which serious discussions (not to mention formal, public statements) concerning these topics were banned for much of the history of EPC, the European Council's list of issues should be considered a major breakthrough for European foreign policy. It set a clear institutional benchmark to encourage specific security-related actions in the CFSP, and embedded these priorities in a broader normative framework involving human rights, democracy, the rule of law, stability, and other EU values. In evaluating the CFSP record in this area we also should keep in mind that the EU plays a vital indirect role in promoting European security by virtue of its "civilian" powers (chiefly trade and aid policies) and its enlargement decisions. However, in terms of actual policy performance, the CFSP clearly was not very aggressive in this area. Most EU states were far more preoccupied with the broader transatlantic debate concerning the future role of NATO and its enlargement than with applying the CFSP's new capabilities in this area. Conflicting American attitudes toward the EU's ambitions in this domain complicated matters as well; the US has consistently demanded greater burden-sharing by its NATO allies yet has not always supported an institutional or operational expression (at the EU level or elsewhere) of such increased European capabilities.

Thus, by the start of the EU's IGC in March 1996, only six minor security-related issues had been addressed directly by the CFSP through specific joint actions: a directive on assistance with UN mine-clearing efforts; preparation for the renewal of the Nuclear Non-Proliferation Treaty (NPT); the control of exports of dual-use goods; the goal to prohibit blinding laser weapons; preparation for a conference on the

---

[49] The Helms–Burton Act (1996) was enacted by the US to punish foreign companies for doing business with Cuba. It was addressed by a CFSP joint action on extra-territoriality in November 1996, but by then both the US and the EU had basically resolved their differences on this issue and the US has neglected to implement the legislation.

[50] The security issues decided at Edinburgh involved the CSCE/OSCE process, disarmament and arms control in Europe, non-proliferation of weapons of mass destruction, and the economic aspects of security (especially technology transfer). The Extraordinary European Council in Brussels defined the general objectives of European security as preserving the territorial integrity and political independence of the EU, its democratic character, its economic stability, and the stability of neighboring regions.

non-proliferation of biological and toxic weapons; and the EU's participation in the Korean Peninsular Energy Development Organization (KEDO). Several common positions also touched upon security issues; most were used to support the joint actions noted above, with the exception of a general plan to evacuate EU nationals from third countries. In the rest of this section, I first examine the general institutional lessons gleaned from the CFSP's security actions, then turn to the CFSP's operational relationship with the WEU.

Security-related actions

While it is true that the CFSP's security-related efforts were limited in scope and ambition, it should first be kept in mind that the very idea of discussing security affairs in the context of the CFSP was (and is) still controversial for several EU states. In addition, fear that the EU framework would contaminate decisions about security with supranational EC procedures was still strong. Finally, the EU was attempting to implement the CFSP in the face of serious external problems (such as Yugoslavia) and while conducting much broader debates about the future of other security-related institutions, such as NATO and the WEU. Under these circumstances, the fact that the CFSP was able to take any actions at all concerning security represents no small achievement. Three of these actions (control of dual-use goods, the NPT conference, and KEDO) also involved EC competencies to varying degrees, yet another confirmation of the ability of the CFSP to overcome long-standing prejudices regarding the institutionalization of EU security cooperation and the role of EC actors in security affairs. The NPT action in particular was "an outstanding success," according to Müller and van Dassen (1997: 65), for it "combined the efforts of member states towards a common goal, provoked activities that would otherwise most likely not have been undertaken, and made a discernible, significant contribution to the successful extension outcome." Beyond this important diplomatic "force multiplier" effect, the action also helped to socialize its participants in terms of thinking about the kinds of specific contributions the CFSP could make to international security.

Similarly, the combined CFSP joint action/EC regulation to control European exports of dual-use goods showed the ability of the EU to erode the barrier between the EC and the CFSP in security affairs. Even before the CFSP, the Luxembourg European Council of June 1991 had listed seven criteria for conventional weapons exports which were common to all EU states. At this time, however, the European Council focused on a common approach involving the harmonization of national policies, not the use of EC tools. Later proposals for action in this area were produced by EU states, the EP (1991; 1992), and the Commission (1992a), which carried out a comprehensive survey of national export controls in 1991. The Council of Ministers set up an ad hoc high-level working group to examine the issue, and in August 1992 the Commission (which has continually called for the deletion of Article 223) made a formal proposal for a Council regulation on the control of dual-use goods (1992b). The resulting EC regulation,[51] which entered into effect on July 1, 1995, represented a major step forward for the CFSP's security dimension in general and its relationship to the EC in particular.[52]

The EU's involvement in KEDO also can be considered a security is-sue, although perhaps more indirectly. In any event, it was a "classic" CFSP issue in the view of the EU officials who took part, as it involved synthesizing the economic, technical, legal, financial, and security aspects of the EU's external relations through the EC/CFSP linkage. In terms of substantive coherence, then, KEDO was indeed a success. The KEDO episode also demonstrated the potential importance of the new "CFSP counselors" (see Chapter 8). As EU states could not agree on an appro-priate collective contribution to this project, the KEDO file went from the CFSP working group on nuclear non-proliferation, to COREPER, to the Council of Ministers, then to the CFSP counselors, where the arrangements for the EU's initial contribution to the organization were finally worked out. Like the New Transatlantic Agenda discussed above, the EU's involvement in KEDO also strongly depended on the US lobby-ing the Commission, which in turn helped to engineer intra-EU support for the new organization.[53]

Before turning to the WEU–CFSP relationship, a final word about cri-sis response is in order. The TEU did not improve the mechanisms here, and they were not invoked during the time period under consideration.[54] However, many officials suggest that the frequency of CFSP meetings at all levels eliminates the need for formal crisis procedures.[55] In any event, there were several opportunities for the CFSP to get more involved in cri-sis situations, but performance was very uneven. On the positive side, the advent of CFSP counselors may have improved the quick response abil-ity of the CFSP, such as during the executions in Nigeria of playwright Ken Saro-Wiwa and eight other political activists in November 1995.

[51] Council Regulation (EC) No. 3381/94 of December 19, 1994.
[52] For details, see Cornish 1997.
[53] Interviews with officials from the US mission to the EU, the Commission, and COREPER, Brussels, 1995–96.
[54] Article J.8 of the TEU generally followed EPC's crisis procedures.
[55] Interviews with various CFSP officials, Brussels, 1995–96.

Since the CFSP's African working group (like most others) meets infrequently, the CFSP counselors, together with the Commission, stepped in to consider proposals on how the CFSP should react. The new arrangement undoubtedly helped speed up the EU's response in this situation, although it did not prevent the executions in the end.[56]

On the negative side, however, the EU was unable to do anything during the early 1996 crisis between Greece and Turkey over the Aegean island of Imia/Karadak. The US ultimately stepped in to prevent the conflict from escalating; this lack of action on the part of the EU stems from giving the EU presidency primary control over the day-to-day CFSP agenda. In this case, the Italian presidency did not call for more decisive moves by the EU, and the leadership vacuum was not filled. These crisis management problems crowded the already-full agenda of items under consideration at Amsterdam, as we shall see in Chapter 8.

The CFSP and the WEU

Concerning the CFSP/WEU linkage specifically mentioned in Maastricht, operational results were extremely modest through the 1990s.[57] It is beyond the scope of this chapter to analyze in detail the complex relationship between the CFSP, the WEU, and NATO, but some basic judgments can be made. Most fundamentally, although the WEU increased its operational capability during the 1990s (mainly during the Persian Gulf War and the Balkans conflicts), no WEU actions had been taken in conjunction with or at the request of the EU under Article J.4.2 by the start of the IGC in mid-1996.[58] In fact, only one EU decision under Article J.4.2 had been taken: the Council Decision of June 27, 1996 to have the WEU prepare contingency plans to support the emergency evacuation of EU citizens from a third country if necessary.[59] Later, during the Kosovo crisis, the WEU decided (using its own authority, not

---

[56] One CFSP counselor compared their role to that of a "fire brigade" used to handle problems in between regular CFSP ministerial and working group meetings, or when other CFSP officials fail to reach agreement. Interview, Brussels, 1996.

[57] For a more detailed examination of this period, see Taylor 1994; Martin and Roper 1995; Duke 1996; Jopp 1997; Rummel 1997; Coffey 1998, Smith 1998a.

[58] WEU support of the EU's administration of Mostar was not an official request by the EU made under Article J.4.2. Nor did the EU ever "avail itself" of the WEU (Article J.7) in order to implement its decisions regarding defense.

[59] This action was not published in the *Official Journal of the EU* because of Danish reservations. According to insiders, it was as much a symbolic decision for the IGC (to show critics of reform that nearly all CFSP instruments had been used at least once) as it was a practical CFSP action. Also, Denmark "opted out" of this decision, but the Danes also said they would not impede the development of closer cooperation among member states in this area. Interview with a COREPER official, Brussels, 1996.

that of the CFSP)[60] in May 1997 to send a "Multinational Advisory Police Element" (MAPE) to Albania, consisting of ninety-four officers from twenty-three WEU member states. This action was in response to the exodus from Albania to Italy of about 14,000 refugees beginning in March 1997. Although this was not a CFSP-related joint action, MAPE was supported by EU funds from the PHARE program in the amount of 4.8 million ECU (MECU) during 1998–99. In short, despite the fact that some EU states ultimately did send troops,[61] the episode undoubtedly called into question the EU's true commitment to undertaking its own independent military operations, with or without the WEU. The WEU was rarely if ever present at CFSP meetings in the Council during the 1990s, and institutional links between the Commission and the WEU were poorly developed. According to EU insiders, Commission relations with NATO were much better than those with the WEU.[62]

However, rather than devise pragmatic ways for the CFSP and WEU to implement joint actions together, the EU was practically paralyzed in the mid-1990s over the larger issue of fully merging the WEU into the EU. This was due in part to the fact that after 1995 fully one third of EU member states (Austria, Denmark, Finland, Ireland, and Sweden) did not enjoy full membership of the WEU and thus were extremely wary of including it in CFSP matters. Instead, decisions by the WEU and NATO during ministerial meetings in mid-1996, following the French *rapprochement* with NATO, finally confirmed that the WEU, and/or "Combined Joint Task Forces" (CJTF) with NATO, could carry out military operations without US involvement but with the logistical support of NATO.[63] These decisions (and previous changes by NATO)[64]

---

[60] The Dutch EU presidency tried to involve the CFSP in the Albanian crisis but to no avail. Several EU states proposed sending EU troops once Albania explicitly appealed to the European members of NATO, but Germany, Sweden, the UK, and other neutral EU states were able to block the idea.

[61] 7,000 multinational troops, led by Italy and France, were deployed in April 1997 (Operation Alba) to assist with elections and to distribute food and medicine; there was no support for a peacekeeping or peacemaking mission. These troops left after the Albanian elections in July and were replaced by 600 policemen, mostly Italians (with some help by the WEU).

[62] As one Commission official put it (interview, Brussels, 1996), the EU's growing ambitions at this time also represented the ultimate death of the WEU, while NATO's existence and independence were assured.

[63] See the "Birmingham Declaration" of the WEU ministerial meeting (May 7, 1996); and the final communiqué of the North Atlantic Council ministerial meeting in Berlin (NATO doc. M-NAC 1-96-63), June 3, 1996.

[64] For example, NATO's "out of area" problem has been addressed, its membership has expanded to the East, cooperation with Russia has taken place, and flexible provisions have been adopted and utilized to permit the participation of NATO non-members in its operations.

helped lay the groundwork for the institutional changes within the EU achieved at Amsterdam and beyond, and ultimately may help prevent clashes over the division of labor among Western security institutions that inhibited effective cooperation in the Balkans. If not, responsibilities will continue to be determined on a case-by-case basis (if at all), and could lead to uncertainties, delays, and operational ineffectiveness. The next chapter will consider the extent to which these and other institutional problems were resolved in the late 1990s, thus impacting the CFSP and the EU's broader ambitions in external relations.

Part III

Residual institutional issues

8   Unfinished business: coherence and the EU's global ambitions

European foreign policy cooperation has expanded considerably since the first tentative steps made under EPC in the early 1970s. Compared to the situation then, the CFSP today involves a far more sophisticated institutional structure and has produced a greater variety of complex common foreign policy actions. Moreover, compared to other regional organizations, such as the Organization of American States or the Association of Southeast Asian Nations, the EU's progressive and determined efforts to cooperate in foreign policy are highly unique. Despite these positive results, however, many observers and EU officials remain dissatisfied with the CFSP's procedural elements and its substantive output. We can describe these limitations as part of the "unfinished business" of the Maastricht era, where certain issues were raised but ultimately sidestepped owing to both general political differences and more specific questions about institutional architecture. These issues have intensified the pressures for institutional change since the late 1990s and deserve some attention here, given the EU's own growing ambitions and the major challenges faced by the CFSP since its implementation.

This chapter explores these difficult institutional questions, focusing in particular on the EU's goal to make its external relations functions more coherent. Improving the effectiveness and coherence of the EU's external capabilities was a key motivation behind the TEU and its single institutional framework. As we saw in the previous chapter, *substantive* coherence in the CFSP has clearly improved compared to EPC. This involves the application of multiple EU external policy tools or competencies (such as development aid, tariff concessions, and political dialogue) toward a single external goal. *Procedural* coherence has been more problematic, as it involves rationalizing the EU's external competencies in terms of decision-making, policy implementation, representation, and a host of other institutional questions. In other words, while there often may be agreement on external policy ends, choosing the institutional means for achieving those ends still provokes uncertainty, controversy, bureaucratic intrigue, turf battles, and ideological debates.

The problem of coherence is complicated further by the expansion of the CFSP to include more security issues and a true European Security and Defense Policy (ESDP). Here a number of EU states, as well as the US, are still not in complete agreement about the ultimate purpose of a truly independent European military force and its relationship to NATO. As space limitations prevent me from fully exploring the ESDP as a separate EU policy domain (which includes complex issues such as command, training, logistics, and armaments production), I instead confine myself to an examination of how this new ambition relates to the existing institutional framework for EU foreign policy. Despite a number of internal and external obstacles, the EU continues to make gradual institutional breakthroughs in this area, and they deserve a closer examination. Exploring how this has taken place, particularly in light of the Amsterdam and Nice Treaties, will conclude my analysis of the institutionalization of EU foreign and security policy.

Institutions, coherence and external relations

The CFSP/ESDP are embedded in the EU's broader and constantly evolving institutional architecture for external affairs. To understand how, we must change the scope of analysis from the EU's foreign policy activities (essentially derived from EPC practices) to include the EU's other external relations capabilities, most of which involve supranational institutional mechanisms. As we saw in the previous chapter, Maastricht established a single institutional framework to govern all of these policies, whether involving the supranational Community method (for foreign economic policy) or the intergovernmental methods of EPC/CFSP and Trevi/Schengen (for Justice and Home Affairs, or JHA). How this framework institutionalized coherence, and the extent to which it has achieved this goal in terms of performance, are the subjects of this section.

The institutionalization of coherence

To help counterbalance the compartmentalization of the EU's external relations that had been established by EPC, the principle of coherence appears throughout the Maastricht Treaty. Under Articles A and C, the EU was charged with ensuring the coherence of its actions, in particular "the consistency of its external activities as a whole in the context of its external relations, security, economic, and development policies" (Article C). Title V (Articles J.1 and J.8) also mentioned the concept as a guiding principle behind the CFSP. And the very fact that the TEU established a *single* institutional framework covering all three EU pillars further demonstrates the importance of coherence in the constitutional structure of European integration.[1]

Despite these various references to what seems to be a fundamental principle in the EU, coherence has not received a great deal of attention.[2] However, it also should be noted that the concept of coherence as mentioned in the TEU is not entirely new; it continues a trend that had been developing for some time in the EU's external affairs under EPC, as we saw in Chapter 5.[3] In addition, becoming a "cohesive force in international relations" was an explicit incentive behind the inclusion of EPC in the SEA (Article 30.2[d]). Maastricht merely attempted to clarify, reinforce, and broaden this principle across all three pillars of the EU. In a sense, then, the CFSP represented another stage in the general transition from EPC's primary focus on negative integration toward more positive integration. This major change in emphasis – coherence across external policy domains or organizational fields – created additional pressures for a shift in institutional design.

Before examining the extent to which the principle of coherence plays a role in how the EU governs its external activities, I must qualify what I mean by coherence. First, I focus on what Tietje (1997: 211) has called "horizontal coherence," or the extent to which the various mechanisms for external policymaking in the EU, whether informal or formal, are logically connected or mutually reinforcing. A full investigation of "vertical coherence," or the extent to which the foreign policy activities of individual EU states actually mesh with those of the Union, would require a study equal in scope to the present one.[4] Second, although it is clear that the creation of the EU and its external capabilities was originally motivated by the changes in its external context noted above, most of the post-Maastricht institutional changes discussed in this chapter have been influenced by internal dynamics. As there are no major distributional issues surrounding the specific question of coherence, institutional contests about coherence are often legal or ideological in nature (i.e., involving the institutional logic of appropriateness). These contests take

---

[1] For more on this point, see Curtin 1993.

[2] For exceptions, see Neuwahl 1994; Krenzler and Schneider 1997; and Tietje 1997. In fact, the term itself is not used consistently in various translations of the TEU. As Tietje (1997: 211–12) points out, the English translation favors "consistency" (or the absence of contradictions) while most continental languages use the term "coherence" (meaning positive connections). Tietje argues that coherence is evidently the favored term for most EU states and it clearly sets a higher standard for the EU's policies. Thus, I favor the term here.

[3] For example, see Lak 1989; Coignez 1992.

[4] On this question, see especially Hill 1983b, 1996; de la Serre 1988; Manners and Whitman 2000.

place at all levels of decision-making in the EU, and the central battle is about the constitutional structure of the EU and the right of EU states to preserve their own foreign policy autonomy within that structure. Moreover, by attempting to create a closer link between the EC and the EU's other external capabilities, the drafters of the TEU unwittingly created tensions, inconsistencies, and gaps between the rules governing these domains at the organizational and even individual levels. Such problems provided openings for EU member state governments and EU organizational officials to influence the system. The fact that the EU was also *legally* required to present a coherent front on the international stage provided an additional opportunity and motivation (particularly among the EU's legal advisers, if not the ECJ itself) to improve the practical working relationships among the EU's external activities. These issues would have to be resolved once the TEU entered into its implementation phase.

Third and finally, it is beyond the scope of a single chapter to analyze all EU policy areas that affect external relations; instead, they may be categorized according to their basic institutional structures and dynamics. Under Maastricht, the EU's external policies were structured according to these three institutional categories (which differ from the EU's three *pillars*), some of which privilege EU member states, and others which privilege supranational EC organizations:

(1) External policy domains where supranational EC organizations (chiefly the Commission and Court) and procedures (qualified majority voting, or QMV) dominate.
(2) Domains that involve interaction between EC organizations/ procedures and intergovernmental forums (chiefly the European Council and Council of Ministers) and procedures, and where economic concerns coexist with other goals, such as political stability.
(3) Domains where intergovernmental forums and procedures clearly dominate, such as security and defense.

Beyond these divisions, also note that the Council of Ministers and the Commission were directed to ensure the coherence of the Union's external policies, thus giving these bodies (one an intergovernmental forum, the other a supranational organization) a joint role in this responsibility. Equally important here is the fact that the ECJ was *excluded* under the TEU (Article L) from exercising its jurisdiction over the activities of the second and third pillars. Thus we cannot rely on Court decisions to determine how coherence has fared as a general principle; we must look to decision-making and policies.

In addition to the way they affect normal policymaking, each of the categories also conditions institutional change within its respective sphere. In areas where the EC dominates, institutions are often self-sustaining,

Table 8.1 *The TEU's organization of external relations*

	EC/supranational competencies	Mixed competencies	Intergovernmental competencies
Dominant focus of policy domain	Economic issues	Political issues	Security and defense
Examples	Trade, aid, development	Dialogues, CFSP, certain aspects of JHA	CFSP/ESDP
Decision rule	QMV is allowed	QMV is allowed under special circumstances	Consensus only
Agenda-setting and implementation	Commission	States/Commission	Primarily states
Policy resources	Primarily EC	EC/states	Primarily states
Legally binding?	Yes	Depends	Depends
ECJ involved?	Yes	Very limited role	Highly unlikely

as EC actors (chiefly the Commission) can produce new rules, and even new competencies, when initiating or implementing policies (for example, through secondary legislation) or otherwise (for example, when the Commission creates new consultative forums). These rules then condition later initiatives. This functional "spillover" is well known and has occurred in other external EU policy areas such as environmental policy and the extra-territorial application of competition policy. In areas where intergovernmentalism is the rule, like JHA and the CFSP, most formal institutional changes, even the most unassuming, still often require tense discussions or bargains among EU governments or their representatives. Informal changes are more common, as participants in these domains work behind the scenes to fill in the gaps left by each major EC/EU treaty. Areas of mixed competency are the most problematic for institutional change, as some EU member states have opposed Commission involvement (or required the Commission to justify its involvement) in such areas or have blocked the use of EC procedures or resources for external political activities.

In fact, we can break down these TEU external policy categories in terms of their institutional provisions, the actors and stakes involved, and the types of external behavior (i.e., foreign policy tools) each one has the capability to produce.

These categories are not discrete, of course. In fact, it is their tendency to interfere with, or even contradict, each other, and thus undermine coherence, that generates many of the institutional problems examined in this chapter. Still, they establish an initial set of reference points against which we can assess institutional performance and change.

Coherence and institutional performance

Given the way Maastricht organized the EU's external capabilities, how did the system perform once it was implemented? Or more accurately, how did *perceptions* of performance among EU elites, defined mainly in terms of coherence, create pressures for further institutionalization? To answer this question, we can examine the EU's record of external policies toward a region or problem that have involved more than one type of the three decision-making competencies as described above (EC-dominant, mixed competency, and intergovernmentalism-dominant), *and* that have produced conflicts between EC organizations and EU governments. These areas include EU activity in the Balkans (perhaps the EU's single most important foreign policy challenge in the 1990s), EU activity regarding arms control or non-proliferation, and various actions toward South Africa, Russia, Central/Eastern Europe, and the Middle East.

More specifically, it is possible to break down institutional incoherence into several areas that have affected policy performance in the view of several observers (Regelsberger and Wessels 1996; Ginsberg 1997a; Smith 1998b); these problems in turn help create a demand for new rules and procedures. In the rest of this section, I analyze the relationship between institutional change and actor perceptions of the TEU's performance by focusing on several sets of institutional problems. Again, I am not attempting to evaluate all of the EU's external policies, only those which have raised serious institutional problems in terms of policy performance and coherence. As I covered institutional problems related to the security provisions of the CFSP in the last chapter, here I primarily focus on conflicts between EC competencies and the CFSP's foreign policy aspects.

Decision-making rules   Perhaps the most common post-Maastricht complaint about incoherence between the pillars in terms of external relations was that rules for decision-making have not been applied uniformly where competencies overlap. Recall that the CFSP is expressed through two primary instruments, *common positions* and *joint actions*, which take the place of normal EC legal instruments (under Article 189). However, in the first place, QMV for CFSP joint actions (and JHA joint actions as well) has not been utilized. As we have seen, the rules for QMV under Maastricht were so convoluted that it was nearly impossible to apply them quickly, consistently, and efficiently. As a result, CFSP decision-making has been "slow and cumbersome."[5] EU member

---

[5] Cameron 1998: 65. Also interviews with numerous CFSP officials, Brussels, 1995–96, 2001.

states blocked the use of QMV primarily for ideological reasons: the fear that one QMV vote on any CFSP action, no matter how trivial, would set a precedent leading to the contamination of the second pillar with supranationalism. These fears are somewhat justified; to help encourage coherence, lower-level CFSP officials have tended to draft policy texts with the understanding that legal precedents are being set, even where EC treaty articles do not apply.[6]

Second, when a policy action generates a conflict between CFSP and EC decision-making rules (particularly the use of economic sanctions), the procedures of the CFSP tend to dominate. Article 228a in the TEU was supposed to clarify the legal conflict between Article 113 (the common commercial policy, which allows QMV) and the largely intergovernmental rules of the CFSP; however, CFSP's intergovernmental procedures (i.e., unanimity) usually prevail.[7] Some CFSP (and JHA) decisions even undermined the EC's own competencies (thus contaminating the EC with intergovernmentalism), a development that led to many Commission complaints during the preparatory stages of Amsterdam.

Third, Article 116, which obliged member states to adhere to common positions (decided by QMV) in international economic organizations, was conspicuously omitted by the TEU. This article was not often invoked before the TEU removed it, but it did impose a certain discipline on member states to coordinate their actions with those of the EC in external economic affairs. Commission officials argued that the absence of Article 116 led to "a marked change in climate. More and more often the opinion is expressed that the complicated rules of the CFSP regarding settlement on a common position (Article J.2) replace Article 116" (da Fonseca-Wollheim 1996: 2). Since these rules required unanimity rather than QMV, it became more difficult to arrange compromises in such matters. This is additional evidence of the way some rules of the intergovernmental pillars have apparently undermined the EC's own supranational procedures.

External representation/policy implementation   In a related fashion, external representation and implementation created problems of coordination in areas where the EC (and thus, the Commission) does not

---

[6] Interviews with legal advisers in the Commission and Council Secretariat General, Brussels, 1995–96.

[7] Article 228a was established to govern the way economic (under Article 113) and financial (under Article 73.1) sanctions could be applied against non-EU states after years of confusion about whether EPC was allowed to impose such sanctions. Under Article 228a, such sanctions could be imposed only by reference to a competence provision of the EC (which allows QMV), or under a CFSP common position or joint action (which stresses unanimity).

enjoy exclusive competency. Maastricht was fairly vague on the division of labor in the CFSP between the EU presidency and the Commission. Within this pillar, arrangements for their respective roles generally were worked out on a case-by-case basis, which created delays at best and confusion at worst. Depending on the issue at hand, representation has been handled by national representatives, Commission officials, the EU presidency, the "tandem" formula (or the "bicephalous" presidency), the "Troika" formula, or by the designation of special representatives on an ad hoc basis. Another formula, the "quint" (France, Germany, Italy, Spain, and the UK), was used to handle EU relations with Turkey (Cameron 1998: 61), while the use of "Contact Groups" with Russia and the US also undermined the EU's own attempts to play a unified role in areas like the Balkans.[8] The EU presidency was the most common form of representation, but its effectiveness naturally depended on the commitment, experience, resources, reputation, and domestic situation of the state holding it. And although multiple forms of representation provide a great deal of flexibility for the EU, outside interlocutors still have trouble determining who represents the EU in external affairs, while those who claim to represent the EU have to compete with other EU representatives. Even within the Commission disputes arose over the division of labor between Commissioners, particularly Leon Brittan for trade and Hans van den Broek for the CFSP, even in areas where the Commission dominated, such as trade.[9]

Financing the EU's external relations   Institutional mechanisms regarding financial resources for external actions also opened up a series of problems after Maastricht. The CFSP/JHA pillars began operating under a rule that the "operational" side of their respective joint actions would be funded by national contributions (unless decided otherwise), while "administrative" expenditure would be drawn from the EC budget. This seemed to be a clear improvement on EPC's norms, which said little about funding joint actions. In practice, however, the arrangements for providing operational funds from national contributions became subject to conceptual and logistical problems compounded by domestic difficulties in EU member states. The EU's administration of Mostar revealed

[8] For the view of an outsider regarding this problem, see Holbrooke 1998. For an insider's view, see Owen 1995.

[9] Interviews with various Commission officials, Brussels, 1995–96. As one insider put it, the basic DG-IA framework (for external relations) was strongly resisted within the Commission and by EU member states. DG-IA was partly staffed by DG-VIII (development) officials, so some also complained that the Commission's approach to the CFSP suffered from a "development mentality."

how difficult it would be to fund the CFSP's operations through national means. Nearly a year after the initial Council decision (November 8, 1993) to support the operation in part with national contributions, only three EU member states (Denmark, Greece, and Ireland) had contributed to it (Hagleitner 1995: 6–7).

Additional problems arose over the basic distinction between administrative and operational expenditures under Articles 199, J.11 (CFSP), and K.13 (JHA) of the TEU. Simply defining what constituted "operational" expenditure became a most difficult issue under the new arrangements. Moreover, the TEU (Article J.5) provided that the EU presidency was responsible for implementing CFSP *joint actions*, but that the Commission (Article 205) would implement the EC *budget*, so several EU member states suggested that QMV be used (under Article 205) to implement the later financing stages of the joint actions in the former Yugoslavia that had been decided unanimously. This led to protracted debates over "joint action implementation" (by the EU presidency) and "budgetary implementation" (by the Commission). The UK adamantly refused to use QMV procedures in this area, and every phase of the EU's actions in the Balkans required a tedious repetition of the consensual decision-making process at the highest levels, when normal disbursements of EC funds could have been made with QMV decisions.[10]

Democratic oversight   Finally, to the extent that the EU's external relations must be subject to democratic oversight by the EP, which is more of a legitimacy issue than a capability issue, some problems of coherence have emerged. The EP is directly involved in some external policy domains (the EC), only consulted in others, and largely ignored in others. Indeed, according to some observers (Stavridis 1997), the democratic deficit is one of the primary deficiencies of the CFSP, and of the EU in general. The continued dominance of certain aspects of the CFSP/EU by the European Council makes it difficult for Euro-enthusiasts to claim that the EU is becoming more transparent and open. Although members of the European Council are elected in their respective states, this body is not a Community institution under the terms of the Treaty of Rome, has a dubious legal identity, meets in secret, does not publish its deliberations, and does not provide for any institutionalized criticism of itself. In addition, since Maastricht the EP has increasingly complained about being ignored by the Council of Ministers. The EP wants consultation to take place before policies are decided; the Council often prefers to provide information *post hoc*. The EP also threatened to use its leverage over the

---

[10] Interviews with Commission and COREPER officials, Brussels, 1995–96.

CFSP budget if its views were not taken into consideration (particularly regarding external agreements), and continually pushed for institutional changes on these issues.[11] These and similar problems increasingly influence public debates about the general institutional architecture of Europe, where democratic oversight remains one of the most fundamental principles of European integration.

Institutional gaps   Beyond the above problems, which were generally raised by existing provisions in the TEU, coherence was hindered by at least three other more fundamental institutional "gaps" or omissions that were not fully addressed at Maastricht.

First, since the EU lacks its own legal personality, it has been difficult to conclude international agreements or join international organizations where the Community (which enjoys legal personality) is not a signatory.[12] This negatively affected the timely implementation of the CFSP, and was especially problematic for the EU's membership of international organizations when competencies appeared to cross pillars.[13] The problem of legal personality similarly complicates the manner by which the EU (or CFSP/JHA), once it finally decides on a negotiator, attempts to implement a policy by way of an agreement with non-EU states or other actors. According to numerous insiders, EU legal officials must continually remind CFSP diplomats that they lack the legal authority to make a particular agreement on behalf of the EU.[14] Similarly, the principle of "exclusivity," which means that EU states are not permitted to join international organizations where the EC has exclusive competence, had to be clarified in terms of cross-pillar issues. This point was raised during a heated debate when France and the UK (as the EU's only nuclear powers) wanted to sit on the board of KEDO while the EU (through the CFSP) was pursing that goal as well. In the end, the parties agreed to have the EC (by virtue of its Euratom competencies) represent the EU on KEDO's board, though with delegations from both the Council and Commission.

Second, Maastricht said little about how to ensure compliance with CFSP/JHA decisions so there was no way to evaluate or punish

---

[11] Grunert 1997; also interview with an EP official, Brussels, 1996.
[12] For more detailed examinations of this problem, see Cheyne 1994; Sack 1995; Wessel 1997.
[13] This has been a problem even within the EC's exclusive sphere of competency, such as trade in services and intellectual property.
[14] Interviews with legal advisers in the Commission and Council Secretariat General, Brussels, 1995–96.

defections.[15] The TEU conferred this responsibility on the Council of Ministers, but since it decides such matters by consensus, a single member state could block effective censure of itself. Of course, domestic compliance after the fact has not been much of a problem since few CFSP actions have required it, and since many joint actions are implemented by the Commission. Still, although the Commission is fully associated with all aspects of the CFSP and must ensure coherence, in this domain it clearly does not enjoy the extremely important monitoring and enforcement role it actively plays in the EC (Article 155). As we have seen, one of the most visible examples is the EU's administration of Mostar, where most EU member states did not make their financial contributions to the operation in a timely fashion. This case especially contributed to later debates over the CFSP budgetary process (see below). Given its institutionalized preoccupation with economic integration, the Commission still chooses its battles carefully and has not emerged as a major enforcer of compliance in external political affairs. It was decidedly reluctant to invoke Articles 34, 35, or 192 of the Euratom Treaty (which involve Commission participation in nuclear tests) to halt French nuclear tests in the Pacific for fear of a backlash, and did not attempt to censure Greece for its unilateral actions regarding the former Yugoslav Republic of Macedonia (although it did take Greece to the ECJ). A related problem was the temptation for EU states to pursue their interests unilaterally or in other forums like the UN Security Council, NATO, or various "Contact Groups," since there was no independent way for the EU to prevent its member states from doing so, or even to require that they make regular use of the CFSP beyond merely consulting with each other.

Third and finally, the ECJ was effectively excluded from second and third pillar issues, so there was no independent dispute resolution procedure in these domains. As noted above, under Article L the ECJ could not exercise any jurisdiction over the CFSP and JHA pillars. This may not seem to be a problem for the EU as its member states tend to assume that disputes cannot arise from decisions made by consensus. Even when they are dissatisfied when the foreign policy actions of other EU states conflict with common EU policies, EU governments do not complain too loudly for fear of inviting future criticisms when their own foreign

---

[15] Article F.1, TEU, does allow the Council (with the assent of the EP) to determine whether a "serious and persistent breach" of the EU's fundamental principles (liberty, democracy, respect for human rights and fundamental freedoms, and the rule of law) by an EU member state has occurred. This could apply to a failure to comply with CFSP decisions. However, this would be highly unlikely in practice as the Council (composed of *EU heads of state and government*, not foreign ministers, under Article F.1) must first decide such a breach by unanimity (excepting the vote of the member state in question).

policies fail to conform to those of the EU. Thus it would be highly un-likely that they would take each other to Court over such matters, even if they enjoyed the legal right to do so. However, Article M provides that nothing in the TEU shall affect the treaties amending the EC (except for certain stated provisions to that effect). In other words, CFSP/JHA activ-ities cannot be used or allowed to modify Community competencies. Yet the ECJ had made no major rulings in this area during the time period under consideration, so we can conclude that its jurisdiction over these questions is still more conceptual rather than operational.

Informal post-Maastricht institutional reforms

In this section I analyze how some institutional inconsistencies or gaps were resolved informally (that is, through the use of customs, or learning-by-doing, rather than treaty changes) following the implementation of Maastricht. To the extent that solutions to the problems of incoherence discussed above became standard operating procedures for the EU's ex-ternal relations, we can say that they have been institutionalized. As with the Maastricht negotiations themselves, this reform process was encour-aged in part by exogenous factors, such as American pressures or the need to improve the EU's position in certain international forums. One major exogenous incentive has been the need to clarify the relationship between the EU's emerging capabilities in security/defense policy and those of other functionally related institutions, namely NATO and the WEU. Yet these pressures have always been part of the EU's internal de-bate about external coherence, and they did not necessarily increase in any dramatic fashion since 1991 (especially compared to the events sur-rounding Maastricht). A notable exception here was the EU's evaluation of its role in the Kosovo crisis, as we shall see below. Even so, these ex-ternal events explain only the general incentives for greater institutional coherence, not the specific choices made by the EU.

Instead, most of the changes discussed in this section are better ex-plained by endogenous processes, most of which involve the ongoing, EU-level debates between supranational and intergovernmental visions (or rule-systems) of external policymaking, largely cast in terms of policy effectiveness and appropriateness. Arguments about *effectiveness* favor the (supranational) Commission by virtue of its policy implementation and evaluation functions, which often require it to establish new procedures to carry out these tasks. Arguments involving *appropriateness*, however, still give EU states (that is, intergovernmentalism) the upper hand, as foreign and security policy are still special domains and EU governments feel they would be acting irresponsibly (if not illegitimately) were they to surrender this right to supranational EC actors. A related strand of argument derives from simple disagreements about what the rules actually mean, particularly concerning the division of labor across the external relations functions. This area of disagreement is about the legalities of certain behaviors within respective spheres of competence; not surprisingly, those who know the rules best (particularly the EU's expanding and complex body of rules) often have the upper hand in this argument.

Given these ongoing debates, plus the inherently unpredictable nature of foreign affairs, there is a strong inherent tendency here toward informal, flexible procedures whose obligations are less demanding (and also are not justiciable by the ECJ). As we saw in previous chapters, this tendency dates back to the formative years of EPC, which relied on a host of unwritten rules or customs about appropriate behaviors in this domain and in terms of its overall relationship to the EC's own formal rules. CFSP insiders have continued this tradition by devising a number of informal procedures (many developed under EPC) to fill in the gaps between the TEU's external relations competencies.

In the sphere of *decision-making*, the EU found several compromises to circumvent the application of QMV procedures in the CFSP; these were used to guide later decisions. For example, the first "dualist" EC/CFSP act, a policy to control the EU's exports of dual-use goods, required much debate among EU officials (particularly those in the legal services) over the extent to which EC regulations (namely Article 113) should be applied. The ultimate solution to this problem involved a "mixed agreement": a CFSP joint action combined with an EC regulation. This was acceptable to both sides of the supranational/intergovernmental divide.[16] More importantly, these discussions later encouraged the establishment of "model common positions" as templates for avoiding time-consuming legal debates over EC/CFSP decision-making.[17] Also, casting combined EC/CFSP agreements as "administrative" in nature has reduced disagreements about the application of decision-making rules to joint EC/CFSP decisions.[18] Similarly, the Commission has pursued its strategy of embedding foreign policy issues within broader EU

---

[16] A CFSP joint action (94/942/CFSP) established the content of the policy (i.e., lists of affected products and technologies) and an EC regulation (3381/94/EEC) was used to implement it.

[17] See the "Mode d'emploi concernant les positions communes définies sur la base de l'Article J.2 de Traité sur l'Union Européenne," internal Council document 5194/95 of March 6, 1995, obtained by the author.

[18] An "administrative" agreement or action is intended to help implement a policy that has already been approved using decision-making procedures appropriate to each competency (EC or CFSP) involved in the policy.

agreements or policies where its authority is more secure.[19] These agreements are in fact specialized institutionalized frameworks to help achieve coherence among the EU's policies toward important areas of interest. Finally, rather than relying on QMV in the CFSP, EU states have occasionally refrained from forcing a vote (i.e., "refrained from insisting on unanimity," in the words of Declaration No. 27, TEU) on uncontroversial CFSP implementation decisions.[20] Although this type of decision-making is probably not what the architects of the TEU had in mind, CFSP officials temporarily managed to find a middle ground between strict intergovernmentalism through unanimity and the use of supranational QMV procedures.

These efforts to improve decision-making without resorting to QMV were enhanced by informal changes in the sphere of *policy-implementation*. Since Maastricht did not delegate complete responsibility to the Commission here, EU officials attempted to improve policy coordination at the organizational level despite the greater number of actors involved at this level. Most importantly, the relationship between the Political Committee (composed of national Political Directors) and COREPER needed to be clarified after Maastricht, as the CFSP would be formally handled by EU foreign ministers acting in Council, an EC institution.[21] After much debate and experimentation, three important changes to COREPER took place. First, COREPER began to prepare all Council ministerial meetings,[22] and technically it has the last word to ensure coherence between CFSP (prepared by the Political Committee) and EC affairs (prepared by COREPER). In other words, the Political Committee reports through COREPER, rather than directly to EU foreign ministers in Council as in EPC (although neither body has clear institutional primacy over the other). The Political Committee does not meet frequently enough (about once a month, as opposed to weekly COREPER meetings) to direct the CFSP actively, and Political Directors at home naturally devote only a portion of their attention to the CFSP. Also, the Political Committee has

---

[19] These "all inclusive" agreements, however, raised other problems. First, since they involved competencies that crossed pillars, they usually had to be negotiated by Commission officials and an official from a member state (usually the EU presidency). Second, assuming this "tandem" approach resulted in an agreement, certain aspects of such agreements (i.e., those involving the second and third pillars) had to be ratified by individual EU states, a long and complicated process.

[20] Examples include: financial sanctions against Bosnia-Herzegovina, the embargo against Haiti, disbursements of some funds for the EU's administration of Mostar, and the EU's anti-personnel mine-clearing directive. Interviews with Commission and COREPER officials, Brussels, 1995–96.

[21] The division of labor between the Political Committee and COREPER in the CFSP could not be agreed at Maastricht; see the Declaration No. 28, TEU.

[22] Articles 151 and J.8.5, TEU.

not engaged in effective monitoring or crisis management, nor does it possess detailed knowledge about operationalizing the link between EC and CFSP affairs. Thus, COREPER gained more ground as the main institutional bridge between capitals and Brussels for the CFSP, just as it is for EC business, but it also complicated the Political Committee's role in the CFSP.[23]

To clarify this "bridging" function, a second change in the CFSP process involved the attachment of a new "CFSP counselor" to each Permanent Representation to the EU after a decision agreed under the German EU presidency in July 1994.[24] These were in place among all EU states by January 1995, although some member states began creating the position in November 1993. After a year of experimentation, COREPER officials recommended that a number of new CFSP working procedures be adopted. CFSP counselors began to meet as a group on a regular basis (two times a week or more), along with a representative from the Commission, to provide continuity in the CFSP and to contend with the demands of foreign ministers or Political Directors who did not always take into account the legal and technical links between the CFSP and the EC.[25] More important is that the CFSP counselors now handle *all matters* relating to the imposition of sanctions as a CFSP instrument, currently one of the strongest CFSP policy tools. This role inevitably places COREPER at the center of many day-to-day decisions concerning the implementation of CFSP actions in specific cases.[26]

Third and finally, all relevant CFSP working groups (i.e., for issues where both EC and EPC working groups already existed) were merged with their EC counterparts into single units and subsumed into the Council Secretariat in order to improve the coordination between EC and CFSP issues. The EU also established a few "tri-pillar" working groups

[23] Interviews with COREPER, Commission, and member state foreign ministry officials, 1995–96.

[24] "Creation du groupe de conseillers PESC," internal COREPER document of July 26, 1994. This change was based on a Political Committee decision of July 1–2, 1994, "Recommendations of the Political Committee to the General Affairs Council," internal Council document, July 18, 1994. Both documents were obtained by the author. CFSP counselors are only attached to COREPER; they are not fully integrated into the system.

[25] For example, in a notorious episode before the TEU, EC foreign ministers worked out an agreement on sanctions against Haiti while meeting as EPC in New York, only to find out later in Brussels (while meeting as the Council of Ministers) that provisions of the plan were contrary to the Lomé Convention of the EC and to the GATT regime as well (de Schoutheete de Tervarent 1997).

[26] According to one CFSP counselor, a "loyalty problem" rapidly emerged in the group as it became difficult to determine which foreign policy goals (national or EU ones) were to take precedence during decision-making. Interview with a CFSP counselor, Brussels, 1995.

(EC/CFSP/JHA) for certain countries and regions (such as the US). According to an internal Council legal decision in April 1995,[27] the Political Directors must chair all working group meetings, but in reality a principal-agent situation has developed (as it often does between foreign ministries and their embassies) where COREPER can use its knowledge of the EU's political situation, and of the legal and budgetary complexities of the EC, to influence member states and help bring about a common position (although COREPER could not change the substance of CFSP policy decided by the Political Committee). The mergers of the working groups were somewhat problematic, however, as some groups switched chairs during meetings, and different officials represented member states at different times, depending on the agenda. Still, some EPC working groups were preserved largely intact and these continued to work effectively under the CFSP.[28] Thus, if knowledge of a political system's rules is a source of power for institutionalizing (and legalizing) a policy domain, then COREPER and the CFSP counselors in particular were now in a far more advantageous position since they are the primary nexus between the EU's increasingly complex political-legal system and the foreign policy structures of individual member states.

Other phases of the CFSP policy process required informal reforms as well in the years prior to Amsterdam. In the area of *financing external policies*, the June 1994 decision to use a GNP scale as a general rule to determine national CFSP contributions became problematic. Given the compliance problems noted above regarding the Mostar operation, EU states increasingly looked to the EC budget for CFSP funds, making Commission and EP involvement in the process certain. Until then, lack of policy guidelines meant that petty ideological disputes over funding often held up actions; even something as uncontroversial as the EU's election-monitoring mission to Russia led to months of internal wrangling over how to pay for buses to transport the monitors. Against the wishes of their EU partners, France and the UK supported financing the CFSP's operational expenditure under the *Council's* line in the budget, to be used at the member states' discretion. Naturally the EP was adamantly opposed to this idea; instead, it adopted a resolution in 1994 to establish a CFSP operational line (line III-B-8) within the *Commission* budget (which includes money for actions previously decided in Council

---

[27] Interview with a CFSP Secretariat official, Brussels, 1996.

[28] These include the groups for Africa, arms control, conventional weapons exports, the UN, human rights, nuclear non-proliferation, non-proliferation of chemical and biological weapons, security, and others. Interviews with Commission, Council Secretariat, and COREPER officials, Brussels, 1995–96.

and a "general CFSP reserve fund").[29] Transfers of funds would still be approved by the EP. In an important victory for the Parliament, this was the solution adopted, and the Commission and the EP now have more discretion than ever before over the disbursement of CFSP operational funds.[30]

While this temporary solution was being worked out, EU states engaged in creative financing by "raiding" CFSP operational funds from the EC budget, particularly that for development. For example, the Council of the EU charged the costs of supporting Belgian "Blue Berets" in Somalia to the EC Development Fund Budget, a clear EC support of a military operation. The excuse was that the EC was not able to spend its own Somali aid due to unrest there, so EC officials argued that "military assistance to the civilian power" in Somalia was a proper charge to the EC development budget. Disbursing these EC funds for CFSP-related actions also raised legal questions, since the EP had the right to participate in the EC's budgetary process (Article 209) and the right to approve all non-compulsory expenditure (Article 203), such as the CFSP. These institutional problems, and the general activism by the EP following Maastricht, led to the solution discussed above.

One final informal rule involved the problem of legal personality. To overcome the lack of such authority, the EU/CFSP has tended to rely on somewhat convoluted "mixed agreements" (which provide for both EC representation and representation by individual EU states) or "administrative agreements" that refer to both CFSP and EC competencies. These formulas not only help prevent tedious debates about decision-making rules, they also help provide the EU with an informal type of legal personality. In other cases, the EU has relied on "memorandums of understanding" negotiated on its own (mainly for CFSP activities), which were not always binding under international law.[31] Although these agreements are difficult to negotiate, nearly impossible for the EP to oversee, and raise unresolved questions about their enforcement, they represent a pragmatic and creative way to circumvent the legal personality problem. Without such informal mechanisms, the EU would be extremely limited in its capacity to implement its second and third pillars. The EU's legal officials were partially responsible for devising these solutions, and they reflect the continued importance of common understandings about the rule of law in explaining the dynamics of European integration.

[29] See the European Parliament 1994.

[30] For more on this issue, see Hagleitner 1995; Monar 1997a, 1997b.

[31] For example, the dispatch of European observers during the cease-fire between Slovenia and Croatia and the EU's administration of Mostar relied on such memorandums of understanding (Lopandic 1995).

Taken together, these informal institutional changes have improved the coherent performance of the CFSP while also helping to break down the institutional distinction between the first and second pillars of the EU. In fact, steps were taken during the Amsterdam and Nice negotiations to expand and codify some of these customs, as we shall see below.

Formal institutional reforms: from Amsterdam to Nice

In this section I examine a number of formal mechanisms codified by the Amsterdam and Nice Treaties, both of which prioritized the institutional reform of the EU's external capabilities. In their official contributions to the 1996–97 IGC, most EU states and organizations admitted some disappointment with the EU's external relations in general and the CFSP in particular. The Commission[32] and the European Parliament[33] were the most critical of these difficulties, while even the official Council report on the functioning of the TEU[34] also referred to the frustration felt by member states about the performance of the CFSP. The ideas outlined in these reports were seriously considered by the "Reflection Group" charged with preparing the agenda for the IGC between June and December 1995.[35] Later, at the formal opening of the IGC in Turin on March 29, 1996, EU foreign ministers specifically directed their representatives to:

1. Define principles for the CFSP and the areas it covers;
2. Define the action needed to defend the EU's interests in areas reflecting these principles;
3. Create procedures and structures for taking joint decisions; and
4. Agree upon suitable budget provisions for taking joint actions.[36]

The Amsterdam Treaty (June 1997) was signed by EU member states on October 2, 1997 and ratified by all EU states by March 1999.[37] To avoid redundancy of material covered previously, I will focus on only the major institutional changes regarding the CFSP.

---

[32] See the High Level Group of Experts on the CFSP 1995–96; Commission 1995a and 1996a.

[33] European Parliament 1995.

[34] For general official EU consensus on the initial performance of the CFSP, see Reflection Group 1995: 39–49; Council of the European Union 1995: Part V.

[35] Interviews with Reflection Group members and IGC negotiators, Brussels, 1995–96; and Reflection Group 1995.

[36] EU Heads of State and Government 1996, 1997a.

[37] The Amsterdam Treaty is officially titled the "Consolidated Version of the TEU." To help distinguish it from the Maastricht TEU, I prefer the term "Amsterdam Treaty." Note also that the Maastricht article numbers were renumbered at Amsterdam; I use the new numbering beginning in this section.

CFSP reforms under Amsterdam

To help improve coherence, and given the Commission's successful experiences with comprehensive external agreements, the Amsterdam Treaty provides for *common strategies* (Articles 12–13). While a CFSP policy tool, these can actually involve all three EU policy pillars and help orient and mobilize them toward a single foreign policy goal.[38] The first such common strategy was established for the EU's relations with Russia in July 1999. In addition, Amsterdam (Article 11) slightly expanded the definition of fundamental objectives of the CFSP, which now include:

1. Safeguarding the common values, fundamental interests, independence, and integrity of the Union in conformity with the principles of the United Nations Charter.
2. Strengthening the security of the Union in all ways.
3. Preserving peace and strengthening international security, in accordance with the principles of the United Nations Charter, as well as the principles of the Helsinki Final Act and the objectives of the Paris Charter, including those on external borders.
4. Promoting international cooperation.
5. Developing and consolidating democracy and the rule of law, and respect for human rights and fundamental freedoms.

Number three above deserves special mention, as it references external borders for the first time. The Amsterdam negotiations immediately followed the 1995 enlargement of the EU, which brought Sweden, Finland, and Austria into the fold. This action extended the EU's frontiers to Slovakia, Hungary, and most importantly, Russia. With this explicit reference to its external borders, long a highly contentious issue, the EU has entered the first phase of securing an area of freedom, security, and justice among its member states.

Beyond these general provisions concerning coherence and common interests, the Amsterdam Treaty made key reforms in three other areas of foreign policy: decision-making, implementation, and financing.

First, concerning *decision-making*, Amsterdam codified the new doctrine of "flexibility" in such matters, effectively opening the door for the first time to two classes of membership in the CFSP. The principle of flexibility was based on a decision reached at the 1996 Florence European Council, where EU states first attempted to devise specific rules to allow states to "opt in" to certain actions, so that the EU could avoid succumbing to the wishes of the most recalcitrant member state(s). However, the

---

[38] As one CFSP insider put it, common strategies have "completely changed the landscape of the CFSP" and helped move it toward a true operational capability. Interview with a Commission official, Brussels, 2001.

new provisions (Articles 17 and 23) for CFSP decision-making failed to extend QMV procedures to security or defense cooperation, as some (such as the smaller EU states) suggested. Instead, unanimity remains the rule here, and Amsterdam attempted to accommodate both pro- and anti-defense factions in the EU by allowing non-WEU members to participate in all CFSP activities, even those related to security and defense, on a case-by-case basis. EU states are thus permitted to abstain (and make a declaration stating their reasons) from any CFSP actions, although they must "accept that the decision commits the Union" and must "refrain from any action likely to conflict with or impede Union action based on that decision and the other Member States shall respect its position" (Article 23.1). This appears to be a major exception to the long-standing rule of consensus in EPC/CFSP. However, if such abstaining members represent more than one third of the votes in Council, the decision will not be adopted. This provision may become a formidable barrier to the formation of "coalitions of the willing" within the CFSP, yet the compromise on flexibility also allowed more specific provisions regarding defense in an EU treaty, as we shall see.

With non-defense related CFSP actions, including those based on common strategies, the Council can act *automatically* by QMV (that is, without first unanimously deciding to "define decisions" where QMV could apply, as under Article J.3.2 of Maastricht) under two circumstances: when adopting joint actions, common positions or taking any other decision on the basis of a common strategy; or when adopting any decision implementing a joint action or a common position. However, as under the TEU, there is still a powerful escape clause that may paralyze the EU: if a member of the Council declares that, "for important and stated reasons of national policy, it intends to oppose the adoption of a decision to be taken by qualified majority, a vote shall not be taken" (Article 23.2). The Council may, acting by QMV, request that the matter be referred to the European Council for decision by unanimity, but this action requires at least sixty-two votes in favor, cast by at least ten members. Thus, Amsterdam still provides enough loopholes to ensure that consensus remains the practical rule in the CFSP. And, as usual, none of these provisions applies to decisions having military or defense implications, which must always be taken by consensus.

Second, Amsterdam also modified certain provisions on *policy implementation and external representation*. Article 18 provides for the EU presidency, associated with the Commission, to represent the EU in CFSP affairs. However, the presidency "shall be assisted by the Secretary-General of the Council who shall exercise the function of High Representative" for the CFSP (Article 18.3). The High Representative also was given responsibility for the new "CFSP Policy Planning and Early Warning Unit" housed in the Council General Secretariat (along with the current CFSP Secretariat).[39] The decision to establish this new permanent Unit, and invest it with clear policy responsibilities (monitoring, assessments, early warning, and policy options), was made with relatively little discord, especially compared to the original EPC Secretariat, as most IGC negotiators clearly felt that the EU's difficulties in situations such as the Balkans were due in part to a lack of a common definition of the problem.[40] Thus, it was expected that this Unit, which has about twenty staff, would establish greater cooperation among the Commission and EU member states to help ensure the coherence of the EU's external actions.

The provision for a new high official provoked more debate (particularly on the part of smaller EU states and Commission President Santer), but at least Amsterdam did not reflect the original French proposal to establish a new grand political official (a "*Monsieur PESC*")[41] to speak for the CFSP. Instead, the function of the High Representative is performed by the Council Secretary General, and is still subordinate to (i.e., "assists") the EU presidency.[42] The first CFSP High Representative (Javier Solana, former NATO secretary-general and Spanish foreign minister) was appointed at the Cologne European Council in June 1999. There was some concern that whoever held the position would be only a figurehead,[43] but the eventual choice of someone like Solana, a high-profile, respected, competent diplomat and administrator, helped to allay those fears. The choice also was made with remarkably little discord, especially compared to the embarrassing debacle over choosing the first head of the European Central Bank and the headaches over appointing an entirely new Commission after the EP forced the resignation of Santer's team in 1999. Although there is potential for conflict with other EU external representatives, particularly those in the Commission, Solana seemed willing and able both to raise the profile of the CFSP and to oversee the eventual merger of the EU and the WEU.

In short, then, Amsterdam basically recast the original EPC/CFSP Troika arrangement to comprise the CFSP High Representative, a Commission official (usually its vice-president in charge of external policies),

---

[39] See the "Declaration Attached to the Final Act on the Establishment of a Policy Planning and Early Warning Unit," appended to the Amsterdam Treaty.

[40] Interviews with Reflection Group members and IGC negotiators, Brussels, 1996.

[41] Named after the French acronym for the CFSP.

[42] Amsterdam also created the new position of *Deputy* Secretary General in the Council Secretariat to assist with the normal administrative tasks of the Secretariat.

[43] For example, the Secretariat General's existing Director General for External Relations/CFSP (Brian Crowe at the time) could have assumed the position of High Representative.

and an EU presidency official, rather than the immediate past, present, and immediate following holders of the EU presidency.[44] Whether this new "modified Troika" framework will aid or impair the EU's external policy coherence (particularly in terms of overlapping with other Commission responsibilities)[45] remains to be seen. Since the EU presidency still represents member states (intergovernmentalism) in the new Troika, and the Commission speaks for European institutions (supranationalism), one must ask who Solana represents in this framework. At least this new arrangement should help to provide greater continuity and visibility compared to an EU presidency-dominated system that rotates its members every six months.[46] Solana and External Relations/CFSP Commissioner Chris Patten also managed to work out a basic division of labor; Patten generally focuses on the CFSP's economic or EC aspects (particularly those linked to development policies, which he helped streamline) while Solana plays more of a political/outreach role.[47] However, Solana still faces two potential difficulties: he cannot initiate policies (unlike Commission officials or member states), and he has far fewer resources (staff and otherwise) than the Commission. Therefore it will still be vital for him to maintain good relations with the Commission and the holder of the EU presidency, not to mention other EU actors.[48]

---

[44] Amsterdam (Article 18.4) does still allow the immediate *following* holder of the EU presidency to assist in its tasks; if this provision is applied, it would actually *expand* the Troika to four participants, not including any "special representatives" appointed for particular policy issues.

[45] It should also be noted that the Commission endured yet another reorganization after the EP forced the resignation of the entire Santer Commission over a corruption scandal in 1999. The Commission abandoned the previous division between relations with the developed and developing worlds in favor of individual portfolios for development/humanitarian aid, enlargement, trade, and external relations/CFSP.

[46] For example, in major American newspapers Solana is usually referred to as the "EU's foreign policy chief," the "EU's top diplomat," or the "EU's foreign policy spokesman." Patten is often referred to as the "head of external relations for the Commission, the EU's executive arm."

[47] As one Commission official put it (interview, Brussels, 2001), Patten is "more subtle" than van den Broek and has been more effective at using the Commission's inherent policy tools in the CFSP. Patten has also been able to prevent Solana from interfering in EC affairs, and he has good relations with trade commissioner Manuel Marin, unlike van den Broek's relations with Brittan.

[48] Solana and the Commission did manage to produce a joint report on conflict resolution for the Nice European Council; see the EU Heads of State and Government 2000b. However, Commission officials later complained that the report was structured to make it look as if Solana had produced it on his own. Moreover, in a September 2000 speech, Commission president Romano Prodi complained that Solana and Patten were not getting along as well as they could be. He also noted the difficulty of maintaining the separation between the political and economic aspects of the CFSP as reflected by the institutional roles of Solana and Patten. Prodi even suggested bringing Solana into the Commission as a vice-president, an idea firmly rejected by Solana. Interview with a Commission official, Brussels, 2001.

Third and finally, given the budgetary problems of the CFSP/JHA over the past several years, the Amsterdam Treaty also outlined more specific provisions in the area of *CFSP financing* (Article 28) and JHA financing (Article 41). Under these articles, both CFSP/JHA administrative expenditures and operational expenditures are to be charged to the budget of the EC, under its normal procedures, which inevitably involve the Commission and the EP. Thus, the Amsterdam Treaty finally made it clear that the EC budget is to be the *primary source* for CFSP funds, although there are, as usual, key exceptions to these procedures for expenditures arising from operations having military or defense implications and cases where the Council, acting unanimously, decides otherwise. In keeping with the new doctrine of flexibility, EU member states which formally abstain from military or defense actions according to the above provisions are not required to finance such actions.

The Treaty also finalized a unique inter-institutional agreement between the EP, the Council, and the Commission concerning CFSP financing, which includes sections regarding the funding of various types of external actions.[49] Considering the haphazard nature of CFSP funding since 1993, and disagreements among EU member states regarding this issue, this agreement could be a key improvement to the CFSP budgetary process. The CFSP also benefited from a major budget increase for the first time since it was established. It had languished in the range of 20–25 million euro during its first few years, but CFSP budgets around the time of the Amsterdam talks included annual amounts in the range of 40–70 million euro.[50] This budgetary increase, the choice of Solana, and the related institutional changes suggest that the EU is still committed to making the coherence of its external relations a reality, although this ambition does not yet fully extend to defense-related cooperation or funding.

Concerning security/defense affairs in particular, operational linkages involving the EU–WEU were overshadowed in part by questions about more general institutional issues involving the CFSP, NATO, the WEU, and the ESDP. Some of these problems were resolved in stages in the period between the Maastricht and Amsterdam Treaties; others remain in place.[51] The overall point to keep in mind here is that NATO remains

---

[49] These include: (1) the observation and organization of elections or participation in democratic transition processes; (2) EU envoys; (3) prevention of conflicts/peace and security processes; (4) financial assistance to disarmament processes; (5) contributions to international conferences; and (6) urgent actions.

[50] This spending, however, still comprises only a tiny fraction (less than one-tenth of 1 percent) of the entire EC budget. Thus EU member states still possess far greater financial resources for foreign policy than the EC itself.

[51] For more detailed examinations of these issues, see Taylor 1994; von Staden 1994; Art 1996; Duke 1996; Smith 1998a; Andréani 2000.

the dominant European security institution while the EU has yet to undertake its own military missions, although individual EU states continue to cooperate in this area. For its part, the WEU attempted to define possible missions for itself since Maastricht, such as the 1992 declaration on so-called "Petersberg tasks" (humanitarian and rescue tasks, peacekeeping tasks, and tasks of combat forces in crisis management, including peacemaking) and plans for a common European defense policy on May 9, 1994. It also attempted to clarify its relationship to NATO and the EU.

In 1996 the Italians and the British managed to adopt a joint declaration on taking steps to increase EU/WEU institutional links, adapt the WEU's "Humanitarian Task Force" for use by the EU, and conduct WEU military exercises. Similarly, the May 7, 1996 "Birmingham Declaration" of the WEU made it clear that the organization was ready to serve as the defense arm of the EU and to perform Petersberg tasks with NATO's logistical support. The WEU established several new permanent organizations to support itself: a Planning Cell, a Situation Center, a Satellite Center, and the Institute for Security Studies.[52] Finally, the WEU itself moved its Secretariat from London to Brussels and shortened its presidency from one year to six months to facilitate a full merger with the EU following the Amsterdam Treaty.[53] And although Amsterdam did not establish an independent defense capability for the EU, it did fully incorporate the Petersberg tasks as general foreign policy objectives of the EU, and affirmed that the WEU was an "integral part of the development of the Union" (Article 17). However, as with the TEU, EU member states also could not agree to *instruct* the WEU to serve the EU; instead, Amsterdam provides that the EU "will *avail itself* of the WEU to elaborate and implement decisions and actions of the Union which have defense implications." Once more, this tortured wording reflected lingering differences over the specific institutional links between the EU and the WEU, and the long-term goal of an ESDP. Amsterdam also set down a number of new arrangements, mainly involving joint meetings and personnel exchanges, for enhanced cooperation between the EU and the WEU, and between the EU and NATO. The Commission as well began to suggest greater defense industry consolidation during this period (see European Commission 1996b). Still, all of these arrangements reaffirmed that NATO was the "essential forum" for Atlantic defense.

---

[52] For more on these reforms, see Coffey 1998.
[53] See the "Declaration Relating to Western European Union" attached to the Amsterdam Treaty.

The CFSP and ESDP after Nice

Although these Amsterdam decisions regarding the WEU and NATO were highly significant in terms of specifying the EU's own role and capabilities in security/defense, actions on the ground at the time (in this case, Kosovo) once again intruded on the EU's internal CFSP deliberations and stimulated ideas for additional reforms that were finalized in the Treaty of Nice. NATO's effective though somewhat controversial military intervention starting in March 1999 was dominated by US assets and ultimately resulted in Yugoslavia's agreement to end its military campaign against ethnic Albanians in that province. This campaign, and perhaps more general sensitivities to inconsistent US leadership, encouraged a British change of position at their summit with France at St. Malo in late 1998, where both sides finally agreed to pursue greater defense cooperation in light of the limited European contribution to the Kosovo operation. This summit led to more intense discussions about the ESDP at the European Councils in Cologne (June 1999), Helsinki (December 1999), and Santa Maria da Feira (June 2000), which involved a European military force, the integration of the WEU into the EU, and EU armaments cooperation.[54] The centerpiece of the ESDP was to achieve, by 2002, the goal of being able to deploy a "European Rapid Reaction Force" (RRF) of 60,000 troops within sixty days of taking such a decision. These plans provided a major focal point of talks concerning the ESDP during the Nice summit.

The final Treaty of Nice agreed at the December 2000 European Council attempted to address much of the unfinished business of Amsterdam. Early signs were not promising, as EU member states could agree on neither the composition of an expert committee to do the preparatory work (thus delegating this task to COREPER), nor on the scope of the IGC agenda. The Commission's resignation crisis in 1999 and the EP's own internal divisions about the scope of the IGC severely limited their influence during the talks (although they made their usual written contributions).[55] The EU's imposition of diplomatic sanctions against one of its own (Austria) at the start of the IGC in early 2000 further complicated the situation, as did the insistence of several EU states, chiefly Belgium, the Netherlands, and Portugal, on improving the general decision-making ability of the EU (whether in terms of QMV or "flexibility") in light of enlargement and the more parochial concerns of smaller EU states. As the French assumed the EU presidency in the

---

[54] EU Heads of State and Government 1999a; 1999b; 2000a.
[55] European Commission 2000a and 2000b; European Parliament 2000.

second half of 2000, the talks failed to coalesce around precise areas of agreement, and the Commission was unable to assume its usual role of an honest broker.[56] In addition, and unlike the preparations for Maastricht and Amsterdam, no major policy papers or position statements emerged to serve as a focal point for debate, possibly because the issues involved at this point were so sensitive and detailed as to discourage bold attempts to synthesize competing views. The French were concerned with maintaining their equal status with Germany (in terms of Council decision-making rules) despite its larger population, and President Chirac's plan for a core group of EU states to take the lead in advancing integration sounded suspiciously like the *directoire* approach greatly feared by the smaller EU states. Not surprisingly, this plan fell on deaf ears at Nice, and Chirac later admitted that his unyielding position had complicated the negotiations.[57]

As reform of the CFSP was not on the Nice agenda, the final Treaty mostly provided incremental changes and cleaned up the wording in a few areas.[58] More specifically, although the ESDP was a key topic of the Nice discussions, and although the WEU was effectively merged within the EU by this time, specific treaty provisions in this domain actually were quite few. In fact, only Article 25 of Nice indirectly relates to the ESDP by changing the Political Committee to the "Political and Security Committee" and charging that committee with exercising (under the responsibility of the Council) "political control and strategic direction of crisis management operations" as determined by the Council. Decision-making by QMV was extended to two minor CFSP areas beyond those agreed at Amsterdam: for the appointing of a special representative with a mandate for particular foreign policy issues, and when concluding an agreement with non-member states or international organizations when implementing a joint action or common position. As usual with such extensions of QMV, there is a related escape clause, in the form of Article 24.5, which should limit the application of this rule. Nice also provided no specific provisions on CFSP compliance, although it did (in light of the Austrian controversy) slightly modify Article 7 on this point, which now allows for a four-fifths majority of EU states (as opposed to a unanimous decision, under Amsterdam) to suspend certain rights of an EU

---

[56] The Commission's limited role at Nice is based on an internal memo by its secretary-general, David O'Sullivan, and was confirmed by other Nice participants, according to Quentin Peel, "Britain and Spain Rated the Biggest Winners at Nice," *Financial Times*, December 14, 2000.

[57] Robert Graham, "Chirac Admits to Failures of Nice Treaty," *Financial Times*, February 27, 2001.

[58] EU Heads of State and Government 2001a.

member state for violating the EU's fundamental principles.[59] However, it would be highly unlikely for EU states to invoke this provision for failing to comply with a CFSP action or position, particularly given the inherent loopholes in most CFSP decisions.

Beyond these minor changes, the most important CFSP-related provisions of Nice concern the evolution of the principle of "flexibility" into a more sophisticated set of rules on "enhanced cooperation," largely based on provisions previously established in the area of Justice and Home Affairs (JHA) under the Maastricht and Amsterdam (Article 40) Treaties. The incorporation of these provisions in the CFSP provides a clear example of mimetic institutional effects: after copying certain CFSP provisions for the JHA portion of the Maastricht Treaty (Turnbull and Sandholtz 2001), the CFSP then drew upon JHA provisions at Nice. In particular, Article 27 of Nice, which previously covered only the association of the Commission in the CFSP, was modified to spell out arrangements for enhanced cooperation in foreign policy. It clearly stipulates that enhanced cooperation must aim at safeguarding the values and serving the interests of the EU when asserting its identity as a coherent force on the international scene (Article 27a). Toward this end, any actions based on enhanced cooperation must also respect: (1) the principles, objectives, general guidelines, decisions, and consistency of the CFSP; (2) the powers of the EC, and (3) consistency between all of the Union's policies and its external activities.

However, enhanced cooperation in the CFSP applies to only the implementation of a joint action or common position; it does not relate to matters having military or defense implications (Article 27b). The British successfully opposed the extension of enhanced cooperation to defense matters, which, in their view, could prevent non-EU member states, such as Turkey, from participating in the RRF. Although this argument certainly has some merit (and the Turks also support it), the exclusion of defense from enhanced cooperation is a potentially crippling limitation; if there is any area of the CFSP that might require a "coalition of willing" to take charge, it is in the area of military/defense issues. Moreover, enhanced cooperation (at least in the CFSP) really "permits" EU states to do what they can already do: act on their own as long as such action does not violate EU treaty obligations. Beyond these qualifications, the rules for such cooperation are fairly onerous in that proposals for enhanced cooperation shall address a request to the Council, and the Commission and EP shall provide information and opinions regarding the request

[59] These principles are liberty, democracy, respect for human rights and fundamental freedoms, and the rule of law.

(Article 27c). The High Representative for the CFSP is given the task of ensuring that the EP and all members of the Council are kept fully informed of the implementation of enhanced cooperation in the CFSP field (Article 27d). Finally, the wording also implies that enhanced cooperation in the CFSP can not involve more general institutional reforms.[60]

These provisions clearly limit the scope of enhanced cooperation within the CFSP (and in the EU in general), and it is entirely possible that EU states might cooperate on their own without even invoking them, which raises the question of how the provision will be enforced. In any event, enhanced cooperation is not likely to alter the fundamental principles on which cooperation in this area is typically based: consensual, pragmatic decision-making among transgovernmental experts with a view to improving the general coherence of the EU's external activities, using economic measures rather than military tools. This can be seen in the EU's initiatives at the time of the Nice Treaty, such as in the Middle East, where the EU is well positioned to continue its tradition of political and economic engagement as the largest aid donor to the region. At the Asia–Europe Meeting (ASEM) in Seoul, South Korea, in October 2000, the EU also managed to secure agreement to (among other things) "promote and protect human rights" despite the initial opposition of China. ASEM was conceived as a forum for economic issues, but political and security issues have increasingly dominated thanks to the input of the EU. And especially since the advent of the Bush administration in 2001, the EU has showed more coherence in challenging US positions on numerous issues: national missile defense, banning land mines, the Kyoto Protocol on global warming, controlling small arms, the International Criminal Court, the death penalty, and numerous trade/economic disputes. In short, EU foreign policy cooperation is alive and well, yet it remains to be seen if this solidarity will extend to tougher security and defense issues, especially in light of enlargement and the Nice Treaty provisions on this subject.

However, as always we must look beyond formal treaty rules to appreciate fully the extent of EU cooperation in this area. For example, the EU defense ministers met for the first time in November 1999 to discuss moves toward the ESDP. At the Helsinki European Council a month later, a "Military Committee" of EU chiefs of staff was created, with its

---

[60] These provisions are further subject to Articles 43–45, which require that such activities must further the objectives of the EU/EC, respect the EU's single institutional framework, not undermine the single market, and perhaps most importantly, involve a minimum of eight EU member states. Such cooperation may be undertaken only as a "last resort," and only those agreeing to take part in enhanced cooperation may adopt decisions to do so in EU institutions.

own "Military Staff" of 136 officials. Although these arrangements are not part of the Nice Treaty, and their specific legal status remains in doubt, informal plans for the ESDP have proceeded quite regularly. In March 2001 the EU voted to appoint a new Military Committee chief, Gustav Hagglund of Finland, although there was some acrimony on how the choice was made.[61] However, this temporary setback did not prevent a number of EU states from agreeing to contribute to the RRF. The commitments from thirty European states inside and outside the EU amounted to 100,000 ground troops, 400 aircraft, and 100 ships in line with the so-called "headline goals" agreed at a Commitment Conference on November 20, 2000.[62] In addition, although Nice failed to provide details about greater European arms cooperation and more defense spending to support the ESDP, EU member states have worked to consolidate their arms industries and engage in joint procurement projects.

Still, the Nice Treaty could have greatly simplified existing arrangements (especially the rules on enhanced cooperation) and clarified new obligations (such as the ESDP) in more detail. And although EU–NATO cooperation has continued since Amsterdam and Nice, chiefly in the form of common ministerial and ambassadorial meetings each year, they have not solved a more fundamental problem: within NATO, non-EU states (such as Turkey) could effectively block the use of NATO assets for the ESDP, and within the EU, neutral states (such as Ireland) could block ESDP decisions. In other words, veto points in each institution (not to mention in their member states) will easily prevent the effective transfer of NATO assets to the ESDP. Even beyond this basic problem, key differences about the ESDP remain. Sweden, which is not a NATO member, prefers the EU's RRF to focus on civilian policing operations, although it has become somewhat more lenient in its general commitment to neutrality, a key element of Swedish identity for a hundred years. Sweden is also hesitant to join peace operations that do not have a UN Security Council mandate. Finland said it would not take part in peace enforcement operations whether or not they are sanctioned by the UN, although it, like Sweden, has made available a pool of about 1,500 troops. Both states, along with Germany, clearly prefer to emphasize the crisis-management

---

[61] In particular, Italy complained that Denmark (whose vote clinched the decision and resulted in the rejection of the Italian candidate, Mario Arpino) participated in a defense-related decision when it had previously chosen to opt out of such decisions under its annex to the Amsterdam Treaty (Protocol 5, Article 6). But Italy did not raise the objection until after the vote was taken because of its confidence in Arpino's appointment, and in the end the Italians said they would not question Hagglund's appointment. Judy Dempsey, "Italy Set to Challenge EU on Defence Appointments," *Financial Times*, April 7, 2001.

[62] See the EU Presidency 2000.

aspects of the EU military forces rather than collective defense. The UK continued to insist that its support for the RRF was conditioned on the dominance of NATO in European security affairs, and that the ESDP could undertake its own operations only within NATO's existing military structures. British officials also warned that the reaction force must not represent a "European army" governed by the EU in Brussels and must not unnecessarily duplicate NATO's assets.[63]

Given these problems, piecemeal "enhanced cooperation," whether sanctioned by the EU or not, may be the only way for some EU states to engage in selective learning-by-doing (and thus institution-building) for the possible benefit of the EU as a whole, but we cannot fully assess this possibility until several EU states actually attempt an independent military operation. Since EU member states are permitted to veto collective action in foreign policy without fear of retribution from their partners, will the EU finally have to resort to hard bargaining over security operations, as in normal EC policy domains? And will the Commission be allowed to engineer such a deal? Both possibilities are unlikely given the consensual norms that have matured in this area over the past three decades. It is also hardly likely that EU member states would exclude one another over a foreign policy matter as the realist theory of abandonment predicts; EU states are embedded in such a dense network of common norms that consensus-building, not naked coercion, is still the dominant tendency. Threatening abandonment would risk disrupting the political cohesion that is the foundation of EPC/CFSP and the EU, and this is not a viable option. Moreover, many security problems in Europe also involve the US and NATO, whose membership largely overlaps with that of the EU. The US will always have some degree of interest in European security, and abandonment still seems unconvincing as a predictor for future EU foreign policy actions, whether in the CFSP or ESDP. Instead, discussions about institutional arrangements still dominate the agenda of EU foreign policy and transatlantic cooperation, an argument I will reiterate in detail in the conclusion to this volume.

---

[63] Moreover, several of the EU's new members (the Czech Republic, Hungary, and Poland) are also new members of NATO and they are unlikely to allow EU ambitions to undermine those of NATO given their security concerns to the East. Poland's strong pro-American stance may upset cohesion within the EU, and in early 2003 it proposed a new "Eastern (European) dimension" to EU foreign policy. How Poland's "special relationship" to the US, like that of the UK, will affect the future of the ESDP is an open question.

Conclusion: beyond the CFSP: institutions, defense, and the European identity

> The principal purposes to be answered by union are these: the common defense of the members; the preservation of the public peace, as well as against internal convulsions as external attacks; the regulation of commerce with other nations and between the states; the superintendence of our intercourse, political and commercial, with foreign authorities.
>
> Alexander Hamilton, 1787

Hamilton's concise case for replacing the weak Articles of Confederation with a federal union of the American states helped inspire support for ratification of the US Constitution. Over two hundred years later his argument seems increasingly pertinent to the debate over European integration. The links between European economic and political objectives, both internal and external, are now extremely difficult to disentangle, and EU foreign/security policy coordination represents a major achievement for a regional economic organization. However, although a union of some unique type, federal or otherwise, may ultimately result from these efforts, I have instead framed this study in terms of cooperation among independent, sovereign states. For European states remain the ultimate locus of authority in developing the EU's institutional future, which has involved a variety of complex behaviors since the 1970s: bargaining, information-sharing, leadership, the establishment of formal organizations, the generation of norms, and delegation to technical specialists. The EU continues to strengthen its intergovernmental elements during key episodes of institutional reform, and EU states still must approve, tacitly or explicitly, any major expansion of EU competencies, such as the ESDP. I also have attempted to structure these factors – intergovernmental, transgovernmental, and supranational – by examining more general processes of institutionalization and their relationship to cooperative outcomes. I have argued that there is a reciprocal relationship between institution-building and cooperation, and I have demonstrated this relationship empirically by focusing on the two-way relationship between *specific processes* of institutionalization and the *types of cooperation* encouraged by that institutionalization.

Institutionalization and cooperation revisited

In the case of European foreign policy, these activities clearly have led to a progressive expansion of both the institutional mechanisms and substantive outcomes of cooperation. There is no denying this linkage if one simply examines the output of EU foreign policy since 1970. Indeed, the EU's conduct of its external political relations has matured considerably since the uncertain days of the Luxembourg Report and its progeny, EPC. Despite a deliberately modest beginning, EPC resulted in a gradual but persistent expansion of the EU's political relationships with third states and with many other regional and international organizations. The tools of EPC grew from the use of mere declarations and joint démarches to the use of economic tools, peace plans, political dialogues, joint actions, common strategies, and other measures. Links between EPC and the EC also became more pronounced in terms of the problems faced and the solutions proposed. These trends have continued with the institutional development of the CFSP, and many recent policy outcomes have exhibited a very high degree of cooperation as I defined it in Chapter 2: the taking of proactive measures on common problems and the regular use of EC resources to implement those measures. In this sense, the CFSP clearly represents international cooperation in terms of *regular, substantive policy outcomes* in addition to *explicit aspirations or goals*.[1]

I have also suggested a number of factors that make institutional change more likely. Although material power can be a useful starting point in explaining the potential for state influence over institutional development (which suggests a focus on France, Germany, and the UK), such apparent power does not necessarily explain final outcomes. In this study, three additional logics played key roles in explaining specific choices: a functional logic, a logic of normative appropriateness, and a logic of socialization. These general logics can be further related to two sets of situational factors, exogenous and endogenous, that encourage specific institutional changes. These elements of institutionalization are summarized in Table 9.1.

Thus, exogenous factors have included changes in the socioeconomic or political context in which institutions are embedded, enlargements, crises, and changes in functionally related institutions. As we have seen throughout this study, exogenous events such as enlargements and periodic IGCs have acted as "institutional moments" during which EU member states reconsidered the ends and means of their cooperation.

---

[1] Only the latter are stressed in much of the literature on international regimes.

Table 9.1 *General logics and causes of institutionalization*

	Functional logic	Appropriateness logic	Socialization logic
Exogenous causes	Major systemic changes (end of the Cold War) EU enlargements Crises Demands of non-members Relations with, and changes in, related institutions (EC, WEU, NATO)	Relations with, and changes in, related institutions (EC, WEU, NATO)	Learning-by-doing (involving links to related institutions, chiefly the EC)
Endogenous causes	Bargaining Problem-solving Policy failures Internal contradictions/gaps New policy ideas/ successes	Internal contradictions/gaps New policy ideas/ successes	Turnover Imitation Leadership Learning-by-doing

Indeed, the tendency for the EU to use enlargement decisions as an excuse for institutional development is a defining characteristic of European integration. Crises such as Afghanistan, the Falkland Islands War, the Gulf War, and Yugoslavia have prompted similar institutional changes. Pressures from outside actors (chiefly the US, but also other states, such as those in the Arab world) played an indirect role here, particularly following the creation of the CFSP at Maastricht. The need to coordinate CFSP/WEU responsibilities with those of NATO provided a convenient excuse for the US to assert its preferences regarding the organization of EU foreign policy. This occurred with US criticism over the EU's Troika arrangement, its desire to have the EU organize a contribution to KEDO and to collective actions in the Balkans, and its questions over the more general division of labor between the CFSP and a changing NATO (Peterson 1998: 12–13). These changes in related institutions generally represent the functional logic (i.e., which institution is best equipped to perform a certain task), but they have also involved logics of appropriateness (in terms of determining the "correct" normative or even legal division of labor between related institutions) and even socialization (in terms of the tendency for officials to rotate among similar positions in these institutions). Additional research will be required to tease out the specific cause–effect relationships among these exogenous factors, particularly where institutions share functions, legal norms, and official participants.

Moreover, institutional change has also been profoundly influenced by endogenous factors in the EPC/CFSP system itself, such as bargaining, problem-solving, policy failures, learning-by-doing, imitation, turnover of officials, and leadership. Although new EPC/CFSP rules generally involve logics of functionality and appropriateness, the most common such functional process in the literature – bargaining regarding the future course of institutional change – played only a limited role in this analysis. While EU states did bargain over the broad structure of the EC/EU (such as linking EMU with progress on political union at Maastricht), such bargains generally reflect practices or proposals that had already developed within the system due to other, less formal processes. Institutional reforms based on new ideas or internal contradictions/gaps are especially interesting, as they can be justified not only in terms of their potential effectiveness (functional logic) but also in terms of their conformity with the existing normative culture (appropriateness logic). In other words, bargaining often can help explain the eventual *codification* of institutional reforms by EU governments, but not their *ultimate source* or *justification*. To explain these facets of institutional reform fully we need to consider the creative ability – or social skill – of lower-level policy officials and EC organizations to work out the practical details of normal policymaking in the face of contradictions or omissions in the treaties. We also must pay close attention to the evolving normative/legal culture within which those activities take place. Thus, by allowing their social interactions to grow beyond mere bargaining-based processes, EU states have created a more stable, rule-based, innovative, and legitimate system of international cooperation. Judging by the expansion of EU policies in this domain since 1970, this system seems far more dynamic than expected of a regional intergovernmental organization.

Finally, I have shown that these institutional changes did not necessarily take place in a haphazard fashion despite the numerous factors involved. In general, EPC/CFSP participants organized their cooperation on the basis of two fundamental principles, one functional (do not attempt to codify working procedures until they have proved their necessity) and one normative (always respect the EC's own legal culture). Thus most changes to the system can be understood in terms of a sequential process of institutional development. These stages involved the establishment of the policy domain, the creation of a transgovernmental communications network, the creation and codification of procedural and substantive norms of behavior, the involvement of permanent organizations in the process, and the creation of mechanisms of governance to oversee the new policy domain of European foreign and security policy cooperation. These processes also led to the gradual internalization (or "Europeanization") of

Table 9.2 *Specific causes and components of EU foreign policy institutionalization*

Major causes	Institutional component
Bargaining in the face of enlargement	Establishment of the EPC policy domain
Learning-by-doing, problem-solving	Transgovernmental network
Imitation, learning-by-doing, turnover, crises, policy failures, bargaining, internal contradictions/gaps, links to other institutions (primarily for legalization)	Norm-creation/codification/ legalization
Problem-solving, internal contradictions/gaps, new policy ideas	Involvement of EC organizations
Enlargement, changes after the Cold War, links to other institutions	Governance mechanisms
Imitation, learning-by-doing, problem-solving	Penetration into the domestic politics of EU states

EPC/CFSP procedures and policies in EU member states, although this was not directly mandated by EU treaties. Still, to the extent that shared understandings and procedures regarding EU foreign policy cooperation prompted sympathetic institutional and political changes in EU member states, the prospects for both cooperative outcomes and additional institutional changes were improved.

Table 9.2 attempts to link major components of the institutionalization of EU foreign policy cooperation with dominant factors that encouraged such institutionalization. This treatment is only subjective, however, and it must be emphasized that most factors were in operation at all stages. Still, it is possible to suggest key factors for each part of the process, and to list them in order of their probable influence based on the historical record.

Although we cannot definitively weigh the importance of these causes relative to each other since they often overlapped, we can make several assessments about how they fit together. First, exogenous forces typically provide only an opportunity or excuse for debate over institutional change, but they do not dictate the specific outcome. Second, endogenous processes within EPC/CFSP (chiefly learning-by-doing, problem-solving, imitation, and turnover) generally provide the range of possible options. Third, specific choices are almost always incremental and progressive (owing to their origins in terms of the aforementioned processes) rather than revolutionary. New procedures usually must show some degree of correspondence with existing ones (assuming a catastrophic institutional crisis has not occurred), especially in complex institutional domains. Fourth, these incremental choices are almost always based primarily on operational experiences and pragmatic concerns (involving the collective evaluation of cooperative outcomes), and secondarily on ideological, legal, or strategic debates within the EU (or within related institutions). The CFSP under Maastricht is particularly representative of these findings: even at a time of major structural change (the end of the Cold War) where EPC seemed to have been overshadowed by outside forces, EU states managed only to rationalize and codify existing EPC procedures, and refused to include more robust, unequivocal provisions concerning defense cooperation, majority voting in the CFSP, Commission responsibilities, and ECJ involvement. Nor can current moves toward the ESDP be considered merely as a delayed reaction to the end of the Cold War; as we saw in Chapter 8, the EU's difficulties in the Balkans, chiefly Kosovo, ultimately led key players such as the UK to reconsider the idea of EU military cooperation.

Fifth and finally, although this *general* process of institutionalization encouraged more cooperation over time, *specific* institutional elements may in fact complicate or undermine the process of policy coordination. Such unintended consequences are especially likely in systems, such as EPC/CFSP, that developed by virtue of multiple sources of institutionalization rather than as a result of a single, coherent blueprint. In turn, various participants in EU foreign policy themselves may respond to, or defend, one logic of change over another, based on their own foreign policy traditions and the problem at hand. Some individuals (such as those representing the UK) are motivated to find pragmatic solutions to recognized operational problems, while others (such as those representing France) are driven by a grander vision of the EU's (and thus France's) proper place in the world. And still others (such as Commission officials) are required to satisfy all different logics of institutional change: as the chief policy initiators and administrators (functional logic), as legal guardians of the EU's large body of treaties and rules (appropriateness logic), and as the primary locus of the EU's institutional memory and its operating and training procedures (socialization logic). Disentangling and evaluating these motivations at various stages of institutional change will require additional research at the domestic and even individual levels of analysis.

Of course, institutional debates are partly a symptom of more fundamental problems: uncertainty about the need for an ESDP, a lack of political will, divergent national interests, and honest disagreements over policy. But to the extent that these issues are in fact defined in terms of institutions, and more importantly, to the extent that institutional ideas and mechanisms increasingly condition these debates and conceptions of interests, they deserve our attention. Moreover, EU states and EC organizations are never content to let these problems lie still; since the EU is a work in progress, there are constant pressures for reform and improvisation. In fact, questions about institutional design have become part of the regular political discourse at the EU and national levels about Europe's purpose, values, and identity. I will return to this question later in the chapter; in the section that follows I will summarize more specific findings of this research in terms of the five questions outlined in the introduction to this study.

Five puzzles of European foreign policy

In the introduction to this volume, I argued that the evolution of European foreign policy cooperation has prompted five related sets of basic questions in the growing literature on the subject. I also argued that an institutional analysis of this cooperation would shed some light (though to varying degrees) on each of these questions. In this section I attempt to recap the major findings of this study in light of the five questions.

1   *The existence, endurance and expansion of European
     foreign policy*

The most fundamental finding of this study concerns the ways by which institutional development both preserved and encouraged cooperation in foreign policy. As we have seen, the expansion of such cooperation cannot be linked to changes in the external environment alone. Realists tend to focus on crises and external threats as mechanisms to induce cooperation, yet there is no consistent relationship between threats and common action. In comparison with other crisis-prone regions of the world, such as the Middle East or East Asia, where effective foreign/security policy coordination is lacking, the EU's efforts in this domain are puzzling for realists, particularly since the EU's security is provided by the most successful alliance in history: NATO. Within the EU, some crises (such as the Persian Gulf War) did not prompt a major collective response, and, conversely, there have been other areas, such as Central America and South Africa, where EU states acted on the basis of common principles and understandings, not fears about external threats.

These common understandings resulted from a constant, increasingly institutionalized debate about foreign policy cooperation. At first, EU states merely attempted to share information about their own foreign policies. They only hoped that such policy coordination would prevent unilateral external actions from interfering with EC business; the idea of joint action was not seriously pursued. Later, EU states reached agreements on positions or actions to be taken unilaterally but still in the service of common interests. Only after these foundations were established – thus creating an atmosphere of trust and predictability in foreign policy – did EU states begin to engage regularly in collective action using EC resources. Nearly all of these actions in turn were institutionalized on the basis of precedents and problem-solving, not self-interested bargaining. Communications, working groups, and the lending of officials to each other also created an environment highly conducive to the establishment of norms. As norms proved their practical usefulness to the officials involved in the system, governments were more likely to upgrade the status of those norms by codifying them as legal rules. Together, these processes contributed to the stability and progressive development of European foreign policy.

A related point concerns the question of whether the CFSP is likely to persist or instead will be rolled back because it is ultimately unworkable. The experience of the EU in general, and of its external relations capacities in particular, suggests that reproduction and incremental adaptation are more likely. EU foreign policy rests on the foundation of EPC and a large body of Community provisions, so the logics of functionality and appropriateness are now even more salient in the EU's pursuit of coherent external relations as compared to EPC. New rules here must be respectful of both the functional track record of EC/EPC rules and of the legitimacy those rules have earned based on that track record. Moreover, new informal working methods and formal improvements (particularly in terms of decision-making, funding, and external representation) have helped EU states strike a balance between institutional stability (to promote coherence) and flexibility (to allow a variety of responses and participants). These new provisions also demonstrate the continuing ability of EU actors to exploit institutional gaps and contradictions with new mechanisms. In other words, these institutions are increasingly self-sustaining among the EU elites who are most intimately involved with them. As with the Maastricht Treaty, however, the real test will come during implementation: when the EU first attempts to make operational its formidable goal of defense cooperation under the new doctrine of "enhanced cooperation," particularly after the next enlargement (see below).

2   *EU foreign policy and the external world*

Does the EU influence actors and events beyond its own territory? Before answering this question, I must once again stress several points made in the introduction to this study. Above all, we must always keep in mind that EPC was originally intended to help reinforce European economic integration, not to solve complex international political problems. Widespread acceptance of the idea that Europe should play an international political role equal to that of its economic role came later. In addition, for much of its history EPC was devoted to helping European states understand each other's foreign policies (i.e., confidence-building), not to the undertaking of common actions. Finally, it is misleading to argue that the EU will never have a common foreign policy as long as it is not a unitary state with centralized decision-making and its own army. As long as the EU remains a collection of states, this comparison is entirely inappropriate. However, when compared to other regional groupings such as the OAS and ASEAN, or even the Commonwealth of Independent States, the EU exhibits a remarkable degree of cooperation in many areas beyond economics, only one of which involves foreign policy.[2] We should also keep in mind that most states are not always able to coordinate all of their external policies in all areas of the world effectively; thus, we should not expect this of the EU.

Still, it is worth asking whether EU foreign policy has had an impact on the external world. Indeed, for many observers this is the *only* question worth exploring. Although this study has not been explicitly directed toward this question since it involves policy *performance* rather than policy *coordination*, there is evidence in the form of existing case studies, memoirs, and other sources to show that non-EU states have been influenced by EU foreign policies.[3] Even during EPC's early years, when foreign policy cooperation was expressed only in the form of declarations and démarches, non-EU states (particularly in the developing world) took note of Europe's attitude toward various global issues. Some developed states, such as Japan and Norway, have been known to align themselves with the EU on certain issues. And as EPC/CFSP developed its policy tools in the form of economic aid and sanctions, its influence has

---

[2] Although the OAS was founded in 1948 (and its roots extend back to the International Union of American Republics in 1890) it was not until 1991 that the OAS adopted Resolution 1080, which set up procedures to react to threats to democracy in the Western hemisphere. It has been invoked only four times. ASEAN, founded in 1967, pledges to promote regional peace and stability, yet its institutional mechanisms for doing so involve mainly economic, social, technical, scientific, and administrative issues. Cooperation within these fields is only sporadic at best.

[3] For a very persuasive analysis of this question, see Ginsberg 2001.

broadened. This has been demonstrated in crisis situations (such as the Falklands War), long-range security issues (such as the CSCE process), and in areas where the EU has attempted to institutionalize a long-range policy into a dialogue (such as the Middle East, East/Central Europe, South Africa, and Central America). South Africa especially demonstrates the ability of the EU to sustain and expand its external policies toward a single area, starting with the Code of Conduct for EC firms with business in South Africa and ending with the post-apartheid transition. The case of Central/Eastern Europe similarly illustrates how the EU can remake other areas in its own image (Mayhew 2001), while EU–US relations deserve more attention to help determine the impact of European norms on American foreign policy, particularly regarding common problems, past and present, such as the Soviet Union/Russia and the Middle East (Risse-Kappen 1995b).

These cases aside, we should also appreciate that the EU's external relations are varied and complex, that there are dense links between political and economic aspects of these relations, and that the CFSP at present constitutes only a small part of the EU's external policies (Smith 1998). The mere hope of securing greater access to the EU market undoubtedly encourages non-member states to respect the political goals of the EU, especially now that requirements for political conditionality are a fundamental part of such agreements. But it is also true that the CFSP represents an important, and much higher profile, expansion of the EU's external agenda. The CFSP is *overtly political* and *specifically oriented* toward non-EU states, which significantly raises the stakes involved (positive and negative) in the EU's external relations. A single CFSP declaration could do serious damage to the EU's other policies if it offended an important external actor. In this sense the CFSP can easily affect EU economic goals in the same way that the lack of foreign policy cooperation adversely affected Europe during crises such as the October 1973 war in the Middle East and its associated oil shocks. The CFSP is also increasingly concerned with crisis management, and here it has the potential to complement the EC's usual long-term solutions to external problems. As Hill notes (1998: 31–33), demands for favors from, and special relationships with, the EU continue to increase among developing states, applicants for EU membership, and other actors interested in general political dialogue (as with Central America, ASEAN, Japan, and India). Thus, to the extent that the EU increasingly integrates CFSP goals and actions with those of its first pillar, which is clearly taking place, its political influence abroad has great potential. Whether this ambition also requires an independent EU military capability will be discussed below.

3   EU foreign policy and European integration

I argued in Chapter 1 that linkages between institutions could act as a powerful source of institutional change, particularly when those institutions share functional tasks or personnel. This observation is highly applicable to the case of European foreign policy, where two separate policy domains (the EC and EPC/CFSP) with their own procedures grew closer together over a period of three decades. Although several EU states hoped that EPC/CFSP would be self-contained, it most certainly did not develop in a vacuum and has had to reconcile itself constantly with the actors, policies, and procedures of the EC. In general, policies and procedures in both domains became linked on the basis of clearer, even shared, norms and rules. For the most part, this involved normative change on the part of EU foreign policy; rules in this domain were less developed than those of the EC, and EPC/CFSP officials increasingly looked to EC rules and organizations for guidance. Today these domains are subsumed under a broader institution, the European Union, and they are expected to perform their activities in a coherent, coordinated manner to improve the effectiveness of the EU's external policies.

The growth of linkages between these two domains was as much an accident as a design. Some architects of EPC certainly hoped or expected the economic and political dimensions of European integration would grow closer together, but they had no idea what form the merger would take, or if it would happen at all. At the time, it was difficult to conceive of a clearly defined middle ground between intergovernmental and supranational/federal visions of policymaking. However, EPC/CFSP eventually found this middle ground, using a combination of broad agenda-setting at the intergovernmental level, transgovernmental communications, rules concerning EC/EPC/CFSP interactions, and regular participation by the Commission. Through a long process of trial-and-error, contradictions and inconsistencies between the two domains were worked out during normal business and later codified in the form of EPC reports and treaties. Of course, it is also true that EPC had a "ready-made" legal culture (that of the EC) to learn from, plus a set of EC officials who were able to insert themselves into the policy process, often to the irritation of EU member states. Other actors, such as the EP, play supporting roles in EU foreign policy thanks to the EC's increasing concern with democratic legitimacy, an important norm of its own. However, these were relatively minor influences in the institutionalization of EPC/CFSP when compared to the roles of communication and norms, and would not have been permitted at all by EU member states without the culture of trust that had been previously established. What really matters here is not the

CFSP in isolation but its synergistic interaction (represented by inherent functional overlaps but also by institutional mechanisms and socialization processes) with other EU policy domains, internal and external. This tendency for related institutions and policy domains to influence each other through political, functional, and even normative spillover will only increase with the EU's growing complexity and scope. Now that the CFSP's relationship with the economic dimension of European integration (the EC) is becoming more coherent, the next step is for the relationship between the CFSP and the defense dimension of European integration to be substantially enhanced, assuming such a goal can be agreed within the EU.

4   The mechanisms and resources of European foreign policy

The extent to which EU foreign policy, as an institution, began to draw upon (and even imitate) the procedures of the EC is just one aspect of a major focus of this study: the development of EPC/CFSP decision-making mechanisms. Passive information-sharing on foreign policy was not problematic, but cooperation involving formal obligations, financial commitments, and eventually, EC resources, was another matter. Yet EU states, through collective trial-and-error and the establishment of pragmatic ground rules, gradually began to define their cooperation in precisely these ways. In other words, changes in institutional procedures changed diplomatic relations among EU states, which then encouraged external expressions of cooperation in foreign policy. With so much uncertainty surrounding the early years of EPC, norms not only helped to make EU member state behaviors more predictable, they also laid the foundations for a sense of common purpose. Over time, the most fundamental norms of EPC – problem-solving, *domaines réservés*, consultation, confidentiality, and consensus – led to a far more goal-oriented and coherent policy process, even a system of governance, in the form of the CFSP.

The close attention to norms in this analysis rejects realist assumptions about state interests and the centrality of material forms of power in explaining state behavior. Norms are part of the liberal tradition in international relations theory, which has increasingly focused on cognitive factors such as ideas, beliefs, learning, lessons of history, knowledge, and language. However, the "power" of such ideas also depends on some consensus regarding their content, the standards for their application in policymaking, and their linkages to existing policies and procedures. In addition, theories of policy learning/ideas are often used to explain a single change or shift in policy (and usually economic or social policy)[4] in a state or two states, which limits its application in multilateral settings. In short, an idea will have limited policy or behavioral consequences, especially in groups of more than a few states, unless it is cast as a specific behavioral norm and thus institutionalized, or at least preserved as a justification for policy or a standard of behavior. Thus, I have deliberately framed this study largely in terms of norms rather than ideas or discourse, as it has been concerned with *multilateral* foreign and security policy cooperation, with the *persistence* of learning or ideas over time in different situations, and with the effects of these factors on *state behavior*, expressed as collective foreign policies.

Still, even as a norm-governed policy process, the CFSP cannot yet be considered in terms of communitarization or supranationalization, although it is certainly less "garbage-can like" and more systematic and bureaucratic (even too bureaucratic, in the view of some insiders) than EPC. The CFSP can be understood in terms of some mechanisms of governance as I outlined in Chapter 7, yet EU member governments still exert a large degree of influence in the CFSP; the CFSP "executive" in the form of the EU presidency, High Representative, or the Commission is fairly weak; the EP and ECJ have severely limited roles relative to other EU policy domains; and public opinion or lobbying rarely intrude on CFSP deliberations in any significant way. Moreover, I have not argued that EPC/CFSP has always been successful. It does have its limits, particularly in areas touching upon crisis management, security, and defense. It would be naive to argue, for example, that a mere change in rules could have enabled the EU to "solve" a situation as complex as the breakup of Yugoslavia. However, although each individual institutional change may not have unequivocally improved the prospects for cooperation, the system as a whole has made it far easier for EU states to cooperate over the past thirty years than if it had not existed. EU member states are also finding it increasingly difficult to prevent the transfer of more CFSP authority to EC institutions, and they all now agree that the system will be unworkable, especially after the next enlargement, if they demand consensus at every stage in the process. Thus the CFSP continues to endure regular institutional reforms, both informal and formal, and this pattern will likely continue with the ESDP (see below).

---

[4] However, studies of security policy also reveal the importance of how an idea, strategy, or new technology can become a norm. For example, the "cult of offensive" in World War I could be considered a norm to the extent that it conditions thinking and behavior among a set of actors (Snyder 1984; Van Evera 1984).

5   *EU foreign policy and domestic politics*

Finally, this study has identified some key processes by which European foreign policy penetrates into the domestic politics of EU member states, thus encouraging cooperation. This argument may seem unusual, considering that EPC/CFSP does not usually command the attention of interest groups, powerful businesses, or other domestic actors concerned with European integration. However, a number of observers have pointed to the importance of elite socialization in the development of EPC/CFSP, and I have confirmed that argument throughout this study. The constant, direct involvement of EU foreign ministers and their subordinates in EPC/CFSP was vital for both institutional change (rule-making) and cooperative outcomes. Moreover, I have shown that membership in EU foreign policy has far more pervasive effects on EU states than one might otherwise expect from the obligations set out in treaties. Although these treaties never explicitly called for such changes, EU states found themselves creating entirely new administrative positions, expanding and reorganizing their foreign ministries to cope with the EPC/CFSP workload, and in some cases even reinterpreting their national constitutions in light of EPC/CFSP norms.[5]

Finally, the growing amount of EPC/CFSP activity has clearly entered the public's consciousness in Europe. This has occurred even though foreign policy is an area where it can be difficult for the Commission to mobilize support among EU citizens for EPC/CFSP initiatives in the same way it has for EC policies. Although it is still not as high profile as other EC policy goals, such as monetary union, by 1995 a majority of citizens in all EU states had agreed that foreign and security policy cooperation is an acceptable and desirable goal of European integration.[6] This broad base of support for the CFSP should act as a positive force for both institutional reforms and specific cooperative outcomes.

These are no small achievements for a regional organization. And although the CFSP is fairly unique as a system of cooperation, I have attempted to explain its development in terms of institutional processes which have been shown to work elsewhere. Information-sharing, transgovernmental networks, norms, organizations, and governance structures are common features in world politics; the singular contribution

---

[5] For a more comprehensive discussion of these tendencies, see Manners and Whitman 2000; Smith 2000.

[6] Eichenberg 1997. Recent (2001–2002) Eurobarometer surveys indicate an average of 65 percent support for a common foreign policy and 73 percent support for a common defense policy. This was despite a decline in general support for the EU, to an average of 48 percent.

of European foreign policy cooperation was the way it gradually, but persistently, linked these processes together in a fairly rational manner while embedding them in the larger architecture of economic integration. And unlike NATO, whose consensual decision-making (and resource base) is clearly dominated by a single member state, the EU has managed its achievement while still respecting, as far as possible, the ideas and unique interests of even its smallest member states. The EU's information-sharing and confidence-building mechanisms alone might be extremely useful for regions attempting to promote reconciliation or peaceful integration, such as the Middle East or Southeast Asia. Participants in EPC/CFSP certainly feel its mechanisms are applicable elsewhere; as I showed in Chapter 6, a major goal of the EU (and the Commission in particular) is to spread regional cooperation/integration elsewhere by encouraging others to imitate its own methods.

Beyond institutions and cooperation: toward a European identity?

Although we can appreciate the EU's expanded foreign policy cooperation today relative to the 1970s and relative to other regional organizations, we must also consider Europe's new ambition to be a "global superpower." Policy effectiveness as well must be factored into the equation, and the EU has been known to make questionable policy decisions (such as the CAP and the stability and growth pact) despite the use of supranational Community procedures. In particular, if the EU truly intends to intensify its cooperation in security/defense affairs to play a greater role in world politics, its member states will have to delegate more responsibilities to a common authority (the EU presidency, Commission, or otherwise) and place more limits on the rule of consensus in this domain. The CFSP/ESDP also needs better mechanisms and criteria to measure policy effectiveness and compliance. Without these reforms, and despite its high degree of civilian/economic cooperation, EU foreign policy may amount to little more than "social work" in the eyes of the international community. Enhanced cooperation may not be enough to provide a true joint operational capability for issues with a crisis/security/defense dimension, especially after the next series of enlargements (although all applicants have met the basic membership criteria for the CFSP).

Concerning the ESDP in particular, timid institutional reforms, shrinking defense budgets, and uncertain political will, coupled with the costs of enlargement and the presence of NATO, suggest that the ESDP may be little more than a psychological insurance policy to back up the Atlantic alliance. It will be a very expensive insurance policy, however, in terms of the financial commitments it requires, and in terms of the backlash it provokes, if an EU-led military operation is viewed as a failure by the outside world and by the EU's own citizens. Although the Commission has taken steps to improve its civilian conflict prevention[7] and crisis management procedures,[8] the EU is still finding its way in handling crises with a military or defense dimension, and the measures outlined in the Göteborg European Council in June 2001 can not fully address this problem.[9] Most proposed changes are still too focused on the margins – consultation, committees, statements of purpose, dialogue with NATO[10] – rather than on the root cause of the problem: the limits of decision-making by consensus in an EU of twenty-five or more states, plus its complex forms of external representation revolving around a rotating EU presidency. Would the US, for example, be a superpower if each of its fifty state governors ran the federal government for six months at a time?

EU states will also need to give serious attention to the key elements of a defense pact: a mutual security guarantee, a truly unified command structure, force modernization, more defense spending, a nuclear weapons policy, and possibly some form of associate membership for non-EU states. Without these measures, the ESDP will appear impotent as a deterrent against attacks on the EU given the dominance of NATO in the European theater. And unless the ESDP provides for more streamlined decision-making coupled with more resources (especially air power and surveillance), it is highly doubtful it could be used to compel other actors to change their behavior in line with EU interests.

However, there is still another rationale for pursuing the CFSP in general and the ESDP in particular: to promote a common European identity for its own sake, rather than for any specific operational mission to defend a common interest. If monetary union can serve this purpose, in part, so too may the ESDP, which may become a powerful symbol of

---

[7] See the European Commission 2001a.

[8] As mandated by the Helsinki European Council (December 1999). The Commission's proposal for a regulation establishing a Rapid Reaction Mechanism (RRM) was adopted by the General Affairs Council in February 2001. The RRM is intended to speed up the use of civilian Community instruments (including policing) in crisis situations, and allows for a number of policy tools to be combined in a single CFSP/ESDP joint action. It also provided for a new RRM budget line, in the amount of 25 million euros for 2002.

[9] In particular, the report of this summit notes that EU crisis management will be undertaken only after a request by lead organizations like the UN or OSCE, and that EU member states will take the ultimate decision to participate in such operations. In light of this report, numerous consultation mechanisms (an EU Military Committee and Military Staff, among others) were set up to facilitate more cooperation, yet the report says nothing about enhancing decision-making capabilities or requiring EU states to provide military assets to an EU-led force. See the EU Presidency 2001.

[10] For example, see the EU Heads of State and Government 2002.

European unity whose effects could reach far beyond EU treaties and European Council reports. Symbols have consequences, even political and economic costs, and can unite as well as divide people inside and outside the EU. This may be especially true with symbols or policy goals directed primarily toward, or in opposition to, non-EU member states, such as the US. Indeed, like the creation of EPC in the 1970s, the EU's very act of developing the ESDP on paper has prompted various reassessments of the transatlantic relationship since the idea was first proposed.

A full exploration of these dimensions of European foreign policy is beyond the scope of this chapter. However, some concluding observations about the relationship between identity and institutionalized cooperation are in order. Most generally, we need more systematic examinations of policy and preference changes within individual EU member states. I have argued only that participation in EPC/CFSP impacts on EU member states in terms of elite socialization, bureaucratic changes, constitutional interpretations, and public opinion. This should influence their general propensity to cooperate in foreign/defense policy, but these factors can vary greatly across EU states, specific policy actions, and time. An exploration of these variables could be enhanced by additional work on how CFSP/ESDP as an institutionalized policy domain penetrates into domestic political cultures, perhaps in terms of other indicators such as political campaigns, party competition and platforms, domestic bureaucratic politics, interest groups, media attention, and so on. All of these factors deserve more attention and comparative analysis, particularly if one intends to demonstrate changes of preferences or identities among EU states.

This type of comparative research may allow us to push this institution–identity nexus even further, by moving from the relationship between norms, domestic politics, and common policies to the construction of common interests and identities, as theorists more sensitive to social constructivism have suggested. These analysts are attempting to recast Deutsch et al.'s (1957) vision of a "pluralistic security community" based on shared values, sensitivity to each other's needs, communication, predictable behavior, and international institutions. For example, Ruggie refers to the EU in his argument about the distinction between "modern" and "post-modern" forms of territorial political organization. In his terms (1993: 172), the EU might be the first "multi-perspectival polity" to emerge in the (post)-modern era. In such a polity, the constitutive processes whereby each EU member state "defines its own identity – and identities are logically prior to preferences – increasingly endogenize the existence" of all other EU states. Similarly, Wendt (1994: 386) argues that "Identification is a continuum from negative to positive – from conceiving the other as anathema to the self conceiving the other as an extension of the self. It also varies by issue and other."[11] Positive interests lead states to think of others' needs as extensions of their needs (such as in a collective security system); negative interests lead to exploitation and manipulation (as in the case of alliances, where states "cooperate" only in the face of an outside threat). Hence social constructivism and neorealism should be viewed as opposite ends of a single spectrum depending on the states and issues involved: "As the degree of common fate increases, so does the incentive to identify with others. As interdependence rises, in other words, so will the potential for endogenous transformations of identity, with consequences that go beyond those analyzed by rationalists" (Wendt 1994: 389–90). He further cites the unique example of the EU as a text-book case of positive interests among a given set of states across several issue-areas.[12]

However, this more nuanced conception of identity as a positive sum, not zero sum, feature of modern states needs to supplemented by explaining how identity is expressed as *behavioral* obligations and adjustments, not just as ideas or discourse. What really matters here are the circumstances by which one identity takes precedence over another (even temporarily), and how that process causes behavioral changes, rule-based or otherwise, among group members. As Commission president Romano Prodi put it in a speech to the EP in February 2001: "Do we realize that our nation-states, taken individually, would find it far more difficult to assert their existence and their identity on the world stage?"[13] This statement was linked to an appeal for a wide-ranging debate about the EU's fundamental purpose and the institutional reforms necessary to achieve that purpose. It also recognizes that institutions both shape and reflect collective identity, which can be manifested as cooperation, the chief focus of this study. The larger question is how the EU can defend its central common principles, required of all member states, in light of its new doctrine of enhanced cooperation in policy domains (such as the ESDP and

[11] Mercer (1995: 249–51) has also argued for a "third way" between positivist realism and social constructivism, and he suggests the example of the EU as an area for research into collective identity. A closely related "epistemic communities" school of thought examines the role of transnational knowledge networks in shaping ideas and behavior; see Müller and van Dassen 1997: 68–69.

[12] Wendt (1999) also applies several concepts from more orthodox international relations theories to support his argument: a common fate, interdependence, and the increasing "dynamic density" of interactions owing to trade, capital, and technological flows help create a system conducive to collective identity formation. However, as I have argued throughout this volume, these factors by themselves will not necessarily lead to specific cooperative outcomes.

[13] Michael Mann, "Prodi Urges Fundamental Debate on the Future of EU," *Financial Times*, February 13, 2001.

monetary union) that traditionally define national sovereignty, while both expanding to the East and maintaining a single European institutional space.

Unfortunately, there is little consensus on how to define and measure identity in empirical terms, nor have many analysts applied these arguments to the EU in any systematic way.[14] As I have stressed in this volume, European foreign policy as an institution is based on interdependence, confidence-building, communication, common definitions of problems, explicit behavioral standards, and the equality of its participants, all of which may encourage a sense of common identity. To the extent that a common identity is expressed by rules and common external policies, the EU clearly possesses such an international political identity. And to the extent that this body of actions is used as a point of reference in the way EU states determine their values and make policies, their identity has changed as well.

This is also a two-way process; as the EU takes an increasing number of principled actions in world politics through the CFSP and other policy instruments, and as the outside world responds to those actions, the CFSP helps provide a valuable social commodity for the EU: internal unity. Here there is the possibility of a true constructivist or reflectivist interpretation, by which a European identity is constructed over (or in addition to) existing national identities and in response to outside actors. National foreign policy rests on the idea of a shared identity among individuals, preserved and developed by collective historical experiences and state institutions, but this has taken time in the EU given the lack of a central authority powerful enough to assert its view of the common interest over the strongly-entrenched national traditions of individual EU member states. There is also no prominent external threat or actor to act as a catalyst, and to the extent that EU governments cling to traditional notions of national sovereignty, the EU's global identity will take time to develop. Instead, and for the moment, such a European foreign policy identity will have to come from within the EU itself, whereby elite officials attempt to "create a collective memory based on shared myths" (Smith 1992) in the manner of European state-building.

A common defense policy symbolizes this identity-building process, but it also raises additional problems of governance. Although it has generally worked for EPC/CFSP, a decentralized, consensus-based, transgovernmental approach to the ESDP may prove unworkable on a practical

---

[14] For exceptions, see Wæver 1996; Whitman 1998; Checkel 2001. Another recent study (Cederman 2000) focuses on the EU's external identity but does not discuss foreign policy in great detail, while Hemmer and Katzenstein (2002) examine the role of regional identity in the creation of NATO.

level. Fundamentally, EU states still seem to disagree on the key functional role of the ESDP: as a support arm for NATO (the UK), as an independent EU force (France), or solely as a peacekeeping/humanitarian force (Germany and Sweden). Moreover, some actor must ultimately take on the risks of leadership and accountability, which is especially problematic in foreign policy (not to mention defense policy) in light of rotating EU presidencies, a weak Commission, different national values and capabilities, and a foreign policy spokesperson with no real resources or mandate. There is still a huge conceptual and operational gap between "normal" CFSP activities and military-related actions, and it is possible that only a major external crisis and/or a major change of policy in the US (such as withdrawing from NATO) would lead the EU to transform its weak ESDP plans into an effective independent military force. While EU states may have a common interest and even shared identity in developing such a force, their political will to act still varies a great deal, their decision-making methods are onerous, they are unwilling to delegate to another institution, and they have not committed the necessary financial resources to back up their common interests in the ESDP. And the ultimate goal of using the ESDP to provide a formal security guarantee for EU member states, including the role of nuclear weapons toward that end, is still an open question.

Europe's constitutional future and the CFSP/EDSP

As this volume goes to press, several recent events further demonstrate the difficulties that remain in forging a common European defense policy: the crisis in Macedonia, the war in Afghanistan following the September 11, 2001 terrorist attacks in the US, and the confrontation with Iraq over its weapons of mass destruction. In all three cases, although the EU showed some solidarity in approving a general position on the issue (occasionally supported by civilian/economic measures),[15] it soon became divided over the need for a specific military response, if any. EU states also clashed over whether the EU should be involved in organizing the response, and in all three cases they chose national and/or NATO contributions instead of the EU's own RRF. On a more positive note, Macedonia at least showed the effectiveness of close cooperation between George Robertson of NATO and Javier Solana of the EU, with a supporting role for the OSCE (in the form of civilian monitors protected by NATO). This division of

---

[15] For example, the EU's "Action Plan" of seventy-nine anti-terrorism policy initiatives (including a blacklist of terrorist organizations and a European arrest warrant) was proposed at the Ghent summit in October 2001 and agreed by the Laeken European Council in December 2001. See the European Commission 2001b.

labor – NATO threatens short-term punishment while the EU simultaneously offers long-term rewards – could be the future model, assuming
both institutions agree on the political priorities in such cases (i.e., supporting fragmentation or unification) and on the same balance between
carrots and sticks. After September 11, NATO invoked Article 5 for the
first time in its history, which facilitated the use of some NATO assets, but
not its command structure, for the war in Afghanistan. These changes,
not to mention the way NATO countries served on missions to protect
US airspace, would have been nearly unthinkable without the terrorist
attacks against the US. On the negative side, however, some Europeans
resisted a reorientation of NATO toward anti-terrorism efforts in the immediate aftermath of the attacks.[16] The refusal in early 2003 of some
European NATO members (including France and Germany) to allow
the use of NATO assets for a US attack on Iraq also raises the specter of
a future US refusal to allow the ESDP use of those same assets.

These types of problems clearly reflect fundamental tensions among
EU states, some of whom also criticize the US for being insensitive
to human rights, disrespectful of the UN, and too unilateral in its approach to foreign/security policy.[17] Even more problematic for the EU,
in December 2001 the Belgian EU presidency (in the person of Belgian
foreign minister Louis Michel) prematurely announced at the Laeken European Council that the ESDP was "operational" and that the EU would
provide up to 4,000 troops for the peacekeeping force in Afghanistan.
This could have been the first deployment of the EU's RRF, yet France,
Germany, and the UK (among others) quickly denied the announcement
and insisted that they would deploy troops on their own accord, not under

---

[16] In fact, the US tried at the 1999 NATO summit in Washington to give NATO a counter-
terrorism role by broadening the definition of "attack" to include terrorism, sabotage, and
organized crime. The Europeans refused, which led to a compromise in the communiqué
(Article 24) issued after the summit: "Any armed attack on the territory of the allies,
from whatever direction, would be covered by Article 5 of the Washington (NATO)
Treaty"; and in addition that "alliance security interests can be affected by risks of
a wider nature, including terrorism, sabotage, and organized crime." European allies
thought this might prevent NATO from assuming a true counter-terrorism role, but the
September 11 attacks effectively led NATO, in the interest of showing solidarity with the
US, to incorporate Article 24 into Article 5 with little debate over the legalities. But some
allies began questioning this *fait accompli* soon after it was decided. See Judy Dempsey,
"EU Doubts Grow over 'Switch' in NATO Role," *Financial Times*, September 18, 2001;
Judy Dempsey, "NATO Help Likely to Go Beyond Bin Laden Attack," *Financial Times*,
October 5, 2001.

[17] These episodes also call into question the need for greater intelligence cooperation in
the EU, whether in the form of spy satellites or other means. Here the UK prefers to rely
on its special relationship with the US, while the French (among others) prefer a more
independent EU capability. The EU Council of Ministers established its own modest
intelligence unit in late 2001, but its resources are unquestionably surpassed by NATO
and the national services of EU member states.

the institutional umbrella of the EU. The EU did, however, later decide to take over NATO's peacekeeping mission in Macedonia as one of its first ESDP actions.[18] If this operation proceeds as planned, there is no reason the EU cannot apply its time-tested method of learning-by-doing to the creation of new rules for military deployments in the ESDP.

Assuming the EU manages to overcome its deficiencies in political will, decision-making, and resources, it must also contend with public opposition to the very idea of using military force in situations that do not involve a direct military attack. Both the Kosovo and Afghanistan military campaigns were marked by intense concerns about civilian casualties, collateral damage, and other humanitarian issues. These concerns always threaten to undermine political cohesion and military effectiveness, even when one state, such as the US, assumes most of the risk. As difficult as it is for the EU to undertake its own military operations, it will face even more obstacles in sustaining public support and collective political will once EU troops are committed and casualties begin to mount. Civilian oversight of the armed forces during a military operation is always a difficult and contentious task, and it is questionable whether the EU's institutional machinery, as presently structured, can handle these responsibilities, even if delegated to do so by its member states. It is also unclear how EU member states could inspire their citizens to risk their lives on behalf of the ESDP.[19] Finally, we must also consider the effectiveness of Petersberg-task type deployments once the barriers of decision-making and public opinion are surmounted. If the experience of the UN in places like Srebrenica is any guide, these missions are still dangerous and can be extremely costly, both politically and economically. The Dutch government learned this lesson when it resigned in April 2002 in response to a report on the failure of Dutch UN peacekeepers to prevent the 1995 massacre of Muslims in Srebrenica. How will the EU be able to explain to its 450 million citizens (post-enlargement) why it should absorb such costs when other institutions (such as NATO or the UN) may be willing to do so, and in light of so many other expensive, pressing tasks, such as enlargement, unemployment, and competitiveness?

In light of these complications, and given the CFSP's track record with civilian/economic tools, it is worth asking a final question: whether the

---

[18] As decided during the June 2002 Seville European Council, which also affirmed the EU's willingness, under the ESDP, to provide civilian police forces to Bosnia starting in January 2003. Eighteen non-EU countries also agreed to participate in this operation.

[19] On this point, France and Germany did propose an EU defense college at their 77th summit in June 2001 to promote a culture of European security and defense. If implemented, this could provide a military counterpart to the integrationist mindset embodied in the Commission's own bureaucratic and diplomatic corps.

EU actually would be wiser to concentrate its efforts in areas where it has demonstrable strengths: the EC, the CFSP, and (potentially) the foreign/security components of JHA. The EU's use of deadly force will almost certainly undermine its "soft power" and its positive image as a civilian actor in world politics, which may give it a rhetorical edge over the US in the view of many other states (particularly in the developing world, where the EU is the largest aid donor). Although the US–EU partnership can be formidable, the EU may be more influential as a global actor by celebrating its differences with the US and NATO rather than by attempting to imitate those actors. Unlike the US, which tends to disdain "state-building," the EU seems both willing and able to remake other troubled states and regions in its own image. Even if it cannot yet help enforce peace agreements or prevent conflicts through military means, the EU can still be a powerful force for democratization, civil society, and long-term development, which are as important to global stability as crisis management. If the EU still decides to proceed with the ESDP in the absence of more radical institutional changes in this domain (which could involve a federal Europe), the only way to achieve cooperation in military affairs would be to allow either a "concert" approach (whereby the ESDP is effectively led by the EU's most willing states) or an institutionalized two-speed Europe, both of which could undermine the cohesion that the EU is supposed to facilitate. Even with these changes, the ESDP is likely to be operational only in situations where NATO (i.e., the US) clearly refuses to participate. Finally, how all of this will take place while upholding the Commission's principles of "good governance" in the EU – openness, participation, accountability, effectiveness, and coherence – remains to be seen.[20]

Thus, the EU faces yet another momentous decision. Its next enlargement will be the most ambitious ever, and will require an equal degree of institutional reform to accommodate so many new member states. A model of intergovernmental, transgovernmental, and supranational governance based on an elite bureaucracy, secret European Council decision-making, 80,000 pages of rules, and multiple policy networks may not be effective enough to bridge the numerous potential foreign policy cleavages after the next enlargement. The emergence of diffuse threats such as terrorists, biological weapons, and organized crime also will put huge stresses on the EU's cumbersome arrangements for security cooperation. Past experience in the EU, involving the deepening of functional, organizational, and even social linkages between enlargement and political cooperation (in the form of EPC, CFSP/JHA, and ESDP), also

---

[20] European Commission 2001c. For a more detailed examination of this question, see Siedentop 2001.

suggests that enlargement must be justified by more than narrow economic considerations. How the EU rationalizes its purpose and growth will be a fundamental question for the EU's "Convention on the Future of Europe" in 2003–2004. At a minimum, this convention hopes to convert the EU's current constitutional order from a patchwork of complex EU/EC treaties into a single, coherent, simple document. At a maximum, it could produce a path-breaking new blueprint for Europe's future development.

At the time of writing (January 2003), however, one of the most widely debated ideas inspired by the convention is a proposal involving a new "EU president" (of the European Council, in addition to rotating EU presidencies) chosen by EU heads of government to represent the EU over a long term, such as five years. The Commission would retain its own president who could be appointed by the EP rather than by member states. France and Germany agreed to this "twin-presidency" plan at a meeting in early 2003, and several other EU states (Denmark, Italy, Spain, Sweden, and the UK) also endorsed the idea, as did convention chair Valery Giscard d'Estaing. Although the two presidency officials could enjoy some measure of democratic legitimacy, it is difficult to see how they would compete with the existing authority and resources of EU member states,[21] especially in security/defense affairs, where EU states would still enjoy veto rights. If EU states block ESDP decisions or fail to invest the EU president or Commission with the resources and responsibility for the CFSP/ESDP, they will have succeeded only in merging the chief virtue of the current CFSP High Representative – greater permanence and a higher profile – with the chief virtue of the current EU presidency: as representative of the collective will of EU member states. This also may involve combining the functions of the CFSP High Representative and the Commissioner for External Relations into a single "EU foreign secretary" Commissioner.

The Commission is likely to oppose the creation of a new European Council president with strong foreign policy powers;[22] this plan could also be derailed if any smaller EU state refuses to sign on or if large EU states insist that one of their own occupy the top position. Would France, for example, really agree to be represented in global affairs over a five-year term by someone from Greece or Estonia? How would the European

[21] The Franco-German plan does propose that the EU foreign secretary would preside over meetings of EU foreign ministers, and would be backed up by a European diplomatic service working closely with those of EU member states.

[22] The Commission does support merging the functions of the CFSP High Representative and the Commissioner for External Relations into a "Secretary of the European Union," a special new role for the vice-president of the Commission. See the European Commission 2002 for its contribution to the convention.

Council president coordinate his/her responsibilities with the rotating EU presidency, the EU foreign secretary, the president of the Commission, other external relations Commissioners, ad hoc EU special envoys, and the top representatives of large EU states? What "authority" would these officials have to enforce compliance, particularly in EU policy domains where member states are free to opt in or opt out on a case-by-case (ESDP) or permanent (Schengen) basis? And would the EU president or foreign secretary have the legal authority/personality to negotiate and conclude agreements on behalf of the EU?

Although it is an unprecedented exercise for the EU, the convention is likely to find it extremely difficult to take final decisions on these matters. In fact, delegates to the convention overwhelmingly denounced the Franco-German plan for a twin-presidency only a few days after it was proposed. Ultimately, if any version of this general plan is agreed, the EU will have taken the path of least resistance that we have seen throughout the institutional history of EPC/CFSP summit-level agreements: a modest compromise that raises as many institutional problems as it solves by simultaneously altering the intergovernmental and supranational elements of European integration without fully reconciling the two. This in turn will require far more transgovernmental coordination – and new rules – among lower-level participants, especially as the EU expands to twenty-five member states.

And yet, even if the EU fails to agree on taking European integration to the federal level, and even if it never fields an independent, operational ESDP, we can still appreciate the unique accomplishment of foreign policy cooperation in a regional economic organization, the primary focus of this volume. Despite the institutional and practical problems discussed in this chapter, there is still no serious thought among EU states of returning, as a normal practice, to their old self-interested, short-sighted, unilateral approaches to foreign policy problems. Through complex processes of institutionalization, the EU has fundamentally changed the way its member states define and pursue their interests. In the face of challenges to those interests, EU member states still generally tend to respond by enhancing their institutions, not by dismantling them, even in the sensitive domain of security/defense policy. As this process continues, we would do well to remember that the EU has surprised the world before with the strength of its commitment to institutionalized integration, most recently with the successful launch of a common currency and the decision on Eastern enlargement. Perhaps it will do so again by creating a truly functional and independent military force to support its well-developed Common Foreign and Security Policy.

References

EUROPEAN COMMUNITY SOURCES (ONLY MAJOR
PUBLICATIONS LISTED)

Council of the European Union (1995). *Report of the Council on the Functioning of the Treaty on European Union*. Luxembourg: Office of Official Publications of the EC.

Court of Auditors of the European Communities (1996). *Special Report No. 2/96 Concerning the Accounts of the Administrator and the European Union Administrator, Mostar*. OJ C 287/1, September 30.

EC/EU Heads of State and Government (1986). "The Single European Act." In *European Political Cooperation* (5th ed., 1988). Bonn: Press and Information Office of the Federal Republic of Germany.

(1991). *The Treaty on European Union*. Luxembourg: Office of Official Publications of the EC.

(1993). *Presidency Conclusions: Brussels European Council* (October 29).

(1996). *Presidency Conclusions: Turin European Council* (March 29).

(1997a). *An Effective and Coherent External Policy. Report of the Intergovernmental Conference of the Amsterdam European Council,* June 16–17. Luxembourg: Office of Official Publications of the EC.

(1997b). *Consolidated Version of the Treaty on European Union*. Luxembourg: Office of Official Publications of the EC.

(1999a). *Presidency Conclusions: Cologne European Council* (June 3–4).

(1999b). *Presidency Conclusions: Helsinki European Council* (December 10–11).

(2000a). *Presidency Conclusions: Santa Maria da Feira European Council* (June 19/20).

(2000b). *Presidency Conclusions: Nice European Council* (December 7–9).

(2001a). *The Treaty of Nice*. Luxembourg: Office of Official Publications of the EC.

(2001b). *Presidency Conclusions: Laeken European Council* (December 14–15).

(2002). *Presidency Conclusions: Brussels European Council* (October 24–25).

EU Foreign Ministers (1970). "First Report of the Foreign Ministers to the Heads of State and Government of the Member States of the European Community of 27 October 1970" (Luxembourg or Davignon Report). In *European Political Cooperation* (5th ed., 1988). Bonn: Press and Information Office of the Federal Republic of Germany.

(1973). "Second Report of the Foreign Ministers to the Heads of State and Government of the Member States of the European Community of 23

July 1973" (Copenhagen Report). In *European Political Cooperation* (5th ed., 1988). Bonn: Press and Information Office of the Federal Republic of Germany.

(1992). *Report to the European Council in Lisbon on the Likely Development of the Common Foreign and Security Policy (CFSP) with a View to Identifying Areas Open to Joint Action vis-à-vis Particular Countries or Groups of Countries.* Annex I to the *Presidency Conclusions, Lisbon European Council,* June 26–27.

EU Presidency (2000). *Presidency Report on the European Security and Defense Policy.* Attached to the *Presidency Conclusions of the Nice European Council,* December 7–9.

(2001). *Presidency Report to the Göteborg European Council on European Security and Defence Policy,* June 11.

European Commission (1972). "Necessary Progress in Community Energy Policy (13 October)." *Bulletin of the European Communities,* supplement, November.

(1986). *Proposal for a Council Directive Suspending New Direct Investment in the Republic of South Africa by Residents of the Community, 86/522.* Brussels, European Community, September 24.

(1990). *Commission Opinion on the Proposal for Amendment of the Treaty Establishing the European Economic Community with a View to Political Union.* COM (90)600 final (October 23). Luxembourg: Office of Official Publications of the EC.

(1992a). *Export Controls on Dual-Use Goods and Technologies and the Completion of the Internal Market.* SEC(92)85 final.

(1992b). *Proposal for a Council Regulation (EEC) on the Control of Exports of Certain Dual-Use Goods and Technologies and of Certain Nuclear Products and Technologies.* COM (92)317 final (August 31).

(1995a). *Commission Report on the Functioning of the Treaty on European Union.* Luxembourg: Office of Official Publications of the EC.

(1995b). *Report on the Promotion of Intra-Regional Cooperation and Good Neighbourly Relations.* Luxembourg: Office of Official Publications of the EC.

(1996a). *Commission Report on Reinforcing Political Union and Preparing for Enlargement.* COM (96)90 final. Luxembourg: Office of Official Publications of the EC.

(1996b). *Commission Communication on the Challenges Facing the European Defence Industry* (25 January). Brussels: Commission's Spokesman's Service.

(1996c). *Top Decision Makers Survey: Summary Report.* Brussels: DG-X Survey Research Unit, September.

(2000a). *Adapting the Institutions to Make a Success of Enlargement: Commission Opinion.* COM (2000)34 final (January 26). Brussels.

(2000b). *Adapting the Institutions to Make a Success of Enlargement: Commission Report to the Presidency.* COM (2000)592 final (December 3). Brussels.

(2001a). *Communication from the Commission on Conflict Prevention.* COM (2001)211 final (April 11). Brussels.

(2001b). *Overview of EU Action in Response to the Events of the 11 September and Assessment of Their Likely Economic Impact.* COM (2001)611 final (October 17). Brussels.

(2001c). *European Governance: A White Paper*. COM (2001)428 final (July 27). Brussels.

(2002). *For the European Union: Peace, Freedom, Solidarity. Communication of the Commission on the Institutional Architecture*. COM (2002)728 final/2 (December 11). Brussels.

European Parliament (1977). "Political Committee of the European Parliament Draft Paper on European Political Cooperation" (Blumenfeld Report). *PE 49335* (October 12).

(1981). "Report on European Political Cooperation and the Role of the European Parliament" (Elles Report). *EP Working Document*, 1–335/81. Luxembourg: European Parliament.

(1982). "Scott-Hopkins Report of the Political Affairs Committee on Southern Africa." *EP Working Document*, 1–657/82. Luxembourg: European Parliament.

(1991). "Report on the Outlook for a Common European Security Policy" (Poettering Report). *EP Documents* 146/269 (April 29).

(1992). "Resolution on the Community's Role in the Supervision of Arms Exports and the Armaments Industry." *EP Documents* 161/873 (September 17).

(1994). "Report on the Financing of the CFSP" (Willockx Report). *EP Documents* 209/630 (October 18).

(1995). 'Report on Progress Made in Implementing the Common Foreign and Security Policy (November 1993–December 1994) of the Committee on Foreign Affairs and Security" (Matutes Report). *EP Documents* 211/241 (April 24).

(2000). "Report on the European Parliament's Proposals for the Intergovernmental Conference" (April 13). Brussels.

High Level Group of Experts on the CFSP (1995–96). "European Security Policy Towards 2000: Ways and Means to Establish Genuine Credibility" (Durieux Report). Brussels: European Commission.

Reflection Group (1995). "Reflection Group's Report for the 1996 IGC." Luxembourg: Office of Official Publications of the EC.

BOOKS AND ARTICLES

Allen, David (1978). "The Euro-Arab Dialogue." *Journal of Common Market Studies* 16: 323–42.

(1982). "European Political Cooperation and the Euro-Arab Dialogue." In Allen, Rummel, and Wessels (eds.).

(1997). "EPC/CFSP, the Soviet Union, and the Former Soviet Republics: Do the Twelve Have a Coherent Policy?" In Regelsberger, de Schoutheete de Tervarent, and Wessels (eds.).

(1998). "Who Speaks for Europe? The Search for an Effective and Coherent External Policy." In Peterson and Sjursen (eds.).

Allen, David and Alfred Pijpers, eds. (1984). *European Foreign Policy-Making and the Arab-Israeli Conflict*. The Hague: Martinus Nijhoff Publishers.

Allen, David, Reinhardt Rummel, and Wolfgang Wessels, eds. (1982). *European Political Cooperation: Towards a Foreign Policy for Western Europe*. London: Butterworths.

Allen, David and Michael Smith (1994). "External Policy Developments." *Journal of Common Market Studies* 32: 67–86.

Allen, David and William Wallace (1982). "European Political Cooperation: The Historical and Contemporary Background." In Allen, Rummel, and Wessels (eds.).

Al-Mani, Saleh A. (1983). *The Euro-Arab Dialogue: A Study in Associative Diplomacy*. London: Pinter Publishers.

Anderson, Jeffrey J. (1995). "The State of the (European) Union: From the Single Market to Maastricht, from Singular Events to General Theories." *World Politics* 47: 441–65.

Anderson, Scott (1992). "Western Europe and the Gulf War." In Rummel (ed.).

Anderson, Stephanie B. (1998). "Problems and Possibilities: The Development of the CFSP from Maastricht to the 1996 IGC." In *The State of the European Union*, vol. IV: *Deepening and Widening*, Pierre-Henri Laurent and Marc Maresceau (eds.). Boulder: Lynne Rienner.

Andréani, Gilles (2000). "Why Institutions Matter." *Survival* 42: 81–95.

Art, Robert J. (1996). "Why Western Europe Needs the United States and NATO." *Political Science Quarterly* 111: 1–39.

Artner, Stephen (1980). "The Middle East: A Chance for Europe." *International Affairs* 56: 430–31.

Axelrod, Robert (1984). *The Evolution of Cooperation*. New York: Basic Books.

(1986). "An Evolutionary Approach to Norms." *American Political Science Review* 80: 1095–1111.

Barbé, Esther and Ferran Izquierdo (1997). "Present and Future of Joint Actions for the Mediterranean Region." In Holland (ed.).

Baun, Michael J. (1995–96). "The Maastricht Treaty as High Politics: Germany, France, and European Integration." *Political Science Quarterly* 110: 605–24.

Bodenheimer, Susanne J. (1967). "The Political Union Debate in Europe: A Case Study in Intergovernmental Diplomacy." *International Organization* 21: 24–54.

Bonvicini, Gianni (1982). "The Dual Structure of EPC and Community Activities: Problems of Coordination." In Allen, Rummel, and Wessels (eds.).

(1983). "Italy: An Integrationist Perspective." In Hill (ed.).

Botcheva, Liliana and Lisa Martin (2001). "Institutional Effects on State Behavior: Convergence and Divergence." *International Studies Quarterly* 45: 1–26.

Bretherton, Charlotte and John Vogler (1999). *The European Union as a Global Actor*. London: Routledge.

Buchan, David (1993). *Europe: The Strange Superpower*. Aldershot: Dartmouth Publishing.

Bull, Hedley (1977). *The Anarchical Society: A Study of Order in World Politics*. New York: Columbia University Press.

Bulmer, Simon (1983). "Domestic Politics and European Community Policy-Making." *Journal of Common Market Studies* 21: 349–63.

(1985). "The European Council's First Decade: Between Interdependence and Domestic Politics." *Journal of Common Market Studies* 24: 89–104.

(1991). "Analyzing EPC: The Case for Two-Tier Analysis." In Holland (ed.).

Bulmer, Simon and Wolfgang Wessels (1987). *The European Council: Decision-Making in European Politics*. London: Macmillan.

Cameron, Fraser (1998). 'Building a Common Foreign Policy: Do Institutions Matter?' In Peterson and Sjursen (eds.).

(1999). *The Foreign and Security Policy of the European Union: Past, Present and Future*. Sheffield: Sheffield Academic Press.

Caporaso, James A. and John T. S. Keeler (1995). "The European Union and Regional Integration Theory." In *The State of the European Union*, vol. III: *Building a European Polity?*, Carolyn Rhodes and Sonia Mazey (eds.). Boulder: Lynne Rienner.

Carlsnaes, Walter and Steve Smith, eds. (1994). *European Foreign Policy: The EC and Changing Perspectives in Europe*. London: Sage.

Cederman, Lars-Erik, ed. (2000). *Constructing Europe's Identity: The External Dimension*. Boulder: Lynne Rienner.

Chayes, Abram and Antonia Handler Chayes (1993). "On Compliance." *International Organization* 47: 175–205.

Checkel, Jeff (1998). "The Constructivist Turn in International Relations Theory." *World Politics* 50: 324–48.

(2001). "Why Comply? Social Learning and European Identity Change." *International Organization* 55: 553–88.

Cheyne, Ilona (1994). "International Agreements and the European Community Legal System." *European Law Review* 19: 581–98.

Christensen, Thomas J. and Jack Snyder (1990). "Chain Gangs and Passed Bucks: Predicting Alliance Patterns in Multipolarity." *International Organization* 44: 137–68.

Coffey, Joseph I. (1998). "WEU After the Second Maastricht." In *The State of the European Union*, vol. IV: *Deepening and Widening*, Pierre-Henri Laurent and Marc Maresceau (eds.). Boulder: Lynne Rienner.

Coignez, Veerle (1992). "A Test Case of Consistency: The San José Dialogue." In Rummel (ed.).

Corbett, Richard (1989). "Testing the New Procedures: The European Parliament's First Experience with its New 'Single Act' Powers." *Journal of Common Market Studies* 27: 359–72.

(1992). "The Intergovernmental Conference on Political Union." *Journal of Common Market Studies* 30: 271–98.

Corbett, Richard, Francis Jacobs, and Michael Shackleton (1995). *The European Parliament*. London: Cartermill.

Cornish, Paul (1997). "Joint Action, 'The Economic Aspects of Security' and the Regulation of Conventional Arms and Technology Exports from the EU." In Holland (ed.).

Cortell, Andrew P. and James W. Davis Jr. (1996). "How Do International Institutions Matter? The Domestic Impact of Rules and Norms." *International Studies Quarterly* 40: 451–78.

Cram, Laura (1997). *Policy-Making in the European Union: Conceptual Lenses and the Integration Process*. London: Routledge.

Crawford, Beverly (1996). "Explaining Defection From International Cooperation: Germany's Unilateral Recognition of Croatia." *World Politics* 48: 482–521.

Crawford, Beverly and Peter W. Schulze, eds. (1990). *The New Europe Asserts Itself: A Changing Role in International Relations*. Berkeley: University of California Press.

Curtin, Deirdre (1993). "The Constitutional Structure of the Union: A Europe of Bits and Pieces." *Common Market Law Review* 30: 17–69.

Curtin, Deirdre and R. van Ooik (1994). "Denmark and the Edinburgh Summit: Maastricht Without Tears." In O'Keeffe and Twomey (eds.).

da Costa Pereira, Pedro Sanchez (1988). "The Use of a Secretariat." In Pijpers, Regelsberger, and Wessels (eds.).

da Fonseca-Wollheim, Hermann (1981). *Ten Years of European Political Cooperation*. Brussels: Commission of the European Communities.

—— (1996). "Towards a Coherent European Trade Policy." Typescript.

de Bassompierre, Guy (1988). *Changing the Guard in Brussels*. New York: Praeger / Center for Strategic and International Studies.

Dehousse, Renaud and Joseph H. H. Weiler (1991). "EPC and the Single Act: From Soft Law to Hard Law?" In Holland (ed.).

de la Serre, Françoise (1988). "The Scope of National Adaptation to EPC." In Pijpers, Regelsberger, and Wessels (eds.).

de la Serre, Françoise and Philippe Moreau Defarges (1983). "France: A Penchant for Leadership." In Hill (ed.).

de Schoutheete de Tervarent, Philippe (1980). *La Coopération Politique Européenne*. Brussels: F. Nathan Editions Labor.

—— (1988). "The Presidency and the Management of Political Cooperation." In Pijpers, Regelsberger, and Wessels (eds.).

—— (1997). "The Creation of the Common Foreign and Security Policy." In Regelsberger, de Schoutheete de Tervarent, and Wessels (eds.).

Deutsch, Karl, et al. (1957). *Political Community in the North Atlantic Area: International Organization in the Light of Historical Experience*. Princeton: Princeton University Press.

Dinan, Desmond (1991). "European Political Cooperation." In *The State of the European Community*, vol. I: *Policies, Institutions & Debates in the Transition Years*, Leon Hurwitz and Christian Lequesne (eds.). Boulder: Lynne Rienner.

Duke, Simon (1996). "The Second Death (or Second Coming?) of the WEU." *Journal of Common Market Studies* 34: 167–90.

Duran, Esperanca (1988). "Western Europe's Role in the Central American Crisis: Possibilities and Limitations." In *Central America: Crisis and Possibilities*, Rigoberto Garcia (ed.). Stockholm: Latinamerika-Institut.

Eaton, M. R. (1994). "Common Foreign and Security Policy." In O'Keeffe and Twomey (eds.).

Edwards, Geoffrey (1984). "Europe and the Falklands Islands Crisis, 1982." *Journal of Common Market Studies* 22 (June): 295–313.

—— (1992). "European Responses to the Yugoslav Crisis: An Interim Assessment." In Rummel (ed.).

(1997). "The Potential and Limits of the CFSP: The Yugoslav Example." In Regelsberger, de Schoutheete de Tervarent, and Wessels (eds.).

Edwards, Geoffrey and Simon Nuttall (1994). "Common Foreign and Security Policy." In *Maastricht and Beyond: Building the European Union*, Andrew Duff, John Pinder, and Roy Price (eds.). London: Routledge.

Edwards, Geoffrey and Elfriede Regelsberger, eds. (1990). *Europe's Global Links: The European Community and Inter-Regional Cooperation*. London: Pinter Publishers.

Eichenberg, Richard C. (1997). "Does Europe Want a Common Security Policy (Anymore than it Ever Did?)." Paper presented at the International Studies Association Conference, Toronto, March 19–23.

Elles, James (1990). "The Foreign Policy Role of the European Parliament." *The Washington Quarterly* 13: 69–78.

Elster, Jon (1989). "Social Norms and Economic Theory." *Journal of Economic Perspectives* 3: 99–117.

Evangelista, Matthew (1989). "Issue-Area and Foreign Policy Revisited." *International Organization* 43: 147–71.

Finnemore, Martha (1996). "Norms, Culture, and World Politics: Insights from Sociology's Institutionalism." *International Organization* 50: 325–47.

Fligstein, Neil (1997). "Fields, Power, and Social Skill: A Critical Analysis of the New Institutionalisms." Typescript: University of California, Berkeley.

Fligstein, Neil and Jason McNichol (1998). "The Institutional Terrain of the European Union." In Stone Sweet and Sandholtz (eds.).

Foot, Rosemary (1979). "The European Community's Voting Behavior at the United Nations' General Assembly." *Journal of Common Market Studies* 17: 350–59.

Forster, Anthony and William Wallace (1997). "Common Foreign and Security Policy." In *Policy-Making in the European Union*, Helen Wallace and William Wallace (eds.). Oxford: Oxford University Press.

Franck, Christian (1983). "Belgium: Committed Multilateralism." In Hill (ed.).

Freestone, D. (1985). "The EEC Treaty and Common Action on Terrorism." *Yearbook of European Law 1984* (Oxford): 207–30.

Fursdon, Edward (1980). *The European Defense Community: A History*. London: Macmillan.

Gaddis, John Lewis (1986). "The Long Peace: Elements of Stability in the Post-war International System." *International Security* 10: 98–142.

Galloway, David (1995). "Common Foreign and Security Policy: Intergovernmentalism Donning the Mantle of the Community Method." In *The Council of the European Union*, Martin Westlake (ed.). London: Cartermill Publishing.

Garrett, Geoffrey (1992). "International Cooperation and Institutional Choice: The European Community's Internal Market." *International Organization* 46: 533–58.

Garrett, Geoffrey and George Tsebelis (1996). "An Institutional Critique of Intergovernmentalism." *International Organization* 50: 269–99.

Ginsberg, Roy H. (1989). *Foreign Policy Actions of the European Community: The Politics of Scale*. Boulder: Lynne Rienner.

(1991). "European Community Foreign Policy Actions in the 1980s." Paper presented at the Second Biennial International Conference of the European Community Studies Association, Washington, May 22–24.

(1994). "The European Union's Common Foreign and Security Policy: An Outsider's Perspective on the First Year." *ECSA Newsletter* 7: 13–16.

(1995). "Principles and Practices of the European Union's Common Foreign and Security Policy: Retrospective on the First Eighteen Months." Paper presented at the Fourth International Biennial Conference of the European Community Studies Association, Charleston, May 11–14.

(1997a). "The EU's CFSP: The Politics of Procedure." In Holland (ed.).

(1997b). "Transatlantic Dimensions of CFSP: The Culture of Foreign Policy Cooperation." In Regelsberger, de Schoutheete de Tervarent, and Wessels (eds.).

(1998). "U.S.–EU Relations: The Commercial, Political, and Security Dimensions." In *The State of the European Union*, vol. IV: *Deepening and Widening*, Pierre-Henri Laurent and Marc Maresceau (eds.). Boulder: Lynne Rienner.

(1999). "Conceptualizing the European Union as an International Actor: Narrowing the Theoretical Capability-Expectations Gap." *Journal of Common Market Studies* 37: 429–54.

(2001). *The European Union in International Politics: Baptism by Fire.* Lanham, MD: Rowman & Littlefield.

Gordon, Philip H. (1997–98). "Europe's Uncommon Foreign Policy." *International Security* 22: 74–100.

Govaere, Inge and Piet Eeckhout (1992). "On Dual Use Goods and Dualist Case Law: The Aimé Richardt Judgment on Export Controls." *Common Market Law Review* 29: 940–65.

Grieco, Joseph M. (1988). "Anarchy and the Limits of Cooperation: A Realist Critique of the Newest Liberal Institutionalism." *International Organization* 42: 485–507.

Grosser, Alfred (1980). *The Western Alliance.* London: Macmillan.

Grunert, Thomas (1997). "The Association of the European Parliament: No Longer the Underdog in EPC?" In Regelsberger, de Schoutheete de Tervarent, and Wessels (eds.).

Haagerup, Niels Jorgen and Christian Thune (1983). "Denmark: The European Pragmatist." In Hill (ed.).

Haas, Ernst B. (1958). *The Uniting of Europe: Political, Economic, and Social Forces, 1950–1957.* Stanford: Stanford University Press.

(1961). "International Integration: The European and the Universal Process." *International Organization* 15: 366–92.

(1964). *Beyond the Nation-State: Functionalism and European Integration.* Stanford: Stanford University Press.

(1980). "Why Collaborate? Issue-Linkage and International Regimes." *World Politics* 32: 357–405.

Haas, Peter M. (1990). *Saving the Mediterranean: The Politics of International Environmental Cooperation.* New York: Columbia University Press.

Haggard, Stephan (1991). "Structuralism and Its Critics: Recent Progress in International Relations Theory." In *Progress in Postwar International Relations*, Emmanuel Adler and Beverly Crawford (eds.). New York: Columbia University Press.

Hagleitner, Thomas (1995). "Financing the Common Foreign and Security Policy." *CFSP Forum* 2: 6–7.

Hemmer, Christopher and Peter J. Katzenstein (2002). "Why is There No NATO in Asia? Collective Identity, Regionalism, and the Origins of Multilateralism." *International Organization* 56: 575–607.

Hertogs, Erik Jan (1985). "Western European Responses to Revolutionary Developments in the Caribbean Basin Region." In *Towards an Alternative for Central America and the Caribbean*, George Irvin and Xabier Gorostiaga (eds.). London: George Allen and Unwin.

Hill, Christopher (1983a). "National Interests – The Insuperable Obstacles?" In Hill (ed.).

ed. (1983b). *National Foreign Policies and European Political Cooperation.* London: George Allen and Unwin.

(1988a). "Research into EPC: Tasks for the Future." In Pijpers, Regelsberger, and Wessels (eds.).

(1988b). "European Preoccupations With Terrorism." In Pijpers, Regelsberger, and Wessels (eds.).

(1992). "EPC's Performance in Crises." In Rummel (ed.).

(1993). "The Capability-Expectations Gap, or Conceptualizing Europe's International Role." *Journal of Common Market Studies* 31: 305–28.

ed. (1996). *The Actors in Europe's Foreign Policy.* London: Routledge.

(1998). "Closing the Capability-Expectations Gap?' In Peterson and Sjursen (eds.).

Hill, Christopher and William Wallace (1979). "Diplomatic Trends in the European Community." *International Affairs* 55: 47–66.

(1996). "Introduction: Actors and Actions." In Hill (ed.).

Hix, Simon (1994). "The Study of the European Community: The Challenge to Comparative Politics." *West European Politics* 17: 1–30.

Hoffman, Stanley (1965). "The European Process at Atlantic Crosspurposes." *Journal of Common Market Studies* 3: 85–101.

(1966). 'Obstinate or Obsolete? The Fate of the Nation-State and the Case of Western Europe." *Daedalus* 95: 862–74.

(2000). "Towards a Common European Foreign and Security Policy?" *Journal of Common Market Studies* 38: 189–98.

Holbrooke, Richard (1998). *To End a War.* New York: Random House.

Holland, Martin (1987). "Three Approaches for Understanding European Political Cooperation: A Case-Study of EC South African Policy." *Journal of Common Market Studies* 25: 295–313.

(1988). *The European Community and South Africa: European Political Cooperation Under Strain.* London: Pinter Publishers.

(1991a). "Sanctions as an EPC Instrument." In Holland (ed.).

ed. (1991b). *The Future of European Political Cooperation: Essays on Theory and Practice.* London: Macmillan.

(1995a). *European Union Foreign Policy: From EPC to CFSP Joint Action and South Africa.* Basingstoke: Macmillan.

(1995b). "Bridging the Capability-Expectations Gap: A Case Study of the CFSP Joint Action on South Africa." *Journal of Common Market Studies* 33: 555–72.

(1997a). "Introduction: CFSP . . . Reinventing the EPC Wheel?" In Holland (ed.).

(1997b). "The Joint Action on South Africa: A Successful Experiment?" In Holland (ed.).

ed. (1997c). *Common Foreign and Security Policy: The Record and Reforms.* London: Pinter Publishers.

Huntington, Samuel (1973). "Transnational Organizations in World Politics." *World Politics* 25: 333–68.

Hurd, Douglas (1981). "Political Cooperation." *International Affairs* 57: 383–93.

(1994). "Developing the Common Foreign and Security Policy." *International Affairs* 70: 421–28.

Hurwitz, Leon (1975). "The EEC in the United Nations: The Voting Behavior of Eight Countries, 1948–1973." *Journal of Common Market Studies* 13: 224–43.

(1976). "The EEC and Decolonization: The Voting Behavior of the Nine in the UN General Assembly." *Political Studies* 24: 435–47.

Ifestos, Panayiotis (1987). *European Political Cooperation: Towards a Framework of Supranational Diplomacy?* Aldershot: Avebury.

Ikenberry, G. John and Charles A. Kupchan (1990). "Socialization and Hegemonic Power." *International Organization* 44 (Summer): 283–315.

Jarausch, Konrad H. (1994). *The Rush to German Unity.* Oxford: Oxford University Press.

Jervis, Robert (1978). "Cooperation Under the Security Dilemma." *World Politics* 30: 167–214.

Johnston, Mary Troy (1994). *The European Council: Gatekeeper of the European Community.* Boulder: Westview Press.

Jopp, Mathias (1997). "The Defense Dimension of the European Union: The Role and Performance of the WEU." In Regelsberger, de Schoutheete de Tervarent, and Wessels (eds.).

Judge, David, David Earnshaw, and Ngaire Cowan (1994). "Ripples or Waves: The European Parliament in the European Community Policy Process." *Journal of European Public Policy* 1: 27–52.

Kanter, Arnold (1970). "The European Defense Community in the French National Assembly." *Comparative Politics* 2: 203–28.

Keal, Paul (1983). *Unspoken Rules and Superpower Dominance.* London: Macmillan.

Keatinge, Patrick (1997). "The Twelve, the United Nations, and Somalia: The Mirage of Global Intervention." In Regelsberger, de Schoutheete de Tervarent, and Wessels (eds.).

Keohane, Robert O. (1984). *After Hegemony: Cooperation and Discord in the World Political Economy.* Princeton: Princeton University Press.

(1988). "International Institutions: Two Approaches." *International Studies Quarterly* 32: 379–96.

Keohane, Robert O. and Lisa L. Martin (1995). "The Promise of Institutionalist Theory." *International Security* 20: 39–51.

Keohane, Robert O. and Joseph S. Nye (1974). "Transgovernmental Relations and International Organization." *World Politics* 27: 39–62.

(1977). *Power and Interdependence.* Boston: Little, Brown.

Keohane, Robert O., Joseph S. Nye, and Stanley Hoffman, eds. (1993). *After the Cold War: International Institutions and State Strategies in Europe, 1989–1991.* Cambridge: Harvard University Press.

Kindleberger, Charles P. (1986). "Hierarchy Versus Inertial Cooperation." *International Organization* 40: 841–47.

Kintis, Andreas G. (1997). "The EU's Foreign Policy and the War in Former Yugoslavia." In Holland (ed.).

Knopf, Jeffrey W. (1993). "Beyond Two-Level Games: Domestic–International Interaction in the Intermediate Range Nuclear Forces Negotiations." *International Organization* 47: 599–628.

Kohler, Beate (1982). "Euro-American Relations and European Political Cooperation." In Allen, Rummel, and Wessels (eds.).

Krasner, Stephen D., ed. (1983a). *International Regimes.* Ithaca: Cornell University Press.

(1983b). "Structural Causes and Regime Consequences: Regimes as Intervening Variables." In Krasner (ed.).

(1984). "Approaches to the State: Alternative Conceptions and Historical Dynamics." *Comparative Politics* 16: 223–46.

Kratochwil, Friedrich V. (1989). *Rules, Norms, and Decisions: On the Conditions of Practical and Legal Reasoning in International Relations and Domestic Affairs.* Cambridge: Cambridge University Press.

Krenzler, Horst-Gunter and Henning C. Schneider (1997). "The Question of Consistency." In Regelsberger, de Schoutheete de Tervarent, and Wessels (eds.).

Krenzler, Horst-Gunter and Astrid Schomaker (1996). "A New Transatlantic Agenda." *European Foreign Affairs Review* 1: 9–28.

Ladrech, Robert (1994). "Europeanization of Domestic Politics and Institutions: The Case of France." *Journal of Common Market Studies* 32: 69–88.

Lak, Maarten W. J. (1989). "Interaction Between European Political Cooperation and the European Community (External) – Existing Rules and Challenges." *Common Market Law Review* 26: 281–99.

Lasswell, Harold (1960). "The Structure and Function of Communication in Society." In *Mass Communications*, Wilbur Schramm (ed.). Urbana: University of Illinois Press.

Legro, Jeffrey W. (1995). *Cooperation Under Fire: Anglo-German Restraint During World War II.* Ithaca: Cornell University Press.

(1997). "Which Norms Matter? Revisiting the 'Failure' of Internationalism." *International Organization* 51: 31–63.

Lewis, Jeff (1998). "Is the 'Hard Bargaining' Image of the Council Misleading? The Committee of Permanent Representatives and the Local Elections Directive." *Journal of Common Market Studies* 36: 479–504.

Lieber, R. J. (1976). *Oil and the Middle East War: Europe in the Energy Crisis.* Cambridge: Harvard Center for International Affairs.

Lindemann, Beate (1976). "Europe and the Third World: The Nine at the United Nations." *The World Today* 32: 260–69.

——— (1982). 'European Political Cooperation at the UN: A Challenge for the Nine." In Allen, Rummel, and Wessels (eds.).

Lippert, Barbara (1997). "Relations with Central and Eastern European Countries: The Anchor Role of the European Union." In Regelsberger, de Schoutheete de Tervarent, and Wessels (eds.).

Lipson, Charles (1984). "International Cooperation in Economic and Security Affairs." *World Politics* 37: 1–23.

——— (1991). "Why Are Some International Agreements Informal?" *International Organization* 45: 495–538.

Lodge, Juliet (1988). "The European Parliament and Foreign Policy." In *Foreign Policy and Legislatures*, M. L. Sondhi (ed.). New Delhi: Abhinav.

——— (1989). "European Political Cooperation: Towards the 1990s." In *The European Community and the Challenge of the Future*, Juliet Lodge (ed.). New York: St. Martin's Press.

Long, David (1997). "Multilateralism in the CFSP." In Holland (ed.).

Lopandic, Dusko (1995). "Les Mémorandums d'Entente: Des Instruments Juridiques Spécifiques de la Politique Étrangère et de Sécurité de l'Union Européenne: Le Cas de l'Ex-Yougoslavie." *Revue du Marché Commun et de l'Union Européenne* 392: 557–62.

McGoldrick, Dominic (1997). *International Relations Law of the European Union.* London: Longman.

Macleod, I., I. D. Henry, and Stephen Hyett (1996). *The External Relations of the European Communities: A Manual of Law and Practice.* Oxford: Clarendon Press.

McManus, Claire (1998). "Poland and the Europe Agreements: The EU as a Regional Actor." In Peterson and Sjursen (eds.).

Manners, Ian and Richard G. Whitman, eds. (2000). *The Foreign Policies of European Union Member States.* Manchester: Manchester University Press.

March, James G. and Johan P. Olsen (1984). "The New Institutionalism: Organizational Factors in Political Life." *American Political Science Review* 78: 734–49.

——— (1989). *Rediscovering Institutions: The Organizational Basis of Politics.* New York: Free Press.

March, James G. and Herbert A. Simon (1958). *Organizations.* New York: Wiley.

Marks, Gary, Liesbet Hooghe, and Kermit Blank (1996). "European Integration from the 1980s: State-Centric Versus Multi-Level Governance." *Journal of Common Market Studies* 34: 342–78.

Martin, Lawrence and John Roper, eds. (1995). *Towards a Common Defence Policy.* Paris: Institute for Security Studies of the WEU.

Martin, Lisa L. (1992). "Institutions and Cooperation: Sanctions During the Falklands Islands Conflict." *International Security* 16: 143–78.

Mastanduno, Michael (1988). "Trade as a Strategic Weapon: American and Alliance Export Control Policy in the Early Postwar Period." *International Organization* 42: 121–50.

May, Ernest (1984). *Knowing One's Enemies*. Princeton: Princeton University Press.

Mayhew, Alan (2001). *Recreating Europe: The European Union's Policy Towards Central and Eastern Europe*. Cambridge: Cambridge University Press.

Mearsheimer, John J. (1994–95). "The False Promise of International Institutions." *International Security* 19: 5–49.

Menon, Anand, Anthony Forster, and William Wallace (1992). "A Common European Defense." *Survival* 34: 98–118.

Mercer, Jonathan (1995). "Anarchy and Identity." *International Organization* 49: 229–52.

Merton, Robert K. (1957). *Social Theory and Social Structure*. Glencoe: The Free Press.

Mitchell, Ronald B. (1998). "Sources of Transparency: Information Systems in International Regimes." *International Studies Quarterly* 42: 109–30.

Mitrany, David (1966). *A Working Peace System*. Chicago: Quadrangle Press.

Monar, Jörg (1997a). "The Financial Dimension of the CFSP." In Holland (ed.).

(1997b). "The Finances of the Union's Intergovernmental Pillars: Tortuous Experiments with the Community Budget." *Journal of Common Market Studies* 35: 57–78.

Moravcsik, Andrew (1991). "Negotiating the Single European Act: National Interests and Conventional Statecraft in the European Community." *International Organization* 45: 19–56.

(1993). "Preferences and Power in the European Community: A Liberal Intergovernmentalist Approach." *Journal of Common Market Studies* 31: 473–524.

(1994). "Why the EC Strengthens the State: Domestic Politics and International Cooperation." Typescript: University of Chicago.

(1998). *The Choice for Europe: Social Purpose and State Power from Messina to Maastricht*. Ithaca: Cornell University Press.

Morrow, James D. (1994). "Modeling the Forms of International Cooperation: Distribution Versus Information." *International Organization* 48: 387–423.

Müller, Harold (1992). "West European Cooperation on Nuclear Disarmament." In Rummel (ed.).

(1995). "The Internalization of Principles, Norms, and Rules by Governments: The Case of Security Regimes." In *Regime Theory and International Relations*, Volker Rittberger (ed.). Oxford: Clarendon Press.

Müller, Harold and Lars van Dassen (1997). "From Cacophony to Joint Action: Successes and Shortcomings of the European Nuclear Non-Proliferation Policy." In Holland (ed.).

Nadelmann, Ethan A. (1990). "Global Prohibition Regimes: The Evolution of Norms in International Society." *International Organization* 44: 479–526.

Ness, Gayl D. and Steven R. Brechin (1988). "Bridging the Gap: International Organizations as Organizations." *International Organization* 42: 245–73.

Neunreither, Karl-Heinz (1990). "The European Parliament: An Emerging Political Role?" In Edwards and Regelsberger (eds.).

Neuwahl, Nanette (1994). "Foreign and Security Policy and the Implementation of the Requirement for 'Consistency' Under the Treaty on European Union." In O'Keeffe and Twomey (eds.).

North, Douglass C. (1990). *Institutions, Institutional Change, and Economic Performance*. New York: Cambridge University Press.

Nugent, Neill (1995). "The Leadership Capacity of the European Commission." *Journal of European Public Policy* 2: 603–23.

Nuttall, Simon (1986). *Yearbook of European Law 1985*. Oxford: Oxford University Press.

(1988). "Where the European Commission Comes In." In Pijpers, Regelsberger, and Wessels (eds.).

(1990). "The Commission: Protagonists of Inter-Regional Cooperation." In Edwards and Regelsberger (eds.).

(1992a). *European Political Cooperation*. Oxford: Clarendon Press.

(1992b). "The Institutional Network and the Instruments of Action." In Rummel (ed.).

(1993). "The Foreign and Security Policy Provisions of the Maastricht Treaty: Their Potential for the Future." In *The Maastricht Treaty on European Union*, Jörg Monar, Werner Ungerer, and Wolfgang Wessels (eds.). Brussels: European Interuniversity Press.

(1994). "The EC and Yugoslavia: Deus ex Machina or Machina sine Deo?" *Journal of Common Market Studies* 32: 11–25.

(1995). "The European Commission's Internal Arrangements for Foreign Affairs and External Relations." *CFSP Forum* 2: 3–4.

(1996). "The Commission: The Struggle for Legitimacy." In Hill (ed.).

(1997a). "The CFSP at Maastricht: Old Friend or New Enemy?" Paper presented at the Fifth Biennial International Conference of the European Community Studies Association, Seattle, WA, May 29–June 1.

(1997b). "Two Decades of EPC Performance." In Regelsberger, de Schoutheete de Tervarent, and Wessels (eds.).

(2001). *European Foreign Policy*. Oxford: Oxford University Press.

Øhrgaard, Jakob C. (1997). "'Less than Supranational, More than Intergovernmental': European Political Cooperation and the Dynamics of Intergovernmental Integration." *Millenium: Journal of International Studies* 26: 1–29.

O'Keeffe, David and Patrick M. Twomey, eds. (1994). *Legal Issues of the Maastricht Treaty*. London: Wiley Chancery Law.

Owen, David (1995). *Balkan Odyssey*. New York: Harcourt Brace.

Oye, Kenneth A. (1986a). "Explaining Cooperation Under Anarchy: Hypotheses and Strategies." In Oye (ed.).

ed. (1986b). *Cooperation Under Anarchy*. Princeton: Princeton University Press.

Pescatore, Pierre (1979). "External Relations in the Case-Law of the Court of Justice of the European Communities." *Common Market Law Review* 16: 615–45.

Peterson, John (1995). "Decision-Making in the European Union: Towards a Framework for Analysis." *Journal of European Public Policy* 2: 69–96.

(1998). "Introduction: The European Union as a Global Actor." In Peterson and Sjursen (eds.).

Peterson, John and Helene Sjursen, eds. (1998). *A Common Foreign Policy for Europe? Competing Visions of the CFSP*. London: Routledge.

Pfetsch, Frank (1994). "Tensions in Sovereignty: Foreign Policies of EC Members Compared." In Carlsnaes and Smith (eds.).

Philippart, Éric and Pascaline Winand, eds. (2001). *Ever Closer Partnership: Policy-Making in U.S.–EU Relations*. Brussels: P.I.E.-Peter Lang.

Piening, Christopher (1997). *Global Europe: The EU in World Affairs*. Boulder: Lynne Rienner.

Pierson, Paul (1993). "When Effect Becomes Cause: Policy Feedback and Political Change." *World Politics* 45: 595–628.

Pijpers, Alfred (1983). "The Netherlands: How to Keep the Spirit of Fouchet in the Bottle." In Hill (ed.).

(1991). "European Political Cooperation and the Realist Paradigm." In Holland (ed.).

Pijpers, Alfred, Elfriede Regelsberger, and Wolfgang Wessels, eds. (1988). *European Political Cooperation in the 1980s: A Common Foreign Policy for Western Europe?* Dordrecht: Martinus Nijhoff Publishers.

Pollack, Mark A. (1997). "Delegation, Agency, and Agenda Setting in the European Community." *International Organization* 51: 99–134.

(1998). "The Engines of Integration? Supranational Autonomy and Influence in the European Community." In Stone Sweet and Sandholtz (eds.).

Polsby, Nelson (1968). "The Institutionalization of the U.S. House of Representatives." *American Political Science Review* 62: 144–68.

Powell, Walter W. and Paul J. DiMaggio, eds. (1991). *The New Institutionalism in Organizational Analysis*. Chicago: University of Chicago Press.

Putnam, Robert D. (1988). "Diplomacy and Domestic Politics: The Logic of Two-Level Games." *International Organization* 42: 429–60.

Putnam, Robert D. and Nicholas Bayne (1987). *Hanging Together: Cooperation and Conflict in the Seven-Power Summits*. Cambridge: Harvard University Press.

Regelsberger, Elfriede (1988). "EPC in the 1980s: Reaching Another Plateau?" In Pijpers, Regelsberger, and Wessels (eds.).

(1991). "The Twelve's Dialogue with Third Countries: Progress Towards a Communauté d'Action?" In Holland (ed.).

(1993). "European Political Cooperation." In *The New Europe: Politics, Government and Economy Since 1945*, Jonathan Story (ed.). Oxford: Blackwell.

(1997). "The Institutional Setup and Functioning of EPC/CFSP." In Regelsberger, de Schoutheete de Tervarent, and Wessels (eds.).

Regelsberger, Elfriede, Philippe de Schoutheete de Tervarent, and Wolfgang Wessels (1997a). "From EPC to CFSP: Does Maastricht Push the EU Toward a Role as a Global Power?" In Regelsberger, de Schoutheete de Tervarent, and Wessels (eds.).

eds. (1997b). *Foreign Policy of the European Union: From EPC to CFSP and Beyond*. Boulder: Lynne Rienner.

Regelsberger, Elfriede and Wolfgang Wessels (1996). "The CFSP Institutions and Procedures: A Third Way for the Second Pillar." *European Foreign Affairs Review* 1: 29–54.

Richardson, Jeremy J. (1996). "Policy-Making in the EU: Interests, Ideas, and Garbage Cans of Primevel Soup." In *European Union: Power and Policy-Making*, Jeremy J. Richardson (ed.). London: Routledge.

Risse, Thomas (2000). "'Let's Argue!' Communicative Action in World Politics." *International Organization* 54: 1–39.

Risse-Kappen, Thomas, ed. (1995a). *Bringing Transnational Relations Back In: Non-State Actors, Domestic Structures, and International Institutions.* Cambridge: Cambridge University Press.

(1995b). *Cooperation Among Democracies: The European Influence on U.S. Foreign Policy.* Princeton: Princeton University Press.

(1996). "Exploring the Nature of the Beast: International Relations Theory and Comparative Policy Analysis Meet the European Union." *Journal of Common Market Studies* 34: 53–80.

Ross, George Ross (1995). *Jacques Delors and European Integration.* Cambridge: Polity Press.

Ruggie, John Gerard (1993). "Territoriality and Beyond: Problematizing Modernity in International Relations." *International Organization* 47: 139–74.

Rummel, Reinhardt (1982). "The Future of European Political Cooperation." In Allen, Rummel, and Wessels (eds.).

ed. (1990). *The Evolution of an International Actor: Western Europe's New Assertiveness.* Boulder: Westview Press.

ed. (1992). *Toward Political Union: Planning a Common Foreign and Security Policy in the European Community.* Boulder: Westview Press.

(1996). "Germany's Role in the CFSP: 'Normalitat' or 'Sonderweg'?" In Hill (ed.).

(1997). "The CFSP's Conflict Prevention Policy." In Holland (ed.).

Sack, Jörn (1995). "The European Community's Membership of International Organizations." *Common Market Law Review* 32: 1227–56.

Sandholtz, Wayne (1996). "Membership Matters: Limits to the Functional Approach to European Institutions." *Journal of Common Market Studies* 34: 403–29.

Scharpf, Fritz W. (1988). "The Joint Decision Trap: Lessons from German Federalism and European Integration." *Public Administration* 66: 239–78.

Schimmelfennig, Frank (2001). "The Community Trap: Liberal Norms, Rhetorical Action, and the Eastern Enlargement of the European Union." *International Organization* 55: 47–80.

Schmuck, Otto (1991). "The European Parliament as an Institutional Actor." In *The State of the European Community*, vol. I: *Policies, Institutions & Debates in the Transition Years*, Leon Hurwitz and Christian Lequesne (eds.). Boulder: Lynne Rienner.

Schneider, Gerald and Claudia Seybold (1997). "Twelve Tongues, One Voice: An Evaluation of European Political Cooperation." *European Journal of Political Research* 31: 367–96.

Schneider, Heinrich (1997). "The Twelve/Fifteen's Conference Diplomacy: Has the CSCE/OSCE Remained a Successful Platform?" In Regelsberger, de Schoutheete de Tervarent, and Wessels (eds.).

Siedentop, Larry (2001). *Democracy in Europe.* Princeton: Princeton University Press.

Smith, Anthony D. (1992). "National Identity and the Idea of European Unity." *International Affairs* 68: 55–76.

Smith, Hazel (1995). *European Foreign Policy and Central America*. New York: St. Martin's Press.

Smith, Michael (1998). "Does the Flag Follow Trade? 'Politicisation' and the Emergence of a European Foreign Policy." In Peterson and Sjursen (eds.).

Smith, Michael E. (1998a). "European Security Cooperation: The EU's Evaluations and Responses." In *NATO and the European Union: Confronting the Challenges of European Security Cooperation*, S. Victor Papacosma and Pierre-Henri Laurent (eds.). Kent: Lyman L. Lemnitzer Center for NATO and EU Studies.

(1998b). "What's Wrong with the CFSP? The Politics of Institutional Reform." In *The State of the European Union*, vol. IV: *Deepening and Widening*, Pierre-Henri Laurent and Marc Maresceau (eds.). Boulder: Lynne Rienner.

(2000). "Conforming to Europe: The Domestic Impact of European Foreign Policy Cooperation." *Journal of European Public Policy* 7: 613–31.

(2001a). "Diplomacy by Decree: The Legalization of EU Foreign Policy." *Journal of Common Market Studies* 39: 79–104.

(2001b). "The Quest for Coherence: Institutional Dilemmas of External Action from Maastricht to Amsterdam." In Stone Sweet, Sandholtz, and Fligstein (eds.).

Snyder, F. (1993). *Soft Law and Institutional Practice in the European Community*. Brussels: European University Institute Working Paper, LAW 93/5.

Snyder, Jack (1984). *The Ideology of the Offensive: Military Decision Making and the Disasters of 1914*. Ithaca: Cornell University Press.

Soetendorp, Ben (1994). "The Evolution of the EC/EU as a Single Foreign Policy Actor." In Carlsnaes and Smith (eds.).

(1999). *Foreign Policy in the European Union*. London: Longman.

Stavridis, Stelios (1997). "The Democratic Control of CFSP." In Holland (ed.).

Stavridis, Stelios and Christopher Hill, eds. (1996). *Domestic Sources of Foreign Policy: Western European Reactions to the Falklands Conflict*. Oxford: Berg Publishers.

Stein, Arthur A. (1983). "Coordination and Collaboration: Regimes in an Anarchic World." In Krasner (ed.).

(1990). *Why Nations Cooperate: Circumstance and Choice in International Relations*. Ithaca: Cornell University Press.

Steinmo, Sven, Kathleen Thelen, and Frank Longstreth, eds. (1992). *Structuring Politics: Historical Institutionalism in Comparative Analysis*. Cambridge: Cambridge University Press.

Stone, Alec (1994). "What Is a Supranational Constitution? An Essay in International Relations Theory." *The Review of Politics* 56: 441–74.

Stone Sweet, Alec and Thomas L. Brunell (1998). "Constructing a Supranational Constitution: Dispute Resolution and Governance in the European Community." *American Political Science Review* 92: 63–81.

Stone Sweet, Alec and Wayne Sandholtz (1998a). "Integration, Supranational Governance, and the Institutionalization of the European Polity." In Stone Sweet and Sandholtz (eds.).

eds. (1998b). *Supranational Governance: The Institutionalization of the European Union*. Oxford: Oxford University Press.

Stone Sweet, Alec, Wayne Sandholtz, and Neil Fligstein, eds. (2001). *The Institutionalization of Europe*. Oxford: Oxford University Press.

Stubb, Alexander C.-G. (1996). "A Categorization of Differentiated Integration." *Journal of Common Market Studies* 34: 283–95.

Taylor, Phillip (1979). *When Europe Speaks With One Voice: The External Relations of the European Community*. Westport: Greenwood Press.

Taylor, Trevor (1994). "West European Security and Defense Cooperation: Maastricht and Beyond." *International Affairs* 70: 1–16.

Thelen, Kathleen and Sven Steinmo (1992). "Historical Institutionalism in Comparative Politics." In Steinmo, Thelen, and Longstreth (eds.).

Tietje, Christian (1997). "The Concept of Coherence in the Treaty on European Union and the Common Foreign and Security Policy." *European Foreign Affairs Review* 2: 211–33.

Tindemans, Leo (1976). "European Union." *Bulletin of the European Communities* (Supplement), No. 1.

Turnbull, Penelope and Wayne Sandholtz (2001). "Migration and Policing: The Evolution of European Policy Spaces." In Stone Sweet, Sandholtz, and Fligstein (eds.).

Ueta, Takako (1997). "The Stability Pact: From the Balladur Initiative to the EU Joint Action." In Holland (ed.).

Van Evera, Stephen (1984). "The Cult of the Offensive and the Origins of the First World War." *International Security* 9: 58–107.

van Praag, Nicholas (1982a). "Political Cooperation and Southern Europe: Case Studies in Crisis Management." In Allen, Rummel, and Wessels (eds.).

    (1982b). "European Political Cooperation and Southern Africa." In Allen, Rummel, and Wessels (eds.).

von der Gablentz, Otto (1979). "Luxembourg Revisited, or the Importance of European Political Cooperation." *Common Market Law Review* 16: 685–99.

von Groll, Götz (1982). "The Nine at the Conference on Security and Cooperation in Europe." In Allen, Rummel, and Wessels (eds.).

von Jagow, Peter (1990). "European Political Cooperation: Concerted Diplomacy in an Inter-Regional Context." In Edwards and Regelsberger (eds.).

von Staden, Alfred (1994). "After Maastricht: Explaining the Movement Towards a Common European Defence Policy." In Carlsnaes and Smith (eds.).

Wæver, Ole (1996). "European Security Identities." *Journal of Common Market Studies* 34: 103–32.

Wallace, Helen (1986). "The Conduct of Bilateral Relationships by Governments." In *Partners and Rivals in Western Europe: Britain, France, and Germany*, Roger Morgan and Caroline Bray (eds.). Brookfield: Gower.

Wallace, Helen and Geoffrey Edwards (1976). "European Community: The Evolving Role of the Presidency of the Council." *International Affairs* 53: 535–50.

Wallace, William (1982). "National Inputs into European Political Cooperation." In Allen, Rummel, and Wessels (eds.).

(1983a). "Political Cooperation: Integration through Intergovernmentalism." In *Policy-Making in the European Community*, Helen Wallace, William Wallace, and Carole Webb (eds.). London: John Wiley & Sons.

(1983b). "Introduction: Cooperation and Convergence in European Foreign Policy." In Hill (ed.).

Wallace, William and David Allen (1977). "Political Cooperation: Procedure as Substitute for Policy." In *Policy-Making in the European Communities*, Helen Wallace, William Wallace, and Carole Webb (eds.). London: John Wiley & Sons.

Walt, Stephen M. (1988). *The Origins of Alliances*. Ithaca: Cornell University Press.

Waltz, Kenneth N. (1979). *Theory of International Politics*. New York: McGraw-Hill.

Weiler, Joseph H. H. (1985). *The Evolution of the Mechanisms and Institutions for a European Foreign Policy*. Florence: European University Institute Working Paper, No. 202.

(1993). "Neither Unity Nor Three Pillars – The Trinity Structure of the Treaty on European Union." In *The Maastricht Treaty on European Union: Legal Complexity and Political Dynamic*, Jörg Monar, Werner Ungerer, and Wolfgang Wessels (eds.). Brussels: European Interuniversity Press.

Weiler, Joseph H. H. and Wolfgang Wessels (1988). "EPC and the Challenge of Theory." In Pijpers, Regelsberger, and Wessels (eds.)

Wendt, Alexander (1994). "Collective Identity Formation and the International State." *American Political Science Review* 88: 384–96.

(1999). *Social Theory of International Politics*. Cambridge: Cambridge University Press.

Wessel, Ramses A. (1997). "The International Legal Status of the European Union." *European Foreign Affairs Review* 2: 109–29.

Wessels, Wolfgang (1982). "European Political Cooperation: A New Approach to European Foreign Policy." In Allen, Rummel, and Wessels (eds.).

White, Brian (2001). *Understanding European Foreign Policy*. Basingstoke: Palgrave.

Whitman, Richard (1998). *From Civilian Power to Superpower? The International Identity of the European Union*. London: Macmillan.

Williamson, Oliver E. (1983). "Credible Commitments: Using Hostages to Support Exchange." *American Economic Review* 73: 519–40.

Winn, Neil (1996). *European Crisis Management in the 1980s*. Aldershot, UK: Dartmouth.

Wood, Pia Christina (1993). "European Political Cooperation: Lessons from the Gulf War and Yugoslavia." In *The State of the European Community*, vol. II: *The Maastricht Debates and Beyond*, Alan W. Cafruny and Glenda G. Rosenthal (eds.). Boulder: Lynne Rienner.

Woodward, S. L. (1995). *Balkan Tragedy: Chaos and Dissolution after the Cold War*. Washington: Brookings Institution.

Yee, Albert S. (1996). "The Causal Effects of Ideas on Policies." *International Organization* 50: 69–108.

Young, Oran R. (1989). *International Cooperation: Building Regimes for Natural Resources and the Environment*. Ithaca: Cornell University Press.

   (1992). "The Effectiveness of International Institutions: Hard Cases and Critical Variables." In *Governance Without Government: Change and Order in World Politics*, James M. Rosenau and Ernst-Otto Czempiel (eds.). New York: Cambridge University Press.

Index